Everyman, I will go with thee,
and be thy guide

Wace and Lawman

THE LIFE OF
KING ARTHUR

Translated and introduced by
JUDITH WEISS
Robinson College, University of Cambridge

and

ROSAMUND ALLEN
Queen Mary and Westfield College, University of London

EVERYMAN
J. M. DENT · LONDON
CHARLES E. TUTTLE
VERMONT

This edition first published in Everyman Paperbacks in 1997

J. M. Dent
Orion Publishing Group
Orion House, 5 Upper St Martin's Lane,
London WC2H 9EA
and
Charles E. Tuttle Co., Inc.
28 South Main Street,
Rutland, Vermont 05701, USA

Printed in Great Britain by
The Guernsey Press Co. Ltd, Guernsey, C. I.

British Library Cataloguing-in-Publication Data
is available upon request.

ISBN 0 460 87570 1

CONTENTS

NOTE ON THE AUTHORS
AND TRANSLATORS

WACE was born *c.* 1110 in Jersey and educated at Caen in Normandy. He continued his studies in the Île de France and then returned to Caen to begin his literary career. Of his early poetry, three saints' lives survive, but he made his name with *Le Roman de Brut*, a history of the British, in French octosyllabic couplets, translated from Geoffrey of Monmouth's *Historia Regum Britanniae*, which he finished in 1155 and dedicated to Eleanor of Aquitaine, wife of England's first Plantagenet king, Henry II. Between 1165 and 1169 he received a canonry at Bayeux. He started writing another chronicle in 1160, on the dukes of Normandy, *Le Roman de Rou*, but, after some 11,000 lines, left it unfinished because his patron, Henry II, had commissioned another poet to write on the same subject. He died between 1174 and 1183.

LAWMAN, who flourished in the late twelfth and early thirteenth centuries, was a priest of Ernley (Areley Kings in Worcestershire). *Brut* is his translation, into Middle English verse, of the history of Britain provided by Wace.

JUDITH WEISS is a Fellow of Robinson College, Cambridge. Her published work includes articles on medieval English and Anglo-Norman romances and saints' lives, and *The Birth of Romance* (Everyman, 1992), a translation and introduction of four twelfth-century Anglo-Norman romances.

ROSAMUND ALLEN is a Reader in English at Queen Mary and Westfield College, University of London. She has edited *King Horn* and has published a modern English rendering of Richard Rolle's English writings, and articles on medieval romances, on mystical writers, and on editing; she has made several recordings of Old and Middle English Texts with the Chaucer Studio.

CHRONOLOGY OF WACE AND LAWMAN'S LIVES AND TIMES

Year	Age	Life
c. 1110		Wace born in Jersey
		Wace moves to Caen
		Wace moves to Île de France
		Wace moves back to Caen
		Vie de Sainte Marguerite
c. 1130–40	c. 20–30	Wace's *Conception de Notre Dame*
		Other works by Wace, not extant

CHRONOLOGY OF THEIR TIMES

Year	Literary Context	Historical Events
1100		Henry I becomes king of England
c. 1100	Culhwch and Olwen	
1106		Battle of Tinchebrai (Henry I vs Robert of Normandy)
1113		Journey of Laon canons to Cornwall
1114		Henry's daughter Matilda marries emperor of Germany
1120		Loss of the White Ship: Henry's heir drowns
1120s–30s	Caradoc of Lancarvan, Vita Gildae	
1125	William of Malmesbury, De Gestis Regum Anglorum	
1127		Matilda recognized as Henry's successor; marries Geoffrey Plantagenet of Anjou
early 1130s	Henry of Huntingdon, Historia Anglorum	
1133		Henry of Anjou born
before 1135	Geoffrey of Monmouth, Prophetiae Merlini	

Year	Age	Life
c. 1150	*c.* 40	Wace's *Vie de St Nicolas*
		Wace begins *Le Roman de Brut*
		Possibly Wace visits England
1155	*c.* 45	Wace's *Roman de Brut* finished
1160	*c.* 50	Wace starts *Le Roman de Rou*
1165–9	*c.* 55–9	Wace canon at Bayeux
1170–4	*c.* 60–4	Part III of Wace's *Roman de Rou*

Year	Literary Context	Historical Events
1135		Henry I dies; Stephen of Blois becomes king
c. 1135–40	Gaimar, Estoire des Engleis	
1136–8		Welsh rebellion
1137		Eleanor, duchess of Aquitaine, marries Louis VII of France
c. 1138	Geoffrey of Monmouth, Historia Regum Britanniae	Robert of Gloucester renounces allegiance to Stephen
1144		Geoffrey of Anjou becomes duke of Normandy
1147–8		Second Crusade
1148	Geoffrey of Monmouth, Vita Merlini	
1152		Eleanor of Aquitaine divorces Louis and marries Henry of Anjou and Normandy
1154		Stephen dies; Henry becomes Henry II of England
1154–73	Benoît de Sainte-Maure, Roman de Troie	
c. 1160–75	Thomas, Tristan	
c. 1160–90	Marie de France, Lais	
1161		Becket becomes archbishop of Canterbury
c. 1165–80	Béroul, Tristran	
c. 1170	Thomas, Roman de Horn Chrétien de Troyes, Eric et Enide	Young King Henry crowned Becket killed

Year	Age	Life

| 1174 | c. 64 | 'Wascius canonicus' in a charter |
| after 1174 | | Wace's last intervention in *Le Roman de Rou* (mentioning the siege of Rouen) |

Date of death unknown

| 1200–16 | | Lawman, parish priest at Areley Kings in N. Worcestershire, probably working on *Brut* |

Year	Literary Context	Historical Events
1173		Armed revolt by Eleanor and her sons against Henry; Eleanor imprisoned
1174		Siege of Rouen by Louis VII
c. 1176	Chrétien, *Cligés*	
c. 1177–81	Chrétien, *Yvain* and *Lancelot*	
c. 1181	Walter Map, *De Nugis Curialium*	
c. 1181–91	Chrétien, *Perceval*	
1183		Young King Henry dies
1189		Henry II dies; Eleanor released; Richard I king
1189–92		Third Crusade
1191		King Arthur's grave 'discovered' at Glastonbury
c. 1196	William of Newburgh, *Historia Rerum Anglicarum*	
1199		Richard dies; John accedes to throne
c. 1200	Robert de Boron, *L'Estoire dou Graal* and *Perlesvaus*	
1203		Arthur of Brittany dies
1204		Normandy lost to French; Eleanor dies
1208–14		England under papal interdict
1215		Magna Carta

Year   *Age*   *Life*

c. 1250   Both extant manuscripts of *Brut* probably copied
                             Lawman's dates of birth and death are unknown

Year	Literary Context	Historical Events
1216		John dies; Henry III accedes; William Marshal is regent
1220–30	*Prose Lancelot*	
c. 1225	*Queste del Saint Graal*	
1227		Henry assumes his majority
c. 1230–5	*Mort Artu*	
c. 1235	Guillaume de Rennes, *Gesta Regum Britanniae*	
1236		Henry marries Eleanor of Provence

INTRODUCTION TO WACE

The *Brut*s of Wace and Lawman are the earliest extant vernacular chronicles of British history, from the eponymous 'Brutus', supposedly descended from Aeneas, down to Cadwallader and the loss of British supremacy over the island. The climax of this history is the reign of King Arthur, and these are the first sustained accounts in French and English of his career from birth to death. The account largely goes back to Geoffrey of Monmouth and his *Historia Regum Britanniae* (c. 1138), in Latin prose, which Wace translated into octosyllabic French couplets twenty years later. Lawman in turn translated Wace into alliterative and often rhyming English verse around the start of the thirteenth century.

Wace's Life, Work and Historical Background

Wace himself provides us with most of what we know about his life.[1] It was spent in the domains of the dukes of Normandy, most of whom were also, in the twelfth century, kings of England. This accident of history determined the subjects of the two principal works for which Wace is now remembered: the *Roman de Rou*, a chronicle of the Norman dukes, and the *Roman de Brut*, a history of the British.

The island of Jersey was part of Normandy, and here Wace was born, c. 1110. At some early stage he was taken to Caen and taught Latin, preparatory to entering the Church. The city, with its two abbeys erected by William the Conqueror, had belonged since 1105 to William's son Henry I, who had ousted his elder brother Robert from the dukedom, made it his headquarters in Normandy and improved its walls.[2] It was also the birthplace of Henry's bastard son, Robert of Gloucester, who

---

[1] In *Rou*; for a list of the relevant passages, see p. 15.
[2] Houck, *Sources*, p. 163.

became governor of Caen. Wace tells us he moved to the Île de France to continue his studies and stayed there many years; it would seem, however, that he must have been back in Caen by around 1130, at the start of his twenties.

It was near the end of a relatively stable period, in both England and Normandy, but events in the 1120s looked forward to the anarchy to come. Henry I had lost his only legitimate male heir in the White Ship in 1120. He had prevailed on his barons to recognize his daughter Matilda, widow of the emperor of Germany, as his successor, in 1127, but she was not a popular figure, despite producing Henry's grandson in 1133, by her second marriage, to Geoffrey Plantagenet of Anjou. Against this background Wace first began to write. His position is obscure and seems to have been lowly: he later refers to himself as a *clerc lisant*, which perhaps means he was a secretary or notary who had to read aloud.[3] From his first surviving work, the *Vie de Sainte Marguerite*, to the end of his life, he seems to have addressed a lay audience.

This saint's life, judging by its simple style, was the first of a trio of religious works in the vernacular.[4] *La Conception de Notre Dame* (c. 1130–40) and *La Vie de Saint Nicolas* (c. 1150), written for Robert FitzTiout, followed and are all that remain of what seems to have been a large output in Wace's twenties and thirties. Meanwhile, from 1135 to 1138 appeared the first works of Geoffrey of Monmouth. The enormous success of his *Historia Regum Britanniae* (dedicated to Robert of Gloucester) must have made Wace realize he could redirect his talents as a 'translator' from Latin into French ('*romanz*', *Rou* III.151–3), from saints' lives towards secular chronicle. Sometime after 1150 he probably started on his rendering of the *Historia* and made a visit to England.

If he arrived before 1153, it was a turbulent time to travel. Stephen of Blois had seized the English throne in 1135, over the claims of Matilda, and a period of civil war began. The southwest, where it is plausibly conjectured Wace travelled and picked

---

[3] *Rou*, p. 215. Wace also mentions the duty of *clercs* to read stories at feasts so that they are not forgotten (*Rou* III.5–10).

[4] For dates, see Wace, *La Vie de Sainte Marguerite*, ed. Francis, p. xvi, and Arnold, 1 p. lxxv.

up his detailed topographical knowledge,[5] had been cruelly harried by both Henry of Anjou, Matilda's son, and Stephen in 1149, and in 1152 Henry invaded again, to relieve Stephen's siege of Wallingford. Finally, however, the Treaty of Wallingford at the end of 1153 recognized Henry as the legitimate heir to the throne, and in 1154 the duke of Anjou and Normandy became king of England.

It was an excellent moment to present a history of her new land to Henry's queen, as Lawman tells us Wace did,[6] when it was finished in 1155. Eleanor of Aquitaine, like her husband, was intelligent, well educated and a patron of literature. When Wace complains[7] of the stinginess of his aristocratic audience, he makes it clear the king and queen are exceptions, generously giving him presents and, later, making him a canon with a prebend at Bayeux (c. 1165–9). He may now have been accepted as a court poet. Certainly he was proud of his personal knowledge of the 'three king Henrys' (Henry I, Henry II and Henry the Young King), since he twice refers to it.[8] Confident of royal support, in about 1160 he started on the Roman de Rou, another long chronicle, this time of Henry's ancestors, the dukes of Normandy.

Work on this did not go smoothly. Wace wrote the first part, and then abandoned it for a new start in a new and longer metre (now called La Chronique ascendante des ducs de Normandie). A second part was written in the same style. Then the poem was interrupted for several years. By the time Wace resumed writing, in the 1170s, his royal patrons may have been getting impatient, and a rival had made his appearance. Benoît de Sainte-Maure had dedicated his Roman de Troie to Eleanor between 1160 and 1170, and it was to him that Henry now turned for a ducal history. Having brought his own poem up to the year 1106, Wace sadly recognized his rival's success and abandoned his labours. He is named in a charter of 1174 as Wascius canonicus; sometime after 1174 he adds to the Rou an account of a siege of Rouen in that year; but the date of his death is unknown. It is, however, probably before 1183, since in that year the Young King Henry, always alluded to as a living person in the Rou, dies.

[5] Houck, Sources, pp. 220–7.
[6] L 20–3.
[7] In Rou, 'Chronique ascendante' 1–23, III.151–62.
[8] Rou III.177–80, 11430–4.

Literary Background to the Text

Wace, like many other twelfth-century historiographers, wrote for a people with a strong interest in the history and legends of their adopted country. Some fifty years after the Norman Conquest, chroniclers like William of Malmesbury (in the *De Gestis Regum Anglorum*, 1125) and Henry of Huntingdon (in the *Historia Anglorum*, 1139) had begun constructing histories of Britain, though their efforts were somewhat vitiated by a lack of information on pre-Saxon, let alone pre-Roman, times.[9] These Latin works were dedicated to important and politically powerful Normans, Robert of Gloucester and Alexander, bishop of Lincoln, both also patrons of Geoffrey of Monmouth. Meanwhile Geffrei Gaimar, influenced by Geoffrey's *Historia* and using the Anglo-Saxon Chronicle, was writing his *Estoire des Engleis*, the first vernacular chronicle, in the late 1130s, for a somewhat humbler noble household, the FitzGilberts, in Hampshire and Lincolnshire.[10]

The interest in national history helps to account for both the *Historia Regum Britanniae* and Wace's rendering of it, the *Brut*. But while their works belong recognizably to the same genre as those of William of Malmesbury and Henry of Huntingdon, they also differ significantly from them in respect of the figure of Arthur. Though in the Middle Ages 'history' is notoriously a mixture of fact and fiction, some medieval historiographers made more serious attempts than others to distinguish one from the other. Both William and Henry had found references to Arthur in the ninth-century *Historia Brittonum* but did not greatly elaborate on what they found, already aware of many dubious stories in circulation: 'This is that Arthur, of whom the Britons fondly fable, even to the present day; a man worthy to be celebrated, not by idle fictions, but in authentic history.'[11] Henry of Huntingdon was thus 'stunned', when the *Historia Regum Britanniae* appeared, to discover a virtually single-handed creation of Arthur's biography, a celebration indeed,

[9] See Henry of Huntingdon's letter to Warinus, quoted by Roberts in *AOW*, p. 100.

[10] See Gaimar, *Estoire des Engleis*, ed. Bell, pp. ix–xii, xxi, li–lii. The first part of Gaimar's chronicle, the *Estoire des Bretuns*, is lost.

[11] William of Malmesbury, *De Gestis*, trans. Stephenson, p. 11.

but where 'authentic history' played very little part. Where historical evidence on pre-Roman and pre-Saxon times had been scanty or non-existent, Geoffrey of Monmouth had creatively filled in the gaps, and Wace, following him, filled them even more substantially. Yet without them the great flowering of Arthurian romance in the second half of the twelfth century would not have been possible.

The Evidence for Arthur before Geoffrey of Monmouth

Before the twelfth century, information on Arthur and on the late fifth to early sixth century, when he supposedly flourished and fought the Saxons, was sparse. Our earliest source for the story of the Saxon incursions is *De Excidio Britonum* ('The Ruin of Britain'), *c.* 540, by a Welshman, Gildas. He tells us that a 'proud tyrant' (a play on the Welsh title *Gwrtheyrn*, 'superior ruler') let in three ships of Saxons to help him repel invaders from the north. He never mentions Arthur, but he does describe a long period of peace after the Saxons had met successful British resistance under Ambrosius Aurelianus, of noble Roman family, and had been defeated at *mons Badonicus*, Badon Hill. He tells us this was forty-four years earlier, so this battle was around AD 496.[12]

Bede's *Historia Ecclesiastica* (731) used Gildas, repeating the story of the Saxon invaders and adding names: the title of the British ruler has now become his name, Vortigern; the Saxon leaders are Hengist and Horsa; and again he gives the credit for British victories and Badon Hill to Ambrosius.[13] The name 'Arthur' does not appear in chronicle until the 820s, when another, multilingual, Welshman (later called 'Nennius') wrote the *Historia Brittonum*, a synchronizing history drawing on Bede, other narratives of English origin, and Welsh folk-tale, battle-lists, and genealogy.[14] The *Historia Brittonum* is one of Geoffrey of Monmouth's (and perhaps one of Wace's)[15] princi-

---

[12] Gildas, *De Excidio*, ed. and trans. Winterbottom, pp. 1–3, 26, 28 and notes pp. 150–1.

[13] Bede, *Historia Ecclesiastica*, Book I, chs 15–16.

[14] Nennius, *British History*, ed. and trans. Morris. See Dumville, 'Historical value', pp. 1–26, and Charles-Edwards in *AOW*, pp. 15–28.

[15] See Foulon in *ALMA*, pp. 96–7.

pal sources, so those of its contents that relate to his 'Arthurian section' can here be briefly listed:

a   Arrival of Hengist and Horsa; Guorthigirnus (= Vortigern); Hengist's daughter; Octa and Ebissa (chs 31, 36–8)

b   Tale of Emrys, called Ambrosius, and Vortigern's tower; Vortimer's four battles with Saxons and his death (chs 40–4)

c   'Night of the Long Knives': Saxons treacherously kill Britons (chs 45–6)

d   Vortigern's death by fire (ch. 47)

e   Ambrosius as supreme king of Britain (ch. 48)

f   The twelve campaigns of Arthur, *dux bellorum* (battle-leader) against Octa, ending in Badon Hill (ch. 56)

g   The Wonders of Britain (*Mirabilia*), including Lake Lumonoy, Linn Liuan (near the Severn Bore) and the Fount of Gorheli (chs 67, 69–70).[16]

In this often discontinuous history, such stories are not always connected in a coherent narrative: any development from the boy-seer Emrys to Ambrosius the overlord is omitted, and Arthur appears unrelated to anyone except the Saxons he fights and the unnamed kings he fights for. He has no parents, no queen, no throne, no overseas conquests – and no death. This last was supplied briefly and mysteriously in the tenth-century *Annales Cambriae* (Welsh Annals), which, assigning the battle of Badon to 516, also states, by the year 537: 'The battle of Camlann, in which Arthur and Medraut fell.'[17]

The authors of three out of four of these 'historical' sources of material about Arthur and his times are Welsh, though writing in Latin. There exists also a large number of references to, and stories about, Arthur and his followers in Welsh literature, though how many of these were in existence before the first quarter of the twelfth century is difficult to determine; however, there is a handful of reliably early ones which have a bearing on the *Historia Regum Britanniae* and Wace's *Brut*. The name Uther Pendragon, unrelated to Arthur, occurs in *Pa Gur yw y Porthaur* (a source or analogue of *Culhwch and Olwen*,

[16] These seem to be incorporated bodily from an existing written source: see Dumville, 'Historical value', p. 22.

[17] Nennius, *British History*, ed. and trans. Morris, p. 45.

c. 1100, so probably before that date), a long speech of Arthur
to a gatekeeper, celebrating, among others, the warriors Cei and
Bedwyr.[18] *Culhwch* itself has a long catalogue of Arthur's
courtiers, the names of his weapons, ship and queen, and three
giants slain by his men, notably Cei.[19] In a Latin life of St Gildas
written by the Welsh Caradoc of Llancarvan (1120s–1130s),
Arthur's queen, Guennuvar, is violated and abducted by Melwas
to Glastonbury, which Arthur then besieges. There is here,
perhaps, as in the Modena archivolt of 1099–1120, a precedent
to Modred's usurpation of queen and crown in Geoffrey's
Historia.[20]

Geoffrey of Monmouth

Geoffrey of Monmouth was probably born or brought up on
the border of Wales, and his origins were possibly Breton:
Monmouth had been ruled by Bretons since Wihenoc from Dôle
took it over in 1075, and the Bretons play an honourable role in
the *Historia*, supplying the dynasty which produces Arthur. But
Geoffrey may, alternatively, have been Welsh; he was certainly
in touch with Welsh legend and traditional Welsh history as
preserved in genealogies and name-catalogues, whether or not
all these were contained in the (possibly fictitious) 'ancient
British book' he claims was presented to him by Walter,
archdeacon of Oxford. Geoffrey had moved to Oxford by 1129,
probably as a secular canon with teaching duties in the College
of St George, and this was the period when he wrote the
Prophetiae Merlini (before 1135), the *Historia* and the *Vita
Merlini* (1148). He is said to have died by 1155.[21]

To sum up most of what may have been available to the
author of the *Historia Regum Britanniae*: on the one hand, by

---

[18] In the *Black Book of Carmarthen*. See Sims-Williams in AOW, pp. 37–9,
and Bromwich and Evans, *Culhwch*, pp. xxxiv–xxxvi.

[19] For giant-slaying in the Welsh Arthurian tradition, see Roberts in AOW,
p. 108.

[20] See Sims-Williams and Roberts in AOW, pp. 59–60, 110, and Loomis in
ALMA, pp. 60–1.

[21] HRB, I, pp. ix–xix; Roberts, 'Geoffrey of Monmouth', pp. 29–40; Piggott,
'Sources', pp. 269–86. For a recent and plausible argument as to whether
Geoffrey was Welsh and promoting the Welsh, see Gillingham, 'Context and
purposes', pp. 99–118.

the ninth century there were 'historical' accounts of Arthur as a British leader who checked the Saxon advance by his victories in the late fifth or the early sixth century. On the other hand, by the twelfth century or earlier, there were snippets and allusions in Welsh story to a prince with a queen and a band of supporters, whose folkloric exploits were clearly widely known. It was Geoffrey of Monmouth's supreme achievement to bring these elements together in a charismatic figure whose deeds, especially against the Romans, form the longest section and the climax of his chronicle.

For Geoffrey's Norman patrons he created a quite new history of their adopted country. He gave Britons a glorious Trojan origin and, drawing on Gildas and the *Historia Brittonum*, constructed for their past a pattern of rise, decline and final loss tightly connected to moral strength and weakness.[22] A long relationship between Britain and Rome is intrinsic to this pattern, and Geoffrey adds to the Roman invasion under Julius Caesar two other, fictitious, confrontations before and after it, glorifying two British conquests of the Roman empire. The first of these is led by Belinus and Brennius, the last by Arthur, and it is only domestic treachery (a recurrent theme in the *Historia*) that destroys his tremendous achievement.

Although a large part of the *Historia* would seem to have been invention, Geoffrey's chronicle often reads quite plausibly and Arthur himself usually sounds, allowing for exaggeration here and there, like a credible medieval king. There are two notable exceptions in the Arthurian narrative, however, that remind us we are dealing with fiction and folk-tale. The first concerns Merlin and his part in the birth of Arthur. Geoffrey appears to have amalgamated two separate figures, the boy-seer Emrys, in the *Historia Brittonum*, and Myrddin in early Welsh verse, a warrior and mad fugitive in the woods of Caledonia after the northern battle of Arfderydd in 573,[23] and supposedly the author of prophecies. In Geoffrey's *Historia*, he is the mysterious product of a supernatural union and provides a

---

[22] See Roberts in *AOW*, pp. 102–3.

[23] See Jarman in *AOW*, pp. 117–36. Many names and tales of the Northern Welsh and their kingdom of Strathclyde, whose headquarters was at Alclud (Dumbarton) migrated southwards to Wales between the sixth and the eleventh century.

suitably marvellous origin for Stonehenge and for the conception of Arthur. The second concerns Arthur's killing of the giant on Mont Saint Michel, an episode strongly reminiscent of *Culhwch and Olwen* and Welsh traditions of Arthur keeping the land free from giants and monsters.

Wace

'Translate' in the Middle Ages did not have the narrow meaning it does today, and Wace, in bringing Geoffrey's 'history' to a yet larger audience unversed in Latin, felt free to amplify and embellish his chronicle. Yet he stuck very close to the outline, and often even the detail, of the events there. Occasionally a train of incidents is better motivated and ordered (like the Arthurian embassy to Lucius), but for the most part it is in the details Wace adds to the narrative that the atmosphere and flavour of his chronicle is captured. In the Arthurian section (as elsewhere), the details often point to Wace's own conception of the story and what was most important about it for him.[24]

It was natural for Wace to add particulars from his personal familiarity with England and the English. These could add immediacy or verisimilitude, or make better topographical sense, as when the Saxons are, after the battle of Bath, scattered by Cador while crossing the River Teign, instead of at Thanet (as in the *Historia*), at the opposite end of the country. He advertises his knowledge of English, and his awareness of the names in various languages for famous topographical features, like Stonehenge (8175–8). His knowledge of Continental geography and inhabitants also emerges: Langres, near the fateful battleground of Soeïse, 'lies on top of a hill surrounded by valleys' (12285–6); and Bedoer commands the Herupeis, a Norman contingent in Arthur's army to whom Wace gives some prominence.

More specialist knowledge still is displayed in various crowd scenes, clustered around Arthur's coronation and its aftermath.

[24] Many scholars have discussed Wace's additions to Geoffrey's narrative, notably Arnold in his edition (1 pp. lxxix–xci), and Pelan and Houck in their books, *Influence du Brut* and *Sources*. As far as his principal source is concerned, recent criticism believes Wace drew on both the Vulgate and the Variant texts of the *Historia*, with the Variant as his base-text: see *HRB*, II, pp. xvi–lviii.

The list of many different musical instruments used by the entertainers is perhaps less striking than the knowledgeable portrayal of the dice-players.[25] Most impressive of all is the loving description of Arthur's embarkation at Southampton, with its plethora of technical nautical terms (11205–38). All these add richness and plausibility to the chronicle. Wace has a talent for making a scene come to life: the coronation is embellished, not just by the scenes mentioned above, but by the portrayal of the crowds around the queen, the competitive dressing of her attendant ladies, and the knights vacillating between the attractions of church music and women (10385–416). The insulting message from the Roman embassy is received with fury and hubbub (10711–24).

Wace was, however, also exercised by what he did not know. When he introduces his single most important addition, possibly of his own invention, the Round Table,[26] he follows it with a now famous passage on the dubiety of the stories around Arthur:

> En cele grant pais ke jo di,
> Ne sai si vus l'avez oï,
> Furent les merveilles pruvees
> E les aventures truvees
> Ki d'Artur sunt tant recuntees
> Ke a fable sunt aturnees:
> Ne tut mençunge, ne tut veir,
> Tut folie ne tut saveir.
> Tant unt li cunteür cunté
> E li fableür tant flablé
> Pur lur cuntes enbeleter,
> Que tut unt fait fable sembler.   (9787–98)

(In this time of great peace I speak of – I do not know if you have heard of it – the wondrous events appeared and the adventures were sought out which, whether for love of his generosity, or for fear of his bravery, are so often told about Arthur that they have become the stuff of fiction: not all lies, not all truth, neither total folly nor total wisdom. The raconteurs have told so many yarns,

---

[25] Lines 10543–52 and 10556–88. These passages are only in ten of the manuscripts; Arnold thought it was possible they were interpolations, but kept them (I pp. xlix–l).

[26] See Schmolke-Hasselmann, 'The Round Table', pp. 41–75.

the story-tellers so many stories, to embellish their tales that they have made it all appear fiction.)

The careful couplet connection of *pruvees* and *truvees* suggests an inextricable mix of fact (*pruver* = 'to appear, show, demonstrate') and fiction (*truver* = 'to seek, discover, invent'). Referring to an apparent host of oral sources from which one must judiciously select is a common rhetorical topos in the twelfth century, used to increase a writer's esteem, and not necessarily true. It is less common, however, to make frequent suggestions that one's sources might be unreliable, however much one would like to believe them. There are passages both in the *Brut* and in the *Rou* where Wace evinces what has been called 'canny Norman scepticism',[27] especially in his record of a visit to Broceliande and the fountain of Barenton, hoping, in vain, to find their fabled *merveilles*.[28] In consequence, one accords a certain respect to Wace's sceptical reporting of Arthur's end and the legends of his survival; the only thing certain here is uncertainty itself.

Wace is far more interested in human emotions than Geoffrey of Monmouth. This is evident in the way each describes battles, an important and recurrent feature in both works. The *Historia* is precise on tactics and manoeuvres, but Wace prefers to evoke atmosphere and feeling: in his account of the great battle in the Soeïse valley, he captures the terrifying and confusing fray, and his heavy use of anaphora catches the remorseless press of anonymous violence (12563–8). His sympathy extends to the victims on the enemy side: the fleeing Saxons, aghast at Cador's ambush (9389–92), and the starving Scots, especially their womenfolk, whose long and moving appeals elicit Arthur's mercy (9465–526). The heroic parts played by Kei, Bedoer and Walwein are all expanded so that the sadness of their deaths can be more keenly felt; what contempt, on the other hand, is displayed in Walwein's address to the Roman emperor (using the familiar *tu*, 11709–33) and in the flight of Modret's soft and selfish army (13113–30). And in the final battle, Wace again eschews the *Historia*'s military and tactical details for a more powerful, general description of the horror and futility of civil war (13253–74).

[27] Morris, 'The *Gesta Regum Britanniae*', p. 93.
[28] *Rou*, III. 6373–98; see also II. 1366–7 and 1371–2 for Wace's care over sources.

This importation of feeling individualizes martial scenes; another feature of Wace's writing tends, on the contrary, to formalize and stereotype them. This is the epic language and concepts characteristic of the contemporary *chansons de geste*. The battles of Britons versus Romans and of Arthur versus Modret are seen as those of Christianity versus paganism. The kernel of this already lay in the *Historia*, but Wace takes every opportunity to remind us of Rome's heathen, especially Saracen, allies (12523, 12710–20, 12914), bent on destroying Christendom, and to stress Modret's association with pagan Northmen (13226–8). Arthur and his men engage with Saracen foes in individual combats, similar to those graduated, formal encounters in the *chansons de geste*,[29] with the same vaunts over the bodies of the fallen, and the same touches of black humour (11832–8, 12908–11). The lament of Charlemagne over Roland, which sees him as representative of a lost generation of fine youth, *juvente bele*, (*Chanson de Roland* 2916) is echoed by Wace's lament over the battle of Camble: 'Dunc peri la bele juvente . . . e de la gent Arthur la flur/E li plus fort e li meillur' ('thus perished fine youth . . . the flower of Arthur's men, strongest and best', 13266, 13273–4).

Wace introduced no extra people into the Arthurian story, but increased and, in some instances, complicated the roles of the existing characters. A very minor part is played by Guitart of Poitiers in the *Historia*, but he is given more prominence and more valour by Wace, possibly as a compliment to Queen Eleanor, who was also countess of Poitou and could count Guitart as a legendary ancestor. Walwein is a distinctly more memorable character than in the *Historia*, if already showing signs of his split personality in later Arthurian literature. His well-known reply to the warlike Cador (10765–72), extolling the virtues of peace-time pursuits, especially love, marks the beginning of his reputation for *corteisie*, and elsewhere Wace praises him for this and his moderation, yet his insolent hot-headedness, encouraged by the irresponsible at Arthur's court, seems the very opposite of such qualities. The character of his uncle Arthur is enhanced and given more life in many ways, first and foremost through direct speech: for example, he harangues his troops more powerfully and more often than in the *Historia*.

---

[29] See Rychner, *La Chanson de Geste*. The combat of Hyrelgas and Boccus is especially notable.

As a soldier he is a consummate tactician (9301–5, 12309–14); as a king he has complete control over his barons, establishing the Round Table to curb their competitive instincts; as a chivalrous man he ensures the safety of the Roman ambassadors and rewards them, and in return we see him through their admiring eyes as a great king (11059–72). Wace completes his portrait of Arthur by entering imaginatively and emotionally into his relationship with the two members of his family who betray him, his nephew Modret and his wife Ganhumare.

Wace tells us the queen is the epitome of a courtly lady, not only beautiful and well-mannered, but highly articulate. These qualities elicit Arthur's deep love, but the marriage is barren – 'they could have no children' (9653–8). The portrait of the couple is even at this stage tinged with emotion, which is concealed during the magnificent coronation festivities, when king and queen enact their public roles, but which erupts in the highly charged passage describing Arthur's arrangements for the care of the kingdom by his nephew and queen in his absence abroad (11173–88). The disgust and indignation Wace feels for Modret's behaviour is conveyed through rhetorical question and exclamation. Modret betrays Arthur twice: he loves the queen (high treason), and he loves his uncle's wife (incest). Wace hammers home the shame and disgrace of this with an especially strong word, *putage* (11185), and its various meanings of fornication, debauchery and whorish behaviour suggest something new about Ganhumare. Does Modret's carefully concealed love (11180–1) also conceal a yielding by the queen? Is she no victim but complicit? Having planted the suggestion, Wace does not elaborate but significantly closes the subject by lamenting Arthur's transfer of power to Modret *and* to the queen. Once Arthur has beaten the Romans, queen and nephew re-appear, to ruin his victory. At the corresponding moment in the *Historia*, Geoffrey of Monmouth is carefully non-committal: Modret has married the queen 'in abominable passion, in violation of her former vows'.[30] This suggests that the queen could be a victim,

---

[30] *Nuntiatur ei Modredum nepotem suum ... eiusdem diademate per tyrannidem et proditionem insignitum esse reginamque Ganhumeram uiolato iure priorum nuptiarum eidem nephanda uenere copulatum fuisse* (HRB, I, p. 129). Roberts (AOW, p. 110), like Thorpe, translates: '[G.] who had broken the vows of her earlier marriage', but this suggests a more active, and reprehensible, role than Geoffrey does. See Tatlock, *Legendary History*, p. 426 n. 19.

and indeed her later flight to Caerleon, prompted by news of Modred's recovery from defeat and his advance to Winchester, supports this view. Wace is much less restrained; as before, he underlines the disgrace and ignominy of Arthur's position, the family bonds and the sexual disloyalty of Modret, who has 'taken the king's wife to bed, the wife of his uncle and his lord' (13028–9). A little later, the queen flees to Caerleon, but this is because of *Arthur's* advance, not Modret's,[31] and her despairing lament reveals her collusion in adultery: she has wickedly disgraced herself, shamed the king and desired his nephew (13201–12). The character of this nephew is also expanded by Wace: he is both more villainous, through the revelation of long-concealed sexual perfidy and through his desertion of his allies (13173–80), and intermittently more sympathetic, in that we are given glimpses into his thoughts, which from time to time acknowledge his guilt and fear (13075, 13174). In his brief but intense sketch of the eternal adulterous triangle, Wace laid the grounds for many later explorations of a fundamental Arthurian theme.

Did Wace have any aims in 'translating' the *Historia Regum Britanniae*, other than spreading a good story further and eliciting his patrons' generosity? One critic sees the *Brut* as political propaganda for Henry II, promoting his recent succession to the throne and inventing the Round Table as a symbol both of his separation from his barons and of his firm control over them.[32] While this is a plausible explanation, there is always a danger in arguing from literature back to life, which involves elevating some literary features at the expense of others. Though the Arthurian section of the *Brut* celebrates Arthur – and thus, perhaps, Henry – it seriously undermines the character of his queen. Yet we know Wace presented his chronicle to Henry's queen, Eleanor, who had only been married to the king for three years and was busy presenting him with a large brood of children. To insinuate any parallel with Ganhumare would have been insulting. We are on safer ground if we withdraw from close historical connections and notice the care with which Wace leaves open the question of Arthur's return.[33] Geoffrey of

[31] A change already introduced in the First Variant version of *HRB*, §177.
[32] Schmolke-Hasselmann, 'The Round Table', pp. 49, 61–8.
[33] See Morris, 'The *Gesta Regum Britanniae*', pp. 93–4.

Monmouth's works had vacillated on this matter, the *Historia* only mentioning Arthur's 'mortal' wounds – and the Bern MS firmly adding 'Animus eius in pace quiescat' ('May his soul rest in peace') – and the *Vita Merlini* expanding on the trip to Avalon and the possibility of Arthur returning to health. Stories of the Breton belief in Arthur's return had been in circulation for fifty years or more before Wace wrote;[34] with his customary interest in oral tradition, he probably wanted to show he knew them, but treated them with his usual caution, knowing, moreover, that on the one hand the Bretons could treat unbelievers with violence but, on the other, that the new Plantagenet dynasty would not favour a work firmly expressing belief in the return of the rightful king. Shifting the onus squarely on to Merlin, he left the matter safely in doubt.

Note on the poem's text and its prose translation

Wace's *Brut* survives in twenty-six manuscripts and fragments. The text I have used for my translation is that provided by Ivor Arnold in his 1938 edition for the Société des Anciens Textes Français. Out of the twenty manuscripts of the *Brut* at Arnold's disposal, he largely used P and D, both Anglo-Norman and thirteenth-century; in the Arthurian section of the *Brut*, MS D is used from line 12000 on, because at this point MS P has many faulty readings. In 1962 Arnold and Pelan edited the Arthurian section separately, from another manuscript (K), from Champagne.[35] I gratefully acknowledge the help I have received from their text, whose readings I have occasionally adopted, and also from the suggestions in their notes (e.g., those to lines 10546, 12350, 12928).

Wace's octosyllabic couplets describe events soberly and clearly, dramatizing them more vividly than Geoffrey of Monmouth by frequent use of direct speech and of repetition, his

---

[34] Tatlock, *Legendary History*, p. 204; Loomis in *ALMA*, pp. 53–4, 64.

[35] P is a manuscript from Christchurch, Canterbury, formerly in the possession of Boies Penrose, now London, British Library, MS Add. 45103. D is Durham Cathedral Library, MS C iv.27; K is Paris, Bibliothèque Nationale, MS fonds français 794. The text used for the 1912 translation of Wace (Everyman's Library) is MS H, Paris, Bibliothèque Nationale, MS fonds français 1450, the base-text of the *Brut* edition by Le Roux de Lincy (1836–8), which has a number of differences from, and additions to, P.

favourite rhetorical device. I have tried to retain this effect wherever possible, and also tried to render those phrases characteristic of *chanson de geste* and early romance, *es vus* ('behold') and *dunc veïssiez* ('now might you see'), much used by Wace to involve us in his liveliest scenes. On names, I have adopted the policy of usually transcribing them in the form in which they first occur in the text; this, in the case of the principal characters, has the effect, I believe, of removing from them a certain stale familiarity. I have only substituted modern names for places where they are already very close to the original.

Robinson College,   JUDITH WEISS
Cambridge
January 1997

Lawman's Version of the Story of Britain

Wace was still alive in 1174, but had died before Lawman began writing: Lawman writes of him in the past tense. Exactly how long after Wace's death Lawman 'took up his quills' and began his redaction of Wace's version of the *Historia* is still a matter of dispute. In his Prologue, Lawman gives us a piece of information about Wace which that author himself had not divulged: that he presented his book to Queen Eleanor, 'who was the queen of Henry the great king', and critics have tried to use this information to date Lawman's poem – or, rather, the Prologue, which was probably written after the rest of the work was complete. The Eleanor to whom Wace presented his work must have been Eleanor of Aquitaine, whose second husband was Henry II of England. In 1216 another Henry came to the throne, the nine-year-old Henry III, for whom the great old soldier William Marshal, earl of Pembroke, acted as regent, aided by the papal legate, Cardinal Guala. It is argued that, had Lawman been writing after Henry III's accession, he would have distinguished the earlier Henry in some way, and that therefore Lawman's *Brut* must date from between Henry II's death in 1189 (because the past tense is used of Henry and Eleanor in line 22) and Henry III's accession in 1216. Two objections can be made to this: the first, a minor point, is that the expression 'who was Henry's queen' seems to signify that Eleanor herself was dead (she died, in France, in 1204); the second is that Henry is indeed distinguished by an epithet: Eleanor was queen of 'the high/great king' (*þes heȝes kinges*); this might well be a means of distinguishing a man famous for his legal and administrative reforms from a mere boy, and could extend the period of composition to the time when Henry III assumed his majority, 1227. But had Lawman been writing as late as 1236, when Henry III himself married a queen called Eleanor, presumably he would then have distinguished the early Henry and Eleanor more specifically from the later.

Attempts to date the poem by Lawman's doubt about the continued payment of Peter's Pence do not identify any precise date: in 1205 John refused to send the collected monies to Rome, but payment also ceased in 1164 and 1169; the allusion could even relate to the period of the Interdict, 1208–14.

It looks as if Lawman wrote either during the reign of John, or while Henry was still a child: in other words, between 1199 and, say, 1225. Indeed, it might have taken him more than a decade to produce the 16,000 long lines of the *Brut*. It is clear that Lawman admires a king who is strong and consistently motivated (even if this means that at times he is severe in administering justice and its penalties) and one who is in harmony with his barons and his clergy. Perhaps it is not impossible that the vagaries of John's temperament and the vicissitudes of his reign, with the loss of Normandy in 1204, the Papal Interdict imposed from 1208 and not formally lifted until 1214, and the baronial demands which culminated in Magna Carta in 1215, could have led Lawman to postulate an ideal monarch markedly distinct from the actual king. Nevertheless, King John was popular in the West, and was actually buried in front of the high altar in Worcester Cathedral in 1216 (Poole, 1087–1216, p. 486). The Interdict may itself hold the clue to dating Lawman's *Brut*: during this period no priest could say Mass, preach, hear confession, baptize, marry or conduct a funeral for his parishioners; this must have left the clergy with time on their hands, which Lawman might have filled constructively by writing the *Brut* – but this is mere surmise. It is, however, interesting that when translating Wace's account of the apostasy under Gurmund, Lawman adds a line declaring that no bells were rung and no Masses said all through Britain, exactly as happened during the Interdict.

Who, then, could Lawman have been? He tells us in his Prologue that he was a priest, and had a living in Areley in the diocese of Worcester. There are still some stones and one round-headed window dating from the twelfth century in St Bartholomew's Church at Areley Kings, which must have been there in Lawman's time (*VCH: Worcester*, IV, p. 228). The rectors of Martley presented to the living of Areley Kings in the thirteenth century, and Elizabeth Salter shows that Areley Kings was part of the manor of Martley which passed from the king's hands in 1196, first, in part, to Philip de Aire and then entirely to the de Frisa or de Frise family in 1200; they kept it until 1233, when it passed to the Despensers (Salter, *E&I*, p. 67, citing *VCH: Worcester*, IV, pp. 227–30); Madden says the estate went to the de Fruges family, in 1205 (Madden, I, x, n. 2), and adds the information that the advowson of Martley was, since the time of Domesday, in the possession of the Abbey of Cormeilles near Lisieux in Normandy (Madden, I, x, n. 2). The prior of Newent, the English cell of Cormeilles, occasionally presented to the living (*VCH: Worcester*, IV, p. 295), but quite possibly Lawman had an Anglo-Norman monk as his rector, since alien priories continued to present to English livings after the loss of Normandy in 1204.

It is important to see Lawman in the context of his parish near the Welsh marches and in his diocese of Worcester. Although Tatlock asserts that Lawman was an obscure cleric living in a rural backwater (*Legendary History*, pp. 509, 514), in fact he lived only ten miles north of the important ecclesiastical centre at Worcester; during the decade 1208–18 successive bishops of Worcester were called upon to share in pronouncing the Interdict and in supervising the nine-year-old king Henry III, and to direct the burial of King John in front of Worcester Cathedral high altar and beside his patron saint, Wulfstan. It was at Worcester that the great Welsh Prince Llywelyn did homage to the boy King Henry III in March 1218, in return for confirmation of the lands he had conquered from the Anglo-Normans. Llywelyn was a supremely good statesman and soldier, and maintained peace among the princes of South Wales until his death in 1240 (Poole, *1087–1216*, pp. 300–1). In Llywelyn, Lawman might well have seen a second King Arthur or another Cadwathlan, with the inept King John, who had planned a campaign against the Welsh, and had antagonized his own barons into inviting Louis of France to take the kingdom, in the role of the Saxons Colgrim or Edwin.

The long tenure of Bishop Wulfstan in the see of Worcester must have produced a painful transition when Norman episcopal control supervened in 1095; the bishops of Worcester at the turn of the twelfth century were especially uncongenial to native English clerics and layfolk: over the nine years from 1190, three

Normans held the see, the last of whom, John de Constantiis, removed from the cathedral the relics of the English Archbishop Wulfstan, just around the hundredth anniversary of his death. Mauger, his successor, who appealed to the Pope to be admitted to the see despite his illegitimacy, was a money-grabber: he had Wulfstan's relics restored to the cathedral and arranged his canonization in 1203, less out of devotion to the English saint (Norman prelates generally scorned native saints) than out of greed for the income from pilgrims to the shrine, which he was using to defray the costs of rebuilding after a fire in the precinct in 1202 until compelled by the Worcester monks to divide the proceeds. Mauger tried to bully the monks at Evesham, but then fled from King John's anger during the Interdict, abandoning his flock; he died in France in 1212. The next bishop but one abused Saint Wulfstan's relics by personally cutting the bones to fit the new shrine prepared for the rededication of the cathedral in 1218; Wulfstan avenged himself: the bishop died six days later. This kind of behaviour from his ecclesiastical superiors may well account for Lawman's reference to the malicious Normans; see *VCH: Worcester*, II, pp. 11–13).

The Manuscripts of Lawman's Brut

The *Brut* is extant in two manuscripts, both in the British Library. MS Cotton Caligula A ix is a quarto volume of 285 leaves, its first half containing the *Brut* on 192 folios written in double columns, mostly of 34 lines, by two scribes who exchanged stints once, the second resuming and completing the copying, and so transcribing about nine-tenths of the whole poem; there are marginal Latin glosses in black ink offering historical summaries and corrections of Lawman's poem, and the names of the characters in red where they occur in the text; the manuscript has been corrected by a contemporary of the two scribes and further corrected by a later hand (Le Saux, *Sources*, p. 1; B&L, 1, ix). The other manuscript, MS Cotton Otho C xiii, is also in double columns and was originally 155 folios written by one scribe. Only 145 folios survive, many greatly damaged in the fire at Ashburnham House in 1731 and deteriorating when Madden was working on the manuscript, which he had rebound (Madden, 1, xxxvi–viii).

Because MS O, before it was damaged, was a condensed

version of the work, some 3000 lines shorter than C and omitting many of the rhetorical expressions, poetic descriptions and archaic diction of MS C, it was assumed until the 1960s that MS O was fifty years or so later than C. When Neil Ker pointed out that MS C dated from the middle rather than the early thirteenth century, two things became clear. First, MS O was not merely a modernized *Brut*, updated after expressions and grammatical structures in the original had become obsolete, but a conscious representation of the material from a factual rather than an imaginative standpoint. Second, because neither extant manuscript was as early as the beginning of the 1200s, as had been thought, it was quite possible that Lawman himself was writing as late as the mid-thirteenth century. One reason that the poem had previously been thought to date from the mid- to late twelfth century was its archaic language: MS C preserves with reasonable accuracy declined forms of the definite article, and strong adjectives, with traces of grammatical gender in nouns, features which had been levelled in most parts of the country by the early thirteenth century. MS O is an inferior version of the poem, partly written from memory and by a scribe who was not sympathetic to Lawman's aims and methods. There are about eighty half-lines in O not present in C, some of them probably authentic. MS C is probably more faithful to Lawman's original, even though it may have been copied half a century after Lawman wrote.

Whenever Lawman was writing, from the ninth decade of the twelfth century to the middle of the thirteenth, he was using a self-consciously archaic spelling and grammar, perhaps to give an 'antique flavour' to his history, yet his diction was mainly colloquial and up to date, with some older compounds which had survived from Old English, and some new compound forms which he either invented on older patterns or imported from current speech to give sonorance and dignity to his account of the great deeds of great men in British history.

The Audience of the Brut

Lawman tells us he was the son of *Leouenað* and enjoyed his situation, near to Redstone (where the parishes of Astley and Areley meet), and there he 'read Book' (probably the Missal at Mass or his breviary). But this identification is contradicted by

MS O, in which we are told that his father was *Leucais* and that he lived at Areley 'with the good knight', where he read 'books'. In MS C he is a simple country priest (although the illuminated letter *A* which begins MS C contains a miniature of Lawman habited as a Benedictine monk), in MS O a learned man, for his time, and presumably a household chaplain. The two states are not incompatible, successively or even perhaps simultaneously. The difference of roles in the two manuscripts suggests a significant distinction in the aim of writing. A chaplain to a household was presumably assigned a certain topic by a patron and wrote for the entertainment or instruction (or both) of a mixed audience, the household as a whole if the work was read aloud, particular literate members of it if the book was passed around in manuscript, a single auditor, perhaps, if the writer were a tutor. In the simplest form of the relationship presumably the patron would furnish the many parchment sheets needed for a huge work like Lawman's *Brut*. A parish priest in a rural area was not very likely to be writing for his rustic parishioners, and unless he wrote the work for the secular priests of neighbouring parishes, or a college of Augustinian canons, or (like Mannyng, who also translated Wace's *Brut* in 1338) for the lay brothers of a monastic community, it is hard to surmise what the purpose of writing and what the actual or envisaged audience could have been. From the little that Lawman tells us of his 'splendid idea' of writing a history of England, he could have been writing for his own entertainment and with no audience in mind but himself.

For the first thousand lines or so Lawman's *Brut* does not appear to be directed towards any specific audience. Then begins a sporadic use of the second-person-singular pronoun: *þu*. Grammatically, Lawman is conducting a dialogue between himself and one other person; however, the obvious potential for declaiming many of the speeches which he adds to Wace's narrative makes it unlikely that Lawman wrote for a solitary reader. Yet who could have wanted to hear the poem, at this length, and in English? Anyone interested in the customs and ancient history of the country and sufficiently literate to be able to read for himself a work as idiosyncratic as the *Brut*, would either be from the clergy, and therefore capable of reading Geoffrey's Latin and Wace's French, or at least from the administrative class, the estate bailiffs and stewards, who by the thirteenth century were learning French for business purposes, and could at least have managed Wace in the original. I think we must assume that Lawman did indeed write for a patron, for the household of a man of some status but certainly not of the Norman ruling class. It is possible that he was a merchant, of English stock, for whom the traditions of his country, and especially its place-names, were important: Lawman's second-person-singular address frequently occurs at the explanation of a place-name, and several of these are Lawman's own insertions. In the tale of Brian in the *Brut*, Brian adopts the disguise of a merchant; this is not necessary to the plot, since Brian's main and effective disguise is that of a beggar, and the account of Brian's base in Southampton, already in Lawman's time a major port, and a detailed description of the cellar in which he conceals his stock, are quite irrelevant but intriguing details, perhaps a touch of realism to please the patron. Another possibility is that the poem was written with an old soldier in mind: when Arthur has conquered Gaul he sends his veteran soldiers home to retirement, to pray for the undoubted sins their martial life-style will have led them to commit (L 12029–39): his command that they should love God so as to deserve Paradise is not in Wace (cf. W 10135–8). There may also be a mild admonition to young men in his audience when Lawman suggests that Carrais drew his army from those who refused to stay at home and work; by contrast to the neglect with which daughters were often treated, Lawman insists that Ebrauc's thirty daughters were all well clothed and cared for. The poem could have belonged to a family.

There is, then, an enigma about Lawman's status, audience and aims which is partly resolved if we accept MS O, line 3, and assume that he was the chaplain to a household, perhaps tutor to the sons of the family, and that parts of the book might be read aloud to them, while others could be read to the head of the household (or handed over to him if he was literate). There was already something of the compendium in Geoffrey's original work, and Lawman broadened its scope even further, even catering for women and young people in the readership. Clearly he had been reading the romances which had been produced in the seventy-odd years since Geoffrey wrote, and in his presentation of the story of Brian, Lawman highlights even more than Wace the romance motifs and themes. In the latter part of his poem especially, Lawman makes frequent use of the romance narrative transition 'now let us turn to'. This allusion to romance techniques, together with Lawman's rather clumsy attempt to deal with female fashion in the account of Arthur's crown-wearing at Caerleon, the generally compassionate tone of much of the narrative, and his enhancement of the women characters, make it not impossible that he wrote with some particular women in mind; even the apparently disparaging comment on women's ingenuity which he offers in speaking of Gornoille would not be out of place in a family setting, where it becomes a piece of friendly banter. The noticeably moralizing tone of many of Lawman's comments would fit this family setting, as would the generally didactic colouring of the material. Lawman's main contribution to the story of Britain is to present a picture of 'merry Britain' where law and order create a world in which populations thrive and society achieves stability and security. His Arthur is one of many lawgivers, who hands on the tradition he inherited to his successor, and his Gawain, markedly distinct from the source character, praises the delights of God-given peace, when men do better deeds (L 12457).

Lawman's own interest in the law is apparent from his allusions to laws and law-makers. In Geoffrey's narrative there were already many references to law, most notably in the accounts of Dunwallo Molmutius and of the great law-giver Queen Marcia; these reflect Geoffrey's Norman interest in government and also his aim of gaining support from the aristocracy, especially Robert of Gloucester and the Empress Matilda. The many women in Geoffrey's work who take the throne or who are instrumental in running affairs are probably part of Geoffrey's political message in support of Matilda's cause. In his version, Lawman enhances this emphasis on the organization of society, and it is even possible that he worked in some way with legal transactions or records: perhaps his name 'Lawman' is not in fact his given name but a cognomen, reflecting his interest in the past and its customs (MED s.v. laue 9 b. 'national custom'); its spelling may well be a deliberate evocation of the Old English form of this title, rather than 'Scandinavian', as Tatlock maintains (Legendary History, p. 529). Perhaps this spelling was Lawman's deliberate imitation of the Anglo-Saxon form of the word: the OE term laȝmann, probably a late loan from Norse lǫgmaðr, was used in the very specialized senses of 'one of [?twelve] permanent judges' in the five boroughs of the Danelaw, and also, in the tenth-century *Ordinance of the Dunsætas* (see *OED* s.v. *lawman*), of the 'finders of law', six experts in Welsh law and six in English in the border region of rural Hereford called 'Archenfield'. But probably in more general use a *law-man* was 'one of a number of local magistrates administering justice in a borough or town' (*MED* s.v. *laue-man*); three men of the thirteenth century are on record with 'Lawman' as a surname, and *MED* cites Lawman's own name as an instance of the cognomen. Paul Brand has explained (in a private communication) that we know little of early thirteenth-century local courts: the 'suitors' to manorial courts, such as that at Martley, or the hundred courts (in Lawman's area this was Dodingtree) were experienced in the unwritten customs of the land. Such men were important receptacles of knowledge, since little written law as such was in force in England *c.* 1200; it was Magna Carta in 1215 that set the mark for the later thirteenth-century preservation of law in its original form. But if 'Lawman' was an honorary title, it must have acquired the familiarity of a personal name, or 'Lawman' would not have asked for prayers for his soul under this name.

Lawman's Verse Style

In return for writing his poem Lawman expected gratitude and payment in the form of prayers from readers who did not know him personally; in other words, he expected to be read by posterity. He had written a long poem which he assumed would have a lasting appeal.

He had every reason for his self-confidence: the *Brut* is a well-constructed narrative. Its episodes, discrete units which probably constituted sections for an evening's reading (Barron and Le Saux, 'Narrative art', p. 28), are presented at a controlled pace. His tone is more solemn than Wace's, and he frequently directs the action with a conventional 'voice-over' of somewhat trite but stern moralizing; he attempts to lighten this with humour in rather poor taste (which perhaps appealed to some of his audience). Yet the characters' motives are not left obscure, nor does Lawman obtrude on their dilemmas to reduce them to the level of moral exampla. There is a delicate tact in his narrative method: if it is only occasionally that we see into characters' minds; nevertheless people are often presented in close-up, and without the distancing effect of irony, which gives the narrative immediacy and dramatic power; this makes fully credible even outrageous events, like Uther's impersonation of Gorlois. In contrast, where the historical montage is moving much faster and the narrative is focused on more distant views of a swift succession of events or actions, Lawman pinpoints salient features in a clearly visualized setting without clogging the pace with detail. He is especially good at the technique which allows the reader to 'follow the gaze' of his characters as they appraise their situation or re-live their past (for example, Merlin's mother recalling her seduction).

The narrative mode of Lawman's poem is a compound of chronicle, romance, saint's life, and sermon; in some sections the reader is especially conscious of romance procedures, and in the last fifth of the work hagiography is prominent. Several of Lawman's characters deliver sermons, and his lay readers address their auditors using the oral techniques of an expert preacher. Lawman seems to have been familiar with the formal procedures of all four of these literary kinds. He has a certain number of set themes, among which Ringbom identifies 'feasts' and 'voyages' (with the sub-theme 'arrivals'). To these may be added 'battle-conflict' and 'death'. When these themes recur, Lawman recounts them in formulaic diction, in phrases which are very similar but not necessarily identical in each occurrence. Nor are these 'formulaic' phrases confined to set-pieces like battles; there are some 128 such 'epic formulas' which recur throughout the poem in roughly similar circumstances, few if any deriving from Old English, but all with that kind of 'archaic dignity' which Lawman must have considered appropriate to his material.

In addition, Lawman gives his tone epic dignity by using compounds; there are over 400 compound nouns in the *Brut*, only about fifty of them Old English poetic compounds, and many composed by Lawman himself, it seems, to convey two major topics: warfare and 'the people'. He also has a number of formulas denoting sub-themes, on the effects of warfare: notably, the cut and thrust of swords, the breaking of shields and armour, and the falling of the dead and the shedding of blood. Lawman has been called bloodthirsty and savage, perhaps because these phrases seem to occur so often. Yet in fact he abbreviates the high point of Geoffrey's narrative, Arthur's war against the emperor of Rome, and he cuts down battles and the technicalities of warfare (Le Saux, *Sources*, pp. 33, 42). Although there are over thirty occurrences of the formula 'the fated/dead fell there', this is no gloating over gore; rather, as it recurs it becomes a world-weary acknowledgement of the effects of human aggression. In battle description the formulas operate as a distancing device: malice and mortality are an unvarying element in human history; the tone is one of sadness rather than exultation. Far from rejoicing in martial heroism, except where pagans or traitors are being finished off, Lawman's verse technique undercuts these achievements by making each battle sound very like the last one. The only obvious difference may well be the rousing speech which precedes the fight, where he does make distinction, for example, between the stirring rhetoric of Arthur and the crude threats of the emperor.

There is an archaic resonance in Lawman's diction which derives from his use of phrases which are found in Old English prose and poetry; presumably Lawman has imported some of these as literary loans, not necessarily from the Old English works in which they are now extant, but from similar works which he may well have read in some monastic library, perhaps in Worcester Cathedral. Such words as *geddian* 'to speak' (L 1676, cf. *Beowulf* 1253) and poetic compounds like *mod-kare* (L 1556, cf. *Beowulf* 3553) and *sæ-werie* (L 2306, cf. *Beowulf: sæ-mēþe*) or *wunsele* (L 7836, 8784; cf. *Beowulf* 1383) were presumably not in everyday speech, but it is possible that such phrases as *hine braeid sæc* (L 3324, cf. ASC s.a. 1003: *gebræde he hine seocne*) and Lawman's favourite *sæht and sibbe* (cf. ASC s.a. 1140: *sib and sæhte*) could have been in colloquial use, at least in the vocabulary of the English story-teller. More difficult to explain are the verbal and situational parallels between L 13802–4 and *The Battle of Maldon*, and the presence of a passage very reminiscent of Wulfstan's most famous sermon in L 2013–18; Madden and others see a strong resemblance between the Old English *Battle of Brunanburh* and Lawman's diction. Whether or not these are conscious loans from Old English texts, such traditional use of language gives an antique flavour to the *Brut* (Stanley, 'Antiquarian sentiments', pp. 27–30).

The Arthurian section of Lawman's *Brut* is especially noted for its 'long-tailed' or epic similes. There are eight of these in the section covering the war with the Saxons and especially the battle of Bath. Although it has been suggested that Lawman must have used a particular source for this section (Davies, 'Laȝamon's similes'), these similes are merely longer than others which occur throughout the poem, and all resemble instances in both Geoffrey and Wace in which a hero is likened to a fierce animal and his foes to hunted prey (see Le Saux, *Sources*, pp. 206–13); moreover, extended similes even more elaborate than this are a feature of Latin heroic poetry of the late twelfth and early thirteenth centuries, in works known or dedicated to patrons on both sides of the English Channel; they also feature, of course, in Virgil and Statius, who were the inspiration of those medieval Latin poets (*E&I*, pp. 63–5). Like his use of formula and poetic compound, Lawman's similes are a stylistic enhancement of his theme.

All these stylistic features serve to highlight Lawman's main interest: people. His most impressive style demonstrates his admiration for great leaders, but by less flamboyant means he can also show a sensitive awareness of the special problems of women. But the world of artefacts interests him less: he omits the technical details of siege-warfare, musical instruments, ships under sail, and courtly pastimes like gambling, which Wace controls with narrative skill and decorum. Perhaps Lawman did not know the equivalent terms in English; perhaps the concepts were not always familiar to his audience; perhaps borrowing Wace's terms would have been the only way of conveying his substance, and the French words would have clashed with his designedly 'English' lexis. Perhaps his audience would simply not have been interested.

Whereas in the later thirteenth and fourteenth centuries writers gave their work a courtly tone by using loan-words taken over from French, Lawman uses very few French-derived words in the *Brut*, even though he was translating from a French poem: Madden counted under 50 words of French origin in MS C, and no more than 70 in the MS O adaptation (Madden, I, xxii, and nn. 3 and 4; Serjeantson, *History of Foreign Words*, pp. 117–18). Quite possibly, Lawman considered that using French terms for technical detail and courtly settings would clog the narrative and slow the pace and so distract from his theme, the people of this island.

Lawman has a different concept of 'Britain' from Geoffrey and Wace. Geoffrey inverts the accepted view of England as seen from the standpoint of English history, by placing the English in the novel role of interrupters rather than initiators of political history; Wace also sees British history as a sequence of successive political supremacies, but Lawman's emphasis is on continuity. He is more interested in the 'ordinary people' (cf. Le Saux, *Sources*, p. 80), the bedrock of the population which changes far less than the rulers. This he demonstrates in narrative content and technique, and in diction. His rulers constantly confer with their subjects at the 'hustings', a kind of informally constituted parliament not confined to the upper classes (Gillespy, 'Comparative study', pp. 398–401; Le Saux, *Sources*, p. 225). We find repeatedly in the *Brut* that Lawman adds direct speech to Wace's narrative: his characters confer and consult. Prominent in the narrative method of the *Brut* is the 'messenger theme', whereby Lawman adds the figure of a messenger who moves between two characters and gives a verbal report, in place of Wace's bald statement that information was given. This has the effect of showing that ordinary people are essential even in the high enterprises of the great (Le Saux, *Sources*, pp. 48–9). Lawman's use of the word *leod(e)* is ambiguous: the word can mean 'men', 'people' or, in Lawman's use, 'the land, nation'. The concept of an 'English' nationhood developed steadily from the loss of Normandy in 1204, and in his use of this word Lawman seems to evince a sense of national identity: the beautiful country promised to Brutus and surveyed by him with delight is home for a group of peoples whose identity it epitomizes; that identity is threatened by invaders, and it is on invasion and civil war rather than martial prowess for its own sake that Lawman focuses in his battle-scenes; if there is a 'hero-figure' in the *Brut*, it is 'this land' rather than any individual. The 'land' is a metonymic expression for everything which is 'us' to Lawman and his audience; great rulers enhance its people's reputation and protect them; evil ones and traitors prey off the populace or bring in alien favourites. Lawman is not interested, for example, in Wace's explanation of Modred's attitude to Arthur or in his remorse (W 13054, 13073–6): his actions betray and endanger the people, and Lawman simply condemns him outright (L 12728–34, 13925).

Lawman's alliterative technique has strong affinities with the alliterative prose of homilists like Ælfric of Eynsham (Frankis, 'English sources'), and Wulfstan, the writer of *Sermo Lupi*; indeed, there seems to be an echo of this sermon in Lawman's *Brut*. In addition, there are phrases and longer passages reminiscent of parts of the Anglo-Saxon Chronicle, of Ælfric's work, and perhaps of the Blickling Homilies. There are two passages, prayers by Arthur and Gawain, which also seem to contain echoes of Old English religious verse (lines 12760–3 and 14077–8; see Le Saux, *Sources*, pp. 213–17).

Already in Old English verse and rhythmic prose authors brought rhyme into play, and, especially after the first thousand lines, Lawman regularly produces the kind of full rhyme found in the Old English *Rhyming Poem* and sporadically in texts like *The Battle of Maldon*. *The Proverbs of Alfred* is a twelfth-century poem which combines alliteration with rhymes in a manner very similar to Lawman's *Brut* (*E&I*, p. 54). Furthermore, Lawman utilizes another word-echo device which derives from the rhetorical prose of the early Middle Ages: the matching of word-endings, particularly case-endings of declined words, a rhetorical device known as *similiter cadens* (cf. Madden, I, xxiv, n. 2). It is commonly said that Lawman wrote alliterative verse, and it is true that many of his half-lines are linked by alliteration. However, very many do not present this 'initial rhyme', but have either full rhyme in our sense (that is, the stem vowel and following consonant are identical) or have the 'closing rhyme' of identical or rhyming grammatical endings: for example, 12626 *swein: þein* and 12684 *comen* (pret. pl.): *to hireden* (dat. sg.). Still more lines have an identical stem-vowel in the two halves ('assonance') with *similar* consonants, that is liquids (*r*, *l*) or nasals (*n*, *m*); an example is 12609 *honden* ('hands'): *worden* ('words'), where the stem-vowels *o* probably rhyme and the inflexions *-en* certainly do. Or, and this is something we would no longer consider rhyme, they have identical or nearly identical consonants with distinction of vowels: 12717 *stille: halle*; 12688 *londen: þusende*. The resulting verse is something between the long line of Old English verse, with medial caesura, and the short octosyllabic couplet of much French narrative verse. Madden printed the short lines individually, like couplets; Brook and Leslie, in the EETS edition on which this translation is based, followed editors of extracts from the *Brut* like Emerson, and Brandl and Zippel, and print long lines with medial caesura, with some 'short' lines where the scribes (or perhaps in some cases Lawman himself) did not write a full line.

Whatever presentation of the verse the editors use is not important: in the original Lawman must be read with ear rather than eye: the speaking voice, or perhaps one should say the preaching voice, is dominant, with the natural intonation of colloquial English (Bennett, *ME Lit*, p. 83), even where the words are archaic or the construction grandiose. It is for this reason that I have tried to translate into the speech rhythms Lawman used, and tried wherever possible to echo his 'rhymes'. A prose rendering makes Lawman sound all too like Geoffrey of Monmouth and inevitably misses some of Lawman's poetic fervour, his enthusiasm for human endeavour, that continuing ambition which created our past and will always fire great achievements – or indeed misfire into disasters, as Leir's father Bladud crashed when he tried to fly, and as Morpidus died when he took on a monster single-handed.

Lawman's Sense of History

Why Lawman should have chosen to present this exciting narrative of the deeds, and, in his version in particular, the words of ancient British men in an archaic idiom modelled on the language of their Saxon conquerors is something of a puzzle. In all likelihood he chose this old-fashioned form of the language because it was redolent of days gone by, and because those days represented a time when the Anglo-Saxons, like the ancient Britons before them, had had a flourishing culture, literate, administratively sound, and independent of the kind of foreign influence and organization that had overtaken them with the arrival of the Normans. The Anglo-Saxons had used their own native language where the Norman tradition favoured Latin for many of the official records of Church and State, among them the annals and chronicles of monastic historians. The Anglo-Saxon Chronicle, begun under the auspices of King Alfred in the late ninth century, was kept up until the middle of the twelfth century in Peterborough, but had been discontinued (after being translated into Latin in some cases) in other centres. What Geoffrey of Monmouth did for the Britons in recording/inventing their past, Lawman continued by identifying the plight of the Britons under Saxon rule with the situation in

England under the Normans, who antagonized the English by
spurning their saints, traditions and language. He did this
through his use of the older English tongue in its former role:
historical record.

Geoffrey, Wace and Lawman were typical of the period of the
high Middle Ages in their interest in the past, and particularly
the pagan past; a similar tendency is at work in the activities of
Snorri Sturluson in thirteenth-century Iceland, and in Chaucer's
tales with a classical and Celtic pagan setting. Against the
backdrop of a belief system which does not automatically
reward the good and punish the bad after death, the actions of
men, for good or ill, take on new dimensions: people may act
well because it serves their reputation or helps others; they may
equally, however, choose to act selfishly with little expectation
of reprisal, unless chance or a man of extreme courage appears
to redress the balance – or to gain his own advantage from
political chaos. Even the great (nominal) Christians like Arthur
lived in a world threatened by pagan incursions, and in this they
formed role-models for later medieval Europe, threatened by
Muslim invasion, from the south and west via North Africa and
Spain in Lawman's time, and by 1260 a new threat was
developing in the east, with the Ottomans in Turkey and the
Tatars in Hungary.

But Lawman lacked the precise sense of structure that is clear
in Geoffrey of Monmouth, who modelled his work on Bede and
Caesar, and to some extent on the Old Testament. Geoffrey
shows a nation emerging from one dominant individual, reaching its apogee, and declining largely because of the extradition
of its best men and women to people Brittany, a European
version of the Babylonian captivity of Israel, from which the
Britons were still expecting a release, perhaps in the form of
Arthur's Return. Wace does not share Geoffrey's chauvinistic
concern with the British versus all other comers, but does exhibit
the developing interest of the twelfth century in the significance
of the individual and presents his characters against a background of social customs, leisure activities and artefacts. It is,
inevitably, for the most part his own culture he depicts. Lawman
is different again: since his principal interest in this shifting
kaleidoscope of people, races and events is their common
interest in the land itself, he suppresses specific detail by using
formulaic expression. Even Geoffrey's hero Arthur is presented

from the more distant perspective of his liegemen, who fear his anger, and of the weak, who seek his protection, and are kept in comfort and content in his retinue. Lawman's greatly expanded treatment of Arthur resembles the fuller accounts of the kings of Scandinavia, which developed at about the same time from synoptic histories of limited scope into long, imaginative rather than historical biographies: 'the vertical narrow run of historical sequence broadens into a fuller presentation' (Einar Sveinsson, *Njáls saga* (Lincoln, Nebr., 1971)); Lawman was following a current trend in Northern Europe.

Lawman's knowledge of history was less extensive than Geoffrey's and Wace's. Although he claims to have used Bede's *Ecclesiastical History*, he seems not to have used it even for the story of Pope Gregory and St Augustine's conversion of England; apart from Wace, he claims one other source, an unidentified book which he ascribes to Albin and Augustine. This may have been the original Latin version of Bede's *Historia*, for which Albin supplied Bede with material and in which Augustine is the main character in Book I; if so, it was a book he did not (could not?) read, or he would have described it more accurately. Lawman based his *Brut* on Wace's *Roman*, which he translated by taking up large amounts of copy and rendering it freehand, largely from memory. Sometimes he re-orders Wace's text, or omits matter (Tatlock, *Legendary History*, p. 489), and occasionally mistranslates (Madden, I, xiv, n. 3), but most of the time he amplifies, by adding speeches and episodes, and making his account more emphatic, explicit and solemn than Wace's (Le Saux, *Sources*, pp. 42–58). He may also have added some material from local legends of saints like Oswald and Augustine, and may perhaps have found someone to translate for him the Welsh triadic poems and perhaps the *Armes Prydein*. Lawman is not a historiographer, and the mention of Bede's name near the beginning is the closest he gets to history. And yet there is a historical relevance in Lawman's work: it lies in his emphases, what he finds significant in his material: the *mores* of his own times and his sense of the importance of the family and kinship group. His sense of 'England' is made all the more relevant by the loss of Normandy to the French in 1204, forcing the Anglo-Norman magnates to give up their lands in Normandy if they wished to remain in England.

Lawman's Importance and his Achievement

It was Archbishop Usher who first read Lawman in post-medieval times: in 1639 he referred to the names in Lawman's account of the conversion of Lucius' Britain. Lawman was mentioned or quoted about ten times in the following two hundred years, but it was Madden's splendid three-volume edition in 1847 that made the whole text available to post-medieval readers. It was also Madden who emphasized the linguistic importance of Lawman's poem, to some extent over-insisting on the early ('Semi-Saxon') state of the English language pre-1230 and minutely examining and correcting in footnotes and appendix the grammatical features of the language of Lawman's scribes.

Articles on Lawman's language are still appearing, and to some extent this has distracted attention from his creative imagination, his control of narrative pace, ability to select salient details of the action from his source(s) and to give a recognizably 'human', often domestic, setting for the narrative, particularly in the more extended episodes such as Uther's seduction of Ygerne. Many of these episodes are much expanded from Wace, and there are incidents which do not appear in Wace at all.

Especially significant are the 'supernatural' additions in the Arthurian section: the fairies who attend Arthur's birth, the elvish smith who made Arthur's corslet, the marvels of Britain, Arthur's nightmare about Modred, and the mysterious Argante and the boat with two women in it which appears at his end to take him to Avalon. Merlin figures more prominently than in Wace: he is sent for twice, to aid Aurelius and later to help Uther, and Lawman continues to refer to Merlin's prophecies as a device to enhance Arthur's status, after Merlin has disappeared from the narrative: at Arthur's birth, the founding of the Round Table, before the Roman war and at his death. Wace candidly refuses to include the prophecies in his translation, and only alludes to them at Arthur's death, which he claims Merlin had said would be doubtful. Lawman cannot have derived his knowledge of the prophecies of Merlin from Wace.

In the first half of this century critical opinion, following Imelmann, maintained that Lawman's *Brut* derived immediately from an expanded version of Wace's *Roman de Brut* to which material had been added from Gaimar's lost 'History of the

Britons'. Until Visser's *Vindication* (1935), Lawman was regarded as a mere translator. But Madden, and recently Le Saux, have suggested that Lawman used other materials, both written and oral, for his sources. He took from Celtic oral tale the account of Taliesin and probably his expanded treatment of Merlin. He seems to have known Geoffrey of Monmouth, or at least the Prophecies of Merlin, perhaps in an Anglo-Norman version, and may have read Geoffrey's late work, the *Vita Merlini* ('Life of Merlin': Le Saux, *Sources*, pp. 110–16). He talks of books he has found on Dunwallo and on the origin of the name Walbrook, the state of Caerleon, and Carric's change of name. He may indeed have looked at many books, yet in the newly literate world of twelfth- and thirteenth-century vernacular poetry, it had become conventional for a writer of romance to talk of the books which were his source, and the ethos and the style of vernacular romance have influenced Lawman strongly, especially in the later sections of his work, from Constance to Cadwalader.

It is now generally considered that Lawman was a creative artist who may have 'compiled' his material from various Welsh, French, English and Latin sources, both oral and written; in fact, critical opinion has swung to another extreme, of regarding Lawman as a trash-bin rummager for any old bits of fact and fiction. Perhaps it is judicious to regard him as a sensitive writer who invented a great deal of his narrative by subconscious associations and by conscious derivation from narrative commonplaces.

However much Lawman may have derived from sources other than Wace, which today can only be guessed at, it remains true that his presentation of his material often shows the mark of genius. The *Brut* is both an interesting picture of how an educated man in the early thirteenth century thought of his nation's past, and an illuminating portrait of the world of the thirteenth century itself. Lawman was a cleric who wrote a translation of a pseudo-history in a strangely contrived idiolect, yet it is not as cleric, historian or grammarian that he is really to be appreciated, but as a poet of genial pragmatism; his sternness is part of his age: in lawless times *justise* meant physical punishment as well as justice and authority. He was the first poet to tell of Arthur and the British past in English, and as far as we know the first poet to write a long narrative poem in

English since the Norman Conquest, and one of the first to bring
the secular literature of the French aristocrats to the English. He
is best read as a writer who knew how to provide an instructive
message for the youth of his age out of the lessons of the past,
yet who never forgot that his narrative (*spell*) was also for
entertainment.

A Note on the Translation

Lawman's *Brut* is extant in two manuscripts, both formerly in
the collection owned by Sir Robert Cotton, and both now in the
British Library. The more complete is MS Cotton Caligula A ix
(C), from which this translation has been made. The other
manuscript, Cotton Otho C xiii (O), is incomplete today because
it was badly damaged in the fire at Ashburnham House in 1731,
but has always been shorter than the Caligula text: from the
outset it was prepared as an abridgement of Lawman's original.
The two manuscripts derive from a shared ancestor which had
already acquired erroneous readings, but presumably MS C
resembles Lawman's original better than MS O, and I have
therefore translated this, the longer version of the *Brut*. The
errors and inadvertent omissions by the scribes in MS C can
sometimes be corrected by reference to MS O; these emendations
are enclosed in square brackets in the translation, and in such
cases the readings of both C and O are listed in the *Emendations*.

A translator who wished to reproduce in modern English
stylistic effects to match Lawman's would have to imitate Pope's
poetic diction, Spenser's archaic forms, and Hopkins's compound words, while at the same time capturing the idioms and
rhythms of colloquial speech in the racier outbursts of the
characters and some of the narrator's more intimate observations. The modern requirement of consistency of tone makes
such a mode of presentation impossible. I have left some of the
inversions of object and verb that Lawman regularly uses, to
indicate the artificial nature of his formal style. I have retained
as much as was practical of his rhyme and alliteration, which
Lawman seems to have used not for decorative effect but as aids
to comprehension when the work was read aloud, much as
similar devices had done in Ælfric's sermons two hundred years
earlier, and also perhaps to encourage accurate copying, by
blocking scribes' attempts at rewriting and simplifying lines in

transmission. The alliteration and rhyme in the original speed rather than impede the flow of the narrative, and occasionally provide opportunity for witty contrast and jokes, as in the savage pun on *iqueme* and *aquele* in line 8807. Modern English is far less inflected than Lawman's, and the 'light rhyme' on identical inflexional endings, which he often used to give balance, is impossible, although sometimes I have tried to echo it by matching form-words such as prepositions or pronouns in similar clauses but without rhyme (e.g. *about it: all of it*), or I have used 'eye-rhyme' (*killed: kindred*; *have: live*). But rather more often I have used sound-echo which will only be obvious if the reader remembers the sound rather than the appearance of the words (for example, 6904 *learn: worthy*).

A translator into modern English cannot use alternative pronunciations, whereas Lawman can rhyme *man* with *Lateran*, and *mon* with *on*; we are also unaware of the licence by which Lawman (like other Middle English writers) regards *long* and *lond/land* as a rhyme. A close(-ish) translation cannot match all the aural devices Lawman uses, and I have tried simply to give an indication of the kind of sound-pattern he creates; after the first few hundred lines he settles into a fairly regular metre in which the end of the second half of the long line echoes the end of the first half more times than not (even if that echo is confined to a single phoneme: [i] in 8312 *king: him*, and [n] in 8323 *mon: Drihten*), unless additional sound-echo in the form of alliteration is present elsewhere in the line. Often Lawman uses both end-rhyme and alliteration, and I have tried to give an impression of this, and of the variation in his line lengths.

It was to give some idea of the rich aural effects in Lawman's *Brut* that I chose to make a 'verse' translation, but I have tried not to depart too far from the sense of the original merely for the sake of metre; this is not, however, in any sense a close translation which can be used as a crib.

The author of the *Brut* is usually known as Laȝamon in England, and as Lawman, its modern equivalent, in America. He seems to have chosen an archaic spelling for his name (or title) reminiscent of the Old English etymon *laȝu* (pl. *laȝa*) 'law'. 'Layamon' is an inaccurate version of his name, often used by modern critics because the special symbol *yogh* does not occur in modern printers' founts, and *y* is one of its modern equivalents; in this word, however, the modern equivalent is *w*, giving

'Lawemon', and I have further modernized his name to 'Lawman'. His contemporaries would probably have pronounced it 'Lau-a-mon', the first syllable like -lou- in 'loud', with a medial vowel resembling the unstressed indefinite article 'a'.

The Text

* Against the end of a line signals an emendation to the Caligula MS reading. The translated text is set in square brackets at the point where the emended word(s) occur in the original. The reasoning behind the emendations is set out in EMENDATIONS TO THE CALIGULA MS OF LAWMAN (pp. 321–32).

Queen Mary and
  Westfield College
January 1997

R. S. ALLEN

ABBREVIATIONS

ALMA	*Arthurian Literature in the Middle Ages*, ed. Loomis
AOW	*The Arthur of the Welsh*, ed. Bromwich, Jarman and Roberts
Arnold	Wace, *Brut*, ed. Arnold
ASC	Anglo-Saxon Chronical
BBIAS	*Bibliographical Bulletin of the International Arthurian Society*
B-H	Blenner-Hassett, *The Place-Names in Lawman's 'Brut'*
B&L	*Laȝamon: Brut*, ed. Brook and Leslie
B&S	*Early Middle English Verse and Prose*, ed. Bennett and Smithers
B&W	Laȝamon's Arthur, ed. Barron and Weinberg
Brook	*Selections from Laȝamon's 'Brut'*, ed. Brook
C	London, British Library, MS Cotton Caligula A ix
CFMA	Classiques Français du Moyen Age
D&W	*Early Middle English Texts*, ed. Dickins and Wilson

E&I	Salter, *English and International*
EETS	Early English Text Society
EME	*Selections from Early Middle English*, ed. Hall
ES	*Englische Studien*
Engl. Studies	*English Studies*
H	*Layamon's 'Brut': Selections*, ed. Hall
HB	*Historia Brittonum* (= 'Nennius', *British History*)
HRB	Geoffrey of Monmouth, *Historia Regum Britanniae*, ed. Wright
JEGP	*Journal of English and Germanic Philology*
LeedsSE	*Leeds Studies in English*
M/Madden	*Laȝamon's 'Brut'*, ed. Madden
MÆ	*Medium Ævum*
MED	*Middle English Dictionary*
MHRA	*Bulletin of the Modern Humanities Research Association*
MP	*Modern Philology*
NM	*Neuphilologische Mitteilungen*
N&Q	*Notes and Queries*
O	London, British Library, MS Cotton Otho C xiii
OED	*Oxford English Dictionary*

PMLA	*Publications of the Modern Language Association of America*
RES	*Review of English Studies*
Rou	Wace, *Le Roman de Rou*, ed. Holden
SATF	Société des Anciens Textes Français
Serjeantson	Serjeantson, *History of Foreign Words in English*
SN	*Studia Neophilologica*
Thorpe	*Geoffrey of Monmouth: History of the Kings of Britain*, trans. Lewis Thorpe
VCH	*Victoria County History*

Further Abbreviations

13c (or other numeral)	thirteenth (or other) century
gl	glossed (as)
L 16095	Lawman, *Brut* line reference
W 14866	Wace, *Roman de Brut* line reference
ME	Middle English
OE	Old English
om	omitted
OW	Old Welsh
prec	preceding
s.a.	*sub anno*, under the entry for this year
sp	spelling, spelled as
sb	substantive, noun
s.v.	*sub verbo* ('under this word/item')
trans	translated

WACE

Le Roman de Brut:
Arthurian Section

[After the departure of the Romans, Britain is attacked by Scots, Picts, Norwegians and Danes. The Archbishop of London, Guencelin, appeals for help to the Armorican British, who send him Constantine, brother of the king of Brittany.]

6424. Constantine came to Totnes. He had many good knights with him and thought each had the courage of a king. They set out for London, summoning Britons from all sides. Formerly none had appeared, but now they poured out of the woods and mountains, coming forward with large bands of men. Why should I make a long speech of it? They fared so well and did so much that they conquered the wicked people who had wrecked the land. Then at Silchester they held a council, which all the barons had to attend. They elected Constantine king, joyfully crowning him without opposition and without delay, and made him their lord. Then they gave him a wife, of noble Roman birth. Three sons he had from her; the king called the eldest Constant, had him brought up at Winchester, and there made him become a monk. Next came Aurelius, known as Ambrosius. The last born was Uther, and he was the one who lived the longest. Archbishop Guencelin took these two boys into his care.

6455. Had Constantine reigned for a long time, he would have set right the whole land, but he died too soon: his rule only lasted twelve years. One of the Picts in his household was a traitor, an evil wretch, who had long served him but then, I do not know why, began to hate him. He took him into an orchard, as if to confer, and there, as he was advising the king, who had no protection against him, he struck him with his knife and killed him, then fled.

6469. The whole kingdom assembled. They wanted to choose a king but hesitated as to which of the boys it should be. These were young and inexperienced, in the care of a nurse and innocent of wrong. They did not dare take Constant, the eldest and first-born, out of his monk's habit; it seemed foolish and base to remove him from the abbey. They had chosen from among the other two, when Vortigern sprang forward, a man of power, who dwelt in Wales. He was a mighty count, clever and crafty, with influential kin. He had long since plotted what he wanted to contrive. 'Why are you hesitating?' he said. 'Make the monk Constant king. He is the rightful heir; let's remove his monk's habit, for the others are too young. Grant the domain to no other. May any sin be upon my own head: I will remove him from the abbey and deliver him to you as king.' Not a single baron wished the monk to become king; to them it seemed a terrible thing. But Vortigern, bent on evil, came spurring to Winchester. So insistent was he on seeing Constant that, with the prior's leave, he spoke to him in the monks' parlour.

6503. 'Constant', he said, 'your father is dead. The realm is passing to your brothers, but by right of inheritance you should have it first. If you will increase my possessions, and if you love and trust me, I will divest you of your black robe and dress you instead in a royal one. I will take you out of the monastery and restore your inheritance.' Constant, not enamoured of the abbey, coveted power; he was quite weary of the monastery and easy to take away. He promised and swore everything that Vortigern asked of him. And at once Vortigern took him out of the abbey. No one dared gainsay him: what was the point, if he was undeterred? He took off his monk's garb and dressed him in rich robes. From there he took him to London. Few people assembled; the archbishop, who should have anointed the king, was dead, and there was no other to anoint him or who wished to have a hand in it. Vortigern took the crown and placed it upon his head: his only blessing came from Vortigern's hand alone. Constant received the crown and abandoned the vows he should have obeyed; he wrongly abandoned God's rule and thus came to a bad end. No one should succeed through doing what he should not do.

6541. Vortigern held the king and his officers firmly in his control: the king did what he advised, and seized what he commanded. From several occasions early on, he saw that the king, educated in the cloister, knew very little. He saw the two brothers were very young, that the kingdom's barons were dead, that he was the strongest of those still alive, that the people were somewhat quarrelsome, and that time and place were just right for him to seize the realm for himself. Now listen to the wicked man. 'Sire', he said, 'I know for sure, and ought to bring it to your knowledge, that the Danes, and the Norwegians from Norway, are gathering. Because you are no knight, and we are weak, they want to enter this land, to seize and ravage your castles, so you must take steps to defend yourself and your land. Have your towers fortified and guarded. I am in great fear of traitors, so you must hand over your castles to those who well know how to protect them.' 'I have handed everything over to you', said the king, 'so do what you like with it all. I shall not assume charge over you, for you know better than I do. Take total control of the land, so that none of it is seized or burned. I continue to be guided by you: do the best you can. Take my cities, my manors, my wealth and my jewels.'

6579. Vortigern, full of deceit, well knew how to conceal his greed. When he had taken possession of fortresses, wealth and jewels, he said, 'Sire, if it please you, I would advise and counsel you to send for the Pictish mercenaries, from Scotland, to be your knights and to be with you at court, wherever our war should turn. You can easily send for the Picts whenever you need them. Through the Picts and their kin we shall know what state the foreigners are in: they will negotiate, and travel, between us and them.' 'Do what you wish', replied the king, 'make as many as you like come; give them as much as you like, and do the best you can.'

6599. When Vortigern had taken everything into his possession and annexed the jewels too, he summoned as many Picts as he pleased, and they arrived just as he wished. Vortigern did them much honour: he gave them good food and drink and a merry life, so that very often they were drunk. So much did he give them, and so much honour did he pay to each one, that there was not one of them who would not say, in the hearing of anyone who cared to hear it, that Vortigern was more courteous and much better than the king, that he deserved to rule the king's realm – or a greater one. Vortigern gloried in this, and gave them more and more favours.

6617. One day he had given them plenty to drink, and made them well and truly drunk. Then he came among them and greeted them, pretending to be sad. 'I have held you very dear', he said, 'and willingly served you, and will do so, if I have the wherewithal. But this land is all the king's, and I can neither give nor spend anything without rendering account for it. I hold little property in this land; I must go and seek more elsewhere. I have striven to serve the king, and from him I do not have enough to maintain honourably a mere forty men-at-arms. If I win land, then return; for now, by your leave, I shall depart. It grieves me to leave you, but I am poor and can do nothing else. If you hear that I'm doing better, be sure to come to me!'

6639. Then Vortigern turned away, false at heart and speaking falsehood. Those who had drunk well entirely believed the villain: whatever he falsely said, they took as complete truth. Amongst themselves, they said, 'What shall we do if we lose this good lord? Let's kill this foolish king, this monk, and raise Vortigern to be king. He deserves the domain and its rule, and we should elect him to it. What use is this foolish monk to us? Why have we suffered him so long?' Then they entered the king's chamber, seized him and cut off his head. Having severed the head from the trunk, they presented it to Vortigern, shouting, 'Look how we have supported you! The king is dead: now keep us with you, take the crown, become king!' He recognized the head of his lord, and pretended to be overcome with grief. In his heart he rejoiced, but he was cunning and concealed it. In order to hide his wickedness, he called an assembly of Londoners and had the traitors beheaded, not leaving one of them alive. There were many who believed (but said so only in private) that they would never have touched the king, nor viewed him intending to harm him, nor would the thought have ever entered their heads, had Vortigern not ordered it of them.

6675. Those looking after the two brothers feared, when they heard of the king's death, that whoever killed the king would do the same to them. For fear of Vortigern they took Aurelius and Uther and went to Brittany, entrusting them to King Budiz, who received them handsomely. He was their relative and looked after them: he equipped them honourably and knighted them with splendour.

6687. Vortigern possessed strongholds, castles and cities. He made himself king and was very arrogant. But two things worried him. On the one hand, the Picts made war on him, with many threats: they wished to avenge their kin, whom he had beheaded. On the other hand, he was disturbed by the news everyone brought him that the two brothers were armed and would soon return; the barons would receive them and do them homage for their domains. They would avenge Constant, their brother, because with them they would bring a great host. There were many who gave such news. Meanwhile, three little boats appeared, arriving at a harbour in Kent and bringing strangers with handsome faces and fine bodies. Their lords were Hengist and Horsa, two brothers of great height and foreign speech. The news was quickly brought to Vortigern, who that day was staying at Canterbury, that three ships belonging to people from another land had together arrived there. The king commanded that, whoever they were, they should receive pledges of peace and safety, and should peacefully speak to him and peacefully return. They heard his command and came without fear.

6723. The king observed the two brothers, with their shapely bodies and fine faces, who were taller and more handsome than all other young men. 'From which land do you come?' he said. 'Where were you born, and what do you seek?' Hengist, the elder and first-born, replied for them all: 'We come from Saxony', he said, 'there were we born, and dwell. If you want to hear the reason for our quest over the sea, I will tell you the truth, if we have your guarantee of safety.' 'Give us all your explanation', said the king, 'you need not fear us.' 'Good king, noble lord', said Hengist, 'I do not know if you ever heard tell, but our land is more plentifully and abundantly supplied with native inhabitants than any other you know or have heard about. Our people are exceedingly fertile and there are too many children: there are too many men, too many women, and this troubles those you see here. When our people grow so many that the land is too full of them, the prince owning the domain, as is the usage and custom, makes all the young men of fifteen or over assemble. All the strongest and best are sent out of the land, by lot, and go to other realms, looking for lands and houses, to disperse the great numbers which the land cannot bear, for children are born thicker and faster than the beasts at pasture in the fields. Through the lot which fell on us, we have

left our country. We were guided by Mercury, a god who led us
here.'

6767. When the king heard him name the god who guided him,
he asked him which god they had and in which god their people
believed. 'We have several gods', he said, 'to whom we should
make altars: they are Phoebus, Saturn, Jupiter and Mercury. We
have many other gods, following the religion of our ancestors,
but above all others we principally honour Mercury, who in our
language, with great piety, is called Woden. Our ancestors
honoured him so much that they consecrated the fourth day to
him: on account of Woden, their god whom they loved, they
called the fourth day "Wednesday", and so it is still called.
Besides this god I've told you of, we worship the goddess Frea,
greatly honoured by all. To pay tribute to her, our forbears
consecrated the sixth day to her and, with great reverence, called
it Friday, after Frea.' 'You have a wicked faith and a wicked
god', said the king. 'It gives me pain; yet I am glad of your
coming. You seem strong and courageous men, and, if you wish
to serve me, I shall retain you all and make you rich. Scottish
scoundrels make war on me, burning my lands and pillaging my
towns. Please God (because it would be greatly to my advantage), I would like to destroy the Picts and the Scots with God's
help and yours. For the Picts who ruin my realm come from that
land, and flee back to it again. Through your help I would like
to take revenge, either killing or exiling them all. You will of
course get your rations, wages and gifts.' So the Saxons stayed
and hauled their boats to dry land; and before long the court
was full of fine young men.

6817. Not long afterwards, the Picts entered the king's land in
great strength, burning, robbing and destroying. When they
were about to cross the Humber, the king, hearing of it, went to
meet them with his barons, with Saxons and Britons. Then you
might have seen a harsh battle and a great defeat. The Picts,
accustomed to frequent victories, were not in the least afraid of
them; at first they held their ground well and struck boldly,
fighting prodigiously, and suffering prodigiously. Because they
were used to defeating them, they wanted to keep to their usual
habits. But then they lost what was customary to them, and the
Saxons won the field. Through them and their help Vortigern

was victorious. He gave them their wages and improved their rations. To Hengist he gave good manors in Lindsey, and great possessions. So they remained for a long while, and their friendship prospered.

6845. Hengist saw that he was needed to execute the king's affairs. He began to advance himself, as everyone should try and do. He well knew how to get round the king in a lying fashion. One day he found the king in a good mood and gave him some advice: 'You have greatly honoured me', he said, 'and made me many gifts; and I serve you and shall continue to do so: if I have done well, I shall do better. But since I have been in your court, and got to know your people, I have often observed, often heard and often seen, that you have no baron who loves you. Everyone hates you, everyone complains. I don't know who these children are that they speak of, who steal from your people the love due to you. They are their rightful lords, sons of a lawful king of theirs. Soon they will come from overseas and take this land from you. All your men wish you harm: they wish you ill, they wish you a bad end. They greatly hate and greatly threaten you; they seek and strive for your downfall. I have thought of how to help you: I want to send to my country for my wife and children and other kin. You will be more sure of me, and I will serve you better. No longer will you find anyone to deprive you, in warfare, of a single foot of land. I've already served you a long while and made many enemies on your account; I can't rest secure at night without a castle, without walls. Therefore, sire, if it please you, it would bring you profit and renown to give me a city, fort or stronghold where I may lie and sleep safely at night. Your enemies would fear me and stop harming you.'

6893. 'Send for your people', said the king; 'receive and equip them handsomely, and I will give you the means. But you are not of our faith – you are pagan and we are Christian: if I gave you a stronghold, it would not find favour. Consider having something else.' 'Sire', said Hengist, 'let me, at one of the manors I possess, enclose and fortify a stronghold in as much land (I ask no more) as I can stretch out a hide on and cover with the hide round about. Only a bull's hide – and I shall lie more securely.' Vortigern granted it him, and Hengist thanked him. He equipped his messenger and sent for his kin. He took a bull's hide and cut it so as to draw out a thong from it, which surrounded a great hill. He sought out good workmen and constructed a castle, giving it the name of Thongcaster in his land's tongue. Thongcaster takes its name from the hide, and one can otherwise call it *chastel de cureie* in French and *Kaër Carreï* in the British language, because it was measured and marked out with the thong.[1]

6925. When Thongcaster was completed, eighteen ships arrived, full of those Hengist had summoned, of knights and followers. They brought him his unmarried daughter: she was called Ronwen, a young girl extraordinarily fine and beautiful. On a day he had selected, Hengist invited the king to stay with him, to enjoy himself eating and drinking and to see his new followers and his new lodgings. The king came with few retainers, wishing to be private. He saw the castle and observed the building; it was very well done and he gave it much praise. He retained the newly arrived knights in his pay. That day they ate, and drank so much that most of them were drunk. Then out of the chamber came Ronwen, very beautiful and well dressed. She carried a full cup of wine, knelt down before the king, bowed very humbly to him, and according to her custom greeted him: 'Lord king, wassail!' she said.[2] The king, not knowing the language the girl spoke to him, enquired what she meant. The first to reply was Keredic, a good linguist, the first of the British to know the Saxon tongue. 'Ronwen', he said, 'has greeted you and called you lord king. The custom, sire, in her country, when friends drink together, is that the one who is to drink says "Wassail", and the one who is to receive it next says "Drinchail". Then he drinks it all, or half of it. And out of joy

---

[1] *Une cureie* = a thong. Arnold, II, p. 805 suggests that here we have to do with Caister, near Grimsby, called Thongcaster in the medieval period.

[2] A Saxon salutation when drinking, literally meaning 'be in good health'. Wace's text keeps it in Middle English, as does *HRB*, p. 67. The Old English occurs in *Beowulf* 407 as Wes hāl. (Lawman's wæs hæil is West Norse rather than Saxon). See *Rou*, I.7331-4, and also Gaimar's *Estoire des Engleis* 3803-8, for another mention of *weseil*, *drinkheil* and the custom of exchanging kisses. The story of Vortigern falling in love with Hengist's daughter is in *HB*, ch. 37, but *HRB* has added the details of *wassail* and *drinchail*; on the other hand, *HRB* has omitted the name of Vortigern's interpreter, Ceretic, while Wace has preserved it.

and friendship at offering and accepting the cup, it is the custom to exchange kisses.' The king, as soon as he learnt this, said 'Drinchail!' and smiled at her. Ronwen drank and then gave it back to him, and, as she gave it, she kissed the king. It was through these people that the custom first began, to say 'Wassail' in this land and to reply 'Drinchail', to drink the whole, or the half, and to exchange kisses.

6981. The girl had a fine body and a very beautiful face; she was fair and comely, handsome in shape and size. Uncloaked, she stood before the king, who could not keep his eyes off her. He was in good spirits, he had drunk well, and he greatly desired her. The Devil enticed him so much, who has turned so many men to evil; he inflamed him with love and desire to take Hengist's daughter. God, what shame! God, what sin! The Devil led him so far astray, he would not refuse to marry her, though she was a heathen, born of heathens. At once he asked Hengist for her, and Hengist accorded her, but first he took counsel with his brother and his friends. They keenly desired this affair and advised and counselled that he should quickly hand her over and ask for Kent as dower. He gave her to the king, not wanting to do otherwise, and asked for the dower of Kent. The king desired the girl, he loved her and made her queen. She was a heathen, and he made her his wife in the heathen fashion: no priest gave a blessing; there was neither Mass nor prayer; he fell in love with her in the morning and had her in the evening, and made Kent over to Hengist. He seized Kent, held it and owned it: Gerangon, whose inheritance it was, never knew a word about it until he was driven out.

7019. The king loved and trusted the heathen more than the Christians, and the Christians hated him for it and forsook him and his council. Even his sons took to hating him and left him because of the heathen. He had had a wife, but she was dead and gone; he had had three sons from her, who were now all full-grown. The eldest was called Vortimer, the others Paschent and Katiger. 'Sire', said Hengist to the king, 'you are somewhat hated on my account, and I am hated in turn because of you. I am your father, you my son, who took and has my daughter: I thank you for asking for her. By rights I should advise you, and you should trust and help me. If you wish to reign securely and

distress those who hate you, send for my son Octa and his cousin
Ebissa, two excellent fighters and marvellous warriors. Give them
land near Scotland, for your battles always come from there.
They will protect you from hostile people so that nothing of
yours will ever be taken. For all the rest of your life, you can live
in peace this side of the Humber.' 'Do what you like', said the
king, 'summon all those you know to be good.' And Hengist at
once sent a message summoning his son and his nephew, and
they arrived with three hundred ships. There was not one good
knight left, who wished to serve for wealth, whom they did not
make accompany them. Then others often came, little by little,
day by day, with four ships, with five, with six, with seven, with
eight, with nine, with ten. So quickly did the heathen increase,
intermingling with the Christians, that one could scarcely tell
who were Christian and who were not. It greatly annoyed the
Britons, and they spoke to the king, begging him not to trust
these foreigners, for they were openly disloyal. He had collected
too many of these heathens; it was wicked, and a great scandal.
He should disband them, in whatever manner, and send all or
most of them away. The king told them he would do no such
thing: they served him well, and he had summoned them. Then
the Britons assembled, and went to London together. They made
Vortimer king, the eldest of Vortigern's three sons. He defied the
Saxons and threw them out of the cities.

7083. The king, out of love for his wife, kept the Saxons close
to him and did not want to forsake them. And his son kept
harrying and routing them; he was valiant, and well supported.
The war fought by Vortimer and the British against his father
and the Saxons was savage. He attacked them four times, and
four times defeated them. First he fought by Derwent Water,
next at a ford near Epiford. There Katiger, the king's son, and
Horsa came to blows, and each mortally wounded the other, as
each desired. The third great battle was in Kent, by the shore
next to their ships, at a ferry, when the Saxons had fled across
the Humber into Kent: a great rout took place there. Then they
fled into Thanet, an island in the sea. There the British attacked
them and every day felled them with arrows and bolts from
boats and ships. On the one hand they killed them, on the other
hand starved them to death. When they saw that they would not
escape unless they left the country, they sent a message to King

Vortigern, to ask his son Vortimer to let them go scot-free, without further injury. The king was continually with them and never left them. While he went to obtain this truce, the Saxons entered their ships and, rowing and sailing furiously, departed as fast as they could, leaving behind their sons and their wives. They escaped in great fear and returned to their own land.

7131. When they had escaped, the British were reassured, and Vortimer restored to everyone what they had lost through the Saxons. To rebuild the churches and to proclaim God's law, which was poorly observed because Hengist had corrupted it, St Germain came to Britain, sent there by St Romain, who held the apostolic power in Rome; St Lous[3] of Troyes came with him – both good bishops, one from Auxerre, the other from Troyes, who knew the paths to God. Through them religion was restored and the people returned to the faith; through them many a man came to salvation. God made and revealed many a miracle, many a wonder, for these two; all England was the better for it.

7153. When God's law was re-established and Britain again converted, hear what devilry was perpetrated. Through great hate and envy Ronwen, like a wicked stepmother, had her stepson Vortimer, whom she hated, poisoned, because of Hengist, whom he had exiled. When Vortimer knew he was dying and could not be healed by any doctor, he called all his barons together and gave them the many treasures he had collected. Listen to what he asked them: 'Retain knights', he said; 'give them gifts and allowances, protect your land and yourselves and defend yourselves against the Saxons so that you never bring them back. Avenge your suffering and mine. To terrify them, have my body buried on the shore and such a tomb raised as may last a long while and be seen from a great distance at sea, in their direction. Neither dead nor alive will they return where they know my body rests.' The noble lord spoke thus, thus ended, thus died. The body was carried to London and buried in London: they did not bury it where he had bidden them.

7187. Then Vortigern was made king once more, as he had been before. Because his wife begged him to, he sent for Hengist,

[3] St Lupus.

his father-in-law. He summoned him to return, but to bring only a few people with him, so that the British should not take fright and once more interfere. Vortimer his son being dead, there was no need for a great company. Hengist returned willingly, but he brought 300,000 armed men; he feared the Britons and would behave differently from before. When the king knew he was back, and had brought so many men, he was so frightened, he knew not what to say, and the Britons were furious. They said they would attack and drive them from the land. Hengist, who had a wicked heart, sent a treacherous message to the king, asking for peace and a truce and a parley: they loved and desired peace, they wished and sought it. They had no wish for war, or to stay there by force. The Britons should keep only those they chose, and all the rest would depart. The Britons allowed the truce, and it was sworn on both sides.

7219. Who suspected treachery? They appointed a day for the parley. And the king sent to Hengist that he should come with few retainers, and Hengist agreed willingly and suggested in return that no weapons should be carried, for fear of starting a fight. On wide Salisbury Plain, next to Amesbury Abbey, the two sides came for conference, on the first day of May. Hengist had instructed and taught all his friends to be sure to carry sharp two-edged knives in their boots. When they were mingling with the Britons and talking to them, he would call out, 'Grab your knives!' which none of the Britons would understand.[4] Each would then take his knife and strike the Briton next to him. When they were all at the parley, mingling together, and the Britons, unarmed and defenceless, were seated, Hengist cried, 'Grab your knives!' Then each drew his knife and struck the one nearest him. Hengist, next to the king, held him fast by the cloak, and let the carnage happen. And those who held the knives ran the blades through cloaks, through mantles, through chests and bowels. The Britons fell over and down. Soon there were 460 dead there, from among the noblest and mightiest. Some fled, defending themselves with stones. Eldulf, count of Gloucester, held a great stake in his right hand: he had found it lying at his feet and not known who had brought it there. He

---

[4] *Nim eure sexes*; in *HRB Nemet oure saxas*, in *HB Enimit Saxas*. See *HB* ed. Dumville, III, p. 5

defended himself with it, killing and cutting down many. He certainly disposed of seventy men: he was a valiant count, of great renown. He cut through the crowd so that no one could wound him. Many knives were thrown at him, but none touched him. He battled through to his horse, an excellent and speedy one, and fled to Gloucester, fortifying his tower and his city.

7277. The Saxons wanted to kill the king, but Hengist shouted to them, 'Leave the king: he has done much for me and endured much hardship on my account. I should protect him, as my son-in-law. But let us make him render up his cities, and hand over his fortresses, if he wants to save his life.' So they did not kill him but put him in iron chains. They so bound and oppressed him that he swore he would give them everything. He gave them London and Winchester, Lincoln, York and Chichester. To release himself from ransom, and get out of prison, he gave them in fee Sussex and all Essex and Middlesex, because they adjoined Kent, which Hengist held before. They thus were called -sex to commemorate the Treachery of the Knives. Sexes is the English word for knives; there are many kinds of knife amongst the French, but they have somewhat changed their names, so that they do not know what sexes means. The English heard themselves reproached for the treachery they had done, removed the end of the word and completely changed the name for knives, to forget the dishonour committed by their ancestors.

7309. Vortigern abandoned everything to them and fled over the Severn. He travelled deep into Wales, and there he stayed. He sent for his soothsayers and his best men, and sought their advice as to what he should do and how protect himself, how defend himself if a stronger force attacked him. His counsellors advised him to construct such a tower that it could never be taken by force or conquered by any stratagem of man. Once it was equipped, he should live inside so that no evil people could kill him. Then he had a search made to choose a suitable place to build the tower. It pleased and suited him to do it on Mount Erir.[5] He sought out masons, the best he knew, and made them set to as fast as possible. They began to labour, and to lay out

[5] Snowdon.

stones and mortar, but whatever they built during the day sank
into the ground during the night; the higher they built it, the
greater was its fall, down to its foundations. In this way many
days of work sank into the ground. When the king knew and
realized that his undertaking would not succeed, he asked his
soothsayers for advice. 'Indeed', he said, 'I wonder what can
become of this work: earth cannot sustain it. Search and enquire
as to why, and how the earth might support it.' They announced
and predicted – though possibly they were lying – that if he
could find a man born without a father, kill him, take his blood
and sprinkle it on the mortar, then his building would endure
and he could work in safety.

7355. So the king sent throughout Wales, to see that, if ever
such a man were found, he should be brought before him. Many
searchers left for many regions. Two of them, travelling the
same road, together arrived in Kermerdin.[6] In front of the city,
at its entrance, there was a great crowd of children, gathered
there to play, and they began to observe them. Amongst those
at play were two boys quarrelling, Merlin and Dinabuz. One
was angry with the other, opposing him and insulting his family.
'Hold your tongue, Merlin', said Dinabuz. 'Stop, because I am
of a much nobler lineage than you. Don't you know who you
are, you wicked thing? You shouldn't quarrel with me or insult
my family. I am born of kings and counts, but if you consider
your parents, you can never name your father, for you don't
know him, nor will you. You never knew your father, nor did
you ever have a father.' Those who were seeking just such a
man, on hearing the boys and their quarrel, approached the
neighbours round about to enquire who he was, who had never
had a father. And the neighbours replied he had never had a
father; nor did his mother, who had borne him, know who had
begotten him. They knew nothing of his father, but he had a
mother known to them: she was the daughter of the king of

[6] Carmarthen. On the town's onomastic link to Merlin, see Jarman in *AOW*,
pp. 131–2, 137. It is *HRB* that calls the boy Merlin (*qui et Ambrosius dicebatur*,
p. 73) and localizes him here; in Geoffrey's source for this passage, *HB*, he is
Ambrosius (also called *Emrys Guletic*) at *Glywysing* in Glamorgan, who later
drives Vortigern out and is called the 'great king of the British nation' (chs 42,
48) – a reference to the historical British king Ambrosius Aurelianus and his
victories against the Saxons.

Demetia, part of Wales.[7] She was a nun of exemplary life in an abbey in the town.

7401. Then these men went to the town governor. On behalf of the king they asked him for the fatherless Merlin, and his mother, to be taken to the king. The governor did not wish to refuse and had both of them taken to the king. He received them well and spoke pleasantly: 'Lady', he said, 'tell me truly, for only through you can I know it: who begot your son Merlin?' The nun bowed her head. After reflecting a while, she said, 'God help me, I never knew or saw who engendered this boy. I never heard, I never knew if it was a man who gave me him. But this I know to be true, and I will admit its truth: when I was a full-grown novice, something (I don't know if it was an apparition) often came to me and kissed me close. I heard it speak like a man; I felt it as if it were a man, and many times it spoke with me, without ever making itself known. So long did it continue to approach me and to kiss me that it lay with me and I conceived. I knew no other man. I had this boy, I have him still; I know no more and I shall say no more.'[8]

7435. Then the king made Magant come forward, a wise and learned man, and asked him if what the nun said could be true. 'We have found it written', he said, 'that there exists a kind of spirit between moon and earth. For whoever wishes to know their nature, they are partly human and partly supernatural. They are called incubus demons; their realm is the air, and they frequent the earth. They cannot do great wickedness, they cannot cause much harm except to deceive and deride. They easily take human shape, and it agrees well with their nature. They have deceived many girls and ravished them in this way. Thus might Merlin be born and thus might he be begotten.' 'King', said Merlin, 'you have sent for me: why did you do so, what do you want of me?' 'Merlin', said the king, 'you shall know; you wish to hear and you shall hear. I began making a high tower, using stone and mortar, but whatever is constructed during the day sinks into the ground. I don't know if you have heard tell of

[7] Demetia is a Latinization of Dyfed: see Tatlock, *Legendary History*, p. 62.
[8] I have substituted MS H's reading – *Plus n'en soi, et plus n'en dirai* – for MS P's *Plus n'en fu ne plus n'en dirai*.

it: no matter how much is built during the day, it collapses
during the night. I have already wasted much over it. According
to my soothsayers, I shall never finish my tower unless your
blood is inside it, because you were born without a father.'

7473. 'God forbid', said Merlin, 'that your tower should stand
firm through my blood. If you make all those men, who
prophesied about my blood, come before me, I shall have them
considered liars: they were liars and lied.' The king had them
sent for and brought to Merlin. After he had observed them,
Merlin said, 'My prophetic lords, say why this building will not
stand. If you cannot answer me why the tower sinks to the
ground, how can you foretell it will stand up through my blood?
Say what it is in the foundations that makes the tower so often
fall; then say what is needed and what will make it stand. If you
cannot tell us what it is underneath that makes the tower fall,
how is it believable that my blood should stabilize it? Tell the
king of the obstruction; then tell us what is needed.' All the
soothsayers kept quiet and could answer him nothing. 'My lord
king', said Merlin, 'listen. Below your tower, in the foundations,
is a great, deep pool, which makes your tower collapse. And, so
that you believe me, dig up the ground and see.' The king had
the ground dug up and found the pool Merlin had indicated.
'My lords', said Merlin, 'listen: you who searched for me in
order to slake the mortar with my blood – say what is in this
pool.' They were all silent and mute, with never a good or a bad
word. Merlin turned back to the king and called to him in the
hearing of his men: 'Have this pool drained', he said, 'and draw
off the water through trenches. At the bottom are two sleeping
dragons, lying in two hollow stones. One of the dragons is all
white, the other red as blood.'

7523. When the water was drained and all carried off by
trenches, two dragons rose from the depths and fiercely attacked
each other. They fought with great violence so that all the
barons saw them. There you could see them foaming at the
mouth and spewing flame from their jaws. The king sat by the
pool and begged Merlin to tell him what the dragons and their
angry battle meant. Then Merlin made the prophecies which I
believe you have heard, of the kings who were to come and who
were to hold the land. I do not wish to translate his book, since

I do not know how to interpret it; I would not like to say anything, in case what I say does not happen.[9]

7543. The king praised Merlin greatly and considered him an excellent prophet. He asked him when he would die, and by what kind of death, for he was terrified of his end. 'Beware', said Merlin, 'beware of the fire from Constantine's children, for you will meet your end through that fire. Already they have left Armorica and are crossing the sea in strength. Of this you can be sure: tomorrow they will be at Totnes. You have done them wrong: they will do you wrong and exact grim revenge. It was your wickedness that betrayed their brother, your wickedness that made you king, and your wickedness that attracted Saxons and heathens to this land. Dangers await you on both sides; I don't know which you should guard against first. On the one hand the Saxons make war on you and would willingly destroy you; on the other the heirs approach, wanting the realm. They want to claim Britain and avenge Constant, their brother. If, then, you can flee, do so, for both brothers are coming. Aurelius will be king first, and then be the first to die, by poison. Uther Pendragon, his brother, will then hold the kingdom; but too soon he will sicken and be poisoned by your heirs. His son, from Cornwall, fierce as a boar in battle, will devour the traitors and destroy all your kin. He will be valiant and brave, conquering all his enemies.'

7583. Merlin finished speaking, and Vortigern went his way. The next day, without delay, the brothers' fleet arrived in Dartmouth, at Totnes, with knights and equipment. The Britons, fortified by these people, were joyful and happy, Formerly dispersed, they gathered together. Hengist, having wickedly destroyed the barons with knives, had made the rest hide, and flee into the mountains and woods. The British assembled and made Aurelius their king and lord. In Wales, Vortigern heard of the matter and took steps to defend himself. With his bravest men he sought protection in a castle called Genoire by the Wye,

[9] Wace is referring to sections 109–17 of *HRB*, which contain the prophecies of Merlin, in the process demonstrating his own scepticism. This was not to the taste of the scribe of MS L (Lincoln Cathedral, MS 104) of the *Brut*, 'Willelme', who put the prophecies back into his own text.

a fast-flowing river. Those nearby call it Wye, and the region is called Hergrin, on top of Cloart, a mountain; so say those who come from there.[10] Vortigern equipped himself thoroughly, with weapons, provisions and men; if this aided him to escape, it would have been sufficient defence. The brothers took their barons and pursued King Vortigern so hard that they laid siege to him in a castle. There they constantly pelted and shot at him. They were eager to capture him, because they bore him enormous hatred. If the brothers hated him, Vortigern had certainly deserved it: he had killed their brother Constant, and Constantine their father before him, not with his own hands but treacherously, so that it was known to be true.[11]

7625. Eldulf, count of Gloucester, familiar with the customs of Wales, had become Aurelius' man and kept him company amongst the soldiers. 'For God's sake, Eldulf', said Aurelius, 'have you already forgotten my father, who gave you nurture and fiefs, and my brother, who loved you dearly? Both of them willingly honoured you, and gave you much trust and much love. By the cunning of this traitor, this perjurer, this tyrant, they were slain; they would still be alive were it not for his cunning. If you grieve for them, take revenge on Vortigern.' This exhortation alone made them all arm. They made a collection of wood, entirely filling a great ditch with it, and then fired it. The fire caught the castle, and from the castle spread to the tower and to the houses round about. Then you might have seen the castle burning, flames flying, houses falling. The king was consumed, along with all those who had sought refuge with him.

7653. When the new king had conquered and appropriated the land, he said he would move against the heathen and deliver the realm. Hengist knew it, and feared it greatly. He journeyed to Scotland, abandoning all the other lands, and fled over the Humber, because he expected to have help, succour and forces from the Scots, and if his plight grew worse, he could pass into Scotland. As day followed day, the king led his men there, and the numbers of British kept increasing and flocked to him in

[10] On these locations, see Arnold, II, p. 805 (Genoire is Ganarew) and Thorpe, p. 187.
[11] Wace told us earlier that a Pict killed Constantine: see p. 3.

such crowds that no one could number them any more than the sands of the sea. The king found the realm badly laid waste and saw no one was tilling it; he saw castles and cities destroyed, towns burned, churches plundered. The heathen had laid everything waste and spared nothing. He promised everyone compensation if he returned safely from battle.

7679. Hengist knew the king was coming and would not turn back without a fight. He wished to comfort his companions and put heart into them. 'My lords', he said, 'don't be afraid of these second-rate troops. You know well enough they are British and can never hold out against us. If you put up even a little opposition against them, you'll never see them resist again. With very few men you have often conquered and demolished them. If they are many, what does it matter? Their numbers are worthless, and an army with a weak and foolish leader is little to be feared. No one should be afraid of a wretched, leaderless army. He who commands them is a child: he can't even bear arms yet. We are good fighters, tested in many a battle. Let's fight for our lives, for there's no other way of saving our skins.' His exhortation finished, Hengist had all his knights arm. He quickly and quietly rode against the Britons, thinking to find them unarmed and thus to rout them all. But the Britons, fearing the heathens, were armed both day and night. When the king realized they were approaching and wanted a battle, he led his men into a battlefield he thought suitable, and drew them up in order. On the one side, on horseback, he arranged three thousand armed knights, all reckoned to be good warriors, whom he had brought from overseas. He divided the Welsh into two companies and placed one in the mountains, so that the heathen could in no circumstances retreat there. He put the others in the woods, guarding the entrance to the forest, so that the pagans could not rush into it without the Welsh killing them. He made the rest go down into the field, to stand fast and put up good resistance.

7729. When he had arrayed everything as he had been advised, he placed himself with those men true to him, whom he knew to be the most loyal. Next to him he had his standard planted, to which his men gathered and clung. Count Eldulf was at his side, and many of the other barons. 'God, how happy I would be', said Eldulf, 'if I could see the moment when I reach Hengist. Then I ought to remember how, at Amesbury, he killed the whole flower of our kingdom on the very first day of May, when I barely made my escape.' As Eldulf was saying these words and indicting Hengist, Hengist himself and his army appeared in the field, occupying a large part of it. They were not slow to join battle. As soon as they saw each other, they at once rushed together. Then might you see warriors fight, one assaulting the other, these attacking, those defending, receiving and giving great blows, one felling the other, the living trampling the dead. Shields were pierced, lances shattered; the wounded fell, the fallen died. The heathens fought valiantly, the Christians even better. The heathens called on their false idols, the Christians on God. They made their troops scatter and abandon the field. The great and heavy blows these received forced them to turn their backs. When Hengist saw his men retreat and turn their backs to the blows, he spurred his horse towards Conisbrough, thinking to find protection there. But the king kept pursuing him, crying to his men, 'Forward! Forward!'

7775. When Hengist saw they were following him, and would besiege him in the castle, he wished rather to fight outside and risk his person than be inside and let himself be attacked, when he had no hope of help. He withdrew, and reassembled his men, returning them to the fight. Once more there was battle, heavy fighting and a violent fray. The heathens turned back, each rallying the other. Thus the Christians suffered losses, and the heathens captured many of them, because they fell into disarray. But the mounted troop of three thousand appeared to aid and support them. The heathens fought doggedly; no wonder, because they knew well they would never escape alive if they could not defend themselves. Eldulf saw Hengist and recognized him. He hated him and had reason to; now he saw the time and place to accomplish his desire. He ran at him with drawn sword. Hengist was strong and withstood the blow. The two warriors were joined in battle, with bare blades and raised shields. You might have seen their blows redouble and the sparks fly from the steel.

7807. Gorlois, count of Cornwall, came boldly towards the fray. Eldulf saw him approaching; it made him prouder and more resolute. Like a valiant warrior he ran and seized Hengist by the nose-guard, dragging him towards him and forcing down his head, carrying him off by brute force. 'Knights, God be thanked', he said, 'my desire is fulfilled. We have captured and defeated the man who has caused us so much harm. Kill this mad dog, who never had pity on us. He is the source of the war which has laid our land waste. You hold victory in your hands if you kill him.' Then Hengist was properly brought to justice. He was bound and chained and handed over to King Aurelius; they guarded and confined him closely. His son Octa, who was in the field, and his cousin, Ebissa, escaped with difficulty and entered York. They equipped the city within with as many men as they had. Many others had fled, whether to the forest, the plain, the valleys or the mountains.

7837. The king was happy with the glory of the victory God had given him. He entered Conisbrough and stayed three whole days there, in order for the wounded to be cared for and the weary to rest. Meanwhile he spoke to the barons and asked them all together what he should do with the wicked Hengist: should he keep him or kill him? Eldadus rose to his feet, younger brother of Count Eldulf, a pious and most learned bishop. 'I want', he said, 'to do to Hengist, this traitor and enemy, what Samuel once did to King Agag, when he was captured. Agag, the boastful king of the Amalekites, was very arrogant. He constantly made war on the Jews, did them harm and ill-treated them, pillaged and burned their lands and frequently killed them. Then, by mishap, he was defeated and captured. He was brought before Saul, then the crowned king. When Saul enquired what he should do with Agag, who had been handed over to him, Samuel, a holy prophet of Israel, rose to his feet. Nobody in all his life knew a man of greater sanctity. This Samuel seized Agag and divided him into many pieces; he cut him up into bits and scattered him throughout the land. Do you know what Samuel said while he cut up Agag? "Agag, you have injured many men, killed many, impoverished many; you have separated many a soul from its body and grieved many a mother, orphaned many a child, and now are you come to your end. I will make your mother childless and separate the soul from your body." What Samuel did to him, you should do to this man.' Following the example Eldadus cited, Eldulf jumped up and seized Hengist, led him out of the town, drew his sword and cut off his head. The king had the body prepared, interred and buried according to the custom of those who observe the heathen law.

7895. The king acted briskly and did not delay. He came to York with a great army and hemmed his enemies in. Octa, Hengist's son, was inside with some of his kin. He saw he would get no help and could not defend himself. He resolved to surrender, take the risk, and most humbly seek mercy; if he found it, he would be content. He did as he had planned, and his relatives praised him: he left the city on foot, and all his men likewise. Octa, the first to reach the king, held an iron chain. 'My lord', he said, 'mercy, mercy! All the gods we used to trust have let us down. Your God is more powerful: he performs miracles and great wonders, so that through you he has conquered us all. I am conquered, I come seeking your mercy. Take this chain I bear and do what you like with me and with my men too. Everything is at your disposal – to take our lives and our limbs. But if you are willing to keep us alive, you will receive great recompense: we will serve you loyally and become your men.'

7929. The king was filled with compassion. He looked round to see what the barons would say and how they would counsel him. The good priest Eldadus spoke first, like a wise man: 'It is, was, and always will be good', he said, 'for him who seeks mercy to receive it, for God will have no mercy on him who has none on others. These men try to have mercy from you; they seek mercy, and they should have it. Britain, extensive and broad, is in many places deserted. Give them a part of it and make them plough and till it: they can live off what they cultivate. But first take good hostages from them, who will serve you faithfully and fight loyally. Once upon a time, the Gibeonites asked for mercy, when the Jews conquered them. They sought mercy, they found mercy, and the Jews released them. We should not be worse than the Jews were that day. They beg for mercy: they should receive it and henceforth should not die.' The king, as Eldadus advised him, granted them land near Scotland to cultivate. So they went to dwell there, but first they gave him hostages, children from their noblest families.

7963. He then spent a fortnight in the city, summoning his people and holding council. He summoned his barons, clerks, abbots and bishops, restoring to them their lands and their rights. Then he commanded and ordained that the churches which the heathens had destroyed should be rebuilt. Meanwhile, he disbanded his army and created sheriffs and governors who would restore his domains and be in charge of his revenue. He had a search made for masons and carpenters and rebuilt the monasteries; throughout the land, the churches destroyed by war were all restored by the king, to serve and worship God. From there he returned to London, where they longed for his coming. He saw that the city was much damaged and deprived of good citizens, with houses laid waste and churches fallen, and many times he greatly lamented it. He had the churches repaired and made the clerks and citizens return to the observances performed there before. Next the king came to Winchester and rebuilt churches, houses and towers as he had done elsewhere. Then he went to Amesbury to visit the graveyard of those who had been murdered with the knives. He summoned many masons, good engineers and carpenters; he wanted to do honour to the site of the treacherous killing by Hengist with such a monument as might last for ever.

8003. Tremorius, a wise man who was archbishop of Caerleon, asked him to send for Merlin and act according to his advice. No man would counsel him better on what he wanted to do, for neither in action nor in prophecy could one find his equal. The king greatly wished to see Merlin and hear his wisdom. He sent for him at Labanes, a far-off spring in Wales (I don't know where, because I was never there).[12] Merlin came to the king, who had summoned him, and the king paid him great honour, receiving him with respect. He made much of him, treasured him and begged and prayed him to teach and inform him of the time to come: he dearly wished to hear of it from him. 'Sire', said Merlin, 'I will not do so; I will never open my mouth unless it is really necessary, and then only with great humility. If I

[12] In *HRB*, this spring is called *Galabes* (*Galahes* in the First Variant version), in the territory of the Gewissei, who are identified by Tatlock, *Legendary History*, p. 75, as the men of Gwent, though they could also be the West Saxons, originally called Gewisse (Bede, *Historia Ecclesiastica*, Book III, ch. 7).

spoke boastfully, in jest, or arrogantly, the spirit I possess, from whom I know what I know, would leave my mouth and take my knowledge with him, and my mouth would no longer speak differently from any other. Leave secret divination alone; think of what you must do. If you wish to create a durable monument, beautiful and fitting, and remembered for ever, have the Giants' Dance, made in Ireland, brought here. It is a huge and marvellous work of stones set in a circle, one on top of the other. The stones are so many and of such a kind, so enormous and so heavy, that no man nowadays would be strong enough to lift them.' 'Merlin', said the king, laughing, 'since the stones weigh so much that no man can move them, who could bring them here? As if we had a dearth of stones in this realm!' 'King', answered Merlin, 'then you don't know that skill surpasses strength. Might is good, skill better; skill prevails where might fails. Skill and art achieve many things which might doesn't dare to start. Skill can move the stones, and through skill you can possess them. They were brought from Africa, where they were first constructed; the giants who took them from there placed them in Ireland. They used to be most beneficial and useful to the sick. People used to wash the stones and mingle this water with their baths. Those who were ill and suffering from any disease prepared baths from these cleansing waters, bathed themselves and were cured; they never sought any other medicine, for whatever infirmity they might suffer.'

8079. When the king and the British realized what worth the stones possessed, they all had a great wish to go and carry off the Dance of which Merlin made such report. Together they chose Uther – and he himself came forward – to cross into Ireland, taking 15,000 armed men, to fight the Irish if they denied them the stones. Merlin would go with them to manoeuvre the stones. When Uther had summoned his men, he crossed the sea to Ireland. Gilloman, who was king, summoned his people and his Irishmen and began to threaten the British, wanting to expel them from the land. And when he heard what they sought, that they had come for the stones, he derided them at length: those who, seeking stones, crossed the sea to another land, went in search of folly. Not a single one, he said, should they have; nor would they ever carry one off. It was easy to despise them, but hard to defeat them. He despised and threatened them for so long, he looked for them so hard, that he found them. At once the two forces came together and exchanged blows. The Irish were not well armed, or used to combat; they had despised the British, but the British defeated them. The king ran away, fleeing from town to town.

8119. When the British had disarmed and thoroughly rested, Merlin, who was in the company, led them to a mountain where the Giants' Dance, which they had sought, was situated. The mountain, on whose top was the Dance, was called Killomar. They completely surrounded the stones and examined them, and each said to the other that he had never seen such a work. 'How can these stones be raised and how will they be moved?' 'My lords', said Merlin, 'try and see if you can move these stones with the strength you have, and if you can carry them.' They grasped the stones behind, in front and sideways; they pushed and thrust them hard, pulled and shook them hard, but however much force they used, they could not find a solution. 'Rise', said Merlin, 'you will do no more by force. Now you shall see how knowledge and skill are better than bodily strength.' Then he stepped forward and stopped. He looked around, his lips moving like a man saying his prayers. I don't know if he said a prayer or not. Then he called the Britons back: 'Come here', he said, 'come! Now you can handle the stones, and carry and load them into your ships.' As Merlin instructed, as he devised and told them, the Britons took the stones, carried them to the ships and placed them inside. They brought them to England and carried them to Amesbury, into the fields nearby. At Pentecost the king arrived, summoning all his bishops, abbots and barons. Many other people gathered there, a feast was held, and he was crowned. For three days he held a great feast, and on the fourth, after great deliberation, he gave bishoprics to the saintly Dubric of Caerleon and Sanson of York. Both were men of great learning and most holy life. And Merlin erected the stones, restoring them to their proper order. In the British language the Britons usually call them the Giants' Dance; in English they are called Stonehenge, and in French, the Hanging Stones.

8179. When the great feast was finished, the king's court departed. One of Vortigern's sons, Paschent, fearful of Aurelius and Uther, left Wales and Britain and fled to Germany. He acquired men and a fleet for money, but his company was not large. He arrived in northern Britain, destroying towns and laying lands waste, but he did not dare to stay there long, because the king arrived and chased him away. When Paschent was back at sea, he did not dare return whence he had come. He sailed and rowed so far that he came to the shores of Ireland. He spoke to the king of that land and revealed his identity and his plight. Paschent begged the king so urgently, and they conferred with each other so much, that they agreed to cross the sea and fight the British, Paschent in order to avenge his father and claim his inheritance, and the king in order to seek revenge on those who had recently defeated him, robbed his people and carried off the Dance. They both pledged to seek vengeance for each other. When there was a favourable wind, they crossed the sea. They all arrived in Wales and entered Menevia. This was at the time a beautiful city, nowadays called St David's.[13]

8215. Aurelius the king lay sick: he languished in bed at Winchester, infirm, and for a long time between recovery and death. When he heard that Paschent, and the Irish king too, had come to Wales intending to ravage his realm, he sent his brother Uther there; he was distressed he could not go himself. He told Uther he was to seek them out and fight them. Uther summoned the barons and all the knights. Partly because he had to gather men together, partly because of the long journey, he was much delayed, and it was a long time before he reached Wales. While he delayed, Eappas spoke to Paschent. He was a heathen, born in Saxony and most learned, knowledgeable about medicines and fluent in many languages, a wicked man with an evil faith. 'Paschent', he said, 'listen to me! You have long hated the king: what will you give me if I kill him?' 'I will give you a thousand pounds', he said; 'nor will I ever fail you, if you are as good as your word, that you'll kill the king.' 'I don't ask for more', he said. So they struck their bargain: Paschent to give him a thousand pounds, and he to poison the king. Eappas was very cunning, and keen to get the money. He dressed in monk's clothes and gave himself a tonsure, cropping his hair on top. Shorn and tonsured like a monk, and dressed like a monk, with a monk's bearing, he went to the royal court. He was a

---

[13] Wace adds this detail of the city.

scoundrel: he made himself out to be a doctor, spoke to the king and promised him that he would restore him to health shortly, if he would put himself in his hands. He felt his pulse and inspected his urine. He was well aware of the source of the trouble, and was quite able to cure it. Who might suspect such a man? The noble king wished, as any of us might do, to get better. He feared no treachery and put himself in the hands of this villain. And he gave him a potion, all mixed up with poison, then had him warmly covered and made him lie in peace, to sleep. As soon as the king warmed up, the poison penetrated his body – and, God, what agony! He had to die. But when he knew he was to die, he told his men, who watched over him, that if they truly loved him, they should carry his body to Stonehenge and bury it within the stones. Thus he died and came to his end, and the traitor escaped.

8285. Uther entered Wales and found the Irish at Menevia. Then a star appeared, seen by many people. According to the clergy, it was called a comet and signified a change of king. It was extraordinarily bright and only one ray came from it. A flame issuing from this ray was shaped like a dragon, and from this dragon's mouth two beams appeared, one stretching over France and shining as far as Muntgieu,[14] the other towards Ireland and divided into seven rays. Each of the seven shone brightly over land and sea. At the sight of such a sign, the people were quite shaken. Uther marvelled greatly at it and was dismayed by these wonders. He begged Merlin to tell him what such a sign meant. And Merlin was very troubled; he was grieved at heart and spoke not a word. When breath came back to him, he lamented and sighed bitterly. 'Oh God', he said, 'what great grief, what great loss, how many tears, have today befallen Britain! She has lost her noble leader: the king is dead, that valiant warrior who delivered this land from grief and harm and the hands of the heathen.' When Uther heard that his brother, that good lord, had perished, he felt great grief and dismay. But Merlin comforted him thus: 'Uther', he said, 'don't be dismayed; there is no remedy for death. Carry out what you intended; fight your enemies. Victory awaits you tomorrow over the Irish king and Paschent; fight tomorrow and win, and you

[14] The Great St Bernard pass.

will be king of Britain. The sign of the dragon meant you, who are brave and bold; one of its beams signified a son which you will have, of great power, who will be victorious as far as France and beyond. Through the other beam, which diverged here and split into seven rays, a daughter is signified, who will make a Scottish marriage. Many good heirs, who will conquer land and sea, will be born of her.'

8345. When Uther had listened carefully to Merlin's words of comfort, he made his men rest that night, and in the morning had them armed. He wanted to attack the city, but when the Irish saw him coming, they seized their weapons, divided themselves into companies, and came out to fight. They fought fiercely but were soon defeated, for the British killed Paschent, and the king of Ireland too. Those who remained alive on the battlefield turned and fled to their ships. Uther, who followed after them, made them die quite unshriven. There were those who escaped by fleeing to their ships and rushing out to sea, so that Uther could not reach them. When his business was finished, he went back towards Winchester, and the best of his barons with him. On the way he met a messenger, who told him that indeed the king was dead, and how he had died, and that the bishops had with great care put his tomb inside the Giants' Dance, as he had instructed his servants and his barons when still alive. When Uther heard this, he came spurring into Winchester, and the common people came before him, weeping and crying out, 'Lord Uther, for God's sake, mercy! He who protected us and did us great good is dead. Now protect us: take the crown, bestowed on you by right and inheritance. And we, noble lord, beg you to do so, desiring only your honour and profit.' Uther saw that it was to his advantage and that he could not do better. He was glad of what they said, and at once did what they asked: he took the crown, became king, loved the realm and protected the people. In honour and memory of the dragon, which had signified he was valiant and would be king, and would have victorious heirs, Uther, advised by his barons, had two golden dragons made. One of them he had carried before him when going into battle; the other he presented to Winchester, to the bishop's church. Ever after, for this reason, he was called Uther Pendragon: Pendragon was his name in British, Dragon Head in French.

8407. When Octa, Hengist's son, whom the king had given tracts of land and great houses, heard that he who had maintained large armies was dead, he set no store by the new king: he owed him neither oath nor loyalty. He gathered friends and family together, including his cousin Eosa; these two were the boldest, and masters over the rest. They retained as allies those men led by Paschent who had escaped Uther, and had a very great company. They overran on every side all the land from the boundary of the Humber up to Scotland. Then they went to York and attacked the city, and those inside defended themselves, so that the heathen captured nothing, but there were many men besieging them. Uther wanted to rescue his city and help his friends inside. He came at once to York, summoning his men from all sides. He wished to make the heathen give up the siege, and immediately advanced to strike them. The battle was violent and arduous, and many a soul was there parted from its body. The heathen were very powerful and put up a spirited resistance; the brave British could neither do them damage nor force an entrance through them. They had to withdraw far off, and when they wanted to retreat, the besiegers chased them, inflicting great injury. They pursued them so hard, overtaking them from time to time, that they brought them to a mountain, and night then separated them. The mountain was called Danien and at its top was rather steep; there were rocks and huge defiles and dense thickets round about. The Britons made for the mountain, some ascending to the top, others going round its sides. They occupied the whole hill, and the heathen, down below in the plain, attacked them, besieging the mountain round about.

8461. The king was much dismayed, both for his men and for himself. He was doubtful about what they could do and how they could escape. Gorlois, a Cornish count, very brave, sagacious and courteous, was with the king; a man of mature years, he was considered to be very wise. They asked him for advice and put the situation before him, for he would not have acted in a cowardly way to save his limbs or his life. 'You ask me for advice', he said. 'My advice is – if you agree – that we arm ourselves secretly and descend this hill: we shall strike our enemies, who imagine they sleep in safety. They have neither fear nor dread that anyone will ever bear a lance against them

again. They expect to seize us in the morning – if we want to
await them here. Let's go to them by stealth and fall suddenly
upon the whole pack! They will never be able to keep order,
blow a horn or shout a battle-cry. Before they are awake we will
have slaughtered so many of them that none of those escaping
us will ever again resist us. But first let us promise God that we
will make amends to Him, and seek penitence and forgiveness
for our sins, and abandon our wickedness, which we have
committed all our lives. And let us pray to the Saviour to
support us and galvanize us against those who don't believe in
Him and attack His Christians. In this way God will be with us
and rescue us; and once God is with us, who can possibly defeat
us?'

8505. By his advice, and according to his words of counsel,
they humbly promised God to amend their lives. Then they
armed and stealthily came down from the hill. They found all
the heathen lying asleep and quite unarmed. Then might you
have seen great killing and amazing slaughter: speared bellies,
smashed chests, heads, feet and fists flying. Just like the proud
lion, long hungry, who kills sheep, ewes and lambs large and
small, so did the British kill both rich and poor. They were
asleep among the fields, and the next minute they were so
engulfed that they could pay no heed to arming; nor could they
flee the spot. And the British, finding them quite unarmed,
slaughtered them: they pierced bellies and hearts, and dragged
out bowels and entrails. The lords who had started the war,
Octa and Eosa, were captured. They were sent to London,
bound and put in a dungeon. If any escaped from the field, they
were saved by the dark night. He who could flee, fled, not
waiting for any friend; but many more were slain there than
escaped alive.

8541. When Uther left that place, he passed through Northumberland, and from Northumberland into Scotland, with a great
company and great army. He traversed the length and breadth
of the whole land, attracting all those people without government to his allegiance. No previous king had ever established
such peace throughout the kingdom as he did. When he had
finished his business in the north, he made his way straight to
London, and Easter Day approached, when he wished to be

crowned. He summoned by letter and message all those far and near – dukes, counts, castellans – and all the rest of his barons, with their wedded wives and private retinues, to come to London for the feast, for he wanted to hold a magnificent one. Everyone obeyed his summons, and whoever had a wife, brought her.

8565. The feast was properly celebrated and, once mass was ended, the king sat down to eat at the head of the hall, on a dais. The barons were set around him, each according to the importance of his fief. In front of him and opposite was seated the count of Cornwall, and next to him sat Ygerne, his wife. There was no fairer in all the land: she was courteous, beautiful and wise, and of very high rank. The king had heard her spoken of and much praised. Before giving any sign of it – indeed, even before seeing her – he had loved and desired her, for she was exceedingly celebrated. During the meal he kept watching her and gave her all his attention. Whether he ate or drank, spoke or kept silent, he always thought of her, and watched her out of the corner of his eye. As he looked at her, he would smile and make her loving signals. He sent her greetings through his close friends, and presents; he addressed frequent laughs and winks to her and showed many signs of love. Ygerne behaved in such a way as neither to consent nor to refuse. From the jests, the laughs, the signs, the greetings and the gifts, the count was well aware that the king loved his wife and would never be loyal to him if he could have her at his disposal. He sprang up from his seat at the table, took his wife and went out; calling to his companions, he went to mount his horse.

8607. The king sent word after him that to leave his court without permission was a shameful and disgraceful deed. He should do the right thing and return; and if he failed to do this, the king repudiated him, wherever he had gone, and could no longer trust him. Gorlois did not want to return: he left the court without leave. And the king uttered great threats against him, but the count cared little for that, not knowing then what was to come. He returned to Cornwall and provisioned the two castles he possessed. His wife he placed in Tintagel, which had been his father's and grandfather's. Tintagel was easy to defend and could not be captured by any engine of war, being closed in by cliffs and the sea; whoever kept guard just on the door would never fear or worry about men finding entrance elsewhere. There the count confined Ygerne: he did not dare put her elsewhere in case she was seized or abducted. And he led his mercenaries and most of his knights to another castle he owned, which protected the greater part of his domains. The king knew he was getting equipped and would defend himself against him. To attack the count, as much as to approach the countess, the king summoned his men from all directions and crossed the Tambre.[15] He came to the count's castle and wanted to capture it, but the count held out. And he besieged it: he laid siege to it for a week without being able to take it, or the count being ready to yield, for he awaited the king of Ireland, who was to bring help.

8651. The king hated the delay and began to suffer. Love for Ygerne, whom he adored above all else, afflicted him. He secretly called to him Ulfin, a baron who was one of his intimates. 'Ulfin', he said, 'advise me: you are privy to all my secrets. Love for Ygerne has struck me down, completely defeating and conquering me: I can neither come nor go, wake nor sleep, arise nor rest, eat nor drink, without thinking of her. But I don't know how to possess her. Without your advice, I'm a dead man.' 'These are astonishing words', said Ulfin. 'You have harassed the count with war, destroyed his lands and confined him to this castle. Do you think that pleases his wife? You love the wife and make war on the husband! I don't know what sort of help you need; I can't advise you. But send for Merlin: he is steeped in many an art, and he has arrived to join your company. If he can't advise you, no one can be your guide.'

8681. Counselled by Ulfin, the king summoned Merlin to come to him and revealed what he needed. He begged and prayed him to advise him, if he could, for without help he must die, unless he could have his will of Ygerne. He besought him to help him. He would reward him, if that was his wish, for he was in great distress and suffering. 'Sire', said Merlin, 'you shall have her; you shall never die on Ygerne's account. I shall make you have

---

[15] In other manuscripts, the *Cambre* or *Camble*, so there is a choice between the Rivers Camel and Tamar. See n. 66 below; Tatlock, *Legendary History*, p. 60; and Pelan, *La Partie arthurienne*, p. 158.

all your desire, and never shall you give me anything of yours. But Ygerne is strongly guarded, locked inside Tintagel, which is so strong it can never be taken or conquered by force. There will be two good men defending both entry and exit. But I will easily get you inside, using new potions: I know how to change a man's face so that one turns into another, the first seeming to be the second, and the second apparently identical to the first. I will make you assume, without fail, the body, face, bearing, speech and appearance of the count of Cornwall. Why need I say more? I will make you resemble the count while I, accompanying you, will take Bretel's appearance, and Ulfin, who will be with us, will exactly resemble Jordan. The count cherishes these two as his intimate counsellors. Thus you can enter the castle and carry out all you desire: you will never be noticed or suspected to be another man.' The king had complete faith in Merlin and abode by his advice. He secretly handed over to a baron the charge of his men. Merlin performed his enchantment and changed their faces and clothes, and in the evening they entered Tintagel. Those who thought they knew them, received and welcomed them, and joyfully served them. The king lay with Ygerne, and that night Ygerne conceived that king – the good, strong and resolute – whose name you will know as Arthur.

8737. The king's men soon realized that the king was not with the army. There was not a single baron who was not afraid and who did not want to do something. Because they feared delay, they seized their weapons and armed themselves. Without orders or battle formation, they impetuously approached the castle and attacked it from all sides. And the count strongly defended himself, but in the defence he was killed and the castle was soon taken. Some of those who escaped went to tell Tintagel what a misfortune they had had in losing their lord. Hearing their news and their laments over the count's death, the king rose and emerged: 'Silence', he said, 'it is not so. I am quite safe and sound, thank God, as you can see. This news is not true: don't believe everything you are told. However, I shall tell you the reason my men feared for my life. I left the castle without taking leave, and thus speaking to no one; I revealed neither my departure, nor my arrival amongst you, for I feared treason. But now they fear I have been killed, because they have not seen me since the king gained the castle. The death of my men, and the castle they have lost, may give us grave difficulties. But the good news is that I'm alive. I will go out to meet the king, seeking peace, and I will come to terms before he besieges this castle and before worse may befall. For if he surprise us here, we shall have more ignominy in pleading our cause.'

8781. Ygerne, constantly in fear of the king, praised this decision; and he then embraced and kissed her, as he left. Thereupon he left the castle, having gained all his desires. When the king, Ulfin and Merlin were outside and on their way, each regained his own form and was as he should be. They came quickly back to the army. The king wanted to know how the castle was so speedily taken and if the count were slain. There were many who could tell him the truth on both matters. He was grieved the count was slain, he said: that had not been his wish. He was full of regrets and compunction, and angry with his barons. He seemed very distressed, but there were few who believed him. He returned to Tintagel and called to those inside the castle, asking them why they defended it: the count was dead and they should surrender it, since they would get no help from the rest of the country or elsewhere. They knew the king spoke the truth, and they had no hope of rescue. They opened the gates of the castle and yielded the fortress up to him. The king, deeply in love with Ygerne, married her without delay. She had conceived a son that night and in due course bore him. His name was Arthur: his greatness has been celebrated ever since. After Arthur, Anna was born, a daughter who was bestowed on a noble and courteous baron, Loth of Loenois.[16]

8823. Uther reigned peaceably a long time, safe and sound. Then his strength began to fail and he fell sick; he lay for a long time very ill and much enfeebled. The soldiers in charge of guarding the prison in London grew bored with their long task and, sweetened with promises, set free Hengist's son Octa and released him from prison together with Eosa, his friend. Whether for promises or gifts, the guards abandoned the prison and fled, along with the prisoners. When these were in their own lands and had once more gathered their men, they issued great threats

[16] *Loenois* (*Lodonesia* in *HRB*) is Lothian, Scotland.

against Uther and acquired a large fleet. With big crowds of knights, men-at-arms and archers, they crossed into Scotland, burning and wasting the land. Uther, lying sick, and unable to help himself, in order to defend his realm and himself, bestowed upon Loth, his son-in-law, the entire charge of commanding his army and rewarding his knights. He told them to listen to Loth and do what he told them, because he was courteous, generous and very noble and wise.

8857. Octa made war on the British. He had large numbers of men and grew very arrogant. In part owing to the king's weakness, in part to Octa's desire to avenge his father and himself, he terrified Britain, for he gave neither truce nor pledge. Loth often encountered him and often routed him; many times he beat him, many times he was beaten in his turn, for that is the way in such matters, that the loser one minute is the gainer the next. Should Loth defeat him and expel him from the land, the British would encourage each other's arrogance and disdain Loth's commands, because they were just as noble and possessed just as much, and more. Thus the war dragged on, and grew, until the king noticed it and the people told him his barons were a half-hearted lot. Listen to what this man did in his great rage! His illness did not restrain him: he would no longer stay behind, he said, but wanted to see his barons in the army. He had himself carried as if on a bier by horses, in a litter. Now he would see, he said, who followed him and who stayed at home. He summoned and sent for those who formerly had deigned to respond neither to Loth nor to his command, and they speedily came.

8891. The king went straight to Verulam, a city at that period, where St Alban had been martyred; but subsequently the place was laid waste and the city quite destroyed. There Octa had led his men, and installed them within the city; without, the king laid siege. He had engines made to shatter the walls, but they were strong and he could not damage them. Octa and his people, warding off the siege-engines, rejoiced. One morning they opened the gate and came out to fight: it seemed contemptible and base to them that the gate should be shut on account of a king making war on them from a bier and going into battle on a litter. But their pride, I believe, was their downfall, and he

who deserved to conquer, conquered. Octa, and his good cousin
Eosa, were defeated and slain. Many who escaped fled towards
Scotland, and took as their leader Colgrin, friend and cousin of
Octa.

8917. From joy at the victory and the glory which God had
given him that day, the king sprang from his bed as if healthy
and well. He made strenuous efforts to encourage his barons.
When he was on his feet, he said laughing to his barons, 'I'd
rather lie on a bier and grow feeble through long illness than be
healthy and strong and shamefully defeated. Much better to die
with honour than to live long with dishonour. The Saxons
despised me because I lay in my bed; they made a mockery of
me and called me half-dead; but now, it seems to us, the half-
dead have defeated the living. Let's follow these fugitives, who
destroy my lands and yours.' When the king had waited a while,
and spoken to his men, he would have gone after the fugitives
and not been constrained by sickness, but the barons asked him
to stay in the city until God delivered him from ill-health,
because they feared he would suffer from it. So he stayed and
did not follow them; he lay sick, and the army departed. He had
sent all his people away except only for his private household.

8951. When the exiled Saxons re-assembled, they thought,
wrongly, that if they had killed the king he would have no heir
to harm them or deprive them of land. They wished to murder
him by means of poison, venomously and treacherously, because
they did not trust so much to their weapons to kill him. They
chose some wicked men – I cannot tell you who, or when – and
promised them money and lands. They sent them to the royal
court poorly dressed, to spy out in what way they could reach
the king and murder him. These men, fluent in many languages,
stealthily approached the court and spied on its circumstances,
but however hard they spied, they could not reach the king. But
they came and went so much that they saw and heard that the
king used to drink cold water and tasted no other liquid, because
water was beneficial for his illness. He always drank from a
spring near the hall; no other pleased him so much. When those
seeking the king's death, wanting to kill him, saw that they
could not reach him, or slay him with some weapon, they
poisoned the spring and then fled the country, so as not to be

recognized. They waited and listened for when and how the king would die, for his end would come soon. When the king wanted to drink, and drank, he was poisoned and must die; he drank the water, then swelled up, changed colour, darkened, and before long died. And all those who drank the water, after the king's death died, so that the thing was known and the wicked deed recognized. Then the community gathered and blocked up the spring; so much earth was brought that a hill was raised.

9005. After the death of Uther the king, he was carried to Stonehenge and there buried within, by the side of his brother. The bishops sent word to each other, and the barons assembled; they summoned Arthur, Uther's son, and crowned him at Silchester. He was a young man of fifteen, tall and strong for his age. I will tell you what Arthur was like and not lie to you. He was a most mighty knight, admirable and renowned, proud to the haughty, and gentle and compassionate to the humble. He was strong, bold and invincible, a generous giver and spender, and if he could help someone in need, he would not refuse him. He greatly loved renown and glory, he greatly wished his deeds to be remembered. He behaved most nobly and saw to it that he was served with courtesy. For as long as he lived and reigned, he surpassed all other monarchs in courtesy and nobility, generosity and power.

9033. Arthur had not long been king when, of his own free will, he swore an oath that as long as the Saxons were in the land they would have no peace. They had slain his uncle and his father and harried the whole land. He summoned his men and sought mercenaries, making them generous gifts and promises. He summoned so many men, and covered so much ground, that he travelled beyond York. Colgrin, who since Octa's death had maintained and led the Saxons, had a great company of them, and also Picts and Scots, to help him. He marched to meet Arthur and puncture his pride. They met in a pass near the River Douglas; many were felled on both sides, by lances, javelins and bolts, but finally Colgrin was defeated and fled. Arthur, pursuing him, chased him as far as York, where Colgrin occupied the city, and Arthur laid siege to it round about.

9059. Baldulf, Colgrin's brother, was waiting on the coast for Cheldric, the king of Germany. When he heard that Arthur was laying siege to his brother in York, and had chased him from the field, he was full of grief and distress and wished he were with him. He gave up waiting for Cheldric, went five miles away from the army, and lay in ambush in a wood. What with the men of his lineage, and foreigners he had brought, he had with him six thousand armed men. He intended to overwhelm Arthur's army by night and make it give up the siege, but someone who saw them in ambush ran to tell the king. Arthur learned of Baldulf's trap, and took the advice of Cador, count of Cornwall, who even in peril of death would not let him down. He put Cador in charge of six hundred knights and three thousand foot-soldiers and sent them secretly against Baldulf in the ambush. The Saxons never heard a word, or cry, or any sound, until Cador, attacking without delay, shouted his battle-cry. He killed more than half of them, and would not have let a single one escape if the night had not been dark and the wood a painful impediment.

9093. Baldulf turned and fled, taking cover from bush to bush. He had lost the best, and the greater part, of his band, and was at a loss how to help his brother; he wished very much to speak with him, if he dared and had the chance. He went in the guise of a minstrel to the siege and pretended he was a harper; he had learned to sing and to harp lays and melodies. In order to reach his brother, he had his beard shaved off one side of his face, and the hair on his head and his moustache treated likewise, so that he looked just like a scoundrel or a fool.[17] He had a harp round his neck. For a while he behaved in such a way that no one suspected him. He went harping here and there to such an extent that he came close enough to the city for those on the walls to recognize him, and they pulled him up with ropes. They were in despair as to how to fly or escape, when news arrived by ship that Cheldric, with six hundred sail, had landed at a port in Scotland and was coming to the siege in strength. But he

[17] Cf. the hairstyle of the fool in the late twelfth- or early thirteenth-century *Folie Tristan*; and see Weiss, *Birth of Romance*, p. 124 n. 5. *Lecheür* ('scoundrel') may also mean 'lecher'. Severe punishments often included shaving the head.

believed, and indeed said, that Arthur would never wait for him. Nor did he: he did not wait, for his friends advised him in no way to stay for Cheldric, nor to fight him, his men being numerous and fierce. He should retreat to London, and if Cheldric were to follow him there, Arthur would fight more confidently, because he could summon the common people, and the numbers of his men would increase every day.

9135. Arthur trusted his barons and came to London with them. Then a land in disarray could be seen: castles were being fortified, people were terrified. Arthur was advised to send for his nephew Hoel, his sister's son, king of Brittany.[18] There his kin were, his cousins and the best men of his race. Arthur sent letters to Hoel, and a request by messenger, telling him that if he did not help him, he would completely lose all his realm. His lineage would be covered in shame if he thus lost his inheritance. Hoel understood the importance of the matter and looked neither for pretext nor excuse; and his relatives and barons quickly prepared themselves. They soon equipped their ships, laden with men and weapons. There were twelve thousand knights, as well as archers and men-at-arms. The wind was fair and they crossed the sea, arriving at the port of Hamtune.[19] Arthur received them with joy and honour, as was fitting. They wasted no time but greeted each in few words. The king summoned his foot-soldiers and gathered his troops, and noiselessly and without more ado they went together to Nichole,[20] which the wicked Cheldric had besieged but not yet taken.

9171. Arthur made his men arm and, sounding neither horn nor trumpet, fell quite unexpectedly upon the enemy. Such a slaughter, such violent destruction, such a massacre and such suffering were never before inflicted on the Saxons in a single day. They threw down their weapons, left their horses and fled through the mountains and valleys, reeling through the rivers and drowning in large numbers. At their backs, the British gave them no rest; they struck great blows with their swords on

[18] Some domestic confusion here, copied from *HRB*: Anna, Arthur's only known sister, has already been married to Loth of Scotland.

[19] Southampton.

[20] Lincoln; *Kaerluideoit* in *HRB*.

bodies, heads and necks. The Saxons fled as far as Celidon Wood[21] and gathered there from all sides, making it their refuge. And the British guarded the wood, entirely surrounding it. Arthur feared lest the Saxons escape and leave the wood at night. He had some of the trees in one part cut down and made into a thick barrier of interwoven branches, tree crossing tree, and trunk fixed to trunk. He camped on the other side, whereupon no one went in or out.

9201. Those in the wood were in great dismay, since they could neither eat nor drink. There was no one, however strong, wise, rich or influential, who had taken bread, wine, meat and corn in there with him. After only three days they were quite overcome with hunger. When they saw they would die of starvation and could not get out by force, they accepted advice to plead for terms. They would leave their booty and their weapons behind, only keeping their ships, and would give the king hostages, as a sign they would perpetually keep peace with him and give him yearly tribute, if he would let them go alive and depart unarmed in their ships. Arthur accepted this plea and gave them leave to go. He retained the rest as hostages, that the promises to him might be kept, returned all their ships to them, and kept their weapons. And they put out to sea without weapons or booty.

9227. They were far out of sight and had lost the land from view when (I do not know what advice they found, nor who gave it to them), between England and Normandy, they turned their fleet around. They rowed and sailed so hard that they came to Dartmouth; they landed at Totnes. How they harried and

---

[21] The 9c HB, one of HRB's principal sources, attributes twelve named and victorious battles to Arthur (probably derived from a Welsh battle-catalogue poem: see Dumville, 'Historical value', p. 13). Four of them are fought on the River Douglas (cf. W 9049), and the last on 'Mount Badon' (following Gildas' mons Badonicus), interpreted by Geoffrey as Bath. The seventh is fought in silva Celidonis, id est Cat Coit Celidon (in Celyddon Forest: that is, the battle of Celyddon Coed). Welsh poems about Merlin, of the 12c and earlier, mention him going mad after the battle of Arfderydd (dated AD 573 in the Annales Cambriae) and wandering in the Forest of Celyddon (i.e. the Caledonian forest). This legend is picked up by Geoffrey of Monmouth in his Vita Merlini (c. 1150), but in HRB (p. 102) he seems to have thought Celidon Wood was in the south. See Jarman in AOW, pp. 117–33.

killed the people! They swarmed off their ships on to land and
spread through the region, seeking weapons, taking clothes,
burning houses, killing men. They covered the countryside and
took everything they found; they seized the peasants' weapons
and killed them likewise. They ravaged and wasted Devonshire,
Somerset and a large part of Dorset and found no one to hinder
them: the barons who could have done something were in
Scotland with the king. Through the countryside, or along the
roads, carrying booty and grasping loot, the Saxons arrived at
Bath, but those inside the town held out against them.

9255. When Arthur – who was in Scotland vanquishing the
Scots because they had attacked him and aided Cheldric –
learned of the heathens' doings, and their siege of Bath, he
summarily had his hostages hanged. He did not wish to keep
them or to delay further. He left behind Hoel of Brittany, whom
he thought to be in a bad way, lying sick of I know not what
illness in the city of Aclud,[22] and came to Bath as soon as he
could, with as many men as he could muster. He wanted to raise
the siege and save his men inside. Beside a wood, in a great
plain, Arthur had his troops arm.

9273. He divided and arranged his men, and he himself put on
his armour. He donned his greaves, well and finely made, and
put on a handsome coat of mail, worthy of such a king. His
sword Chaliburne was girded on, both long and broad. It was
made in the Isle of Avalon, and brought joy to whoever held it
unsheathed.[23] The helmet on his head gleamed brightly; the
nose-guard in front and the surrounding hoop were all of gold,
and at the top was painted a dragon. Many precious stones were
in the helmet; it had belonged to his father Uther. He mounted
a fine horse, strong, speedy and fleet of foot, with Pridwen, his
shield, round his neck, and resembled neither coward nor fool.

[22] *Aldclud*, in *HRB*. This is Dumbarton, capital of the Northern Welsh
kingdom of Strathclyde: see Hunter Blair, *Anglo-Saxon England*, p. 39.

[23] Arthur's sword is variously spelt *Chaliburn, Calibore, Calibuerne, Caliburn*
in the *Brut* manuscripts, and *Caliburnus* in *HRB. Escalibor* is a variant
introduced in 13c and 14c Continental manuscripts. In the Welsh tale *Culhwch
and Olwen* (c. 1100), Arthur's sword is Caletfwlch, his lance Rongomynyat,
and his ship Prydwen. See Bromwich and Evans, *Culhwch and Olwen*, pp. lxxxi,
64–5, 147.

Inside the shield, the image of my lady St Mary was artfully depicted and painted, in her honour and memory. Ron was the name of his straight lance: its iron was covered with steel at the tip, and it was fairly long and broad, much feared in times of need.

9301. When Arthur had armed his men and disposed his army, he made them advance slowly, not wanting anyone to break ranks until they came to strike. But the Saxons could not withstand them; they turned to a nearby hill and vied with each other to gain the summit. There they held out and defended themselves as vigorously as if they were surrounded by walls. But they were hardly secure, for Arthur attacked them there, hating their proximity. He followed them aloft, exhorting his men. 'Behold before you', he said, 'the false and arrogant wretches who have ruined and destroyed your family and kin, your friends and neighbours, and harmed you yourselves. Avenge your friends, your kin, avenge this great destruction, avenge the losses, the suffering, which they have inflicted on you so many times. I will take vengeance on their perjury and wicked deeds, I will avenge my forefathers and their grief and misery, and I will take vengeance on the return of the Saxons to Dartmouth. If we can rush amongst them and strike them down from this hill, they will never resist us or have any defence against us.'

9337. At these words Arthur spurred his horse, covering his breast with his shield. I do not know which Saxon he reached, but he struck him dead to the ground. Sweeping onward, he shouted, 'May God help us, St Mary! Mine is the first blow', he said: 'I've put paid to this one.' Then the British could be seen joining in, striking and smashing Saxons; they surrounded them on all sides, rushing and thrusting and delivering blows. Arthur fought with great harshness, power and valour. With raised shield and drawn sword, he made his way up, smashing through the throng, killing to right and left. He killed four hundred alone, more than were killed by his whole army, and he brought them to an evil end. Baldulf died, Colgrin died, and Cheldric fled, he and others besides, down a slope; they wanted to get back to the ships, enter them and protect themselves.

9365. Arthur heard that they were in flight and intent on returning to the ships. He had Cador of Cornwall sent after the fugitives, and with him ten thousand of the best and swiftest knights. Arthur then turned towards Scotland, for a messenger came to tell him that the Scots had besieged Hoel and almost captured him. Cheldric was fleeing towards his ships, but Cador was very cunning: through his knowledge of a more direct path to Totnes, he got ahead of Cheldric and his men. He came to the ships and equipped them with men, installing peasants and farmers; then he chased the fugitives. Two by two, and three by three, they fled, as they best could. To run more freely and easily they had jettisoned their arms and only carried their swords. They hastened towards the ships because they thought to escape in them. As they were fording the River Teign,[24] Cador came upon them, shouting his war-cry. The Saxons were utterly aghast and everywhere totally scattered. Climbing the mountain of Teignwic, Cheldric was overtaken and slain. The others, as they came up, died painfully by the sword. Those who could escape, fled from all sides to the ships, and those inside the ships transfixed them with arrows and toppled them into the sea. Some surrendered, some killed themselves. In woods and in the mountains they hid, in large bands; there were so many in hiding that they died of hunger and thirst.

9407. When Cador had carried out this slaughter and restored the land to complete peace, he rode after Arthur, not stopping until he reached Scotland. He found Arthur in Aclud, bringing aid to his nephew; Hoel was found to be quite safe and sound, cured of his illness. The Scots, hearing of Arthur's arrival, abandoned the siege and fled far away, into Mureif,[25] protecting themselves inside the city. There they thought to await Arthur, and there to defend themselves. Arthur knew that they were gathering and rallying against him, and followed them to Mureif, but they had fled further still. In the Lake of Lumonoi[26] they were dispersed amongst the islands. In the lake there are

---

[24] In *HRB* the Saxons flee to the Isle of Thanet; Wace has changed the locality to the West Country.

[25] Moray; Wace seems to think it is a town, not a district.

[26] *Stagnum Lumonoy* is in *HB*, ch. 67, as are the other two marvellous lakes; *HRB* took the name to refer to Loch Lomond, which is not in Moray.

sixty islands, much frequented by birds. In each island is a rock, and there eagles make their nest and eyrie. And, from what I have heard, when wicked people used to come to lay Scotland waste, all the eagles would gather, fighting and crying. You could see them at war for a day, or two, three or four more; it was a portent of great destruction.

9441. The lake was huge and deep, for it was fed by sixty streams from the valleys and mountains, and all of them remained within it except one, which found its way to the sea through one outlet alone. The Scots disappeared into the lake and scattered among the islands. And Arthur hastened after them, collecting boats, barges and ships. He watched them so carefully, attacked them so severely, harried and starved them so much, that in their twenties, their hundreds and thousands, they fell dead on the beaches. Gillomar, an Irish king coming to help the Scots, landed very close to Arthur, and Arthur moved against him; he fought the Irish king and defeated him very easily. He made him and his men flee back to Ireland; then he returned to the lake where he had left the Scots.

9465. Thereupon bishops, abbots, monks and other priests appeared, carrying the remains and relics of saints, and asking for mercy on the Scots. And on the other side appeared the women of the land, their feet and heads quite bare, their clothes torn and their faces scratched, their little children in their arms. With tears and loud cries they all fell at Arthur's feet, weeping and wailing and begging for mercy: 'Mercy, my lord!' they all said. 'Why have you destroyed this land? Have mercy on those wretches whom you, my lord, are starving to death. If you don't have mercy on the fathers, then look at these children and these mothers. Look at their sons, their daughters, their families, ruined by you! Give fathers back to their little sons, husbands back to their wives; give lords back to their ladies, and brothers back to their sisters! We paid sufficient penalty when the Saxons came this way: it was no wish of ours that they should enter this land. It grieves us that they came here: they have exhausted and harmed us. If we harboured them, they harmed us even more; they seized and devoured our property and sent it home to their lands. We had no one to defend us, or protect us against them. And if we did serve them, we did it unwillingly. They had the power; we endured it, not expecting any help. The Saxons were heathen and we were Christian; they molested us all the more for it and treated us all the more wickedly. They did us wrong; you do worse still. Neither honour nor renown will come to you from killing those who ask for mercy, who die of hunger among these rocks. You have conquered us, but let us live; give us land, wherever it may be! If you wish, make us live in slavery, both us and all our family, but have mercy on Christians: we hold the faith you hold. Christianity will be brought low if this land is ravaged, and already most of it is destroyed.' In victory Arthur was magnanimous: he took pity on these wretched people and on the clergy with their holy relics. He spared them life and limb, received their homage and left them alone.

9527. Hoel looked at the lake, and spoke about it to his men. He was amazed by its size, its breadth and its length; he marvelled at its many islands and many rocks, at so many eagles and so many nests, and at their noise and cries. Whatever he saw there he considered extraordinary. 'Hoel, my fine nephew', said Arthur, 'you are amazed at this lake. You will be even more amazed at another lake you can see, nearby in this land. The space it occupies is square, twenty feet long by twenty feet wide, and five feet deep. In the angles of the four corners are four kinds of fish; those in one corner will never cross into another, and yet there is no separation or prohibition of any sort that one can perceive, either by touch or by sight. I don't know whether man contrived it or nature created it.[27] I will tell you of yet another lake which will amaze you: it is near the Severn, in Wales. When the tide rises, it floods into it; yet, no matter how high the sea rises or how much the tide floods into it, it is never filled by the rising tide. Whether the tide rises higher or lower, the lake is never inundated by it and never overflows its banks. But, when the sea round about retreats, and the tide ebbs backwards, then you may see the water rise, cover and swamp

[27] This lake, unnamed in *HRB*, corresponds to *HB*'s *Finnaun Guur Helic*, the Fount of Gorheli; the third, called *Linligua* in *HRB*, corresponds to *HB*'s *Linn Liuan* (*Llyn Lliwan* in *Culhwch and Olwen*) – here the phenomenon of the Severn Bore is described. The author of this part of the *HB* is using an old tradition of listing certain extraordinary geographical features, known as the Marvels of Britain. See Roberts in *AOW*, pp. 88–90; and Bromwich and Evans, *Culhwch and Olwen*, p. 168.

the banks, fly up with great whirlwinds, and water and soak the fields. If a native of the country goes to see it, facing towards it, at once the water will spout up and pour over his clothes and himself, and no matter how strong he is, he will have to fall in. It has in this way made many fall in and many drown. If a man approaches with his back to it, his heels facing it, he can stand on the bank, and as long as he wants to stay, he will never be reached by the water, neither touched nor soaked.' 'This is a great wonder', said Hoel, 'and He who created it is wonderful too.'

9587. Then Arthur had his horns blown and his bugles and trumpets sounded, as the signal to return. He gave his men leave to go back to their homes, all except for the barons who were his close friends. They left joyfully, full of talk about Arthur, their king. Throughout Britain it was said that they had never had such a valiant leader. Arthur went to York and stayed there till Christmas, feasting there on Christmas Day. He saw that the city was greatly impoverished, weakened and damaged; many churches were deserted, and houses fallen and ruined. He made Piram, a wise chaplain who had not served him in vain, take over the archbishopric, in order to maintain the churches and restore the monasteries which the heathen had destroyed. The king had peace proclaimed throughout and set the peasants to work. He sent throughout his realm for those nobles who had been disinherited, restored their inheritances to them, and granted them fiefs and revenues.

9617. There were three high-born brothers, of royal lineage and well-connected, Loth, Angusel and Urien.[28] Their ancestors, and they after them, had held by right, as long as peace reigned, the land north of the Humber, wronging no man. Arthur restored their fiefs to them and increased their heritage. In the first place he returned Mureif to Urien, without payment[29] or charge, and

---

[28] Urien is a historical character, ruler of the northern British kingdom of Rheged, who led Welsh resistance to the English in the second half of the sixth century. See Hunter Blair, *Anglo-Saxon England*, pp. 41-2, and Thomson in *AOW*, p. 160.

[29] Literally, *relief*: the payment a feudal heir would normally have to make to his overlord when he took possession of his estate on the death of his parent.

asked him to be once more its ruler. The lord of the people of Mureif was then called king. He gave Scotland to Angusel, and he claimed it as his fief. To Loth, who had been his sister's husband for a long time, he gave all Loeneis, and other fiefs besides.[30] Walwein,[31] Loth's son, was as yet a young boy.

9641. When Arthur had established his realm, and justice throughout it, and restored his whole kingdom to its former dignity, he took Ganhumare[32] as his queen, a graceful and noble girl. She was beautiful, courteous and well-born, of a noble Roman family. For a long while Cador had had her brought up in Cornwall in excellent fashion, as befitted his close kins-woman; his mother had been Roman. Her manners were perfect, her behaviour noble, and she talked freely and well. Arthur loved her deeply and held her very dear; but the two of them produced no heir, nor could they have any children.

9659. When winter was passed, summer's warmth had returned, and it was safe sailing the seas, Arthur had his fleet prepared. He said he would go to Ireland and conquer it all. He did not delay long but summoned the flower of his young men, and those most experienced in war, rich and poor alike, from his realm. When they had crossed into Ireland, they seized their food from the land, taking cows and oxen and whatever was suitable to eat. Gillomar, king of the country, knew that Arthur had gone in search of these; he knew of the tidings, the brawls, the complaints and laments made by the peasantry, who had lost their herds. He went off to fight Arthur, but was unsuccess-ful, because his men were quite defenceless: they had neither hauberks nor shields; they knew nothing of arrows or how to draw a bow. And the British, who had bows, shot arrows at them in great numbers, so that they dared not expose their eyes; nor did they know where to hide. They could be seen making their escape in large numbers, one hiding next to another,

---

[30] As in *HRB*, Scotland is thus divided into three parts: Scotland, Lothian and Moray, here seen as a region, not a town.

[31] Gawain; *Gwalgwanus* and *Walwanus* in *HRB* (Vulgate and First Variant versions).

[32] Guinevere. Arnold, II, p. 808, lists the many variant spellings, both in *HRB* (where at this point in the Vulgate version she is called *Guenhuuara*) and in Wace, who actually only names her twice (this is MS P's variant at line 11176).

running into woods and bushes, towns and houses, seeking for mercy on their lives. They were defeated and beaten. Their king tried to dodge into a wood but was overtaken and could not escape. Arthur harried and attacked him so much that he caught up with him and took him. But Gillomar did homage to Arthur and received his heritage back from him. He gave hostages in perpetuity, to ensure he paid yearly tribute.

9703. When Arthur had conquered Ireland, he travelled as far as Iceland, taking and conquering the whole land, and subduing it entirely to him: he wanted to rule everywhere. Gonvais, king of Orkney, Doldani, king of Gotland, and Rummaret of Wenelande[33] all heard the news, each from their spies, that Arthur would come their way and destroy all the islands. There was not his equal in the whole world for military might, or anyone who could lead such an army. Afraid he would attack them and ravage their lands, they freely and without constraint went to him in Iceland. They brought him so many of their possessions, promised and gave so much, that peace was made and they became his men, holding their heritage from him. They promised and appointed a truce, and each gave hostages. In this way everybody stayed in peace, and Arthur returned to his ships; he came back to England and was welcomed with great joy.

9731. For twelve years after his return, Arthur reigned in peace. No one dared to make war on him; nor did he go to war himself. On his own, with no other instruction, he acquired such knightly skill and behaved so nobly, so finely and courteously, that there was no court so talked about, not even that of the Roman emperor. He never heard of a knight who was in any way considered to be praiseworthy who would not belong to his household, provided that he could get him, and if such a one wanted reward for his service, he would never leave deprived of

[33] Orkney and Gotland (*Godland, Gollande*) come from *HRB*; Wace has added the mysterious Rummaret of Wenelande, identified by critics since Tatlock with Wendland, of the Slavic Wends, against whom a campaign took place in 1147, while Wace was writing. Arnold's suggestion that it refers to Vinland is, however, supported by Ernest C. York, 'Wace's *Wenelande*: identification and speculation', *Romance Notes*, 22 (1981), 112–18.

it. On account of his noble barons – each felt he was superior, each considered himself the best, and no one could say who was the worst – Arthur had the Round Table made,[34] about which the British tell many a tale. There sat the vassals, all equal, all leaders; they were placed equally round the table, and equally served. None of them could boast he sat higher than his peer; all were seated near the place of honour, none far away. No one – whether Scot, Briton, Frenchman, Norman, Angevin, Fleming, Burgundian or Lorrainer – whoever he held his fief from, from the West as far as Muntgieu, was accounted courtly if he did not go to Arthur's court and stay with him and wear the livery, device and armour in the fashion of those who served at that court. They came from many lands, those who sought honour and renown, partly to hear of his courtly deeds, partly to see his rich possessions, partly to know his barons, partly to receive his splendid gifts. He was loved by the poor and greatly honoured by the rich. Foreign kings envied him, doubting and fearing he would conquer the whole world and take their territories away.

9785. In this time of great peace I speak of – I do not know if you have heard of it – the wondrous events appeared and the adventures were sought out which, whether for love of his generosity, or for fear of his bravery, are so often told about Arthur that they have become the stuff of fiction: not all lies, not all truth, neither total folly nor total wisdom. The raconteurs have told so many yarns, the story-tellers so many stories, to embellish their tales, that they have made it all appear fiction.

9799. Prompted by his own noble disposition, the advice of his barons, and the large body of knights he had equipped and nurtured, Arthur said he would cross the sea and conquer all France. But first he would go to Norway and make his brother-in-law Loth king there. Sichelin the king had died, without son or daughter; on his death-bed he had asked, as he had asked

---

[34] This is the first appearance of the Round Table. See Foulon in *ALMA*, pp. 99–100, and Schmolke-Hasselmann, 'The Round Table', who provides a detailed translation of this passage. In particular, she suggests: 'There sat the vassals, all of them at the table-head [translating the rare word *chevelmant*] ... All were seated *in medio* [a term denoting the seat of honour, rendering *meain*] and nobody was at the far end [*forain*]' (p. 48).

when in health, that Loth should be king of Norway and hold his domain and his kingdom. He was his nephew, he had no other heir, so Loth by right should have everything. If Sichelin had ordained this, and thought it would be so, the Norwegians considered both his command and his decree folly. When they saw that the king was dead, they utterly refused Loth the kingdom. They had no desire to call upon a foreigner or make a foreigner their lord; they would have to be all old greybeards before recognizing him. He would give to others abroad what he should give to them. They would make one of Sichelin's retainers king, who would cherish them and their sons. For this reason they thus made Riculf, one of their barons, king.

9831. When Loth saw he would lose his rights if he did not conquer them by force, he appealed to Arthur, his lord, and Arthur promised him that he would give him all the kingdom, and Riculf had been wrong to accept it. He summoned a large fleet and large army and entered Norway by force. He inflicted great damage on the land, burning towns and plundering houses. Riculf would not flee or leave the country; he thought he could defend himself against Arthur, and gathered together the men of Norway, but he had few men and few friends. He was conquered and slain. So many of the others were killed that very few were left. When Norway surrendered, Arthur gave it all to Loth, on condition that Loth held it from him and acknowledged him as overlord. Walwein had recently returned, a renowned and valiant knight, from St Soplice, the Pope, may his soul rest in glory. He had given him armour, which was well bestowed. Walwein possessed bravery and great moderation; he had no time for pride or arrogance. He would do more than he said, and give more than he promised.

9863. Once Arthur had taken Norway, and Loth had it well under his control, he had the bravest and most valiant warriors selected and gathered, and barges and ships equipped. When he had fine weather and a good wind, he crossed into Denmark, leading his other men as well. He desired the country for himself. Aschil, king of the Danes, considered the British, the Norwegians, the all-conquering Arthur, and saw that he could not resist. He did not want himself harmed or his good land despoiled; he neither wished his gold and silver spent, nor his people killed, nor his towers surrendered. He said, did and strove so much, promised and gave so much, asked and begged so much, that he reached an agreement with King Arthur: he did homage, became his man, and held his whole kingdom in the king's name.

9887. Arthur was pleased with this great achievement and the conquests he was making. It was not yet enough for him. He had the best knights and best archers in Denmark chosen – I do not know how many hundreds or thousands of them – and wished to take them with him into France, which he did without delay. He conquered Flanders and Boulogne, seized towns and took castles. He made his men behave prudently, not wanting the land destroyed, the towns burned or booty taken; he forbade them anything except meat, drink and fodder, and if anyone could be found to sell it to them, it should be bought with good money, not seized or stolen. In those days, France was called Gaul and had neither king nor overlord. It was in the power of Rome, who held it in demesne. It was in Frollo's charge and he had guarded it a long time; he received tribute and revenues and sent them, at set times, to the Emperor Leo in Rome.

9914. Frollo was a man of great prowess; one of the Roman nobility, he was physically afraid of no one. He knew, from many messengers, of the seizures and the damage that Arthur and his men were carrying out, robbing the Romans of their rights. He had all those men able to bear weapons and belonging to Rome's domain, whom he thought could help him and who were in his jurisdiction, summoned, armed and well equipped. He went to do battle with Arthur but was unsuccessful: he was defeated and fled, losing many of his men, whether slain, wounded, captured, or deserting back to their homes. Nor was this surprising, because Arthur had a very large army, for from the lands he had conquered and the cities he had taken there was not a single man left behind, good knight or foot-soldier, of fighting age or ability, whom he did not take along with him or subsequently summon. He sent for many foreigners, in addition to his household, made up of bold knights and proven fighters. The French, those who could and who dared, went over to his side, partly because of his wise words, partly because of his generous gifts, partly because of his nobility, partly out of fear, or for refuge. They went to him, made peace and acknowledged him as their overlord.

9955. After Frollo was defeated, he came to Paris in great haste, not daring to stop anywhere or trust anyone. He was seeking a secure refuge, because he feared Arthur and his army. He had provisions brought into the city from the surrounding towns; at Paris he would await Arthur, and at Paris he would defend himself. Partly from the people who had fled there, partly from its native inhabitants, the city was swollen with men. Each in his own way strove to collect corn and meat and to make walls and doors. Arthur knew Frollo was equipping himself at Paris; he approached him and began a siege, lodging in the surrounding towns. He had a watch set by water and on land so that food could not get in. The French held out well, and Arthur sat there nearly a month. There were many people in the city and soon they were short of food; all that they had acquired and collected in a short time was soon eaten and used up. They were starving! There was little food and many people. The women and children wept and wailed; if it had been up to the poor, the city would soon have surrendered. They kept crying: 'Frollo, what are you doing? Why don't you ask Arthur for peace?'

9991. Frollo saw the people distraught for lack of food, and men dying of hunger, saw they wished to surrender, and saw the city made destitute. He preferred to endanger his body and risk his life rather than totally abandon Paris; he relied upon his valour. He sent word to King Arthur that the two of them should come to the island and fight in single combat, and whoever killed the other, or could take him alive, would have all the other's land and receive all France, so that the people would not die or the city be destroyed. Arthur liked this request very much and it greatly pleased him. He agreed to this combat between the two of them, just as Frollo had requested it. Thus pledges were exchanged and hostages taken on both sides, from the army and from Paris, guaranteeing the agreement.

10015. Then the two armed warriors appeared and entered the meadow on the island. The people could be seen in tumult, men and women coming out, jumping on walls and houses and calling upon God by all His names to let him who would give them peace, win, so that war never came to them again. Arthur's men, on the other hand, were listening and watching, and praying the King of Glory to give their lord victory. Whoever could then have seen the two warriors, seated armed on horse-back, their steeds ready to leap forward, raising their shields and brandishing their spears, could say, and say truly, that he saw two bold fighters. They had good, fast, horses, fine shields, hauberks and helmets; it was not easy to tell, seeing them, who was the stronger or who would win, for each seemed a brave fighter. When they were ready, each removed to a distance, and with reins loosed, shields raised and lances lowered, they both spurred to strike each other with extraordinary violence. But Frollo missed his stroke – I do not know if his horse swerved – and Arthur struck him below the shield-boss, carrying him a spear's length from his horse. He charged at him and drew his sword; the battle would have been over, but Frollo jumped to his feet and stuck his lance out towards Arthur. He hit his horse full in the chest and pierced him to the heart, making horse and rider topple together. You could see how alarmed men were: the British were shouting and seizing their weapons. They would have broken the truce and crossed the water to the island and started a massacre. Then Arthur got to his feet, raised his shield, covered his head and gave Frollo a welcome with his sword.

10069. Frollo was very brave and bold, and neither slow nor scared. He raised his sword aloft and struck Arthur in the middle of the forehead. Frollo was strong, the blow heavy, and the sword hard and keen. It broke and split the helmet, damaged and shattered the hauberk and wounded Arthur in mid-fore-head, so that the blood ran down his face. When Arthur felt the wound and saw his own blood, he was so angry he went pale and livid with fury. He did not fail to rush forward, with Caliburn in his hand, his sword which he had had in many a time of need. He struck Frollo on top of his head and split it down to his shoulders. Pulling out his sword, he pushed, and Frollo fell, scattering brains and blood; he had no more need of helmet or of the hauberk he cherished. For a while his feet kicked; then he died without a word. The people in the city and the army shouted, the former weeping, the latter laughing. The citizens wept for Frollo, yet ran to the gates. They received Arthur, his household and his men, inside. Then the French could be seen coming to offer their homage, and Arthur received it and took hostages as a guarantee of peace. He stayed a long while in Paris, appointing a governor and regulating the peace.

10105. He divided his army into two parts and established two companies. One half he gave to Hoel, his nephew, and asked him to conquer with it Anjou, Gascony, Auvergne and Poitou, and he should conquer Burgundy and Lorraine if he could. Hoel carried out his command as he had ordained it: he conquered Berry, then Touraine, Anjou, Auvergne and Gascony. Guitart, duke of Poitiers, was a brave and good knight. To keep his land and his rights, he fought many times, often in pursuit, often in flight, often winning and often losing. Finally he saw that if he lost, he would have trouble recovering. He made peace and a treaty with Hoel because, apart from towers and castles, nothing was left to destroy: neither plants nor vines to be despoiled. He swore fealty to Arthur, and the king afterwards held him very dear. Then Arthur mightily conquered the remaining parts of France.

10133. When he had brought peace to the whole land, so that no part erupted in war, he presented gifts and wages to the old men and the married ones, who had long been in his army, and sent them back to their own lands. As for the young and unmarried men, with neither wives nor children, who expected more conquests, he kept them with him in France for nine years. In the nine years he held France, many marvels happened to him, he tamed many a proud man and kept many a villain in check. One Easter, he held a great feast for his friends in Paris. He compensated his men's losses and rewarded their deserts, repaying each one's service according to what he had done. To Kei, his chief seneschal, a brave and loyal knight, he gave all Anjou and Angers, which was gratefully received. To Bedoer, his cup-bearer and one of his privy counsellors, he gave in fief all Normandy, which then was called Neustria. These two were his most faithful subjects and knew all his deliberations.[35] And

[35] The seneschal and cup-bearer (*dapifer* and *pincerna*) were two of five great officers of state in the royal household (see Weiss, *Birth of Romance*, pp. 159–60). The importance of Kei and Bedoer in Arthur's household perhaps reflects the fact that they are his main companions in Welsh literature of *c.* 1100 or earlier: see Sims-Williams in *AOW*, p. 39; and Bromwich and Evans on *Pa Gur* in *Culhwch and Olwen*, pp. xxxiv–xxxvi. Cei is referred to in *Culhwch* as *swyddwr* (= *dapifer*).

he gave Flanders to Holdin, Le Mans to his cousin Borel, Boulogne to Ligier, and Puntif to Richier.[36] To many according to their nobility, to several according to their service, he gave what domains were available, and to minor nobles he gave lands.

10171. When he had given his barons fiefs and made all his friends rich, he crossed to England in April, at the start of summer. Men and women could be seen celebrating his return: the ladies kissed their husbands, and the mothers their sons; sons and daughters kissed their fathers, and mothers wept for joy; cousins and neighbours embraced, as did sweethearts who, when opportunity allowed, indulged themselves rather more. Aunts kissed their nephews – for everyone, joy was widespread. In streets and at crossroads many people would congregate to ask the new arrivals how they were and what they had done with their conquests, how they had acted, what they had found and why they had been away so long. They in turn told of their adventures, the harsh and bitter battles, the hardships they had endured and the dangers they had seen.

10197. Arthur honoured all his men, especially cherishing and rewarding the best ones. To display his wealth and spread his fame, he took counsel and was advised to assemble his barons at Pentecost, in summer, and then to be crowned.[37] He summoned all his barons by proclamation to Caerleon, in Glamorgan. The city was well situated and extremely wealthy. Men said at that time that its rich palaces made it another Rome. Caerleon lies on the Usk, a river flowing into the Severn; those coming from overseas could arrive on this river. On one side was the river, on the other the dense forest. There was plenty of fish and a wealth of game; the meadows were lovely and the fields fertile. There were two churches in the city, both prestigious: one called after St Juile,[38] the martyr, where there were nuns to serve God, and the other after his friend, St Aaron.

[36] None of these four is in *HRB* here.

[37] On plenary courts, where the crown could be worn in state, see Thorpe, *History*, p. 226 n. 2.

[38] Julius. These two saints according to Bede, *Historia Ecclesiastica*, Book 1, ch. 7, were citizens of Caerleon and Christian martyrs.

This was the seat of the archbishop, and there were many
noble priests, and most learned canons who knew about astronomy. They concerned themselves with the stars and often told
King Arthur how the works he wished to perform would come
to pass. Caerleon was a good place then; it has deteriorated
since.

10237. Because of the handsome lodgings, the great comforts,
the fine woods and beautiful meadows, because of these excellent places you have heard of, Arthur wished to hold his court
there. He made all his barons come: he summoned his kings and
his counts, his dukes and his viscounts, barons, vassals, bishops
and abbots. And those who were summoned came, as was
fitting, to the feast. From Scotland came King Angusel, dressed
handsomely and well; from Mureif, King Urien, and Ewain the
courteous, his son.[39] Stater came, king of South Wales, and
Cadual of North Wales; Cador of Cornwall, whom the king
held dear, was there, Morvid, count of Gloucester, and Mauron,
count of Worcester, Guerguint, count of Hereford, and Bos,
count of Oxford. From Bath came Urgent; from Chester, Cursal;
and from Dorchester, Jonathas. Anaraud came from Salisbury,
and Kimmare from Canterbury. Baluc, count of Silchester, came,
and Jugein from Leicester, and Argahl from Warwick, a count
with many of his relations at court.

10269. There were many other barons whose lands were no
less: Donaud, son of Apo, and Regeim, son of Elaud; Cheneus,
son of Coil, and Cathleus, son of Catel; the son of Cledauc,
Edelin, and the son of Trunat, Kimbelin. Grifu was there, son of
Nagoid, Run, son of Neton, and Margoid, Glofaud, and Kincar,
son of Aingan, and Kimmar and Gorboian, Kinlint, Neton and
Peredur, called the son of Elidur.[40] I do not want to tell stories

---

[39] Wace adds Ewain here; he appears in *HRB* later on (p. 130). This is Owan
or Ywain, the hero of poems by Taliesin. See Roberts in *AOW*, p. 109.

[40] The list of men at Arthur's court is taken from *HRB*, where it is an element
imported from Welsh genealogies, which preserved ancient British traditions
(Piggott, 'Sources', p. 282, calls it 'a curious fragment of an untranslated group
of pedigrees'). Many names in the group, from *Donaut* to *Kinlith* in *HRB*
(absent in the First Variant version), appear with the Welsh form *map* ('son of'):
e.g., *Donaut Mappapo, Cheneus Mapcoil*. Wace makes a few additions and
changes. In the names from Angusel to Argahl, he sometimes uses the spelling

about those serving in court who were friends of the king and
belonged to the Round Table. There were so many others of
lesser rank there, I could not count them all. There were many
abbots and bishops, and the three archbishops in the land: from
London, from York, and saintly Dubric from Caerleon. He was
the papal legate and a man of great piety: through his love and
prayers, many a sick man was cured. At that time, and subsequently, the see of the archbishopric was in London, until the
English ruled, laying the churches waste.

10301. There were many barons at court whose names I do not
know. Gillomar, king of Ireland, was there, and Malvaisus, king
of Iceland, and Doldani of Godland, a country rather short of
food. Aschil was there, king of Denmark, and Loth, king of
Norway, and Gonvais, king of Orkney, who controlled many
pirates. From overseas came Count Ligier, who held the fief of
Boulogne; from Flanders, Count Holdin; and from Chartres,
Count Gerin, bringing with him, in great splendour, the twelve
peers of France. Guitart, count of Poitiers, came, and Kei, count
of Angers, and Bedoer from Normandy (then called Neustria),
and from Le Mans came Count Borel and from Brittany, Hoel.
Hoel and all those from France had noble bearing, fine weapons,
handsome clothes, splendid trappings and sleek steeds. There
was not a single baron, from Spain to the Rim,[41] near Germany,
who did not attend the feast, provided he heard the summons.
Some came because of Arthur, some because of his gifts, some
to know his barons, some to see his wealth, some to hear his
courtly speech, some for love, some for the proclamation, some
for honour, some for power.

or variations of the First Variant version: *Stather, Caduallo, Kimmare (Eddelin,
Caduan* and *Kinmarc* in the Vulgate version). He adds Guerguint, who as
Gurguint Barbtruc appears in *HRB* (pp. 30–1), and makes Baluc come from
Silchester, as in the First Variant version. Elidur, like *HRB*'s *Eridur*, seems to be
a distortion of Eleuther, Peredur's father in Welsh genealogy. Both Peredur and
Elidur occur earlier in *HRB*, as sons of Morvid, and kings associated with
Dumbarton (*Alclud*). Peredur, like Owain, Urien and Dunaut, seems to be
another hero of the 6c British North. See n. 28 above, and Roberts and Lovecy
in *AOW*, pp. 109, 175–6. Morvid and Mauron also occur in Vortigern's
genealogy in *HB*.
   [41] Rhine.

10337. When the king's court was assembled, a fine gathering could be seen, and the city was in tumult, with servants coming and going, seizing and occupying lodgings, emptying houses, hanging tapestries, giving marshals apartments, clearing upper and lower rooms, and erecting lodges and tents for those who had nowhere to stay. The squires could be seen busy leading palfreys and war-horses, arranging stabling, sinking tethering-posts, bringing horses, tethering horses, rubbing them down and watering them, and carrying oats, straw and grass. You could see servants and chamberlains moving in several directions, hanging up and folding away mantles, shaking their dust off and fastening them, carrying grey and white furs: you would have thought it just like a fair.

10359. In the morning of the feast-day (according to the story in the chronicle), all three of the archbishops, as well as the abbots and bishops, arrived. Inside the palace, they crowned the king and then led him to the church. Two archbishops, one on each side, went with him, each supporting an arm, until he came to his seat. There were four swords of gold – both pommels and hilts[42] – borne by four kings, who walked directly in front of the king. This was their office when Arthur held court and a feast-day. They were the kings of Scotland and North Wales; the third came from South Wales, and Cador of Cornwall held the fourth sword. He was no less dignified than if he had been royal. Dubric, the Pope's legate and the prelate of Caerleon, undertook to perform the office, as it was in his own church.

10385. The queen, for her part, was attended with great pomp. She had invited beforehand, and now gathered round her on the feast-day, the noble ladies of the land, and she made her friends' wives, her female friends and relations, and beautiful, noble girls, all come to her to observe the festival with her. She was crowned in her rooms and led to the nuns' church. To make a path through the great crowd, which would not allow any room, four ladies, walking in front, held four white doves. The ladies were the wives of those who carried the four swords. After the

[42] *Que pont, que helt, que entretor*: the last, hitherto unknown, word may signify another part of a sword. MS D has: *Ki furent pris hors del tresor* (which were taken from the treasury).

queen followed other ladies, joyfully, happily and in the noblest fashion. They were splendidly garbed, dressed and adorned. Many a one could be seen who thought she was as good as many of the others. They had the most expensive garments, costly attire and costly vestments, splendid tunics, splendid mantles, precious brooches, precious rings, many a fur of white and grey, and clothes of every fashion.

10417. At the processions there was a great crowd, with everyone pushing forward. When Mass began, which that day was especially solemn, you could hear a great sound of organs, and the clerics singing and playing, voices rising and falling, chants sinking and soaring. Many knights could be seen coming and going through the churches. Partly to hear the clerics sing, partly to look at the ladies, they kept going to and fro from one church to the other. They did not know for sure in which they were the longest; they could not have enough of either seeing or hearing. If the whole day had passed this way I believe they would never have got bored.

10437. When the service was ended, and the last words of the Mass sung, the king removed the crown he had worn in church and assumed a lighter one, and the queen did the same. They took off the weightier robes and donned lesser, lighter ones. When the king returned from church, he went to his palace to eat. The queen went to another and took her ladies with her: the king ate with his men, and the queen with the ladies, with great joy and pleasure. It used to be the custom in Troy, and the British still adhered to it, that when they gathered for a feast-day, the men ate with the men, taking no women with them, while the ladies ate elsewhere, with no men except their servants. When the king was seated on the dais, in the manner of the land the barons sat all round, each in order of his importance.[43] The seneschal, called Kei, dressed in robes of ermine, served the king at his meal, with a thousand nobles to help him, all dressed in ermine. They brought food from the kitchen and moved about in great numbers, carrying bowls and dishes. Bedoer, on the other side, brought drink from the buttery, and accompanying

---

[43] This more familiar medieval seating-plan would seem to contradict the idea of the Round Table: see Schmolke-Hasselmann, 'The Round Table', p. 51.

him were a thousand pages, handsome and fair and dressed in ermine. They brought wine in cups, bowls[44] of fine gold, and goblets. No man serving was not clad in ermine. Bedoer went before them carrying the king's cup; the pages came close behind, to serve the barons with wine.

10483. The queen also had her servants; I cannot tell you how many or who they were. She and her whole company were served nobly and well. Many splendid dishes could be seen, expensive and beautiful, lavish helpings of food and drinks of many kinds. I neither can nor know how to describe everything, or to enumerate the objects of luxury. Above all the surrounding realms, and above all those we now know, England was unparalleled for fine men, wealth, plenty, nobility, courtesy and honour. Even the poor peasants were more courtly and brave than knights in other realms, and so were the women too. You would never see a knight worth his salt who did not have his armour, clothing and equipment all of the same colour. They made their armour all of one colour and their dress to match, and ladies of high repute were likewise clothed in one colour. There was no knight, however nobly born, who could expect affection or have a courtly lady as his love, if he had not proved himself three times in knightly combat. The knights were the more worthy for it, and performed better in the fray; the ladies, too, were the better and lived a chaster life.

10521. When the king rose from his meal, everyone went in search of amusement. They went out of the city into the fields and dispersed for various games. Some went off to joust and show off their fast horses, others to fence or throw the stone or jump. There were some who threw javelins, and some who wrestled. Each one took part in the game he knew most about. The man who defeated his friends and who was prized for any game was at once taken to the king and exhibited to all the others, and the king gave him a gift of his own so large that he went away delighted. The ladies mounted the walls to look at those who were playing, and whoever had a friend quickly bent her eyes and face towards him. There were many minstrels at court, singers and instrumentalists: many songs could be heard,

---

[44] The *nés* were cups shaped like ships.

melodies sung to the *rote*[45] and new tunes, fiddle music, lays and melodies, lays on fiddles, lays on *rotes*, lays on harps, lays on flutes, lyres, drums and shawms, bagpipes, psalteries,[46] stringed instruments, tambourines and zithers. There were plenty of conjurors, dancers and jugglers. Some told stories and tales, others asked for dice and backgammon. There were some who played games of chance – that's a cruel game – but most played chess or at the dicing-bowl or at something better. Two by two they were joined in the game, some losing, some winning; some envied those who made the most throws, or they told others how to move. They borrowed money in exchange for pledges, quite willing only to get eleven to the dozen on the loan; they gave pledges, they seized pledges, they took them, they promised them, often swearing, often protesting their good intentions, often cheating and often tricking. They got argumentative and angry, often miscounting and grousing. They threw twos, and then fours, two aces, a third one, and threes, sometimes fives, sometimes sixes. Six, five four, three, two and ace – these stripped many of their clothes.[47] Those holding the dice were in high hopes; when their friends had them, they made a racket. Very often they shouted and cried out, one saying to the other, 'You're cheating me, throw them out, shake your hand, scatter the dice! I'm raising the bid before your throw! If you're looking for money, put some down, like me!' The man who sat down to play clothed might rise naked at close of play.

10589. In this way, the feast lasted three days. When it came to the fourth, a Wednesday, the king gave his young men fiefs and shared out available domains. He repaid the service of everyone who had served him for land: he distributed towns and castles, bishoprics and abbeys. To those who came from another land, for love of the king, he gave cups and war horses and some of his finest possessions. He gave playthings, he gave jewels, he gave greyhounds, birds, furs, cloth, cups, goblets, brocade, rings,

---

[45] The *rote* was a triangular zither: see Page, *Voices and Instruments*, p. 123.

[46] The psaltery was an instrument like a dulcimer, plucked with the fingers.

[47] See Jean Bodel's *Jeu de Saint-Nicolas* (*c.* 1200) for extended representations of similar dice-games where 'he who throws most takes the lot' (ed. F. J. Warne, (Oxford, 1972), line 870 and notes pp. 82–8). This description of dice-playing, like those of the music (10543–88), and of Arthur's gifts (10601–20), is not in all the manuscripts: see Introduction, n. 25.

tunics, cloaks, lances, swords and barbed arrows. He gave quivers and shields, bows and keen swords, leopards and bears, saddles, trappings and chargers. He gave hauberks and war horses, helmets and money, silver and gold, the best in his treasury. Any man worth anything, who had come to visit him from other lands, was given such a gift from the king that it did him honour.

10621. Arthur was seated on a dais, with counts and kings around him. Twelve white-haired men now appeared, well dressed and equipped. Two by two they entered the hall, each pair linking hands. They were twelve, and they carried twelve olive branches in their hands. In a slow, suitable and measured fashion, they splendidly crossed the hall, came to the king and greeted him. They came from Rome, they said, and were Rome's envoys. They unfolded a charter, and one of them delivered it to Arthur, on behalf of the Roman emperor. This was the burden of the charter:

10639. 'Lucius, the ruler of Rome and lord of the Romans,[48] sends King Arthur, his enemy, what he has deserved. In my amazement, I am also angry, and in the midst of my anger I am amazed, that in insolence and pride you have dared cast a greedy eye on Rome. I am angry and amazed as to where and by whom you were advised to contend with Rome, so long as you know a single Roman alive. You have been very stupid to attack us, who are entitled to sit in judgement on the whole world and who possess the world's capital. You don't know yet, but you will, you haven't seen, but you will, how grave it is to anger Rome, who has the right to rule over all. You have done what you had no right to do and exceeded your permitted bounds. Do you know who you are and whence you come, that you seize and hold our tributes? You take our lands and our tributes: why do you have them, why are they not restored? Why do you hold them? What right do you have? You will be a fool to keep them. If you manage to hold

[48] In *HRB* there is a difference between the Emperor Leo (p. 108) and Lucius Hiberius, described, somewhat inconsistently, as procurator of the republic (p. 112). Wace appears to confound the two – see line 9913 – making Lucius (whose second name, denoting his Spanish origin, he keeps as *Hiber*, 11085, 12451) emperor.

them for long, without our forcing you to surrender them, you can say (and it will be amazing) that the lion flees the lamb, the wolf flees the kid, and the greyhound flees the hare. It cannot happen thus, nor will nature suffer it. Julius Caesar, our ancestor (but perhaps you respect him little), captured Britain and took tribute from it, and our people have always received it since. We have long taken tribute from the other islands round about. In your presumption you have taken both from us: you are mad. You have also done us a greater injury, which matters more to us than any loss: you have slain Frollo, our baron, and wrongfully hold France and Flanders. Because you have feared neither Rome nor her great authority, the Senate summons and orders you, commands you through its summons, to appear before it in Rome, in mid-August, no matter what it costs you, ready to do reparation for what you have taken and to make amends for the charge against you. And if you reject any of my commands and do not do them, I will cross Muntgieu[49] in strength and deprive you of Britain and France. I do not believe you will wait for me, or defend France against me; it is my conviction you will never dare to show your face beyond the Channel. And if you were overseas, you would never await my arrival. There is no place you'll be able to take cover out of which I won't rout you. I'll bring you in chains to Rome and hand you over to the Senate.'

10711. At these words there was tremendous uproar, and everybody was furious. The British could be heard shouting, swearing by God and taking Him for witness that those who had brought this message would be dishonoured. The messengers would have been received with many reproaches and much abuse, but the king got up and shouted, 'Silence, silence! They are messengers, they shall not be harmed; they are only bearing their lord's message. They can say what they like, but no one shall hurt them.'

10725. When the noise had died down and the court was reassured, the king took all his dukes, counts and friends with him into a stone tower of his, called the Giants' Tower. There he wanted to take counsel on what he would reply to these messengers. The barons and counts were already on the stairs,

[49] See n. 14 above.

side by side, when Cador said, smiling, in the hearing of the king, who was ahead, 'I've often thought and been very afraid that the British would become weaklings through peace and idleness. For idleness attracts weakness and makes many a man lazy. Idleness brings indolence, idleness lessens prowess, idleness inflames lechery, and idleness kindles love-affairs. Much rest and idleness makes youth give all its attention to jokes, pleasure, board-games and other amusing sports. Through long rests and inactivity we could lose our renown. For a while we have been asleep, but, thanks be to God, He has awoken us a little, by encouraging the Romans to lay claim to our country and to the others we have won. If the Romans have so much confidence in themselves as to do what their letter says, the British will recover their reputation for boldness and strength. I never loved a long peace, nor shall I ever do so.' 'Indeed, my lord count', said Walwein, 'you are upset about nothing. Peace is good after war, and the land is the better and lovelier for it. Jokes are excellent and so are love-affairs. It's for love and their beloved that knights do knightly deeds.' As they were saying these words, they entered the tower and sat down.

10775. When Arthur saw them all seated, all attentive and quiet, he was silent a while, thinking. Then he raised his head and spoke: 'Barons here assembled', he said, 'my friends and companions, companions in prosperity and in adversity, if any great battle has come my way, you have endured it with me. In victory or defeat, the renown has been yours as much as mine. You share in my loss, and also in my success when I am victorious. Through you and your help I have had many a victory. I have led you in many a battle over sea, over land, far and near, and always I have found you loyal in conduct and counsel. I have tested you many times and always found you true. With your help the neighbouring lands are subject to me.

10799. 'You have heard the demand and the purpose in those letters, and the arrogance and pride of the Romans' orders. They've insulted and threatened us long enough but, if God preserves you and me, we shall be delivered from them. They are wealthy and powerful, and we shall have to ponder what it is suitable to say and do. When something is planned in advance, it's easier to sustain it in an emergency. Whoever sees the arrow coming should flee or hide; just so should we do. The Romans intend to advance towards us, and we should make ready, so that they can't harm us. They demand tribute of Britain and tell us they should have it, tribute from other islands too and from France in particular. First of all I shall make fitting reply about Britain. They say Caesar conquered it: he was a powerful man and took it by force. The British could not defend themselves; he constrained them to render tribute. But force is not justice, but overweening pride. What is taken by force is not justly held. We are certainly allowed to hold by right what they used to take from us by force. They have shamed us with the harm and losses, the disgrace, suffering and fear they inflicted on our ancestors; they have boasted that they defeated them and took tribute and money from them. We have all the more reason to injure them, and they have the more to restore to us. We should hate those who hated our ancestors, and hurt those who hurt them. They did them wrong, and that shames us; they took tribute and demand it again. They would like to inherit those exactions and our shame. They were accustomed to tribute from Britain, so they want it from us.

10851. 'For exactly the same reason and the same cause we may lay claim to Rome, and easily justify it. Belin, king of Britain, and Brenne, duke of Burgundy, were two brothers, born in Britain, brave and wise knights who went to Rome and besieged it. They attacked it and took it, hanging twenty-four hostages in the sight of all their kin. When Belin came away, he entrusted Rome to his brother. Let us leave Brenne and Belin and speak of Constantine, who came from Britain and was Helena's son. He held Rome and had it in his power. Maximian, king of Britain, conquered France and Germany, crossed Muntgieu and Lombardy and ruled over Rome. These were my close kin, and each had Rome in his hands! Now you can hear and know that I have as much reasonable right to Rome as Rome to Britain, if we look at our ancestors. Rome got tribute from us, and my kin got it from them. They lay claim to Britain, I to Rome! This is the gist of my advice: he who can defeat the other should get the money and the land. They should stop talking about France and the other lands, which we have taken off their hands, if they don't want to protect them. Either they don't want to, or can't, or, perhaps, they have no right to, because

through greed they keep them in fief by force. Now may he who
can get it, have it all: there's no need for any other right! The
emperor threatens us; God forbid he does us any harm. He says
he will take our lands and bring me bound to Rome; he values
us little, he has small fear of me, but, God willing, if he comes
here, before he returns he won't feel like making threats. If I and
he both lay claim, then may he who can take it all, seize it!'

10905. When Arthur the king had spoken and revealed this to
the barons, there were some who spoke next and others who
listened. Hoel spoke after the king: 'Sire', he said, 'upon my
word, you speak most reasonably; no one could better it.
Command your people, summon your men and us who are here
at your court. Cross the sea without delay; cross Burgundy,
France and Muntgieu, and take Lombardy! Disturb and frighten
the emperor who defies you, so he has no chance of hurting you.
The Romans have set in motion a business that will quite
destroy them. The Lord God wants to raise you up; don't
hesitate or delay. He is putting the empire in your power of his
own accord. Remember what the Sibyl said, in her written
prophecies: three Britons would arise from Britain to conquer
Rome by force. Two of those, who were lords of Rome, have
already passed away: the first of them was Belin and the second
Constantine. You will be the third to have Rome and conquer it
by force. In you the Sibyl's prophecy will be fulfilled. Why wait
to seize what God wishes to grant you? Exalt yourself, exalt us,
who desire it. Indeed we can say we fear neither blow nor
wound, neither death, hardship nor prison, as long as we seek
your honour. And, so that your affair be not neglected, I shall
give you for companions ten thousand armed knights; and if
you don't have enough wealth, I shall pledge all my land and
give you its silver and gold. You must never leave me a penny as
long as you have need of it.'

10955. After Hoel's words, the king of Scotland, Angusel,
brother of Loth and Urien, spoke: 'Sire', he said, 'Hoel has
spoken well. And, if you undertake this thing, speak to those
who are here, the best of your barons, who heard the message
from Rome. Know what each will do for you and how each will
help you. Now we need to plan how to get help and advice. All
those from your kingdom, who hold fiefs and land from you,

should help and assist you, and so they shall, as best they can. I never before heard news which seemed so good and fair to me as this of fighting the Romans. I can never like or esteem them. From my earliest understanding, I hated the Romans and their pride. How shameful of a wicked race, who are intent on nothing else honourable, only on amassing wealth, and must defy virtuous people. The emperor acts stupidly and lays up great trouble for himself by sending you a challenge. I believe the day will come when he will wish he had not done so, even for this tower filled with silver.

10987. 'The Romans have begun such a business as will punish them all. And even if they had never begun it, even if they had not spoken of it first, we would have had to begin it and of our own accord make war, to avenge our kin and abate their pride, who think fit to say and assert that we should render tribute. They say our ancestors used to give tribute to theirs; I don't believe they gave or sent tribute. They neither gave it nor rendered it, but it was taken from them by force. And we will wrest it by force from them! We will avenge ourselves and our ancestors. We have won many a battle and carried out many a great war; but what good are any of our conquests if we do not defeat the Romans? Never did I have such a desire for food and drink as I have to see the moment when we attack each other on horseback, spears gripped, shields round our necks, helmets laced. Lord, what wealth! Lord, what treasure (if God protect us), will those who want wealth have; they'll never be poor again. There we shall see fine possessions, handsome manors, splendid castles and strong, speedy horses. I feel I'm already there and already see them defeated. On, then, to conquer Rome! Let us take the Romans' lands! When we have conquered Rome, slain the men, taken the city, we'll cross into Lorraine and conquer it, both Lorraine and Germany, so that no country remains on this side of the mountains which is not yours. No one shall escape us: we shall seize everything, rightly or wrongly. And so that my deeds match my words, I myself will go with you and bring two thousand knights and so many foot-soldiers that no one will ever be able to count them.'

11041. When the king of Scotland had finished, everyone said and shouted all together, 'Shame on whoever stays behind and doesn't do his best!' When each one had spoken his mind and Arthur had heard them all out, he had his letters composed and sealed. He had them delivered to the messengers and saw to it they were greatly honoured and given large gifts from his possessions. 'In Rome', he said, 'you can say I am lord of Britain. I hold France and will hold it and defend it against Romans. And know indeed that I shall shortly go to Rome, not to bring tribute but to demand it.'

11059. The messengers left Arthur, came back to Rome and reported exactly how they found Arthur and where and how they had spoken to him. They said he was very generous, brave and wise, with excellent manners and noble behaviour. Nobody, they said, could support the expenditure he allowed; his retinue was magnificent and very well dressed. It was no use asking him for tribute, for he said *they* would give it to *him*. When the Roman lords heard the messengers' replies and the charters they brought, they recalled their words that Arthur had no intention of paying and would demand tribute from them. They advised the emperor, and this advice was to his taste, that he should summon his whole empire, cross Muntgieu and Burgundy, and fight King Arthur, depriving him of kingdom and crown.

11085. Lucius Hiber did not delay; he summoned kings, counts and dukes to come on the tenth day. They had to be in Rome with him, if they loved honour, all ready to seek out Arthur wherever he might be. Those hearing the summons came very quickly. Epistrod came, king of Greece, and Echion, duke of Boetia; Hirtac came, king of the Turks, with strong and resolute knights; Pandras came, king of Egypt, and King Ypolite from Crete – he had very great power, with a hundred cities at his command. From Syria came King Evander, and from Phrygia, Duke Teucer; from Babylon, Micipsa and from Spain, Aliphatima. From Media came King Boccus, and from Libya, Sertorius; from Bithynia, Polidetes, and King Xerses from the Iturei.[50] Mustensar, who controlled Africa, dwelt afar off, and came from afar; he brought Africans and Moors, and also his great treasure. From the numbers of the Senate, who had high office

---

[50] Arnold and Pelan, *La Partie arthurienne*, p. 160, interpret these as a people in Palestine.

in Rome, came Marcel and Luces Catel, Cocta and Gaius Metel. There were many other barons whose names I have not found. When they were all assembled, they were 400,000 in number, and a total of 180,000, except for foot-soldiers and servants.[51] When they were equipped and ready, they left Rome at the beginning of August.

11125. Arthur concluded his court and asked for help from all the barons. He named them all by their names and summoned each by name to help him as best he could, if he wished to keep his love, and to say how many knights he would bring, each according to the size of his domain. The Irish, those from Gotland, the Icelanders, the Danes, the Norwegians and those from Orkney promised 120,000 men armed in the fashion of their lands: they were not knights, nor knew how to ride. They went on foot, bearing their weapons: axes, javelins, throwing-spears and broadswords. Those from Normandy and Anjou, Maine and Poitou, Flanders and Boulogne, promised without delay 80,000 men in full armour; so many should be useful, they said. Twelve counts from other sovereign states, who accompanied Gerin de Chartres and were called the Peers of France, swelled the numbers by 1200: each promised a hundred knights, saying they should be useful. Hoel promised 10,000 and Angusel, 2000 Scots. From Britain, his own land (now called England), Arthur reckoned he had 60,000 knights with hauberks. I cannot count the number of foot-soldiers, crossbow-men, servants or archers; nor could those who saw the great army assembled. When Arthur knew what people he would have and how many armed men each would lead, he commanded and summoned everyone to come at the appointed time, each with his fleet, to Barfleur in Normandy. When the barons had taken leave, they went home to their lands and made ready the men they would take with them.

11173. To Modret, one of his nephews, a great and valiant knight, and to Ganhumare, his wife, Arthur committed the

---

[51] This confusing statement on the numbers in Lucius's army is taken from equally confusing figures in *HRB* (para. 163): 400,000 'in total' but 160,000 'when all counted'. (The First Variant version has 180,000). Wace follows *HRB*'s figures for Arthur's army too, but wisely does not try to add them up. See Thorpe's note to his translation of *HRB*, p. 235.

charge of his kingdom. Modret was of noble birth but disloyal. He was in love with the queen, but this was not suspected. He kept it very quiet; and who would have believed he could love his uncle's wife, especially the wife of such a lord, whose kin all held him in honour? Modret loved his uncle's wife shamefully and was dishonourable. To Modret and to the queen – alas, how unfortunate that he gave them possession! – Arthur entrusted everything but the crown. Then he came to Southampton, for the sea-crossing. There the ships were gathered and the troops assembled. There you could see many a ship being prepared, moored, anchored, dried out and floated, pegged and nailed, its cordage stretched, its masts raised and its gangplank lowered, loaded with helmets, shields and hauberks, with lances aloft, horses dragged along, knights and servants embarking, and friends calling to each other. Those staying behind and those departing kept exchanging greetings.

11205. When they had all embarked and the tide and the wind were in their favour, then you could see anchors raised, stays pulled, guy-ropes secured and sailors bounding through the ships, unfurling sails and canvas. Some strove with the windlass, others with tacking and with yard-ropes; behind them were the pilots, the best master-helmsmen. Each one applied himself to manoeuvring the rudder, which steers the ship: below the tiller-bar to go left, and above it to go right. To capture the wind in the sails, they brought forward the fore-leeches[52] and drew hard on the bolt-ropes. These weigh on the bunt-lines and somewhat lower the sails, so the ship runs more sweetly. They secured the studding-sails and sheets and tautened all the ropes; they slackened the running-ropes, brought down the sails, hauled and tugged the bowlines and observed the wind and the stars, setting their sails according to the breeze. They strapped the brails[53] to the mast so that the wind did not tug at them from underneath. They took two or three reefs in the sails. How bold and skilled was the man who first made a ship and put to sea before the wind, seeking a land he could not see and a shore he could not know!

[52] *Lisprié* or leech-prows: the leech was the perpendicular or sloping side of a sail (*OED*).

[53] The brails are small ropes on the sail-edges for trussing, or clewing up, the sails before furling (*OED*).

11239. Arthur's men went on their way joyfully, sailing fast with a good wind. At midnight they were crossing the sea, with their course set for Barfleur, when Arthur began to nod: he fell asleep and could not stay awake. As he was sleeping, it seemed to him that he saw a bear, high in the sky, come flying from the east; it was very ugly, strong, mighty and large, most horrible in appearance. From the other direction he saw a dragon, flying from the west, his eyes shooting flame. The land and sea round about glistened from his radiance. The dragon attacked the bear, who strongly defended himself; their onslaughts and blows were amazing, but the dragon gripped the bear and threw him to the ground. When Arthur had slept a little longer, the dream he had seen roused him; he woke, sat up and told the clerics and the barons, in its proper order, the dream which he had had of the dragon and the bear. Some of them answered him that the dragon he had seen signified himself, and the great bear meant some giant he would kill, who would come from a foreign land. The others expounded it in a different way, but nevertheless they all interpreted it favourably. 'It seems to me', he said, 'that it is, on the contrary, the war we must start between the emperor and myself. But may it be all in the Creator's hands.'

11279. Dawn broke at these words; the sun rose and it was fine weather. They arrived in harbour very early, at Barfleur in the Cotentin, and disembarked as soon as they could, scattering through the countryside. Arthur waited for those of his men who had not yet arrived. He had not waited for long when he heard, and was told, of a hulking giant who had come from Spain, seized Hoel's niece Eleine, raped her and set her on the mountain now called after St Michael. There was neither altar nor chapel there; it was surrounded by the sea's tidal waters. There was no man in the land so bold, no young man, whether noble or peasant, however proud or brave, who dared to fight the giant or venture into his neighbourhood. When the people round about assembled and approached the mountain to fight him, sometimes coming from the sea, sometimes from the land, he cared nothing for their efforts: he smashed their ships with rocks, killing and drowning many. They had all let him alone and not dared approach him. You could see peasants all leaving their houses, carrying children, leading women, hustling animals, and climbing mountains or hiding in woods. They fled into forests and wilderness, still fearing to die even there. The whole land was abandoned, all its people fled. The giant was called Dinabuc: bad luck to him!

11319. When Arthur heard of this, he called Kei and Bedoer; the first was his seneschal, the second his cup-bearer. He wished to talk to no one else. At once, as night fell, these two and their squires had their arms and horses made ready. Arthur did not want to take an army with him or reveal this business to everyone; he feared that, if they knew, they would be afraid of the giant, and he thought his own person and worth were quite sufficient to destroy him. All night they rode so fast, they spurred so hard, they travelled so far, that by morning they came to the shore where they knew there to be a crossing. They saw a fire burning on the mountain, visible far and wide. There was also a fire burning on another, lesser, peak, not far from the larger one. This made Arthur hesitate over which mountain the giant was on, and on which mountain he would find him. There was no one who could tell him or who had seen the giant that day. He told Bedoer to go and search both mountains, and to seek until he found him, then to return with the news.

11351. Bedoer got into a boat and crossed to the nearest mountain; there was no other way of approaching it, because the tide was at the full. When he came to the nearest mountain and was climbing it, he heard a great weeping and wailing, great laments and cries. He was afraid and began to tremble, for he thought he heard the giant. But soon he took courage; he drew his sword and went on. He recovered his daring, and thought and wished he could fight the giant and put himself in jeopardy. He would not be a coward, on pain of losing his life. But this thought was in vain for, when he was up on the plateau, he saw only a burning fire and a new-made tombstone. The tomb was recently made; the count approached it with drawn sword. He found an old woman, bare-headed, her clothes torn, lying beside the tombstone. She kept wailing and sobbing and lamenting Eleine, grieving bitterly and uttering loud cries. When she saw Bedoer, she said, 'Wretch, who are you? What misfortune brings you here? If the giant finds you, your life must end today in grief, pain and anguish. Poor unfortunate, fly, be off before the devil sees you!' 'Good woman', said Bedoer, 'speak to me, stop crying. Tell me who you are and why you weep, why you stay on this island, and who lies in this tomb. Tell me everything that has happened to you.'

11395. 'I am a lost creature', she said, 'a miserable wretch, weeping here for a girl I suckled at my breast, Hoel's niece Eleine, whose body lies here under the stone. She was given me to suckle. Alas! Why was she given me? Alas! For what purpose did I feed her so, when a devil raped her? A giant raped her and me and brought us both here. He wanted to ravish her, but she was delicate and could not stand it; he was too huge, too large, too ugly, too gross and too heavy. He made her soul leave her body; Eleine could not endure it. Alas, wretch that I am! The giant shamefully slew my gentle one, my joy, my treasure, my love, and here have I buried her.' 'Why do you not go', said the count, 'since you have lost Eleine?' 'Do you wish to hear why?' she said. 'I see you are a noble and courteous man: nothing shall be hidden from you. When Eleine expired – which made me nearly lose my mind, for I saw her die in shame – the giant made me stay here, to assuage his lechery. By force he kept me here and by force he raped me. I have to yield to his strength, I cannot prevent him. I do not consent to it – I call God to witness! He's come near to killing me, but I'm older and stronger, bigger and tougher, more hardened and more resolute than lady Eleine. But all the same I'm in great pain, all my body is in agony. And if he comes here, as he usually does, to satisfy his lechery, you will be killed, you can't escape. He's over there, on that smoking mountain, and soon he will come, that's his habit. Be quick, flee, my friend; what did you seek here? Do not be captured; leave me alone to weep and wail. If I had my way, I would have died long ago; alas for Eleine's love!'

11450. Then Bedoer had pity and gently comforted her, before leaving her and returning. He came to the king and told him of what he had heard and found: of the old woman and her lamentation, of Eleine and her death, and of the giant, who dwelt in the larger, smoking, mountain. Arthur grieved for Eleine, but he was neither cowardly nor slow and at ebb-tide he made his companions mount their horses. They came in a short while to the larger mountain, as the sea uncovered it. They entrusted their palfreys and steeds to the squires, and all three, Arthur, Bedoer and Kei, began to climb. 'I will go ahead', said Arthur, 'and fight the giant. You will follow close after me. Take care that no one strikes a blow, so long as I am able to help myself and so long as I don't need it. It would look like cowardice if anyone except I were to fight. Nevertheless, if you see I'm in need, help me.' They agreed to what he asked; then all three climbed the mountain.

11481. The giant was sitting by the fire, roasting pork. He had cooked some of it on a spit and roasted part in the coals. His beard and whiskers were filthy with the meat cooked on charcoal. Arthur hoped to surprise him before he could seize his club, but the giant saw him. He was amazed, jumped to his feet and shouldered his club, which was so large and square that two peasants could neither carry it nor lift it from the ground. Arthur saw him standing all ready to strike; he drew his sword, raised his shield and covered his head, fearful of the blow. And the giant gave him one, such that the whole mountain echoed and Arthur was quite stunned by it, but he was strong and did not stagger. He suffered the heavy blow, gripped his sword, raised the blade, with his arm aloft and outstretched, and struck the giant high in the forehead, mangling his two eyebrows, so that the blood ran down into his eyes. He might have brained and killed him, he would never have recovered, had the giant not held up his club high to withstand the blow; he turned his head and stayed upright. Nevertheless, he received such a blow as bloodied his whole face and blurred his vision.

11517. When he realized his eyes were blurred, the giant went mad. Just as a boar, impaled on the spear, long harried by the dogs, rushes at the huntsman, so he furiously dashed at the king and grasped him, not releasing him despite the sword. Huge and strong, he seized him in the middle and forced him to his knees, but the king at once struggled hard, got back on his feet and stood up. Arthur's blood was roused and he was also amazingly wily. Both angry and afraid, he made every effort: he pulled the giant to him and pushed him violently. As he was very strong, he did not fail, but by a jump he dodged sideways and so got out of the enemy's clutches. As soon as he had escaped from him and felt his body free, he swiftly dashed around the giant, now here, now there, repeatedly striking him with his sword. And the giant groped about with his hands, his eyes full of blood, unable to tell black from white. Arthur kept weaving and dodging so much, sometimes behind, sometimes in front, that he drove Caliburn's blade into the giant's brain. He pushed and pulled and the giant fell, kicking, with a cry; in his fall he crashed like an oak felled by the wind.

11553. Then Arthur began to laugh, for now his anger was past. He stood at a distance and looked at him, and told his cup-bearer to cut off the giant's head and give it to a squire; he wanted it carried to the army and exhibited as a marvel. 'I was afraid', said Arthur, 'more than of any other giant, except only Rithon, who mortified so many kings.' Rithon had conquered and defeated so many kings, leaving them alive or dead, that he had had a skin cloak made of their beards which he had stripped off, a cloak for him to wear. Rithon certainly had to be killed. In great pride and arrogance he had ordered Arthur to strip off his own beard and kindly send it to him and, as he was stronger and worth more than other kings, Rithon would honour his beard and use it for the cloak's border. And if Arthur refused Rithon's request, they would come together face to face and fight each other, and whoever killed the other, or took him alive, would get the beard and add it to the cloak as border or fringe. Arthur fought him and defeated him on Mount Arave; he flayed him and stripped off his beard. Never since had he found a giant of such strength or who frightened him so much.

11593. When Arthur had killed the monster, and Bedoer taken his head, they left the mountain joyful and happy and returned to the army, to tell them where they had been and why. Then they showed the head to them all. Hoel grieved for his niece and suffered great distress for a long while, ashamed that she should have died in that way. He had a chapel of Our Lady St Mary, now called Eleine's Tomb, built on the mountain; the name comes from the tombstone where Eleine lay, from the tomb where the body was buried.

11609. When the Irish had arrived, and those others who were due to come, Arthur progressed through Normandy, day after day. He passed by castles and towns, and his army grew and increased, everyone helping him in his task. He crossed France and came to Burgundy. He wanted to go straight to Ostum,[54] because he had news that the Romans were on their way there and overrunning the country; they were led by Lucius Hiber, who held the domain of Rome. When Arthur was about to cross the river you know as the Albe,[55] he was told by the peasants and informed by his spies that nearby he could find the emperor, if he wished. The emperor had pitched his tents and his arbours very close by. He had so many men, he led so many kings and rode with such retinues that Arthur would be mad to wait for him: his men could never match theirs; it was four against one. He should make peace and abandon the fight. Arthur was not dismayed: he was confident and put his trust in God. He had heard plenty of threats. In a secure place on the Albe he built a fort, put there a large number of men, and soon fortified it. He did this so that he might leave his equipment there and, if he were in great danger, return to the fort.

11647. Then he called for two counts, most wise and eloquent and each of high birth. Gerin of Chartres was one, the other Bos of Oxford, who well knew what was right and what wrong. To these he added Walwein, who had spent a long time at Rome. Because they were much esteemed, well known and well educated, the king sent them in a group to the emperor. He commanded him to turn back and not to enter France, which was Arthur's. If he would not turn back, he should come the very first day he arrived to prove in battle which of them had the greater right, for Arthur, so long as he lived, would defend France from the Romans. He had won it and captured it in battle, and long ago the Romans had done likewise. Now battle could once again prove which of them should have France.

11673. The messengers took leave of Arthur and mounted their best horses, wearing their hauberks, their helmets laced up, their shields round their necks, and their swords in their hands. Then certain young knights could be seen, the most irresponsible ones,

---

[54] Autun.
[55] Aube.

going to Walwein, advising him and secretly begging him that, in the court where he was going, he should do something, before he left, to precipitate the war which for so long had been impending. It would turn out badly, when each side had got so close to the other, if they never had the chance of a joust and separated so soon. The messengers crossed a mountain, then a wood, then a plain. They saw the enemy's tents and arrived there very soon. Then the Romans could be seen coming, and knights leaving their tents, to see the three messengers and to discover the news. They kept asking what they sought and if they came to make peace, but the messengers neither stopped nor took heed until they came to the emperor. They dismounted before his tent and had their horses held outside; they went before the emperor and told him of Arthur's command. Each of them said what he pleased and what he knew was right to say. The emperor heard it all and replied at his leisure.

11709. 'We come from Arthur', said Walwein, 'and we bear Arthur's message. We are his men, he is our lord; we must all deliver his message. Through us he orders you, and forbids you (let it be known to all) to set foot in France or concern yourself with it. He holds France and shall hold it, defending it as his own. He orders you to take nothing from it, and if you lay claim to it from him, it must be disputed through battle, and through battle justified. The Romans took it through battle and won it through battle, and he has got it through battle and held it through battle. Through battle it can once more be proved who should control it. Tomorrow, without more ado, come, if you wish to lay claim to France; or go, turn back, be off, there's nothing for you here! We have won, you have lost.'

11734. The emperor replied he had no reason to return: France was his and he would advance. It would grieve him if he lost, he would win if he could; but in his opinion he believed he could conquer and hold France. Quintilien sat by him and spoke next; he was his nephew and very proud, a most refractory knight. 'Britons', he said, 'are boasters and make some very fine threats. They're all boasts and threats; they menace in plenty and do little.' He would, I think, have spoken further and derided the messengers, but Walwein, who was furious, drew his sword, rushed forward and made his head fly from his body. 'To horse!'

he said to the counts, and they both mounted, Walwein with them, they with him. Each seized his horse and quickly left, shields on necks, lances in hand: they took no leave of the Romans.

11761. The court was all in uproar! The emperor shouted loudly, 'What are you doing? They have shamed us! Capture them for me; they'll never get away!' Then knights could be heard shouting, 'To arms, to arms! To horse, to horse! Quickly, quickly, mount, mount, spur, spur, run, run!' The army could be seen in tumult, saddling, seizing horses, gripping lances, girding on swords and spurring to catch up. And the counts were in full flight, looking behind them from time to time. The Romans followed them in disorder, whether along the roads or across the fields, here in twos, there in threes, here in fives, there in sixes, here in sevens, there in eights, here in nines, there in tens. One of them spurred ahead, passing his companions with his good and speedy horse, and he kept shouting, 'Wait, knights, wait! If you don't turn back, you're craven!' Gerin of Chartres turned round, took his shield, drew back his lance and with its whole length knocked him off his good horse. Then he said to him, 'Now you are worse off: your horse is much too frisky. You would do much better to be back in the tents than stay here.'

11793. Bos watched what Gerin did and heard his unpleasant remarks. He wanted to do something similar. He turned his horse's head and rushed towards a knight, who met him unafraid. Bos struck him through the throat as far as the marrow of his neck-bone, and he fell, mouth agape, having swallowed the lance. And the count shouted at him, 'My lord and master, I can feed you on such choice morsels. Be at peace, lie here and wait for those who follow you. Tell those who are to come that the messengers went this way.' One man, born in Rome and of noble Roman kin, was called Marcel and had a very fast horse. He was among the last to mount, and then overtook all those in front. He did not carry a lance: he had forgotten it in the haste of departure. Spurring, he caught up with Walwein and slackened his bridle; already he had begun to jostle him so that Walwein could not move away. He stretched out his hand to grab Walwein, having promised to hand him over alive. Walwein saw he came so quickly and could travel so fast; he drew rein and stopped, and the other man was so close that he overran. As he passed by, Walwein drew his sword and plunged it entirely into his head, splitting it down to the shoulders. The helmet gave him no protection; he fell and his life ended. And Walwein said courteously, 'Marcel, carry a message to Quintilien in hell, where you are going. Through you I inform him, and you must tell him, that the British are pretty confident; they certainly intend to claim their rights and do more than just threaten.'

11839. Then, calling his companions Gerin and Bos by name, Walwein summoned each of them to turn round and fight one of the pursuers. Walwein told them and they did so, at once laying low three Romans. The messengers galloped off, the horses carrying them swiftly, and the Romans pursued them, showing them no mercy. They kept reaching them and striking them with lances; they gave them great blows, now with lances, now with swords, but they could never strike them enough to catch one of them, or wound, unhorse or harm them in any way. There was a cousin of Marcel, on a very swift horse, who was most distressed about his kinsman, whom he saw lying by the road-side. He spurred over the fields and drew level with the three messengers, intending to strike them sideways, but Walwein noticed him, spurred at him and went to strike. He never had an opportunity to turn, but let his lance fall, which he did not need, drew his sword, thinking to strike, and raised his arm and his fist; and Walwein completely cut off the arm he had raised, making sword, arm and fist fly far over the field. He would have given him another blow, but the Romans were pressing him hard. Thus they were pursued until they came fleeing to a wood, which was between them and the castle which Arthur had newly made.

11881. Arthur had sent six thousand knights after the messengers, to scour the woods and valleys and spy out the land. They would be in the messengers' direction and, if need be, they could help them. They had traversed a wood and stopped beside it, sitting on horseback in their armour, when they noticed the messengers and saw the plains quite covered with large bands of armed men. They recognized their messengers and saw the pursuers. With one shout and unanimously, they jumped out at them. The Romans at once withdrew, scattering throughout the fields. There were some who were angry they had pursued so far, because the Britons made a determined attack on them, striking many as they withdrew, reaching and taking many, overthrowing and killing many. There was a noble lord, Petreïus, unequalled in Rome for feats of arms, who had ten thousand armed men under his control: so many were at his command. He heard tell of the ambush which the Britons had made and speedily helped the Romans with ten thousand men. By pure force and compulsion, with the troops he led, he made the Britons retreat to the wood; they could not resist. The pursuit lasted right up to the wood, because they could not stand their ground. In the wood, they fought back, and in the wood they defended themselves. Petreïus attacked them, but lost many of his men, because the Britons cut them down and dragged them inside the wood. The fighting was very heavy between wood and hillside.

11927. When Arthur saw that the messengers were delayed, and that those who had gone after them had not returned, he called Ider, son of Nu,[56] and entrusted him with five thousand knights. He sent them after the others, asking him to look for them. Walwein and Bos were both fighting, and the others were dealing hard blows, there was a great din and clamour, when Ider, son of Nu, arrived. Then the Britons took new heart and recovered the ground in front. Ider spurred forward, shouting his war-cry, and so did those with him. The attack was well carried out and there were many saddles emptied, many horses captured and won and many knights overthrown. Petreïus kept up the fight but checked his men and retreated; he well knew when and how to flee, to turn back, to pursue and to stand fast. There you could have seen splendid pursuits and combats in many places. Whoever was bold found his match in boldness, whoever wanted single combat soon found it, whoever wanted to strike soon struck, and whoever could not hold out fell. The

[56] Ider/Yder (Welsh *Edern*) joins Arthurian legend at an early stage: he is depicted (as Isdernus) on the Modena archivolt (between 1099 and 1120), and is in *Culhwch and Olwen*: see Loomis in *ALMA*, pp. 60–1, and Bromwich and Evans, *Culhwch and Olwen*, line 182 and pp. 70–1.

Britons drove forward impetuously, not caring to be organized into troops: they wanted to joust and to bear weapons, they wanted knightly deeds, and so they often broke ranks. They did not care how the battle went, as long as it started.

11965. Petreïus fought fiercely, keeping his best men close to him; he was experienced in fighting and war, knowing when to wait and when to attack. Sometimes he wheeled, sometimes he rushed forward, rescuing those who fell. Bos of Oxford, who knew the way the fight was going, realized they would not escape without losses unless they slew Petreïus, slew him or captured him, for it was because of him that the Romans held out, and the Britons foolishly rushed around among their men. He secretly called aside to him several of the boldest and best. 'My lords', he said, 'you who loyally love Arthur, speak with me. We have started this battle without the knowledge of our lord. If all goes well with us, it will be well with him; if it goes badly, he will hate us. If we are the losers, and get no honour on this field, we shall be humiliated and harmed and the recipients of Arthur's hate. For this reason we must make an effort to trap Petreïus, so as to take him alive or dead and, alive or dead, hand him over to Arthur. Otherwise, we cannot get away without great losses. Do everything I do and where I spur ahead, follow me.' They said they would certainly do so[57] and would go wherever Bos went.

12001. When Bos had those he wanted with him and had discovered and seen which man was Petreïus, who was upholding all the rest, he spurred most fiercely in that direction, and the others with him. They neither stopped nor stayed till they reached the mêlée where Petreïus was riding, controlling the troops. Bos recognized him, spurred up to him and forced the two horses into close proximity. He threw out his arms and gripped him and, trusting to his companions, of his own accord let himself fall. This was an amazing thing to see! He fell to the ground, in that great throng, with Petreïus clutched in his arms. Bos tugged and Petreïus pulled, struggling hard to escape. The Romans ran to the rescue, and those carrying lances soon broke

---

[57] After this point (11999), Arnold's edition abandons MS P and follows MS D.

them; when lances failed them, they fought with their polished swords. They wanted to rescue Petreïus, and the Britons wanted to help Bos. A fierce clash could be seen, a mighty struggle, a hard mêlée, with helmets bent, shields pierced, hauberks broken, lances shattered, saddles emptied, men wounded and falling. The Britons shouted their lord's war-cry, the Romans shouted theirs. One side strove to get Petreïus, the other side was continually pulling him back; and scarcely could Roman be told from Briton, except by words and cries, so thick was the fray.

12041. Walwein pushed through the great press, making his way with his sword; he struck and smote, fought and thrust, felling many, crushing more. No Roman seeing his blows did not make way for him, if he could. On the other side moved Ider, making great slaughter amongst the Romans, helped by Gerin of Chartres, each fighting hard for the other. They overtook Petreïus and knocked him and Bos over, and the Britons raised Bos to his feet and remounted him. They kept a grip on Petreïus, who had received many blows, and led him through the fray to within the safety of their forces. They left him carefully guarded and then began the battle all over again. The Romans were without someone to control them, like a ship without a pilot, driven by the wind whichever way it wishes, when there is no one to steer her aright. So it was with the troops who had lost their leader; because their commander was missing, they could no longer defend themselves. The Britons kept driving them about and knocking great crowds of them down. They overran the fallen and reached those in flight; they captured some, they killed some, they stripped some and they bound some. Then they pulled their companions back and returned to their prisoners in the wood. They brought Petreïus with them and presented him to their lord, and many other prisoners with him. Arthur thanked them and told them he would increase the domains of each if he were victorious.

12083. Arthur had the prisoners guarded and handed them over to gaolers. He discussed it and took the advice to send them to Paris; they would be kept in prison until he could do what they wished with them, for if he kept them amongst his men, he feared he would lose them, come what may. So he equipped those who would take them and decided on those who would lead them. Cador, Borel, Richier and Bedoer the cup-bearer, four counts of exalted lineage, were asked by the king to rise early and go with the prisoners, escorting them until those conducting them were safe and had crossed through the danger zone. Through his spies, the emperor soon heard the news that those due to escort the prisoners would leave early. He had ten thousand knights mount and asked them to journey all night, in order to get ahead of the prisoners and, if possible, rescue them. Sertorius, lord of Libya, Evander, king of Syria, and Caricius and Catellus Vulteïus from Rome – each of these four had large lands and was experienced in warfare. They were chosen and summoned to go and rescue the prisoners and to lead the rest. That evening ten thousand armed men set out. They were guided by the country folk, who knew the right paths. They rode so hard that night, and advanced so far in their ride, that they met the road to Paris and found a suitable spot to make their ambush. There they quietly remained.

12127. In the morning, there were Arthur's men, riding rather confidently, and yet they feared a trap. They travelled in two bands. Cador and Borel, with their men, rode first, and the Counts Richier and Bedoer, who were in charge of the prisoners, followed them with five hundred men, escorting the prisoners, with their hands tied behind their backs, and their feet tied under the horses. Then those in front came upon the ambush which the Romans had made, and all the Romans rushed out at once; the ground quite shook and shuddered! Boldly they attacked them, and the Britons strongly defended themselves. Bedoer and Richier heard the loud clamour and saw the blows. They had the prisoners seized and removed to a secure place; they handed them over to their squires and ordered them to guard them. Then they gave free rein to their horses, not sparing the spur until they reached their people, when they fought vigorously. Everywhere the Romans were rushing about, intent not so much on defeating the Britons as on rescuing the prisoners. And the Britons together spurred forward and together held back, advanced and retreated together and defended themselves together. And the Romans rushed up and down, seeking the prisoners here and there; they were so intent on finding the prisoners that they lost many of their men. The British divided themselves into companies and established four sections: Cador had the Cornish, and Bedoer the Herupeis;[58] Richier had a troop of his own men, and Borel had with him the men from Maine.

12173. King Evander noticed that their own might and men were diminishing and, since they could not reach the prisoners, he made them all hold back; then he made them keep together and strike in military formation. Then the Romans came off best, and it was the worse for the Britons: they were harried, many of them were captured and four of the best were slain. Er, Ider's son, died there, a strong and brave knight, Hyrelgas of Periron (no one was bolder than him), Aliduc of Tintagel (whose kin were much grieved) and Mauric Cadorkeneneis[59] – I do not know if he was Breton or Welsh. Borel of Le Mans, a noble count very useful to his men, acted boldly and greatly exhorted his troops. But towards him spurred Evander; he forced the iron of his lance through Borel's throat, and he fell, not able to stand. Britons left the field in dismay at losing so many of their men; there were seven Romans for every one of theirs. Soon they would have been captured, killed, taken or destroyed, and would have lost their prisoners, but Guitart, count of Poitiers, who was that day in charge of the foragers, before long heard the news that a party of the Romans was about to rescue the prisoners. He charged in that direction, and with him three thousand knights, as well as the foragers and archers. The Romans were busy striking and discomfiting the Britons, when Guitart arrived, spurring, with his troops, their lances lowered. They unhorsed more than a hundred, who never got up again.

12219. The Romans were quite aghast, and all thought they were done for. They thought Arthur had arrived, followed by his whole army. When they saw so many of theirs fall, they lost hope of escape. The Poitevins attacked them hard, and the Bretons were not far behind; both made every effort for each other and struggled to cut the Romans down. And the Romans

---

[58] This is the earliest mention of the Herupeis, the inhabitants of La Hérupe, an ancient term designating Neustria (the land between the Seine, Marne and Loire). Wace follows *HRB* and contemporary usage in making Neustria and Normandy synonymous: see Houck, *Sources*, pp. 197–200.

[59] From Cahors; but see Tatlock, *Legendary History*, pp. 105–6.

turned to flee, exposing their uncovered, defenceless backs. They wanted to get back to camp; they knew no other place where they could escape. The Britons pursued them a long while and took ample vengeance for their dead; they chased and overtook them, not failing to cut them down. The Kings Evander and Catellus, and five hundred or more of the rest, were hit and struck down, some killed, some captured. The Britons seized as many as they could and as many as they could take away; then they returned to the road where the battle had occurred. They looked for Borel, the good count of Le Mans, and their dead, among the fields. They found the count lying in a pool of blood, breathing his last. They had the wounded borne away, and buried the slain. To those of whom Arthur had requested it, and as he had ordered, they entrusted the first lot of prisoners and sent them to Paris. The rest, recently taken, they had tightly bound. They led them to the castle with them and presented them to their lord, telling him of the events and the ambush, and they all together promised him that if he fought the Romans, he would, without doubt, defeat them.

12263. The emperor learned what had happened and learned of the great defeat, learned that Evander had been killed and the others had been taken. He saw that his men were in great dismay and battle had started; he saw that matters kept going wrong for him and he saw he would acquire nothing. He was grieved and was much dismayed; he thought and thought and was full of doubts. He was in doubt as to what he should do: whether to fight Arthur or await the rest of his vassals, who were to follow after him. The battle gave him much cause for fear because it would profit him nothing. He decided to go to Ostum by way of Langres. He summoned his men and set them on the move; they arrived in Langres late in the evening, encamped in the city and lodged in the valleys. Langres lies on top of a hill, and valleys surround it.

12287. Arthur soon learned what they wanted to do and which way they would take. He knew very well the emperor would not fight until he had more men, and he did not want to let them rest or get close enough to protect him. As far as he could, he secretly had his men summoned and sent for. He by-passed Langres, on his left, and went beyond it, bearing right: he wanted to get ahead of the emperor and block the road to Ostum. All night, until morning came, he travelled with his army, through wood or plain, until he came to a valley called Soeïse.[60] Everyone going from Ostum to Langres had to pass through this valley.

12305. Arthur had his men armed and his troops drawn up, so that, whatever time the Romans came, they could readily receive them. He had the equipment and the camp-followers, who were no use in a battle, stationed beside a hill, in the guise of an armed band, so that if the Romans saw them, they would be terrified of the great numbers. He put 6666 men, all excellent, in a troop in a wood above a hill – whether on the right or the left I do not know. Morvid, count of Gloucester, was to be leader of this group. To them the king said, 'Stay here! Whatever happens, don't move. If need be, I shall move here and direct the others your way, and if the Romans by any chance withdraw in defeat, spur after them and catch them up. Kill them, don't spare them!' And they replied, 'We'll do it.'

12330. Then he took another legion of noble men, vassals, mounted and with helmets laced on, and put them in a more visible spot. They had no commander but him: this was his own retinue, whom he had raised and nurtured. In the midst he had his dragon held aloft, his own personal banner. From all the others he made eight companies, with two commanders in each; half the companies were on horseback, half on foot. He gave commands to all these together, praying and asking that when the infantry was fighting, the mounted men should strike and attack the Romans from the side. Each division numbered 5555 knights, all chosen from the best[61] and all armed from top to toe. The eight companies were drawn up in groups of four – four in front and four at the rear – and in the middle were great numbers of other men, each armed in his fashion.

[60] Sessia/Siesia in HRB: the valley of the Suize, a tributary of the Marne (Arnold and Pelan, La Partie arthurienne, p. 118), or Saussy (Thorpe, History, p. 247 n. 1).

[61] Line 12350 has the obscure phrase: tuz pris en esling. I have adopted Arnold and Pelan's interpretation here (La Partie arthurienne, p. 135).

12358. Angusel of Scotland was in charge of the front of the first division, and Cador of Cornwall of the rest. The second company was controlled by Bos and count Gerin of Chartres; the third, well armed and equipped, was given to Aschil, the Danish king, and Loth, the Norwegian one. Hoel took command of the fourth, and Walwein (no coward he) with him. After these four were four more, ready for combat. Kei and Bedoer the cup-bearer controlled one; Bedoer had the Herupeis, and Kei the Angevins and those from Chinon. Another division was commanded by Holdin, count of Flanders, and Guitart the Poitevin, who willingly led it. Count Jugeïn of Leicester and Jonathas of Dorchester received the seventh company and were its lords and commanders. Cursal, count of Chester, and count Urgen of Bath had charge of the eighth division, and Arthur had great trust in them. He put good servants, fine archers and brave crossbow-men outside the throng, on either side, to be able to shoot well from the flank. All these were in front of the king, and he was behind with his own company.

12393. When Arthur had divided them and drawn up his companies, hear what he said to his retainers, his barons and their sons: 'My lords', he said, 'I am much cheered when I remember your many virtues, your great might, your many conquests. I've always found you ready and bold. Your prowess keeps increasing, keeps growing, regardless of whom it offends. When I remember and reflect that Britain is, in your time and through you and your companions, mistress of thirty realms, I am overjoyed, I glory in it, and I trust in God and in you to conquer yet more, seize and have yet more. Your exploits, your own mighty hands, have twice defeated the Romans. You must know that my heart tells me, and everything ordains it, that today you will defeat them again, and then you will have beaten them thrice. You have beaten the Norwegians, the Danes and the French, and you hold France against their will. You should certainly be able to defeat the worst when you have defeated the best. They want to make you tributaries and extract tribute from us, and they want to recover France. They think to find here the sort of men they are bringing from the East; but one of us is worth a hundred of theirs. Don't be afraid of them, for women are worth as much. We must trust in God and not lose the hope that, with a little daring, we shall easily defeat them.

Never fail me for anyone, and never flee for anyone: I shall certainly know what everyone is doing and certainly see who does best. I shall go everywhere and see everything and be at every fight.' When the words which the king had said and expounded were finished, all those who heard him replied together with one accord that they would rather die there than leave the field without victory. You could hear them mustering, swearing oaths and making pledges that on pain of death they would not fail him, but make the same end as he did.

12451. Lucius was born in Spain, of good Roman stock. He was still youthful, less than forty but more than thirty, bold and courageous. He had already done many brave deeds; on account of his strength and valour he had been made emperor. In the morning he left Langres, thinking to go straight to Ostum. The whole of his great army was on the move; the road was large and wide. When he heard and learned of the trap which Arthur had set in front of him, he saw he would have either to fight or to retreat. He did not deign to retreat, because it seemed cowardly, and his enemies would overtake him and do him great harm, for to fight and fly at the same time is hard to accomplish. He summoned his kings, his princes, his dukes (of whom there were two hundred or more) and senators, and spoke to them:

12477. 'Peers, noble lords', he said, 'good and victorious vassals, you are the descendants of worthy ancestors who conquered large domains. It is through them that Rome leads the world and shall do, as long as Romans are alive. They conquered our great empire; it's shameful if, in our lifetime, it declines. They were noble, and so are you, valiant sons of valiant fathers. Each of you had a valiant father, and their valour appears in you today. Each of you must strive to resemble his excellent father; shame on him who deserves to lose his father's inheritance and who abandons through wickedness what his father conquered for him. I am not saying, you know, that I consider you've gone downhill: you were brave, and you are brave, and I consider you all valiant. My lords, I see and you see, I know and you certainly know, that our way, which ran straight to Ostum, is blocked. We cannot travel along it unless we fight our way through. I don't know which recent robber, which robber or bandit, has closed to us the way ahead by which I was to take you. They thought I would flee and leave the land to them, but I have turned around to lure them out in front. Now they have attacked us. To arms! Seize your weapons! If they await us, we will strike them, and if they flee, we will pursue them. Let us curb their violence and destroy their power!'

12519. Then they leapt to take up their weapons, unwilling to wait any longer. They prepared their army, took their measures and set their men in ranks. There were many pagan kings and dukes mingled with the Christians, who held their fiefs from Rome and for those fiefs were subject to the Romans. By thirties and forties, by sixties and hundreds, by legions and thousands, they divided up their knights, many on foot, many on horseback, some on the hill, others in the valley. Then, all in serried ranks, they advanced against Arthur's men. The Roman army entered the valley at one end; at the other end, in front of them, the Britons had taken possession of the field. Then a great blowing of horns and bugles could be heard. With resolution and calmness they approached and came together, and at this approach many arrows were shot and spears thrown; no one could open his eyes or uncover his face. Arrows flew like hail; the air grew quite dark and murky with them. Then they set to breaking lances and shattering and piercing shields; the lances dealt great blows, and pieces of them flew high in the sky. Next they came to sword-play and huge strokes with shining blades. Then the fray was extraordinary; you never saw a more dangerous one, nor more thick and confused. Anyone keen to strike there had ample opportunity. Those who were stupid or aghast served no purpose; cowards were at a loss. The great crowd and press prevented one man from hitting another. The battlefield could be seen in tumult, one division attacking another, one company colliding with another, some striking, some shoving, some advancing, some withdrawing, some falling, some standing, with lances broken, splinters flying, swords drawn, shields raised, with the strong overthrowing the weak, and the living trampling on the dying, with saddle-girths broken, breastplates smashed, saddles emptied and horses in flight.

12575. For a long time they fought, for a long time they struggled, because the Romans did not withdraw; nor did they gain ground over the Britons. It was not easy to know who should have the victory, until the division approached which was led by Bedoer and Kei. They saw that they were gaining little and that the Romans were holding fast. In anger and pure fury they straightaway rushed with their company upon the Romans, into where they saw the fray was thickest. Bedoer struck hard, Kei struck hard. Lord, what fighters the king had at court! What a seneschal, what a cup-bearer! They performed such service with their steel blades. What a pair of fighters, had they lived a while! They had done much and would have done more. They went smashing through the press, laying many men low. Their large band followed them, pressing forward and knocking down; they took and gave many a blow, slew and wounded many a man. Bedoer rushed into the fray, without respite or rest. Kei, for his part, never stopped; he knocked down many, he laid many flat. If they had beaten a retreat somewhat, and given ground, with their men, until the British could follow them up and the other troops come, they would have gained great renown and great advantage and they would have been protected from death. But they were too hot-headed and eager to keep striking forward; they had no thought of sparing themselves but wished to penetrate the fray, trusting in their great valour and in the numerous men they led.

12617. But they encountered a division led by the king of Media; he was called Boccus and was a pagan, a very brave man, with many troops. The counts joined battle with them, not in the least afraid of their great numbers. It was a well-fought battle and well-sustained conflict, between heathens and Saracens and Herupeis and Angevins. King Boccus held a sword – a curse on his coming! He slashed at the two counts and struck Bedoer in the chest. With his lance he pierced him right through the body. Bedoer fell, his heart broke asunder and his soul left him: Christ protect him! Kei found Bedoer dead. He wanted to bear him away: he had greatly loved and cherished him. With as many men as he had, he made those from Media withdraw and abandon the spot. But, during the wait and delay it took to rescue Bedoer's body, the king of Libya approached. He was called Sertorius and was much renowned; he had a great crowd of heathen men from his own lands. These mortally wounded Kei and killed many of his men. They gave him many wounds, they struck him many blows, but he held on to the body. The rest of his men rallied round to defend it and carried it to the golden dragon, whether the Romans wished it or not.

12655. Bedoer's nephew was Hyrelgas, who had greatly loved his uncle. He took so many of his friends and relations that he had three hundred, with helmets, hauberks and swords, mounted on good, strong and swift horses. He gathered them into a troop and then said to them, 'Come with me: I'm going to avenge my uncle's death.' Then he began to draw near the Romans. He saw the king of Media and recognized him from his banner. At this company he launched himself, continually shouting Arthur's war-cry, like a madman who cannot be restrained. He did not fear anyone or anything which he found, provided that he could avenge his uncle. His companions rushed forward with him, grabbing their shields and lowering their lances. They killed and laid low many and pressed forward over the fallen, reaching the division of the king who had slain Bedoer. Combining the power of good horses with the impetuosity of good vassals, they wheeled right and left, led by Hyrelgas. They never stopped until they reached the banner and King Boccus. Hyrelgas took a good look at him and turned his horse in his direction, rushing ahead out of the throng, and he hit Boccus on top of his head. The knight was strong, his blow was mighty and the blade hard and sharp. It split and broke the helmet and rent the hauberk coif asunder, cleaving him down to the shoulders. His heart burst, his soul fled, and Hyrelgas stretched out his arm to grasp the body before it fell. He pulled it in front of him, across his horse, and held it face up; he pulled it across and before him, and it uttered never a cry or a howl.

12701. The knight was impetuous and the horse powerful; he made his way back to his men unhurt by pagan or Roman. He broke and smashed through the fray, and his companions made way for him. He set Boccus' body down next to his uncle and hewed it all into pieces. Then he said to his friends, 'Come on, you barons' sons! Let's go and kill these Romans, these bastards and sons of whores. They have brought into this land people with no faith or trust in God, to kill us and our friends. Go on, let's kill the heathens, and the Christians likewise who have united with the heathens to destroy Christianity. Come and test your strength!'

12722. Whereupon they returned to the field. Then you might have heard brawls and shouts, and seen heavy fighting, helmets and swords glittering, and sparks flying from the steel. Guitart, the good duke of Poitiers, did not behave like a coward, but kept up the fight around him. He came up to the king of Africa; each gave the other hard blows, but the king of Africa fell, and the count pressed forward, killing Africans and Moors. Holdin, the Flemings' duke, who held Bruges and Lens, wheeled to attack the division of Aliphatima, a Spanish king. They attacked and hit each other so much that Aliphatima was killed and so was Count Holdin. Ligier, count of Boulogne, fought the king of Babylon; I do not know who struck the best, but each brought the other down, and the count and the king both died.

12748. Three other counts died: Baluc and Cursal and Urgent. Each of the three headed many men: Urgent was lord of Bath, and Baluc count of Wiltshire. Cursal was count of Chester, which borders on Wales. These were killed very quickly, attacked from both sides. The men they had to lead, and who followed their banners, withdrew to the division commanded by Walwein and Hoel, his friend, with him; there never were two such vassals. In ages past there have never been two such lords for goodness, courtesy, excellence and chivalry. Those from Brittany followed Hoel, their lord. Their company was so fierce and bold in such a way that they feared neither press nor throng but reached and thrust everywhere. Those who had just been pursuing them and laying them low in heaps, they soon made turn tail, and left many in the throes of death. Through the great blows they dealt and the men they led, they came right up to the banner with the golden eagle on top. There the emperor was, with the flower of his knights, and with him were the noble men and valiant knights of Rome.

12785. There you might have seen a deadly battle; I think you never saw the like before. Kimar, count of Triguel, was in Hoel's company. His valour was great and he did much damage to the Romans. But a Roman foot-soldier struck him dead with his sword. With him died two thousand Bretons, including three noble friends: one of the three was called Jaguz, from Bodloan, the second was Richomarcus, and the third Boclovius. There were not six men in the division with their valour and renown.

Had they been counts or kings, I think there would have been talk ever after of their prowess. They were quite ruthless, and slaughtered the Romans: no one who fell into their hands was not finished off, whether by lance or by sword. They rushed ahead of their troops on to the emperor's company, and the Romans captured them and slew all three together.

12813. Hoel and his cousin Walwein were full of anger and fury when they saw the great slaughter the Romans were making of their men. To destroy their enemies and avenge their friends, they came upon them like lions, like beasts let out of their cage. They demolished and slaughtered Romans, dealing out to them hits and blows. The Romans strongly defended themselves, receiving and giving many a blow. They attacked well and were well attacked, they struck well and were well struck, they pushed well and were well pushed, did great harm and were in turn much harmed. Walwein's violence was ferocious; he never wearied of striking; his strength was always fresh and his hand never tired. He vigorously sought out Romans and vigorously pressed forward in order to get to the emperor and fight with him. He advanced so far and performed so much, rushed forward and backward so often, that he encountered the emperor, and each carefully scrutinized the other. The emperor saw Walwein, and Walwein knew who he was. With great force they hurtled together; both were strong and neither fell. The emperor was tall and strong, young, bold and with great vigour, intelligent and of great prowess; he was joyful and delighted to be fighting Walwein, whose fame was so great. If he could come through it alive, he intended to boast of it in Rome.

12853. They raised their arms, held their shields up and attacked each other with extraordinary blows. They hurt and harassed each other and hit each other in many ways. Each strongly attacked the other and vigorously struck him. Splinters flew from the shields, and sparks from the steel. They fought up and down, both being exceptionally brave. Had they had the field to themselves, an end would soon have been made of one of them. But the Romans recovered: they rallied to the golden eagle and helped the emperor, having nearly lost him. They repulsed the Britons and took possession of the field. Arthur saw his men retreating, the Romans taking heart and occupying the battlefield against him. He could not and would not wait any more. With his company he advanced, shouting, 'What are you doing? Forward! See, I'm here to protect you; don't leave a single man alive. It's Arthur leading you, who never flees the field. Follow me: I'll lead the way, and take care no one gives up. Remember your own greatness, you who have conquered so many realms. I shall never leave this field alive: here I either conquer or die!'

12887. Then you might have seen Arthur in combat, killing men and laying them low, breaking hauberks, splitting helmets, cutting off heads and arms and fists. He brandished Caliburn, covered in blood; whoever he reached, he knocked him down dead. I cannot write down all his blows: with each one, he killed a man. As a lion, driven by hunger, kills whatever animal it can reach, just so did the good king, leaving neither horse nor man alive. Whoever he struck or wounded had no use for a doctor; no one ever survived his blow, however slight the wound. All fled from Arthur's path, like sheep before the wolf. He pursued the Libyan king, called Sertorius, a man of power, and severed his head from his body. Then he said to him, 'Curse you for bearing arms here, to make Caliburn bloody!' But the dead man said not a word. Polidetes was next to him, a wealthy king from Bithynia, a heathen land. Arthur saw him in front of him and gave him an amazing blow: he cut off his head at shoulder-level. The head fell, the trunk remained. At Arthur's blows and words, the Britons attacked the Romans, and the Romans hurt them in return, drawing their swords and shattering their lances. They inflicted great damage on the Britons, opposing force with force. Arthur saw them: it increased his efforts, and he struck huge blows with Caliburn. The emperor did not hang back but killed Arthur's men one after the other. They could not meet or touch each other, so thick was the press between them and so savage the fray.

12933. On both sides men fought well, and soon you could see a thousand die. They fiercely attacked and fiercely slew each other. It was not clear who would win or who would be defeated and slain, when Morvid arrived with his company, who had been in the forest on the mountain, where Arthur was to re-muster his forces if misfortune overtook his army. Six thousand, six hundred and sixty-six knights, on horseback, with bright helmets and white hauberks, straight lances and raised swords, swept down from the mountain, unseen by the Romans. They came up behind and struck them, splitting their army in two, separating one from the other and laying all and sundry low. They trampled them with their horses and slew them with their swords. After that, the Romans could not stand their ground or recover, but fled in great crowds, knocking one another down. The emperor was knocked over and pierced through the body with a lance. I cannot say who laid him low, nor can I say who struck him: he was attacked in the press and in the press was slain. He was found dead amongst the dead, wounded through the body by a lance. Those from Rome and from the East, and the rest too, fled the field as fast as they could. The Britons harried and demolished them; quite weary of killing so many, they trampled the slain underfoot. You could see blood running in streams, corpses lying in heaps, and fine palfreys and war-horses roaming loose over the fields.

12977. Arthur was joyful and delighted that he had tamed the pride of Rome. He gave thanks to the King of Glory, through whom he had gained victory. He had all the slain searched and his men and friends removed; some he had buried there, others carried back to their lands. Many of them he had buried throughout the country, in abbeys. He had the body of the emperor removed and kept with great honour. He sent it on a bier to Rome and informed the Romans he owed them no other tribute from Britain, which he governed; and whoever required tribute from him would be sent back in the same way. Kei, mortally wounded, was carried to his castle of Chinon; Kei planned and built Chinon, and Chinon takes its name from him. He did not live for long but soon died. He was buried in a wood near Chinon, in a hermitage. At Bayeux in Normandy, where he was lord, they buried Bedoer, outside the gate, towards noon. Holdin was taken to Flanders and buried in Terrüene,[62] and Ligier was carried to Boulogne.

13010. Arthur, who stayed in Burgundy, spent all winter there, capturing cities and appeasing them. In summer he wanted to

[62] Thérouanne, in the Pas de Calais (Arnold and Pelan, *La Partie arthurienne*, p. 162).

cross the St Bernard pass and go to Rome, but Modret made him turn back. God, what shame! God, what disgrace! He was his nephew, his sister's son, and had the care of his kingdom; Arthur had entrusted the whole realm to him and put it all in his charge. And Modret wanted to take it all away from him and keep it all for his own use. He took homage from all the barons, and hostages from all the castles. After this act of great wickedness, Modret did another evil deed, because, against Christian law, he took to his bed the king's wife: he treacherously took the wife of his uncle and lord. Arthur heard and certainly realized that Modret bore him no loyalty: he held his land and had taken his wife. He was not grateful to him for such service. He handed over all his men to Hoel and left him France and Burgundy, asking him to look after it all and to make peace throughout. He would return to Britain, taking the islanders with him, and have his revenge on Modret, who held his wife and his land. All his conquests would be of little value to him if he lost Britain, his own domain. He would rather leave Rome to be conquered than lose his own land. In a little while he would return and would, he said, go to Rome. So Arthur arrived at Wissant, lamenting the perjury of Modret, who had made him abandon a great conquest, and prepared his fleet there.

13053. Modret knew of Arthur's return; he neither wished nor deigned to make peace. He sent for Cheldric of Seisuine,[63] a duke, who brought him eight hundred well-equipped ships, all laden with knights. And Modret, for their help and their forces, granted and gave them as a heritage all the land from the Humber to Scotland, and Hengist's land in Kent at the time Vortigern married his daughter. When Modret had gathered his men together, the army was large and splendid. What with the pagan troops and the Christian ones there were, with hauberks and horses, sixty thousand knights. He thought he could await Arthur with confidence, believing he could defend all the ports against him. He did not want to hand over his rights to him, or seek peace, or repent, and he knew himself to be so guilty that to seek peace would be ridiculous.

[63] HRB (Vulgate version) tries to distinguish this leader from Saxony from the Cheldric of Arthur's early career by calling him Chelric. The First Variant version, however, restores the d.

13077. Arthur manned his ships; so many were embarked, I cannot count them. He wanted to land at Romenel,[64] and commanded his ships to travel there, but before he had disembarked, Modret with his men, bound to him by oath, quickly advanced against him. Those in the ships struggled to land, those on land prevented them. Many on both sides attacked each other, shooting arrows and throwing javelins, piercing bellies, chests and heads, and putting eyes out if they reached them. Those in the ships had to pay so much attention to steering the boats and trying to land that they were not allowed to strike or to protect themselves; many of them lay dead in the sea. Sometimes falling, sometimes staggering, they called those on shore traitors. Unloading the ships ashore, Arthur lost many men; there many bodies and heads were severed. There Walwein, his nephew, was slain; Arthur's grief for him was very great, for he never loved any man so much. Angusel, who had dominion over Scotland, was killed with him. There were many others slain, whom the king lamented and mourned.

13107. As long as they were on the beach, Arthur could only lose, but once they were on firm ground and both forces equally on the level, neither Modret nor the great army he had brought could hold out. Modret had assembled men brought up to peace and quiet: they did not know how to protect themselves, to wheel and to strike, as Arthur's men did, who had been brought up to war. Arthur and his soldiers struck them and entertained them with their swords; they killed them by scores and by hundreds, slaying many, taking many captive. The slaughter was huge, and would have been greater had the evening not thwarted them. The light failed and darkness came; Arthur stopped and withheld his men. Modret's men fled. Did you think some of them helped to guide others? No one cared about anyone else, but each thought only of his own skin.

13131. Modret fled all night, in search of refuge he could rely on. He thought he could stay in London, but the Londoners would not receive him. He crossed London and the Thames and did not stop until Winchester. He took up quarters in the city and summoned his men and his friends. From the citizens he

---

[64] Romney; *Rutupiae* (= Richborough) in *HRB*.

took oaths of fealty and homage, against their will, so that they would, as far as possible, support him and show him loyalty and peace. Arthur, full of hatred for Modret, had no wish to delay. He grieved bitterly for Angusel and for Walwein, whom he had lost. His anguish for his nephew was great, but I do not know where he put his body. He turned his anger and fury on Modret, if he could just kill him. He followed him to Winchester, summoning men from all directions; he wished to besiege the city and encamp his men round about.

13155. When Modret saw Arthur and the army encompassing the city, he made it appear he would fight and that he wished to fight, for if he were besieged for long, he would not escape being captured, and if he were captured, he would never escape Arthur alive. He gathered all his men and made them take their weapons and arm themselves. He had them arranged into companies and made them go out and fight. As soon as they ventured out, the whole army fell upon them, and at once there were many blows dealt, and many men killed and wounded. It turned out badly for Modret, because his men could not stand firm. But he gave thought to saving his own skin: his misdeeds were many, and he feared the king. He gathered in great secrecy all his intimates and dependants and those whom Arthur most hated, and left the other men to fight. Taking a path leading to Hamtune,[65] he never stopped till he was on the beach. With promises and bribes he got helmsmen and sailors, and rushed out to sea with them so that Arthur could not reach him. They took him to Cornwall; he willingly fled, because he feared Arthur.

13187. King Arthur besieged Winchester, defeated the people and took the city. To Ewain, son of Urien, who was on good terms with the court, he gave Scotland as heritage, and Ewain did him homage for it. He had been Angusel's nephew and claimed it by right of inheritance, for Angusel had neither son nor wife to take the kingdom ahead of Ewain. He was a man of great valour, having won much renown and honour in the conflict and fighting which Modret had started in England.

[65] Southampton.

13201. The queen knew and heard that Modret had so many times been put to flight; he could neither defend himself against Arthur nor dared await him in the field. She was staying in York, melancholy and distressed. She remembered the wickedness she had done in tarnishing her honour for Modret's sake, shaming the good king and desiring his nephew. He had married her illicitly and she was badly degraded by it. She wished she were dead rather than alive. Filled with misery and dejection, she fled to Caerleon and there entered an abbey. There she took the veil and was concealed; she was neither heard nor seen, neither known nor found, because of the shame of her misdeed and the sin she had committed.

13223. Modret held Cornwall, having lost all the rest of the land. He sent over land and sea, summoning pagans and Christians: he summoned Irish, Norwegians, Saxons and Danes, he summoned those who hated Arthur and feared his service, he summoned those who had no land and who would serve to get it. He gave and promised and begged, as a man does in need. Arthur was mortified and angry that he had taken no vengeance on Modret; it grieved him greatly that the traitor had even a fistful of his land. Modret had already brought men into Cornwall and was trying to get more; he aimed to hold that territory and grab others. Arthur knew this and it disturbed him. He summoned his whole army from as far as the Humber; I do not know their number, but there were many people. The king's army was large, and he sought Modret where he knew him to be, intent on killing and destroying this traitor and his broken faith. Modret had no wish to flee; he preferred to stake his life and risk death rather than so often desert the field.

13253. The battle was beside Camble[66] in the land of Cornwall. They gathered and joined battle in great anger; in great anger was the work begun, great were the numbers of men and great was the slaughter. I cannot say who did best, or who lost or won, or who fell or stood firm, or who died and who lived. The

[66] In other manuscripts *Cambre* or *Tanbre*. In the *Annales Cambriae* (AD 539), Arthur and Medraut fall at the battle of *Camlann*. In *HRB* this has become the river of *Camblan*, which Thorpe identifies as the Camel. (See Thorpe, p. 259, for local legend.)

losses were great on both sides; the plain was strewn with dead and bloody with the blood of the dying. Then perished the flower of youth, tended and gathered by Arthur from many lands, and those of the Round Table, famous throughout the world. Modret was slain in the fray, and the vast majority of his men, and the cream of Arthur's people, both the strongest and the best.

13275. Arthur, if the chronicle is true, received a mortal wound to his body. He had himself carried to Avalon, for the treatment of his wounds. He is still there, awaited by the Britons, as they say and believe, and will return and may live again. Master Wace, who made this book, will say no more of his end than the prophet Merlin did. Merlin said of Arthur, rightly, that his death would be doubtful. The prophet spoke truly: ever since, people have always doubted it and always will, I think, doubt whether he is dead or alive. Truly, 542 years after the Incarnation he did have himself carried to Avalon. It was a great loss that he had no children. To Cador's son, Costentin of Cornwall, his cousin, he surrendered his kingdom, and told him to be king until he returned.

LAWMAN

Brut:
Arthurian Section

To these islands journeyed Constantine the gracious, *Constantine's*
And his army quite secure all at Totnes came ashore. *Arrival*
There arrived the brave man: extremely well was he
    endowed! 6390
And with him two thousand knights; the like no king has owned.
Onward they went marching into London city
And sent for the knights throughout all that kingdom,
And every single brave man, that in great haste they must come
    then.
This was heard by the British where they were living down in pits
In the earth, and in tree trunks they were hiding out like badgers,
In wood and in wilderness, in heathland and in ferns,
So that practically nobody could ever find a Briton,
Unless they were in a castle or in a town enclosed securely.
   When they heard of this word that Constantine was in the land,
There emerged from the mountains many thousand men; 6401
They came springing out of woodlands as if they were wild beasts:
There went loping off to London many hundred thousand,
On streets and through forests all men forwards went marching,
And the brave women dressed in weaponed men's clothing,
And off they all went towards the great army.
When Constantine observed all these folk coming to him,
Then he was more blithe than he'd been ever in his life.
   Off they went on their way for two whole nights and a day,
Until they came, most certainly, on Melga and Wanis. 6410
Together they rushed on them with fiercest rigour:
Fought there with fury; the fated then fell there.
Before the day was quite over slain were Wanis and Melga,
And Picts quite enough and Scots without number,
Danish and Norwegian, men of Galloway and Ireland.
All the time that there was daylight still this slaughter lasted;
When it came to evening-time then called out Earl Constantine,
Asking for route planners to run ahead towards the rivers,
And sprightly men towards the sea, so that there they could spy
    out for them.
One really should have seen that sport, how the ladies all marched
    forward,
Right through woods and right through fields, over hills and over
    dales;

Wherever they detected a single man escaping   6422
Who had been with Melga, with the heathen king,
The women then laughed loudly and ripped him all to pieces,
Praying for his soul – that salvation never neared it!
So the British women were the death of many thousands,
And so they rid this kingdom of Wanis and of Melga,
And Constantine the brave marched to Silchester,
And there held his hustings for all his British feoffs.

    All of the British were bound for the meeting,   6430
And adopted Prince Constantine and made him king of the
    Britons.
Great was the rejoicing there was among mankind,   CONSTANTINE
And afterwards they gave him a wife, a wondrously fair one,
Born of the highest, of the best of all among the British.
From this high-born wife King Constantine had
Among this very people three little sons;
The first son very nearly had his own father's name:
The king's name was Constantine, and **Constance** was the child's
    name.

    When this child had grown till he was old enough for riding,
Then his father had him made a monk, through the bad advice of
    men,
And the child was a monk, enclosed in Winchester.   6441
After him was born another, who was the middle brother:
He was called **Aurelius**, and his surname was **Ambrosius**;
Then last of all was born a child who was specially chosen:
He was known as **Uther**: his honour was excellent;
He was the youngest brother but he lived longer than the others.
Archbishop Guencelin who was most good in serving God,
Took charge of these two children in his love for the king,
But alas that their own father was not able to live longer,
For he maintained good laws all the time he was alive,   6450
But he was not king here for more than twelve years.
Then came the death of the king: now listen through what
    scheming.

    He had in his house a Pict, a courteous knight and very valiant;
He travelled with the king and with all his courtiers,
In no other manner than exactly like his brother.
And so he became very mighty, all his companions were not like
    this;
Then he decided to betray King Constantine the great.

He came in the king's presence and he fell upon his knees,
And this is how that traitor told lies before his lord:
'My lord king, come right now, and speak with your knight
    Cadal, 6460
And I shall instruct you in secret information
Such as you never before on earth have ever heard.'
So up stood King Constantine and off he went outside with him,
But alas that they knew nothing of it, Constantine's knights!
They went such a long while onwards that they came into an
    orchard;
There the traitor then said: 'Lord, here we are, the two of us.'
The traitor sat down, as if to hold secret council,
And bent towards the king as one does for whispering;
A really long knife he grabbed and with this the king he stabbed,
Down into the heart; and he himself slipped off. 6470
Dead there the king lay while the traitor fled away.
The word came to the court of how the king's life was cut short;
There was tremendous sorrow and it spread among the people.
    Then did the British start thinking very hard;
They had no idea of anything they could do about a king
For the king's two sons were both of them little:
Ambrosius hardly knew how to ride a horse,
And Uther his brother was still suckled by his mother,[1]
And Constance the eldest was away in Winchester:
A monk's habit he had on, like those of his community. 6480
Then all those living in this nation came up to London,
To their hustings, and to take advice about a king,
Which way they could act, and how they might tackle it,
And which of these children they could have as their king.
Then the people selected Aurelius Ambrosius
To have as a king over them all.
    This was heard by **Vortigern**, a wily man and wary.
Among the earls he was standing and earnestly he opposed it,
And this he told them (though it was not true):
'I shall now advise you, my advice is the best: 6490
Wait for a fortnight, and let's come back here straight,
And then I will tell you, with very true words,

---

[1] Marcie's son was not made king until he could ride (Lawman 3161) and therefore Ambrosius is not qualified yet. Lawman's Uther is being suckled by his mother, which was rare among the medieval nobility.

What with your eyes you shall behold, and your time you'll well
    bestow.
This same thing we shall await, and to our homes meanwhile ride,
And keep peace and keep quiet with freedom in the land.'
    That assembly all did as Vortigern decreed,
And he himself went off as if going to his lands,
And then turned, right on to the way that down to Winchester lay.
A half share of the Welsh lands did Vortigern have in his hands;
Forty good knights he had in his retinue.   6500
He went off to Winchester where he would find Constance
And spoke with the abbot who was in charge of the convent
Where Constance was a monk, he who was the king of Britain's
    son.
He went into the monastery mouthing humble words;
He said that he wanted to have speech with Constance.
This the abbot granted him and led him to the parlour.
    In this way spoke Vortigern with the monk then and there:
'Constance, listen to my advice, for your father is now dead.
There is Ambrosius your brother, and Uther is the other.
Now all the [elders], the most outstanding in the land,*   6510
Have selected Aurelius, whose surname is Ambrosius
If they can, above everything, they wish to make him king,
And Uther your brother is still suckled by his mother.
    But I have opposed them, and intend to refuse it,
For I have been justiciar of all of Britain's area,
And I'm a powerful earl, different from my fellows,
And a half share of the Welsh lands do I have in my hands;
I have more alone than the others all told.
I have come to you, for you are the dearest of men to me;
If you will swear me oaths, I will strip you of these clothes; 6520
If you will increase my land, and put your affairs into my hand,
And make me your justiciar, over all of Britain's area,
And on my veto do everything you do.
If you give me your hand on it that I shall be in charge,
I will above all things make you Britain's king!'
    This monk sat very quietly; the words worked with his own
    wishes.
Then the child-monk answered with much eagerness:
'Blessings on you, Vortigern, that you have come here.
If ever yet comes that day on which I may be king,
All my affairs and all my land I shall deliver in your hand,   6530

And everything you wish to do, my men shall undertake it.
And I shall swear you oaths that I shall perform this.'
So spoke the monk: he grieved very much
How it all could have been that he was a monk,
For to him black clothes were amazingly loathsome.

Vortigern was wily and wary (that he revealed everywhere):[2]
He took up a cape from off one of his knights;
He put it on the monk and led him out of that place;
At once he took a servant and put the black clothes on him,
And went on whispering with the servant as if he were the
    monk.   6540
Monks were going upstairs, monks were going downstairs,
They saw, as they went by, the servant in monk's habit:
His hood was pulled right down as if covering his tonsure;
It was the thought of every other that this one was their brother
Who was sitting there so soberly, there in the parlour,
In broad daylight among all the knights.

They came to their abbot and greeted him in God's name:
'Benedicite, my lord; we have come to see you to have word,
For it seems very odd to us, what Vortigern is up to,
There in our parlour where he is conversing: 6550
All this whole day no monk is allowed to go in there,
Except Constance alone, and the whole set of knights.
We are deeply anxious that they're guiding him astray.'
Then the abbot answered, 'On the contrary! They're guiding him
    to good:
Telling him to remain in orders because now his father's dead.'

Vortigern remained there while Constance rode away.   *Constance*
Vortigern got up and strode out of the monastery,   *escapes*
And all of his knights marched out straight.
Monks ran in there at once, expecting to find Constance:
Then they saw the clothes lying, there beside the wall;   6560
And each to his neighbour grieved for their brother.
The abbot leaped on horseback and galloped after Vortigern,
And soon managed to overtake Earl Vortigern.
This is what the abbot said to Vortigern as he rode:
'Tell me, you insane knight: why are you committing such a crime?

[2] This episode, expanded by Lawman, is superbly conceived and reminiscent
of fabliau.

You are abducting from us our brother; leave him and take the
   other,
Take the child Ambrosius, and make him into a king,
And do not anger Saint Benedict: don't do him any wrong.'
   Vortigern could hear this (he was wily and very wary),
He turned straight back again, and took hold of the abbot,   6570
And swore by his two hands that he was going to hang him
Unless he would promise him that he would very swiftly
Unconsecrate Constance, the king's son in this land,
And in such great need as this was he must be king of this nation.
The abbot dared not do other than to unconsecrate his brother,
And the child put into the abbot's hands the gift of twenty
   ploughlands,[3]
And then they journeyed onwards up into London.
   Vortigern the most high forbade all his courtiers
Ever to tell any man what they were holding in their command.*
In London Vortigern was staying until came that agreed-on
   day   6580
When to the hustings were to come the knights from this our
   land.*
On the day they arrived, many and uncountable:
They held council, they conferred, those courageous soldiers,
Deciding that they would have Ambrose and elect him king,
For Uther was too little: for some time he'd have to suckle,
And the eldest of them, Constance, was an enclosed religious,
And no, not for anything would they make a monk a king.
   This was heard by Vortigern, who was wily and most wary,
And to his feet he leaped, as a lion springs.
(Among the British none at all knew what Vortigern had
   been up to: 6590
In a room he had secreted Constance the beloved,
Well-bathed and dressed and then by twelve knights guarded).
The following spoke Vortigern (in manoeuvering he was wily):
'Listen to me, princelings, while I speak to you of kings.
I have been in Winchester and there I was successful;
I spoke there to the abbot, who is a holy man and good,
And told him of the crisis which has come upon this nation
With Constantine's death (about that he was distressed)

---

[3] A ploughland was a unit of land-measure denoting the area of land which
one plough and ploughman could cultivate.

And with Constance, only a child, whom he had been holding,
And I begged him for God's sake the monk's hood from the child
    to take,
Since in this great need he ought to be king in the nation, 6601
And the abbot held his chapter and did everything I asked him,
And right here I have his monks, who are good men and gracious,
Who are bound to give evidence before you in audience.
Look now: here is that same child! Let us make a king of him:
I've got the crown here, which we need for the purpose.
Anyone who protests at this must pay the penalty!'
    Vortigern was very strong – the highest man in Britain's land;
There was no one else at all as high with courage to abjure his
    speech;
The archbishop in that very week departed from this world; 6610
There remained no bishop who on his way did not shuffle,
No monk, nor any abbot who on his way did not ride off,
For they dared not in the name of God commit there such a
    sacrilege
As to take an oblate monk and make him into Britain's king.
This noted Vortigern (of evil he was well aware!):
Up did he stand, picked the crown up in his hand,
And placed it upon Constance (which delighted him).
There was no man present to perform the Christian ceremony,
Who could impart the blessing upon the new king,   CONSTANCE
But Vortigern alone did it entirely for them all: 6620
The start was unfitting and so was the ending:
He abandoned holy orders and for that he endured sorrows.
    So the king was Constance, with Vortigern as his justiciar;
Constance put his royal lands all into Vortigern's own hands,
And with all those lands he did just what he wanted.
Then noticed Vortigern (of evil he was all too well aware!)
That Constance the king about his own land knew nothing,
For he had never learned any lessons at all
Except in his monastery of a monk's duties.
Vortigern noticed this (the Devil was very close to him); 6630
Often he thought deeply of what might be his policy,
How by his lying he could mollify the king.
    Now you can hear how this traitor prepared:
The best men of Britain now all lay dead,
And the king's brothers were as yet both quite little,
And Guencelin the archbishop before this had died,

And this very land's own king of its laws knew not a thing.
Vortigern observed this and he approached the king
With most submissive speech his overlord he greeted:
'May you prosper, Constance, ruler of Britain!   6640
I have approached you this closely because of great necessity:
Because of information which has just come to the land
Concerning the gravest danger. Now you must have power;
Now you must have weapons to defend your nation.
Merchants from other lands have come here, as it is customary;
To me they have brought the tax on their imports,
And they have been telling me (its truth they have vouched for)
That the king of Norway decided recently to come here,
And the king of the Danishmen will make request for Danes,
And the king of Russia for the most rigorous of knights,   6650
And the king of Jutland, with a very strong army,
And the king of Frisia (which sets me shivering).
   'Most serious is this news which has arrived here on these
        shores:
It makes me deeply anxious because I can't think of any solutions,
Unless with our authority we were to send for knights
Who are good and strong and who are familiar with the land,
And invest your castles with courageous men;
In this way your realm might be guarded from the aliens,
And your honour be upheld by superior strength,
For there is no kingdom, however wide, however long,   6660
Which cannot rapidly be seized if there are too few soldiers.'
   Then responded the king (about his own land he knew nothing):
'Vortigern, you are justiciar over all of Britain's area,
And you are to govern it according to your wishes.
Send out for knights who are valiant in fight,
And take into your hand all my castles and my land,
And fulfil all your desires, for I shall remain silent,
Save for one single thing: I want to be called king.'
Then smiled Vortigern (he was of evil much aware);
He was never so blithe before this in his life.   6670
Vortigern took his leave and off began to move,
And so he traversed [all Britain's area;
All castles and] all the land he set in his own hands,*
And men's homage he took always wherever he came,
And [then] took his messengers and sent them to Scotland,*
And summoned the Picts, the very best of all knights:

Three hundred came to him, and he wished to do well by them,
And to him those knights came after that very soon.
    Like this spoke the treacherous fellow: 'Sirs, you are welcome!
I have in my hand all this royal dominion;   6680
With me you are to march, for much I shall love you,
And I shall conduct you into our king's presence:
You shall have silver and gold, the best horses in this land,
Clothes and lovely women; I'll do everything you want!
You shall be very dear to me, for the British I find despicable.
Publicly and privately I'll [fulfil your desires],*
If you in this land will regard me as lord.'
Then declared straight each one of these knights:
'We shall completely fulfil all that you will.'
And then they proceeded to Constance the king.   6690
    Towards the king went Vortigern (of evil he was well aware),
And told him of his deeds, how he had proceeded:
'And here I've brought the Picts, who are to become royal knights,
And all of your castles I have very well appointed,
And these foreign knights in our defence shall fight.'
Everything the king believed, as Vortigern intended,
But alas that the king of his thoughts knew nothing,
Nor of his treachery, which he did afterwards and quickly.
    Those knights in the retinue were highly respected;
For fully two years with the king they lived there,   6700
And Vortigern the justiciar over all of them was ruler,
He kept on saying the British were no more use than rubbish,
But he said that the Picts were very good knights.
Constantly the British were deprived of goods,
While the Picts commanded everything they wanted:
They had drink, they had food, and they had great fun as well;
Vortigern gave to them everything they wanted,
And he was as dear to them as their own life,
So they were all saying, in the place where they were dining,
That Vortigern rightly deserved to rule this nation,   6710
In absolutely everything, better than three similar kings.
Vortigern gave these characters a great deal of treasure.
    Now it happened one fine day, as in his house Vortigern stayed,
He took his two attendant knights and sent after the Picts,
Instructing them 'come here', for they were all to dine there.
To him came those knights, to his house straightaway;
He tempted them by talking as they sat there at the table;

He had them served with draughts of many kinds of liquor:
They swilled and they sang and the day slipped away.
When they were so drunk that their legs folded under them   6720
Then announced Vortigern what he'd been thinking long before:
'Now listen to me, knights: I am going to tell you straight
About my very great troubles; I've been most mournful about
    them.
The king entrusted this land to me as his own justiciar;
You are in this life to me the dearest of all men,
But I have no fine things to give out to my knights,
For this king owns all this land, and he is young, moreover strong,
And I have to give him everything I take from off his land,
And if I ruin things of his I must suffer the rule of law,
And my own income I have spent, for I like to give you
    pleasure.   6730
   And now I've got to go from here, far off to some king,
To serve him peaceably and with him obtain property;
I cannot, for fear of great disgrace, retain here this dwelling-place,
But off I've got to go, off to foreign places,
And if the day ever comes when I can gain some goods,
If I can succeed in this so well that you come to the land where I
    have gone,
Then I shall protect you well with the greatest honour;
And so now I wish you good day: tonight I will have to go away;
It is very much uncertain whether you'll see me ever again.'
   These knights did not know what the traitor was thinking.   6740
Vortigern was disloyal, for in this he betrayed his lord,
And the knights took as truth what the traitor was saying.
Vortigern told his servants to saddle his horses,
And nominated twelve men to travel with himself.
On horseback they mounted as if leaving the country.
It was noted by the Picts, those completely drunken knights,
That Vortigern was about to leave; at this they felt very much
    grief.
They went to take counsel, they went to confer;
They all mourned for their very lives, so very much was their love
    for Vortigern,
And like this spoke the Picts, those drunken knights: 6750
'What shall we do now for advice? Who will now advise us?
Who is going to feed us? Who is going to clothe us?
Who at the court is going to be our lord?

Now Vortigern has gone away we must all scurry off.
No, not for anything will we have a monk as king!
But very well we will do; right away to him let's go,
Secretly and quietly and do everything we want;
Into his bedroom, and drink up his beer,
And when we have drunk, let's make a loud din,
And some must go to the door, stand with swords in front
    of it, 6760
And some straight seize the king and his knights,
And strike off the heads – and we ourselves 'll be having court.
And once we've quickly overtaken our lord Vortigern,
Then we above all things can have him as king.
Then can we live the way we find most likeable.'
  Off went the knights to the king in person straight;
In marched they all, right through the hall,
Into the king's bedroom, where he sat by the brazier.
There was no one there who spoke except **Gille Callaet**;
Like this to the king he spoke – he intended to betray him: 6770
'Listen to me now, land-king, it's not lies to you I'm telling.
In your retinue we've been greatly respected
Because of your steward, who has governed all this land.
He has fed us very well, he has clothed us very well.
And the truth is, I can tell you, we dined with him today just now,
But we bitterly regret that we had nothing there to drink,
And now that we are in your bedroom, give us some draughts of
    your good beer.
Then the king replied to them: 'That shall be your least concern,
For you shall certainly have liquor for as long as you would like
    to.'
They were served with their drinks, and they started to get
    noisy. 6780
Then announced Gille Callaet (at the door he stood alert):
'Where are you, you knights? Stir yourselves now, straight!'
And the king they then grabbed and off his head they   *Constance's*
    slashed,   *Murder*
And every one of his knights they killed there outright,
And got hold of a messenger and sent him towards London,
So that he should gallop quickly in Vortigern's wake,
For him to come back quickly and take over the kingdom,
For he must know above all things that slain was Constance the
    king.

This message reached Vortigern (a traitor in deep secrecy);
In this way he instructed the messenger to ride right back,   6790
And told them to 'guard safely all our reputations,
So that not a single one of them must go out of that area:
But all be waiting for me until my arrival,
And then I shall divide this land among us all.'
Off went that messenger and Vortigern at once took another
And sent all over London, to hustings summoning them,
Rapidly and very soon they were all to come.

    All the citizens had come there, very confident they were,
And then up spoke Vortigern (a traitor in deep secrecy),
Without pause he was weeping and painfully sighing,   6800
But it was all from his mind and not from his heart.
Then the citizens asked him, very confident they were:
'O lord Vortigern, what is causing you distress?
You are not a woman to be so sadly weeping.'
Then responded Vortigern (a traitor in deep secrecy):
'I shall to you reveal a too pitiful tale,
Of absolute disaster which has settled on this land.
In this country I have been the steward of your king,
And have been his confidant and loved him as my life,
But he would not in the end [begin to understand,*
Nor in his actions act by my advice]*   6810a
He favoured the Picts, those alien knights,
But to us he did no good, nowhere gave a kind reception,
But to them he was gentle all of their lives.
I could not get from the king any kind of recompense:
I spent my own means as long as they lasted,
And then I took leave to go to my lands,
And when I'd collected my taxes to come back to the court.
When it was noticed by the Picts that the king had no knights,
Nor even any kinsman who would do anything to prevent them,
They forced an entry into the king's bedroom.   6820
I'm telling you the truth of the thing: they have actually killed the
    king!
And they intend to bring downfall on this kingdom and us all,
And they want without delaying to make a Pict the king.
But I was his steward, and I shall avenge my lord,
And let every brave man aid me to do that.
On will I put my armour, and straightway I shall travel.'
    There marched out of London knights numbering three hundred:

They rode and they ran, off with Vortigern
Until they were approaching where the Picts were [stationed];*
And he took one of his knights and sent him to the Picts   6830
To inform them he was coming, if they wished to entertain him.
The Picts showed enthusiasm for their own coming doom,
And put on their best gear – they had there neither shield nor
     spear.
Vortigern, most forthright, weaponed all his knights,
And there came the Picts, bringing the head of the king.
   When Vortigern saw this head he collapsed nearly to the ground,
As if suffering deep emotion, the most of all those men;
With his looks he was lying, for his heart was rejoicing.
Then announced Vortigern (who was a traitor in deep secrecy):
'Let every brave man with his sword lay into them,   6840
And avenge well on this earth the disaster of our lord.'
They did not capture any living, but each one of them they killed,
And went into the house inside Winchester
And slaughtered their servants and their attendants,
Their cooks and their boys – all they deprived of their life-days.
   In this way spread the tidings of Constance the king,
And worldly-wise men had charge of the other children:
Because of their concern about Vortigern they took Ambrose and
     Uther
And carried them abroad into Little Britain,
And graciously entrusted them to **Budiz** the king,   6850
Who as graciously received them: he was their relative and friend,
And with very great pleasure he supervised the children,
And so for very many years they lived with him there.
   In this land Vortigern was elevated to the throne;   VORTIGERN
All the stalwart British were within his power;
For twenty-five years he was king here.
He was crazy, he was wild, he was fierce and he was bold,
In everything he had his desire – except for the Picts who were
     never quiet,
But constantly they entered all across the northern end,
And laid hold on this kingdom with uncountable horrors,   6860
And more than avenged their kindred here whom Vortigern killed.
   Meanwhile there came tidings into this land
That Aurelius (called Ambrosius) had been made a knight,
And so too was Uther: a good knight and very prudent,

And they wished to come to this land leading an army strong in
     numbers.
This was a remark which was frequently repeated;
The messages kept coming to Vortigern the king.
At this he often felt ashamed and his feelings were enraged
For men were saying almost everywhere: 'Here come Ambrosius
     and Uther,
And they wish to avenge Constance, [who was] king in this
     land.*   6870
Their course can be no other: they wish to avenge their brother,
And to kill Vortigern and him to dust and ashes burn;
So all of this land they will set in their own hand.'
So went the gossip every day of all who walked along the ways.
     Vortigern thought carefully of what could be his remedy,
And decided to send messages into other lands,
For knights from foreign places who might be his defence,
And intended to be wary against Ambrosius and Uther.
     Meanwhile there came tidings to Vortigern the king
That across the sea had come some very strange men,   6880
Up into the Thames they had come ashore:
Three ships fine and good had arrived on the flood,
Three hundred knights, to all appearances kings,
Not counting the mariners who were below the decks there.
These were the most handsome men who ever came here,
But they were heathens, the more harm it was!
Vortigern sent to them and asked them their intentions,
Was it peace they were seeking and his friendship requesting?
Wisely they responded as they well knew how,
And said that they wanted to speak to the king,   6890
And lovingly revere him and regard him as their leader,
And so they started moving off to meet the king.
At that time King Vortigern was in Canterbury,
Where he and his court were holding high council;
There these knights arrived before the people's king:
As soon as they encountered him politely they saluted him,
Saying that they wished to serve him in this land,
If he were willing to support them and give them fair treatment.
     Then Vortigern responded (of every evil he was aware):
'For the whole of my life, as long as I've lived,   6900
By day or by night never have I yet seen such knights.
At your coming I'm delighted, and with me you must remain,

And your wishes I'll comply with, by my living life!
But from you I wish to learn, as you are true and worthy,
What knights you may be, and from what place you have come,
And whether you'll be as true, when vows are old, as new?'
Then answered the other, who was the eldest brother:
'Listen to me now, my lord king, and I shall inform you
What knights we are and where it is we say we come from.
I am called **Hengest, Horsa** here's my brother;   6910
We come from Germany, most glorious of all lands,   *Hengest*
From that same area which is called Angle.[4]   *and Horsa*
There are in our land very strange proceedings:
After every fifteen years the people are assembled,[5]
All our national tribes, and they cast their lots:
He upon whom it falls must travel from the land;
Five are allowed to stay; the sixth must set off
Out of the country, into strange regions;
However popular he is, he must depart,
For the population there is huge, higher than they can
    control: 6920
A woman produces children as wild creatures do;
Every single year she'll have a baby there.
The [lot] fell on us so that we had to leave;*
We could not be left out, not for life or for death,
Not ever for any thing, for fear of the people's king.
So [things go on] there and therefore we are here,*
To seek beneath the [heavens] for land and a good lord.*
Now you have heard, my lord the king, the truth about us in all
    details.'
  Then answered Vortigern (of each evil he was aware):
'I believe you, sir, that you tell me the truth all right.   6930
And what are your beliefs which you believe in?
And your beloved god, to whom you all bow?'
Then replied Hengest, of all knights the fairest,
There is not in this kingdom's land a knight so tall nor yet so
    strong:
'We have powerful gods whom we love in our heart,

[4] Lawman's Hengest comes from Germany (*Alemainne*) rather than Geoffrey of Monmouth's Saxony.
[5] The casting of lots every fifteen years is Lawman's misreading of Wace's 'young men of fifteen or over'.

In whom we have hope and whom we serve with our strength.
The first is called Phoebus and the second is Saturn;
The third is called Woden, who is a wealth-giving god;
The fourth is called Jupiter, of everything he is aware;
The fifth is called Mercury, who is the highest over us;   6940
The sixth is called Apollin, who is a god most splendid;[6]
The seventh is called Tervagant, a high god in our land.
In addition we have a lady who is most high and mighty;
High she is and holy – courtiers love her for this:
She is called Frea; well does she direct them.
But before all our dear gods, whom we are bound to obey,
Woden had the highest rule in our elders' days:
To them he was dear, just as much as their life;
He was their ruler and they treated him with respect;
The fourth day in the week [we] give him for his worship.*   6950
To the Thunder [we] give Thursday, because he can give [us] aid.
Frea [our] lady, [we] give to her Friday;
Saturn [we] give Saturday, to the sun [we] give Sunday;
To the Moon [we] give Monday, and to Tidea [we] g[i]ve
    Tuesday.'*
So spoke Hengest, of all knights the handsomest.
    Then responded Vortigern (of every evil he was aware):
'Knights, you are dear to me, but this report to me is dismal!
Your [beliefs] are iniquitous: you do not believe in Christ,*
But you believe in the Devil, whom God himself has damned;
Your gods are just worthless; in hell they lie lowest.   6960
But nevertheless I shall maintain you in my command,
For in the north are the Picts, very valiant knights,
Who often lead into my lands their forces which are very strong,
And often badly disgrace me, and this makes me enraged.
And if you will avenge me, and obtain their heads for me,
Then I'll give you land, much silver and gold.'
Then answered Hengest, of all knights the fairest:
'If it is the will of Saturnus, it shall all happen thus,
And of Woden our lord, in whom we believe.'
    Hengest took his leave, and to his ships did proceed.   6970
There were many knights who were strong: they dragged their
    ships up on the land.

---

[6] Lawman has added to his source the 'Saracen' gods popular in French romance.

Off went the soldiers to Vortigern the king.
At their head went Hengest, and of all men Horsa closest to him,
Then the men of Germany who were noble in their actions,
And afterwards they sent to him their splendid Saxon knights,
Hengest's relatives [of his ancestors'] race.*
Making much bravado they all marched into the hall:
Better were garbed and better were fed
Hengest's servers than Vortigern's landholders.
Then Vortigern's retinue were treated as ridiculous;   6980
The British were saddened by such an appearance.
    It was not very long before there came to the king
Five sons of knights who had travelled with speed;
They reported to the king some recent tidings:
'Now rightaway the Picts have arrived:
They are riding through your land, and ravaging and burning,   .
And all the northern area they've laid flat to the ground.*
You must decide about this or we shall all be dead.'
The king thought carefully what might be his policy:
He sent to their lodgings for all of his soldiers.   6990
There came Hengest, there came Horsa, there came many a man
        most brave;
There came the Saxon men, who were Hengest's kinsmen,
And the German knights, who are excellent in fight.
This observed King Vortigern: happy was he then and there.
    The Picts followed their custom: this side of the Humber they'd
        come,
And King Vortigern of their coming was fully aware.
They clashed together and slew many there;
There was very strong fighting, combat most severe.
The Picts were well accustomed to conquering Vortigern,
And thought they would then also – but then it turned out quite
        another way,
For it was a saving factor that our men had Hengest there,   7001
With those knights so strong who came out of Saxony,
And the bold men of Germany who came this way with Horsa.
Very many Picts they slaughtered in that fight.
Furiously they fought: the fated there fell.
When the third hour had come the Picts were overcome,
And swiftly away they fled, on every side away they sped,
And all the day they were in flight, many and uncountable.
    King Vortigern went to his pavilion,

And always very close to him were Horsa and Hengest.   7010
Hengest was favoured by the king: to him he gave Lindsey,
And he gave to Horsa plenty of treasures,
And all their knights he treated all right.
And for a good space things stood on the same footing:
The Picts were too scared to come into the land,
There were no pillagers nor outlaws who were not swiftly
        executed,
And Hengest most handsomely was serving the king.
   Then it happened at one time when the king was very happy,
On a festival day, among his men of first rank,
Hengest was thinking carefully what should be his policy,   7020
For with the king he wanted to hold a secret conclave.
He went and stood before the king and gave him courteous
        greeting;
The king at once stood up, and seated him beside himself.
They drank and they grew merry: they were full of enjoyment.
Then said Hengest to the king: 'Lord, are you listening?
I want to give you news in very secret whispers;
If you wish to listen well to what you learn from me,
You will not be enraged at what I impart.'
The response of the king was: let Hengest have his wish.
   Then announced Hengest, of all knights the fairest: 7030
'Lord, I have for many a day enhanced your dignity,
And been your loyal man in your luxurious court,
And in every fight the most superior knight,
And often I've been hearing anxious whisperings
Among your retainers: they really hate you deeply,
To the very death, if they dared to reveal it.
Often they speak very softly, and in whispers they discuss
Two young men living a long way from here;
One of them is called Uther, the other Ambrosius;[7]
There was a third called Constance who was king in this
        [country],*
And here he was murdered by treasonable practices;   7040
Now will come the others and avenge their brother,

---

[7] The addition of Hengest's sly allusion to the two rightful heirs to the throne,
and to his daughter Rowena (7059), points up the dramatic irony: in his fear of
reprisals from one family, Vortigern invites into the country another, even more
dangerous to him and to Britain.

And totally burn up your land and slaughter those who live here,
And yourself and your bodyguard they'll drive out of the land,
And this is what your men are saying as they sit together,
Seeing the two brothers are [both] born of a king,*
From Aldroien's race, these nobles of Brittany.
In this way your doughty men silently condemn you.
     But I will give you advice for your great problem,
That you acquire knights who are valiant in fight,   7050
And deliver to me a castle or a royal borough
In which I may reside for the whole of my life;
Because of you I'm hated: for that I expect death.
If I go wherever I may go, I am never free from stress,
Unless I am securely lying enclosed within a castle.
If you will do this for me, I shall accept it with affection,
And I shall speedily send for my wife:
She is a Saxon woman, well endowed with wisdom,
And for **Rowena**, who is my daughter, and very dear to me she is.
When I have my wife, and my close relations,   7060
And I am within your land fully established,
Then all the better will I serve you, if you allow me this.'
     Then replied Vortigern (of each evil he was aware):
'Take knights and swiftly, and send for your wife,
And for your children, the young and the older,
And for your relations: receive them with elation.
When they have come to you, you shall have wealth,
To feed them in luxury and splendidly clothe them.
But I shall not deliver you either castle or borough,
For I should be reviled within my own kingdom,   7070
Since you retain the heathen customs which were current in your
          elders' times,
And we uphold Christ's ways and will for ever do so all our days.'
Then again spoke Hengest, of all knights the handsomest:
'My lord, I will perform your will, in this and in all things,
And make all my actions accord with your advice.
Now I will speedily send for my wife,
And for my daughter, so dear to me she is,
And for bold men, the best from my race,
And you give me as much land to remain for ever in my hands
As a single bull's hide will in each direction cover,   7080
Far from every castle, in the middle of a field.
Then no one can accuse you, the humble nor the aristocrats,

That ever any high town to a heathen man you've given.'
The king granted to him just what Hengest craved.
    Hengest took his leave and off he proceeded,
And sent a message for his wife to his own land,
And he himself went through this land searching for a wide field,
On which he could extend fully his splendid hide.
He came upon an area in a lovely plain;
He had obtained a hide suited to his need[x]   7090
From a wild bull, and it was wonderfully strong.
He had a clever man who was well trained in skills,   *The Bull's*
Who took up this hide, laid it out on a board,   *Hide*
And sharpened his knives, preparing to slice;
From the hide he cut a thong, very narrow and very long;
This thong was not very wide, only like a thread of twine.
When all the thong was slit, it was wonderfully long;
Hengest stretched it round a huge tract of land.
He began to excavate a very deep ditch,
On top of it a stone wall, which was strong over all.   7100
He erected a town, a great one and glorious;
When the town was quite complete he assigned it a name:
He called it, now note this, Kaer Carrai in British,
And the English knights called it 'Thong-chester';
Now and for all time the name remains the same,
And not from any other exploit did the town carry that name,
Until the Danish men arrived, and drove out the Britons:
They applied a third name there, and Long-castle they called it,
And from all these events, the town had these three names.[*]
    Meanwhile Hengest's wife came here, travelling with her
        ships;   7110
She had as her escort fifteen hundred riders,
And with her came, to be specific, eighteen enormous ships,
There arrived in them many of Hengest's own kindred,
And Rowena his daughter, very dear to him she was.
It was after a short while that there came the actual time
When the city was completed among the very best;
Hengest came to the king and offered him hospitality,

---

[*] Lawman dramatizes the construction of Thongcastle. His term 'Long-castle'
(7108) must have been derived from a corrupted reading in Wace. The
traditional site for Hengest's castle is Thong, near Milton, Kent; it was William
Camden (1586) who associated it with Caister, near Grimsby (see W 6924).

Saying that he had a place prepared ready to receive him,
Inviting him to come to it, where he would graciously be welcome,
And the king granted him what Hengest wanted.   7120
   Then arrived the time for the king to proceed,
With the most esteemed men from all of his court.
Off he started travelling until he reached the town;
He gazed at the walls, up and down and all round,
And he liked very much everything he looked at.
He went into the hall, and all his men with him;
Fanfares were sounding; entertainments they were announcing.
The trestle-boards were spread, and knights sat down at them:[9]
They ate and they drank; there was joyful din in town.
   When the courtiers had eaten, even better luck befell them: 7130
Hengest went into the chamber where lodged fair Rowena.
He had her attired with excessive pride: *Rowena*
Every garment which she had on was extremely finely made,
They were among the best, embroidered with gold thread.
She carried in her hand a bowl made of gold,
Filled up with wine which was exquisitely good.
High-born men escorted her to hall,
In the presence of the king, she the fairest of all things.
Rowena went down on her knees and called out to the king,
And said for the first time in the land of the English: 7140
'Lord king, wassail! I am delighted at your coming.'[10]
The king heard this but did not know what she was saying.
King Vortigern asked his knights at once
What were those phrases which the maiden uttered.
Then replied **Keredic**, a knight who was most gifted
He was the best interpreter who [ever] came here:*
'Listen to me now, lord king, and I shall explain to you
What Rowena is saying, the loveliest of women.
It is a custom, in the Saxons' land,
Wherever any band of men is revelling in drink,   7150

[9] Fixed tables were rare before the sixteenth century: food was eaten on removable boards covered with cloths and balanced on trestles, which were removed and stacked away after meals so that the hall could be used for entertainment and sleeping accommodation.
[10] Lawman's comments on English drinking habits (not in Wace's *Brut*) resemble comments by Nigel Wireker (late twelfth century) (Hall, in *EME*, II) and Wace's description of the English before the battle of Hastings (see Wace n. 2).

That a friend should say to a friend with sweet, gracious
    expression:
'Dear friend, wassail'; the other replies: 'Drink hail'.
The one who holds the bowl, he drinks it all up;
A second full goblet is brought there and is offered to his
    companion;
When that goblet arrives, then they kiss three times.
These are the pleasing customs within Saxony,
And in Germany they are considered noble.'
This was heard by Vortigern (of each evil he was aware),
And spoke this in British (he did not know any English):
'Maiden Rowena, then drink happily!'   7160
The girl drank up the wine and had some more poured in,
And had it offered to the king, and three times she kissed him,
And through that same race those customs came to this land:
'Wassail and drink hail'; many a man is glad about that!
   Rowena the lovely sat beside the king;
The king looked at her with desire; he was deeply in love with her:
Again and again he kissed her; again and again he embraced her,
All his feelings and his powers were bent on that girl:
The Devil was very close there (in [such] sport he is rampant);*
The Devil never does anyone good: he disturbed the king's
    emotions.
Sadly he yearned to have the maiden as his wife,   7171
It was a very heinous thing that the Christian king
Was in love with the heathen girl to his nation's harm.
To the king the girl was just as dear as his own life was;
He asked Hengest his tenant to give him that girl-child.
Hengest found this a good idea, to do as the king urged him;
He gave him Rowena, a very lovely woman.
The king found it [agreeable]: he made her his queen,*
All according to the laws they had in heathen days;
There was no Christian rite where the king took that maid, 7180
No priest and no bishop nor was God's book taken in their hands,
But in the heathen ritual he wedded and he brought her to his
    bed.[11]

[11] Where Wace objects to Vortigern's sin in loving a pagan (W 6993),
Lawman is scandalized by the way he twice dispenses with ecclesiastical
authority: for Constans' coronation (6620) and his own wedding.

As a virgin he took her, and the morning-gift he bestowed on her;[12]
When he had disgraced himself with her, he gave her London and
    Kent.
   The king had three sons, who were very courteous men:
The eldest was called **Vortimer**, then **Passent** and **Katiger**.
Garengan was the earl who'd owned Kent a long time,
As had his father before him, and then he through his descent;
When he most expected to retain his land,
Then Hengest had got it in his own hands;   7190
Strange it seemed to the knight what the king intended.
The king loved the heathens, and punished the Christians;
The heathens had all this land to govern under their own hand,
And the three sons of the king often suffered sorrow and care.
Their mother was then dead, for which reason they had less
    guidance;
Their mother was a very good woman who led a very Christian
    life,
But their stepmother was heathen, the daughter of Hengest.
   It did not take long, just a short while,
Before the king gave a really huge banquet;[13]
He invited the heathens to it: he thought to act for the very
    best.   7200
To it came landholders, knights and landworkers,
But all who were literate avoided the banquet,
Because the heathen men had highest rank at the court,
And the Christian courtiers were accounted menials.
Then the heathens were happy because the king loved them so
    much.
Hengest thought carefully about his diplomacy:
He came to the king with a salutation,
And drank to the king.
Then like this spoke Hengest, the handsomest of all the knights
Who in those days were living under heathen laws: 7210

[12] The morning-gift in Germanic law was given by the husband to his new
bride after the consummation of the marriage, to provide her with means of
support in the form of land in the event of her widowhood. Lawman adds
London to this dower-gift.
[13] Lawman has either invented the opening of this feast or was using a more
complete manuscript of Wace than those surviving (see p. 10 above).

'Listen to me, my lord the king: you are my beloved above all
        things:[14]
You have my daughter, who is so dear to me,
And I am to you in people's eyes as if I were your father.
Listen to my instructions: they shall prove attractive to you,
For I wish supremely to assist you to decide.
Your court hate you because of me, and are hostile to me because
        of you,
And those who hate you are kings, earls and leaders:
They advance into your land as a very large invasion.
If you wish to get your own back, with increased dignity,
And do your opponents harm, then send for my son **Octa**,   7220
And for yet one other, **Ebissa** his sworn-brother:[15]
These are the boldest men who ever led an armed band,
And in the northern parts give them some of your lands.
They are magnificent in might and strong in every fight;
They will give defence to your land well among the best;
Then all your life you might wear away in full delight,
With hawks and with hounds enjoying courtly games;
You need never feel anxiety about foreign nations.'
    Then answered King Vortigern (of each evil he was wary):
'Send your messengers out into Saxony   7230
To fetch your son Octa and to fetch more of your friends.
Have him fully instructed to send out his missives
For all of the knights who are valiant in fight
Through all the Saxon nation, that they come to me in my great
        need,
And even if he brings a thousand, to me they are all welcome.'
This was heard by Hengest, of all knights the handsomest:
Then he was more blithe than ever in his life;
Hengest sent his messengers out into Saxony,
And ordered here Octa and his sworn-brother Ebissa,
And all of their relations whom they could obtain,   7240
And all of the knights whom they could acquire.

[14] Hengest is now handling Vortigern as the latter had handled Constance,
ironically presented more amusingly in Wace through similar phraseology (6595;
cf. 7051–2) than Lawman's attempt (6665; cf. 7230).
[15] The sworn or blood-brotherhood, common in romance and saga, was a far
closer relationship than that of siblings; Ebissa is a younger brother in *HRB*,
and a cousin in Wace's *Brut* (7042).

Octa sent messages all through three kingdoms,
Bidding each and every brave man to come to him in haste
If he wanted to get lands, or get silver or get gold.
They arrived at the court as hailstones come tumbling,
To be more specific: in three hundred ships.
They set off with Octa, thirty thousand and yet more,
Bold men and courageous; and Ebissa his companion
Came voyaging after with countless supporters,
And the ships he led, precisely, were a hundred and fifty.   7250
After these came sliding five, and then five,
In sixes, in sevens, in tens and in elevens,
And so they came slipping towards this our land,
Heathen war-lords to the court of the king,
Until this land was so full of the foreign people
That there was no man so wise nor so quick-witted
That he could distinguish between the heathens and the Christians,
For the heathen were so rife, and were so rapidly arriving.
    When the British realized that there was trouble in the land,
They were most distressed about it and gloomy in their
        hearts,   7260
And they went to the king, the noblest in this land,
And addressed him as follows, in sorrowful tones:
'Listen to us now, lord king, from our people's council:[16]
You because of us are the bold king in this Britain,
And you have brought upon yourself danger and much sinfulness,
Have brought in heathen people: it will still bring you harm!
And you abandon God's laws for these foreign people
And refuse to honour our Lord God for these heathen knights,
And we wish to request you for the sake of God's blessing
That you will relinquish them and drive them from your
        land.   7270
Or else, if you're not able to, we'll make a great confrontation,
And drive them from the land or fell them to the ground,
Or else we ourselves dead will lie there, slaughtered,
And let the heathen hordes have control of the kingdom,
Enjoy it in comfort, if they can conquer it.
And if they are all heathen, and you are a Christian,
It won't be for very long that they keep you as king,
Unless you in your days will adopt heathen ways,

[16] Lawman has, as usual, converted statement into a debate.

And abandon God Most High, and love their false idols.
Then you will be destroyed in the kingdom of this world   7280
And your wretched soul will sink down to Hell,
And you will have paid for the love of your bride.'
    Then responded Vortigern (of each evil he was aware):
'I will not relinquish them, by my living life!
For here has Hengest come: he is my father and I his son,
And I have as my beloved his daughter Rowena,
Whom I have wedded and taken to my bed,
And then I sent for Octa and for more of his companions;
So how could I, for shame, shun them so quickly,
Drive from the land my own friends so dear?'   7290
Then the British answered, bent down by sorrows:
'Never any more will we obey your instructions,
Nor come to your court here, nor regard you as king,
Rather, we will hate, with our utmost powers,
All your heathen friends, and with harm treat them.
We pray for our assistance from Christ who is God's son!'
    Off went the earls, off went the warriors,
Off went the bishops, and the book-learned clerics,
Off went the landholders, off went the landworkers,
All the people of Britain, till they came to London.   7300
There was many a noble Briton there at the hustings,
And the king's three sons; there all of them had come:
There was Vortimer, and Passent and Katiger
And very many others who came with the brothers,
And all people came there to the city who loved Christianity;
All the powerful people consulted together,
And took the king's eldest son (to the hustings he had come),
And with many songs of praise they raised him to the throne.
And so was Vortimer the Christian king there,   VORTIMER
And Vortigern his father followed the heathen;   7310
[It all came about as the decision had been made.]*   7310a
    Vortimer the young king had great courage above all things:
He sent word to Hengest and to Horsa his brother
That unless they would hastily travel from his kingdom
He would do them great evil: both blind them and hang them,
And his own father he wished to destroy,
And all the heathen race with most heavy force.
To which replied Hengest, of all knights the handsomest,
'Here we intend to remain, both winter and summer,

To ride and to run alongside King Vortigern,
And all those who side with Vortimer, they shall receive much
    sorrow and care!'
This was heard by Vortimer (he was wise and really aware)   7321
And summoned all his forces throughout all this nation,
Saying all the Christian folk were to come to court.
   Vortimer the young king in London held his hustings:
The king instructed each man who loved the Christian faith
That they must have hatred for the heathen race,
Whose heads they must bring to Vortimer the king,
Twelve pennies to receive as reward for [their] good deed.*
Vortimer the young advanced out of London,
And Passent his brother and Katiger the other;   7330
To them had come word that Hengest was at Epiford,*
Upon that river which people call Derwent.[17]
   There assembled together sixty thousand soldiers,
On one side was Vortimer, Passent and Katiger,
And all people living here who bore love for Our Lord;
On the other side were warriors with Vortigern the king:
Hengest and his brother and many thousand others.
Together they clashed and with force they attacked;
There fell to the ground thirty-two hundred
Of Hengest's men, and Horsa was badly wounded: 7340
Katiger had come there and with his spear had run him through,
And Horsa instantly there badly wounded Katiger,
And Hengest began to flee with all his soldiery,
And Vortigern the king fled off like the wind;
They fled onwards into Kent, and after them went Vortimer;
Upon the sea's edge, there Hengest suffered anguish:
There they made a stand, and fought for very long;
Five thousand there were slain and deprived of their life's days
On Vortigern's side, from the heathen tribes.
   Hengest thought carefully what might be his remedy: 7350
He saw on the side there a very splendid harbour:
Many a good ship there floated on the sea-flood.
They spotted on their right hand a very pretty island:
This is called Thanet: to get to it they moved smartly;
There those Saxon men took to the sea

[17] Lawman conflates two battles, Derwent and Epiford; Epiford (Eoppa's Ford) is recorded as the battle of Aylesford (755) in the Anglo-Saxon Chronicle.

And instantly started going out to the island,
And the British after them with many kinds of craft,
And driving across to them from every direction
With ships and with boats. They started striking and shooting.
Often had Hengest been sad and never till then were things so
     bad: 7360
Unless he took another course, he was going to get killed.
He took a spear shaft which was long and very strong,
And fixed on the tip a finely-made mantle,
And called to the Britons and asked them to wait:
With them he wanted speech and craved the king's peace,
And in peace to send Vortigern to land,
To make agreement with him that he must get away,
To prevent further shame done to the Saxons' land.
    The British went ashore, to Vortimer their king,
And Hengest spoke to Vortigern of very secret matters.   7370
Vortigern went up on land carrying a rod in his hand;
While they were discussing peace, the Saxons leaped aboard,
And dragged high their sails right up to the top,
Travelling with the weather upon the wild sea,
And leaving in this land their wives and their children,
And Vortigern the king, who loved them above all things.
With much grief of heart did Hengest turn to depart:
So long they journeyed until in Saxony they arrived.
    Then within Britain were the British very bold:
They took upon themselves great spirit and did everything they felt
     was needed,
And Vortimer the young was a valiant man above all things,* 7381
And Vortigern his father went faring all through Britain,
But there was no man so feeble who did not pour scorn on him,
And so he went wandering for fully five winters,
And his son Vortimer, great king, was dwelling here,
And all the native people loved him very greatly:
He was gentle with every child and taught the folk God's law,
Taught the old and the young how they must keep their Christian
    faith.
Letters he had sent to Rome to the glorious Pope,
Who was called Saint **Romanus**; all Christendom he made
    rejoice.   7390
He selected two bishops, holy men were they both:

Germanus and **Lupus**, of Auxerre and of Troyes;[18] *Saint Germanus*
They travelled away from Rome until they hither came.
Then more blithe was Vortimer than he had ever yet been here.
He and all his knights made their way direct,
Walking barefoot, going to meet the bishops,
And with great happiness lips there did kiss.
   Now you can hear about King Vortimer,
How he spoke to Saint Germanus of how their coming made him
    glad:
'Listen to me, my lords, your graces: I am king of all this
    race;   7400
My name is Vortimer, this is my brother Katiger;[19]
Vortigern was our father's name: evil doctrines make him foul.
He has brought into this land heathen people,
But we have driven them in exile as our sworn enemies,
And with weapons struck down many thousands of them,
And sent them over the sea-streams so they never succeed in
    coming back,
And in the land we shall love God our Lord,
God's people we shall comfort, and in friendship keep them,
And also be supportive to those who till the land;
Churches we shall erect and heathendom reject.   7410
Let each good man have his rights if these God will grant,
And each slave and each foreign captive will be set free;
And here I donate into your hand quite freely all church land,
And I donate to every widow her lord's legacy,
[And each man will love the other as if they were brothers],* 7414a
And so we shall in our own days bring down low Hengest's laws,
And himself and his heathendom which he has brought here,
[Who] deceived my father with his treacherous wiles:*
Through his daughter Rowena he miscounselled my father,
And my father proceeded most wickedly by renouncing his
    Christendom:
The heathen religion he loved far too much;   7420

[18] Bede says Germanus came twice, in AD 429 and *c*. AD 435–44, while
Hengest and Horsa did not come until 449; but Lawman follows Wace in
moving Germanus' visit from Vortigern's marriage (as in *HRB*) to Vortimer's
insurrection; Wace may have been misled by Bede's arrangement of chapters:
Hengist in I, 15 and Germanus in I, 17.

[19] Katiger is already dead in Wace. Lawman has supplied Vortimer's speech,
and his religious and legal reforms.

These we shall avoid as long as we live.'
     Then replied St Germanus (at such words he rejoiced):
'I give thanks to my lord who created the day's light
That he sends such mercy down to mankind.'
     The bishops travelled round this land and placed it all within
          God's hand,
And Christianity they established and to it folk directed,
And then after this, quite soon, they went off back to Rome,
Informing the Pope there, who was called Romanus,
How they had been acting here, establishing Christianity.
And so for a time things remained the same.   7430
     Let us pick up again at Vortigern (of all kings may he be most
          wretched!);[20]
He loved Rowena of the heathen race,
Daughter of Hengest: she seemed to him so soft.
Rowena thought carefully what should be her policy,
How she could avenge her father and the deaths of her friends.
She kept on sending messages to Vortimer the king;
She sent to him precious things of many different kinds,
Of silver and of gold; the best of any land;
She begged for his mercy that she might go on living here,
With his father, Vortigern, and follow his instructions.   7440
The king at his father's plea granted what she pleaded,
Save that she must behave well and embrace Christianity;
Everything the king requested, all she conceded,
But alas that Vortimer of her intent was not aware!
Alas that the good king of her intent knew nothing!
That he did not know the treachery plotted by the evil woman.
     It happened at one time that she adopted a plan
[That she would travel to meet King Vortimer;   7447a
To act on his advice] in all her needs,*
And to ask what time she could act well by receiving Christianity.
She set off riding, to Vortimer the king;   7450
When she had met him, courteously she greeted him:
'Good health to you, my lord the king, the Britons' own darling!

[20] Acting perhaps on a hint from Geoffrey of Monmouth's *Vita Merlini*
(where Renua, Hengest's *sister*, gives Vortimer poison), Lawman develops a
scene where a woman acts out a prominent role. Rowena is the wicked
stepmother of folk-tale: she poisons her stepson by carrying venom instead of
milk in her breast.

I have come here to you: I wish to take the Christian faith,
On whichever day that you yourself decide.'
  Then Vortimer the king was happy above all things:
He thought it was truth that the she-devil spoke.
Brass trumpets were blowing; there was bliss in the court.
They brought out the water before the king's presence;
They set up the trestles in greatest delight.
When the king had eaten, then the lords' servitors took food: 7460
In the hall they were drinking, harps were resounding.
The deceitful Rowena went over to a wine-tun;
There was stored inside it the king's most precious wine.
She took in her hand a goblet of red gold,
And she began to pour the drinks at the king's high table.
When she saw her time, she filled her cup with wine,
And in the presence of all the company she went up to the king,
And like this the deceitful woman gave him salutation:
'Lord, king, wassail; I am celebrating with you!'
  Now listen how much treachery came from that wicked
    woman,   7470
How she set about it there, her betrayal of King Vortimer.
The king cheerfully received her for what was to be his doom;
Vortimer spoke British, Rowena spoke in Saxon;
The king found it most amusing: her speech set him laughing.
Hear now how she was going on, [this] deceitful woman:*
In her bosom she carried, underneath her breasts,
A flask all of gold, filled up with poison,
And the wicked Rowena drank deep in the bowl
Until it was half drained, on the king's direction;
While the king was laughing, she slipped out the flask,   7480
Set the bowl up to her chin and tipped the poison in the wine,
And then handed the cup over to the king.
The king drank up all the wine and the poison in it.
  The day went past; all the court was rejoicing,
For Vortimer the good king of the treachery knew nothing,
Since he saw there Rowena holding the bowl
And drinking half of the same wine which she had poured into it.
When it came to night time then came the parting of the court
    knights,
And the evil Rowena went to her apartment,
And all her own knights accompanied her straight.   7490
Then she ordered her servants and also the attendants

That they should speedily get their horses saddled,
And they should most silently steal out of the township
And travel right through the night to Thongchester directly,
And there most securely enclose themselves in a castle,
And lie to Vortigern that his son was going to besiege him;
And Vortigern the traitorous king believed in the lying.
  Now Vortimer his son realised he'd taken poison;
Nor could any medicine give him any relief at all.
He took many messengers and sent them round his country,   7500
And ordered all his knights to come over to him straightaway.
By the time the folk came the king was gravely stricken.
Then the king begged their favour and like this addressed them all:
'Of all knights may things be best for those of you who serve a
      king:
There is now no other course except my imminent decease.
Here I bequeath you my land, all my silver and all my gold,
And my entire treasury: your reputation's thus enhanced;
And do you directly send out for knights,
And give them silver and gold and yourselves hold all your land,
And avenge yourselves if you can on every Saxon man,   7510
For as soon as I have departed, Hengest will make great trouble for
      you.
So take up my corpse and lay it in a chest,
And convey me to the sea-shore where Saxon men will come to
      land.
As soon as they know that I am there they will go away again;
Neither dead nor alive do they dare to await me!'
In the middle of this discourse the good king collapsed and died.
There was weeping, there was wailing and gestures of grief.
They took the king's corpse and carried it to London
And beside Billingsgate with ceremony buried him,[21]
And in no way did they carry him to where the king had
      ordered.   7520
So lived Vortimer, and so he died there.
  Then the Britons declined into a disastrous plan:
They at once took Vortigern and proferred him this
      kingdom.   VORTIGERN
Really pitiful there was everything now that Vortigern was again
      king.

[21] Lawman invents Billingsgate as Vortimer's burial-place.

Vortigern took his messenger and sent message to the Saxons,
Saluting well Hengest, of all knights the fairest,
Telling him speedily to come to this land,
And with him he should bring here a full hundred riders,
'For know this above all things, of the death of Vortimer the king,
And in safety here you may come, for dead is Vortimer my
    son.   7530
There is no need for you to bring a large troop along
In case our Britons get angry again
So that once more sorrows slip in between you.'
   Hengest summoned a force from many different places,
Until he had, to be specific, seven hundred ships,
And each ship he supplied with three hundred knights.
In the Thames at London Hengest came to land.
The news came very quickly to Vortigern the king
That Hengest was in harbour with seven hundred ships;
Often Vortigern had been sad, but not till then were things so bad,
And the British were saddened and gloomy in spirit;   7541
They did not know where in the world was a remedy to suit them.
Hengest of evil was well aware (and that he well showed there):
At once he took his messengers and sent them to the king,
And greeted King Vortigern with very courteous words,
And said that he had come, as a father should to his son,
In harmony and concord he'd like to live contented;
Peace he would love, injustice he would avoid;
Peace he would have, peace he would hold to,
And all the people of this land he would surely love,   7550
And Vortigern the king he would love above everything.
But he had brought into this land, from the Saxon people,
Seven hundred ships with heathen folk,
Who are the bravest of all men who live beneath the sun:
'And I wish', said Hengest, 'to conduct them to the king,
On an appointed day, in the presence of his courtiers,
And the king is to arise, and from those knights select
Two hundred knights to conduct to his fights,
Who shall protect the king honourably above all things,
And then are the others to return to their country,   7560
Peacefully and happily going back to Saxon lands,
And I will remain with the best of all men,
Namely Vortigern the king, whom I love above all things.'
The word came to the Britons of what Hengest had promised them:

Then they were delighted because of his fine words,
And arranged the peace and arranged the truce for a specific time
When the king on a certain day wished to review his troops.
    This was heard by Hengest, of all knights the handsomest;
Then was he more blithe than he'd been ever in his life
As he intended to betray the king and his realm.   7570
Here Hengest became the most depraved of knights,
As is every man who betrays the one who freely pays him.
Who would expect, in all this world's extent,
That Hengest thought to trick the king who had taken his
    daughter?
Yet there was never any man who could not be overcome by
    treason.
    They took an appointed day when all the troops must come
Together in truce, and in friendship too,
On a lovely meadow which lay beside Amesbury.
Then the place was Ealing, now it's known as **Stonehenge**.
There Hengest the traitor both in word and in writing   7580
Let the king know that he was coming,
With his body-guard, in the king's honour,
But he would not bring in his force more than three hundred
    knights,
The very wisest men whom he could find,
And the king should bring just as many of his brave supporters,
Who should be the very wisest of all who lived in Britain,
In their best clothing, quite without weapons,
So that they should not come to grief through trusting in the
    weapons.
Like this they proposed it, and then again they broke it,
For Hengest the traitor, like this he taught his men: 7590
That each should take a long knife and lay it beside his leg,
Inside his hose, where [he could hide] it.*
    When they came together, Saxons and British,
Then said Hengest, of all knights the most deceitful:
'Health to you, my lord king, each to you is your   *The British*
    subject,[22]   *Massacre*
If any of your men at all has any war-gear round here,

---

[22] Lawman's contributions to this famous episode are the speeches of Hengest
and Vortigern, the peasant with his club (7610) and the impression of a vast,
apparently happy, crowd.

Let him send it in amity far away from us,
And let us be joyful and treat now of truce,
Now we may in peacefulness live out our lives.'
So the malicious man there deceived the British.*   7600
Then answered Vortigern (this time he was too unaware!)
'If any knight here is so mad as to have weapons at his side,
He must forfeit his hand through his own blade,
Unless at once he sends it far away from here.'
They sent their weapons right away; then they had nothing in their
        hands.
    Knights were walking up the field, knights were walking down
        the field,
Each chatting to the other as if he were his brother.
When the British were mingling with the Saxons,
Then shouted Hengest, of all knights the most deceitful:
'Take up your saxes, my lucky warriors,   7610
And busily bestir yourselves, don't spare any one of them!'
    The British there were noble but they did not know the speech at
        all,
Or what the Saxon men were saying among themselves.
They drew out the saxes in every direction:
They struck on the right side, they struck on the left side,
In front and behind they laid them to the ground;
Everyone they slew whom they came near to;
Of the king's men [instantly] there fell*
Four hundred and five; the king's very life was grief.
Then Hengest seized him in his grim clutches,   7620
And by his mantle dragged him until the strings broke,
And the Saxons set upon him, wanting to kill the king,
And Hengest was defending him, and would not permit it,
But he held on to him very fast all the time the fight lasted.
    There many a fine Briton was deprived of his life:
Some fled hurriedly across the broad field,
And defended themselves with stones, for weapons had they none.
There was a very hard fight: there fell many a good knight.
    There had come from Salisbury a bold peasant fellow;
A huge powerful club he carried on his back.   7630
Then there was a valiant earl who was called **Aldolf**
A knight of the best: he was lord of Gloucester;
He went leaping to the peasant just like a lion,
And snatched away his club which he carried on his back;

Every single one he struck upon the instant died;
In front and behind he laid them to the ground,
Fifty-three there he slew and then towards [his steed] drew off;*
He leaped up on horseback and rode off in a hurry;
He galloped to Gloucester, and locked the gates most securely,
And immediately straight after had his knights get themselves
        armed,   7640
And all over the land they were to take what they found:
They took cattle, they took corn, and everything they found alive,
And brought them to the borough with the greatest pleasure.
The gates they barred firmly and guarded them well.
    Let us leave things standing like that and let's speak of the king:
Saxons leaped towards him and wanted to destroy the king.
Hengest called out straight, 'Stop now, my knights!
You are not to harm him: he's had much trouble on our account,
And he has as his queen my daughter who's so lovely;
But all his fortified places he is to donate us   7650
If he wishes to enjoy his life, or otherwise he's doomed to misery.'
    Then Vortigern was firmly tied up,
Most massive fetters they attached to his feet;
He was not allowed to touch food, nor to speak to any friend,
Before he had sworn to them, upon a relic specially chosen,
That all of his kingly land he would deliver into their hands,
Boroughs and castles and all his [pavilions];*
And he did all of it, as it was determined.
And Hengest took into his hands all this glorious kingdom,
And dealt out to his people a great part of this land.   7660
He gave to an earl all Kent where near London it extends;
He gave his steward Essex,
And to his butler he gave Middlesex there.
The knights received all this and for a while they kept it.
    Meanwhile Vortigern travelled all round this land,
Delivering to Hengest his splendid boroughs,
And Hengest forthwith placed in them his knights.
All this time many lesser folk were located in South-sex,
And in Middlesex very many of the race,
And in East-sex their highest-born youth;   7670
Food they would fetch, everything they found;
They violated women and by them God's laws were broken.
They did in the land just what they wanted.
    The British could see there was disaster in the land,

And how the Saxon men had slipped in beside them.
The Britons devised a name for the land because of the Saxon
    men's disgrace,
And for the treachery which they had performed:
Because it was with knives that they had deprived them of life,[23]
They called all that area East-'sax' and West-'sax',
And the third one Middle-'sax'.   7680
Vortigern the king had given to them all this land,
Till he had left in his hand not a single turf of land,
And he himself, Vortigern, fled across the Severn,
Deep into Welsh country, and there did he remain,
And his troop with him, which had become depleted,
And yet he had in hoard a very great treasure.
He got his men to ride very far and wide,
And made them summon to him some of every kind of man,
Whoever was willing to seek his property from patronage.
    This the Britons heard; this the Scotsmen heard: 7690
To him then they came after that very soon,
From every direction, that way they came riding,
Many a nobleman's son, keen for gold and great treasure.
When he had together sixty thousand men,
Then he assembled the great who well knew how to judge:
'Good men, instruct me by your advice, for I am in very great
    need,
Where in the wilderness I might build a castle
Where I might live inside safe with my men,
And hold it against Hengest with powerful strength,
Until I might the better reconquer boroughs,   7700
Avenge me on my enemies who have felled my friends,
And all who my kingdom's land have snatched out of my hand,
And so have exiled me, being fully my foes.'
    Then responded a wise man who well knew good advice:
'Listen to me now, lord king, I'll show you a good thing:
On the mountain of Reir, as I would advise,
Do you raise up the castle with strongest stone walls,
For there you could dwell and live with delight.
And still you have in your hands much silver and gold
To maintain your attendants who must give you aid: 7710

[23] Perhaps Lawman did not understand Wace's rather obscure comment on
French words for 'knife'.

And so you in your lifetime might live the very best life.'
Then answered the king: 'Have it announced in all haste,
Throughout my great retinue that I intend to go
To the mountain of Reir, there to raise a castle.'
Off marched the king and the army with him;
When they came there they began a ditch at once:
Horns there were blowing, machines there were hacking,
Lime they started burning, through the terrain running,
And all West Wales land they set in Vortigern's hand;
They took everything which they came close to.   7720
When the ditch was dug and completely deepened
They began the wall, on the ditch all way round,
And lime and stone they laid together;
Of amazing machines there were twenty five hundred.
  By day they laid the wall; by night the whole thing fell;
In the morning they repaired it; at night it fell in ruins.
For one whole week in this way [the work] busied them:*
Each day they repaired it; and each night it fell in ruins.
    This upset the king: he was gloomy above all things,
Also all the army was hideously afraid,   7730
For all the time they were watching for when Hengest would come
        on them.
The king was most anxious and sent for advisers,
For worldly-wise men who knew of wisdom,
And asked them to cast lots, and try incantations,
To find out the truth with their divinations,
What it could derive from, that the wall which was so firm
Could never stay upright for the whole of a night.
These worldly-wise men divided in two groups:
Some of them went to the woodland, some of them to the cross-
        ways;
They proceeded to cast lots with their divinations;   7740
For three whole nights their spells they recited:
They could not any way discover by any means whatever
What it could derive from, that the wall which was so firm
Every night fell to rubble and the king lost his labour.
But there was just one wise-man and he was called **Joram**;
He said that he had discovered (but it sounded like fiction)
He said if any one found in whatever land,
Any little boy who had never had a father,
And opened his breast and took some of his blood,

And mixed it with the lime, and laid the wall with that,   7750
Then would it stand for all the world long.
   The message reached the king about all that lying,
And he believed it, although it was lies.
At once he took his messengers and sent them throughout that
     land:
Each as far on any roadway as he for fear of death dared go,
Who in every township must listen to the gossip,
Of where they might discover some mention of such a child.
   These knights travelled off far and wide round the land;
Two of them walked on a way which due westwards lay,
Which led directly in to what now is Caermarthen.   7760
Right outside the borough, on the broad roadway,
All the boys of the town were playing a great game;
These knights were very tired and were feeling most despondent,
And sat down beside the play, and were watching these boys.
After a little while they started quarrelling,
Which has always been the rule where there are children playing!
One of them punched the other and the [blows] landed on him;*
Then towards **Merlin** Dinabus got really cross,   *Merlin*
And **Dinabus** who was punched started shouting this:
'Merlin, accursed man, why have you done this to me?   7770
You've treated me most disgracefully and for that you are going to
     pay.
I am actually a king's son, and you come from just nothing.
You ought not in any place to have a freeman's house,
Seeing that was all the story, that your mother was a whore
And she didn't even know the guy who got her pregnant with you;
Nor did you among human beings ever have a father!
And here in our district you bring us to disgrace.
Among us you've sprung up, and you're not any man's son.
And for all that this very day you are going to die!'
   There on the sidelines those knights were listening;   7780
They stood up and walked closer and felt compelled to [listen]*
To this mysterious story which they were hearing from the boy.
There was in Caermarthen a provost known as **Eli**;
The knights at great speed came to the provost,
And addressed him like this, with most ready lips:
'Here we've just arrived, Vortigern's knights,
And here we have discovered a certain young lad
Who is called Merlin; we have no idea of his family.

Get hold of him quickly and send him to the king
– If you want to stay alive and keep all your limbs! –   7790
And his mother with him, who gave birth to this male child;
If you will do this the king will receive them,
And if you pay no attention, you'll be exiled for it,
And this town will be burned down and the people all
          condemned.'
    To which responded Eli, the provost of Caermarthen:
'I am well aware that all this land stands within Vortigern's hand,
And we are all his men: the greater is his honour,
And we shall do this gladly and perform his wish.'
    Off went the provost with townsmen in company,
And discovered Merlin and his play-fellows with him.   7800
Merlin they arrested and his companions laughed;
When Merlin was led off Dinabus was exultant,
Thinking he was being led off to have his limbs removed,
But quite another fate awaited before it was all finished.
Now Merlin's mother had been strangely beautiful;
In a noble monastery she was a nun professed.
To the place went Eli, the provost of Caermarthen,
And took with him the lady from where she was enclosed
And off he went, running, to King Vortigern,
And a crowd of folk with him, leading the nun and Merlin.   7810
    At once it was announced to King Vortigern's face
That there had come Eli, bringing with him the lady,
And Merlin her son with her there had come.
Then by his life was Vortigern blithe,
And received the lady with many gracious glances,
While Merlin he entrusted to twelve loyal knights,
Who were true to the king and whose role was to guard him.
    Then asked King Vortigern as with the nun he conversed there:
'My good lady, tell me (good fortune shall be yours)
Where were you born? What kind of parents did you have?'   7820
Then the nun responded and her father she named:
'A third part of all this land lay in my father's hand;
Of the land he was king, famed this was far and wide;
He was called **Conan**, lord of many knights.'
Then the king replied, as if she were his close relation:
'Lady, do you tell me (good fortune shall be yours):
Here is Merlin, your son: who begot him on you?
Who among the folk was regarded as his father?'

Then she hung her head, bent it down to her breast;
She sat very quiet beside the king, and for a little while she mused.

    After a time she spoke, and communed with the king: 7831
'King, I shall tell you, a most amazing story:[24]
My father, Conan the king, loved me above everything.
In those days I had a marvellously lovely figure.
When I had advanced to fifteen years old,
I was living in the private rooms, in my own apartment,
My girl attendants with me, all really lovely.
When on my bed I was asleep in my soft slumbers,
Then came before me the loveliest thing that ever was born,
As if it were a huge knight, all in gold clothing.   7840
This I would see in a dream; each night in my sleep
This thing would glide before me and would glisten with gold;
Often it kissed me, often it cuddled me,
Often it approached and came very close to me.

    'In the end when I faced myself this seemed to me most odd:
I couldn't bear my food, couldn't recognise my body;
It seemed to me most odd what it could all mean.
Then in the end I realized I was going to have a baby.
When my time came, this boy here I had.
I don't know in the world what his father was,   7850
Nor who engendered him in this world's kingdom,
Nor whether it was a monster, or on God's behalf appointed.
Look, as I pray for mercy I don't know any more
To tell you about my son, how he has come into this world.'
The nun bowed down her head and arranged her [veil].*

    The king thought carefully what might be his policy,
And called good counsellors to him for counsel,
And they advised him with the best advice
That he should send for **Magan**, who was an unusual man:
He was a learned scholar and was skilled in many crafts,   7860
He knew how to advise well, he knew how to lead far,
He knew of the art which rules in the heavens,
He knew how to recite every kind of incantation.
Magan came to the court where the king resided
And greeted the king with most gracious words:

---

[24] Typical of his greater interest in female concerns, it is Lawman who
constructs a home background for Merlin's mother, with father and attendants,
and dramatizes her youth (7835) and innocence (7846 ff.).

'May you be healthy and fit, Vortigern the king!
I have come to you: show me what your wish is.'
Then the king replied, revealing all to the scholar
Of how the nun had spoken, and asked him there for advice;
From beginning to end, everything he told him.   7870
Then Magan announced: 'I know all about this.
There live in the heavens many kinds of beings
Which are to remain there until Doomsday comes on us.
Some of them are admirable and some of them do evil.
Among them is a very large type which comes down among
        humans;
These are termed, to be precise, *incubi demones*;
They don't commit much wrong, but they make fun of people;
Many a man in dreams often they harass,
And many a pretty woman by their art at once gets pregnant,
And many a good man's child by their magic they beguile.   7880
That's how Merlin was begotten and born of his mother,
And that's how it all goes on', said the scholar, Magan.
    Then Merlin spoke to the king in person:
'King, your men have captured me and I have come to you,
And I want to know what you intend,
And for what reason I've been brought to the king.'
Then the king explained, speaking very clearly,
'Merlin, you have come to this place; you are not any man's son;
You are requesting what you'll find repugnant:
You want to know what's going on: now you shall hear it!   7890
    'I have begun a fort with tremendous efforts
Which have very much consumed all of my great treasure;
Five thousand men are at work on it.
I have lime and stone, in the country there's none better,
Nor in our land are there any workmen as good.
All that they lay in a day, and it's the truth I can say,
Before morning the next day, all of it's down,
Each stone away from the next, thrown down flat on the ground.
Now my wise men and my wizards are all of them saying
That if I take your blood out of your breast,   7900
For making my wall, and mix it in with my lime,
Then it will stand all the world long.
Now you know everything that's going to happen to you.'
    All this Merlin heard, and was furious in mood,
And spoke these words in spite of his wrath:

'The very God himself, who is leader of good men
Would not have your castle stand because of my heart's blood,
Nor your stone wall standing firm and still.
For all your wise men are outright deceivers:
They pronounce lies in front of you yourself;   7910
This you'll discover in this same day's duration.
Now Joram has said this (he is openly my enemy);
The information makes me laugh: I was born to be his destroyer.
Get Joram your wise man to come into your presence,
And all his confederates, right here and now,
Who announced all that lying in front of the king.
And if I shall tell you in my own true words
All about your wall and why it keeps on falling,
And so declare truthfully that their tales must be lies,
Then give me their heads, if I improve your works!'   7920
    Then the king announced, speaking very clearly,
'As my hand may help me, I'll have this agreement with you!'
To the king was brought Joram the wise one
And seven of his confederates (all were doomed to die).
Merlin grew angry and spoke very grimly:
'Say to me now, you traitor, Joram, loathsome in my sight,
Why this wall keeps falling down to ground-level;*
Say to me why it falls out that the wall tumbles.
What can be found in the base of the moat?'
Joram was silent: he could not explain it.   7930
Then Merlin spoke these words: 'King, keep your promise!
Have this ditch dug out seven feet deeper.
They will uncover there a stone, amazingly lovely,
It is massive and pretty for people to look at.'
    The ditch was dug out seven feet deeper
And at once they found, right away, the stone.
Then Merlin spoke these words: 'King, keep your promise!
Say to me now, Joram, most hateful of men to me,
And announce to this king what kind of things
Have taken up their station underneath this stone here.'   7940
Joram was silent; he could not explain it.
    Then Merlin made a strange remark: 'There is a pool under here;
Take away this stone and you'll find the pool at once.'
They took away the stone in the king's presence at once,
And they found the pool there. Then Merlin spoke:
'Ask Joram for me (he is openly my enemy),

After a certain space to tell you of the abyss:
What inhabits that pool there, in winter and summer?'
The king enquired of Joram, but he knew nothing about it.
   Then once more Merlin spoke the words: 'King, keep your
     promise!   7950
Have this water drawn off, and drain it away;
There are living in its depths two powerful dragons:
One is on the north side, the other on the south side;
One of them is milk-white, unlike any other being,
The other one is red as blood, the boldest of serpents.
In the middle of each night they begin to fight,
[And because of their fighting] your building works fell:*
The earth started to tremble and your wall to totter;
Through marvels like these your wall has collapsed;
It occurred in this flood and not because of my blood!'   7960
   This water was all drawn off; the king's men were relieved;
Great was the rejoicing in the presence of the king –
Yet straightaway afterwards they were saddened again:
Before the day came to an end they heard the tidings.
When the water was all drawn off, and the pit was empty,
Then these two dragons came out, and made a terrific din,
Fighting ferociously down in the ditch;
Never was seen by any knight a more loathsome fight:
There flew from their mouths fiery flames.
The monarch surveyed their monstrous appearance;[25]   7970
Then he was wondering what in this very world
This could be the sign of, as he looked there in the depths,
And how Merlin knew of it when no other man could know.
First the white one was on top and then it was underneath,
And the red dragon had wounded it to death,
And each one went to its hole, and no man born saw them ever
    after.
So proceeded this thing which King Vortigern was watching,
And all those who were with him much admired Merlin,

---

[25] At this point there follow in *HRB* the Prophecies of Merlin (originally a separate work). Lawman, like Wace, omits these, but clearly knows them from some other source since he refers to them five times (9411-20, 11492-517, 13530 ff.; 14200-2, 14288-97). The authority invested in the prophetic child Merlin is reinserted in Lawman's presentation as a witty role-reversal where the bastard child rebukes his monarch for asking the wrong question (7996).

While the king hated Joram, and had his head removed,
And those of his seven friends who were there with him.   7980
   To his tent went the king, and with him he led Merlin,
And said to him with much love: 'Merlin, you are welcome!
And I shall give to you everything which you desire
Here from these my lands, of silver and of gold.'
(He thought that through Merlin all that land he would win,
But things went quite otherwise before the day's end came.)
   This question asked the king of his dear friend Merlin:
'Say to me now, Merlin, most beloved of all my men,
What do the dragons signify which were making all that din?
And the stone and the pool and that terrifying fight?   7990
Tell me if you please, what all this signifies;
And afterwards you must advise me how I must conduct myself,
And how I may regain the kingdom that is mine
From Hengest, my wife's father, who has most gravely harmed
      me.'
Then Merlin replied to the king who addressed him:
'King, you are unwise, and your plans are silly!
You enquire about the dragons which were making all the din,
And what their fight signifies and their ferocious attacks.
They signify kings who are still to come,
And their fights and their behaviour and their doomed folk.   8000
But if you were as wise a man and as clever in thinking
As to have asked me about your many troubles,
Of your own great anxiety which is coming upon you,
Then I would tell you about your own troubles.'
   Then said Vortigern the king: 'Dearest friend, Merlin,
Tell me about the things which are destined to come to me.'
'Gladly', replied Merlin in very bold tones,
'I will inform you, but you will always regret it!
King, see to yourself! Trouble is to be your lot
From Constantine's family: his child you got murdered.   8010
Constance you had killed, who was king in this land:
You arranged for your Picts to betray him horribly,
And for that you will suffer the greatest of disasters.
Since you drew upon you the alien people,
The Saxons to this land, you shall therefore be disgraced.
   'Now out of Brittany the barons have arrived,
That is, Aurelius and Uther, and now you are aware of this.
They are coming tomorrow, certain it is, into this land at Totnes,

I inform you specifically, with seven hundred ships;
Even now on the sea they are sailing swiftly!   8020
You have done great evil to them and now you must take
     harshness from them;
On both sides you're faced by those who plot your downfall:
Your opponents ahead of you and your enemies in your rear!
But fly, fly, on your way, and protect your life!
Yet fly wherever you may fly, after you they'll quickly hie:
Ambrosius Aurelius will first of all have this kingdom;
But through a drink of deadly poison he shall suffer death;
And then shall Uther Pendragon inherit this kingdom;
But your own descendants will with venom destroy him,
Yet before enduring death he will make an outcry.   8030
Uther shall have the one son: out of Cornwall he shall come.
That will be a wild boar bearing bristles of steel;
The boar will burn down the loftiest boroughs;
All of the traitors he will demolish by sheer terror;
All your powerful descendants with torments he'll destroy.
He shall be a very valiant man and of noble virtue.
From here as far as Rome this same man will rule.
He shall fell to the ground all of his foes.
I have spoken true things to you, but no softer do they strike you;
But flee with all your forces: your foes are coming to you at your
     court.'*
     Then ceased the speech of Merlin the sage,   8041
And the king had men blow thirteen brass trumpets,
And went off with his forces furiously fast.
After this things went apace but a single night's space
Before the brothers came, both of them together,
To the sea shore, true it was, at Dartmouth near Totnes.
The news came to the British, who were truly glad at this.
They rushed out of the woodlands, and from the wilderness,
Here sixty and there sixty, and there seven hundred,
Here thirty and there thirty and there many thousand.   8050
When they all assembled very good did it seem to them.
     The brothers to this country brought a countless army,
And before them came all these bravest Britons,
An uncountable force which [covered] all the plain,*
Those who once were dispersed, desperate in the woodlands
Because of the great terror and because of the great trouble,

And because of the great misery which Hengest had made for
    them,
After he had murdered all their chieftains with those long knives
And with sword blades had sliced through the sturdy landholders.
The Britons set up their hustings; with great common sense,   8060
They settled on Aurelius (the elder brother) at once   AURELIUS
In the highest hustings, where they raised him up as   AMBROSIUS
    king.
Then were the British all filled with happiness,
Happy at heart were those who had been grieving.
Then this information came to King Vortigern,
That Aurelius was chosen and raised to the throne.
   Then Vortigern was wretched (and later even worse);
Vortigern went off, far away to a castle:
Ganarew it was called, high on a hilltop;
Cloard was the hill's name and Hergin the district's,   8070
Right beside the Wye, which is a lovely river.
Vortigern's men captured all that they came close to:
They seized weapons and provisions of many different types,
To the castle they carried as much as they cared to,
Until they had enough (though it helped but little).
   Aurelius and Uther were aware of Vortigern,
Where he was, up on Cloard, enclosed in the castle.
They had brass trumpets blown, to bring together their army,
An uncountable host from many different countries.
They marched upon Ganarew where Vortigern lay: 8080
There was a king outside; there was a king inside!
Knights there were fighting with furious onslaughts;
Every single good man got himself ready.
When they could see that they had not yet conquered
Then off to the woodlands went a wonderfully big force:
They felled the wood right down and dragged it to the castle
And filled in all the ditch, which was wonderfully deep.
With fire they ignited everywhere inside
And called out to Vortigern: 'Now you'll be nice and warm in
    there!
That's for killing Constance who was king here in this land,   8090
And then Constantine, his son; now Aurelius has come,[26]

---

[26] Lawman, or the Caligula scribe, has transposed father (Constantine) and
son (Constance).

And Uther, his brother, who will bring you to destruction!'
The wind wafted the fire so that wonderfully it burned:
The castle started burning, the chambers were consumed;
The halls all fell in, fast collapsing to earth.
Not a single knight there could get control of the fire;
The fire spread right through it all and burned house and burned
        wall,
And also King Vortigern, inside he began to burn,   *Vortigern's*
And it consumed everything alive that was there inside.   *Death*
And so in great anguish Vortigern was finished.   8100
    Then in Aurelius's hand stood the whole of the land.
There was an honourable earl, Aldolf he was called;
He came from Gloucester, the cleverest of knights.
For all the land Aurelius made him his justiciar.
Aurelius by then and Uther his brother
Had felled all their foes and because of it were happier.
This was heard by Hengest, of all knights the strongest,
And then he was terrified, tremendously greatly.
He hustled his hosts and hastened to Scotland,
And Aurelius the king marched after him hurrying.   8110
Now Hengest thought he would flee, with all his host of men,
Should he be attacked, off into Scotland,
So that with ingenuity he could escape from there,
In case he could not make a stand against Aurelius in that land.
    Aurelius marched forth and led his men due north,
With his full strength for one full week's length.
The British were the bravest and advanced over the forest;
By then Aurelius had an enormous army;
He found there waste land, people all slaughtered,
Churches fire-gutted, Britons burned to death.   8120
Then declared King Aurelius, the darling of the Britons:
'If I'm to survive so that back again I ride,
If it is willed by Our Lord who made the daylight with his word
That I may in safety obtain what is my heritage,
Then churches I shall raise, and the true God I will praise;
I will to each knight give what is his right,
And to every single man, both to the old and young,
I shall be kindly,
If God will grant me to regain my own country.'
    To Hengest came the tidings of Aurelius the king,   8130
[That he was bringing a force of innumerable folk];*   8130a

Then spoke Hengest, of all knights the falsest:
'Hearken now, my men! honour now is granted you;
Here comes Aurelius, and his brother Uther also;
They're bringing very many troops, but all of them are doomed,
For the king is stupid, and so are his knights,
And a mere boy is his brother – the one just like the other!
In consequence the British will be much less courageous:
When the head is pretty feeble, the [forces] will abate,*
So hold well in your memories what I'm about to mention:
Better are fifty of our men than a whole five hundred of them, 8140
And that on many occasions they have had to find out
Ever since they landed to test out the people,
For tales are widely told of our retaliation,
That we are stalwarts, elite among the best.
Against them we shall stand and drive them from our land,
And rule over the realm just as we wish to.'
Thus the bold Hengest, of all knights the handsomest,
Emboldened his forces as they stood on the field.
Yet quite otherwise it came about before a week was out.
　　On then sped the tidings to Aurelius the king   8150
Of where Hengest was lodged, up high on the mount.
Aurelius had supporters, thirty thousand riders,
Very bold Britons who uttered their vows,
And also he had Welshmen, wonderfully many.
He insisted his knights, by day and by night,
Should always be weaponed as if going off to war,
For always he was anxious about the heathen hordes.
Then to Hengest came news that Aurelius was close:
He marshalled his army and marched out against him.
　　When Aurelius was aware that Hengest was going to come
　　　　there   8160
He moved into a field and was well weaponed behind shield;
He took with him straight ten thousand knights
Who were the best born and most select from his force,
And positioned them in the field, on foot behind their shields;
Ten thousand Welshmen he sent off to the woodland;
Ten thousand Scots he sent out on the flanks
To encounter the heathen on tracks and on paved street.
He himself took his earls and his excellent warriors,
And the most loyal men whom he had in his land,
And he formed up his shield-wall like a winter-hoary wood;   8170

Five thousand were on horseback, all these people to protect.
    Then shouted Aldolf, who was earl of Gloucester:
'If the Lord should grant it me, he who governs every outcome,
That I'm allowed to be alive when Hengest comes here riding
(Who has so long remained here in this our land,
And betrayed my friends and loved ones with his long saxon
        knives,
Close beside Amesbury, to an atrocious death),
If however, from that earl I might win myself the glory
Then I could utter my own true declaration
That God himself had granted good things to me –   8180
If I could fell all my foes to the ground at once
And avenge my dear kinsfolk whom they have laid down low!'
Scarcely was this speech spoken to the end
When they saw Hengest advancing over the down
With an enormous force of men; furiously they advanced.
    Together they came, and [fiercely] they struck;*
There the stern men rushed straight together:
Helmets were resounding, knights there were falling,
Steel struck against bone, destruction there was rife,
Down the roads went gushing rivulets of blood;   8190
The fields were fallow coloured and the grass all faded.
    When Hengest saw that his help was failing
He dashed from the fight and fled to the sides,
And after him his people pressed on very fast;
The Christians coming in pursuit pounded them with blows,
And called upon Christ the son of God to give them assistance,
And the heathen people also called out loudly:
'Our own god, Tervagant, why do you fail us this time?'
When Hengest saw the heathens were surrounded
And the Christian men came down upon them   8200
Then Hengest fled on and on until he came to Conisbrough;
Into the city he went seeking its security,
And King Aurelius went after him at once,
Calling to his people in a loud bellow:
'Keep on running, on, now, on: it is northward Hengest's gone!'
And after him they turned until they came to the town.
    Then Hengest and his son watched all the army coming after
        them.
Then declared Hengest (of all men the angriest!):
'I refuse to fly any more, now instead I want to fight,

And my son Octa, and his sworn-brother Ebissa,   8210
And all my army of men. Now draw your weapons,
And let's march against them and make havoc-raids,
And if we don't fell those men, then it's we who're fated,
Laid out on the field and bereft of our friends.'
   Hengest moved out into the [field], left behind all his tents,*
And formed up his shield-wall entirely from his heathen men.
Then Aurelius the king arrived, and many thousands with him,
And began a second fight there which was frighteningly strong:
Many a great blow was dealt there in that combat.
There the Christian men were all but overcome.   8220
Then arrived galloping the five thousand riders
Whom Aurelius had there to fight men from horseback:
They struck at the heathen so they hurtled downwards;
There was a very stiff fight, most severe battle-ardour.
Into the fight came the Earl Aldolf of Gloucester
And discovered Hengest, of all knights the wickedest,
Where he was fighting fiercely and felling down Christians.
Aldolf drew his good sword and on Hengest he smote,
And Hengest threw his shield in front of him, or else his life would
     have been lost,
And Aldolf struck into the shield so that it split in two,   8230
And Hengest leaped upon him as if he were a lion
And struck at Aldolf's helmet so it fell into two pieces.
Then they hacked with their swords – the swipes were very savage:
Sparks sprang from the steel over and over again.
After quite a time Aldolf jumped down to the ground
And caught sight of **Gorlois**, and he was brave, most certain this is;
He was the earl of Cornwall and he was famous far and wide;
Then the warrior Aldolf because of that was much bolder,
And heaving high his sword let it come slashing down,
Until it struck Hengest's hand and made him drop his blade.   8240
Instantly he grabbed him with a grim expression
By the coif on the cuirass, which was covering his head,
And by his own sheer brute force smashed him right down,
And then bounced him up again as if he wanted to break him up;
With his arms he encircled him and off then he led him.
   Now Hengest had been captured through Aldolf's skill in action.
Then announced Aldolf who was earl of Gloucester:
'Hengest, you're not as jolly as you were by Amesbury,
Where you drew those saxon-swords and struck down the Britons!

With the grossest treachery you killed my kinsfolk.   8250
Now you must pay out compensation and your own friends shall
    perish,
And with gruesome torments you will go off from this world!'
Hengest walked silently: he could see no help at all;
Aldolf was leading him to his sovereign lord,
And greeted his liege lord with most loyal words:
'All hail to you, Aurelius, of most exalted rank!
I am bringing here before you the destroyer of your kinsfolk,
Hengest the heathen who has perpetrated harm for us.*
God has indeed allowed me to get him in my grip!
Now to you I'm going to give him, for you are dearest to me of all
    men,
So let the children of your courtiers play games with this pet
    dog,   8261
Shoot at him with arrows and put a stop to his race quickly!'
    Then the king made reply with a clear and eager voice:
'Blessings on you, Aldolf, best and noblest of earls!
I love you like my own life: you shall be a leader of this people!'
Here Hengest was seized and there Hengest was tied up;
There, by then, was Hengest of all knights the saddest!
    This fight was then concluded and the heathen folk had fled;
Then Octa noticed that his father was in trouble,
And with Ebissa his sworn-brother joined forces together   8270
And fled inside York city amid every misery,
And got ready the walls and demolished the halls.
Certain of the heathen went off to the woodland
Where the foot-soldiers laid them flat on the ground.
    Then Aurelius the king was well content above all things.
He went into Conisbrough with his household guard
And gave thanks to God for all such prowess.
For three days and three nights the king stayed there all right,
To doctor all the wounds of his most dear knights,
And to bathe in that borough all their weary bones.   8280
When the third day had come, and they had said the hour of
    nones[27]

---

[27] Timing of the liturgical hours varied with the changing length of the natural
day from season to season; in high summer 'nones' would be about 3 p.m.

Then the king had trumpets blown and brought his earls together
So that they might come to hustings to Aurelius the king.
   When they had assembled the king asked them at once
What they would advise him, those who were his associates,
As to what kind of torture should form Hengest's execution,
And how he might best avenge his own dearest friends
Who beside Amesbury lay buried in the ground.
   Then up stood **Aldadus,** and he addressed the king like this
(He was good and in God's favour and was a holy bishop   8290
And was Earl Aldolf's brother – he hadn't any other):
'My lord king, listen to me now, to what I shall relate to you:
I shall pronounce to you the sentence on how he is to be struck
   down.
Because for us who live here of men he is most loathsome,
And has slaughtered our kinsmen and deprived them of their days
   of life,
And he is a heathen hound, so he must go down to hell:
There let him sink because of his treachery.
Lord king, hearken to me, to what I want to tell you:
There was a king in Jerusalem, Saul was his name,
[And] in the heathen territory a king of great power,*   8300
Agag he was called, and Jerusalem he hated,
He was king of the Amalekites (to him the Evil One was close);
All the time he hated Jerusalem to its greatest harm;
Never would he give them any peace but always he opposed them:
He burned them, he killed them, he gave them many sorrows.
   'It happened at one time that the sun began to shine
And Agag the king was sitting on his high throne,
And his doomed blood was stirred and put him in mind of
   marching.
He called to his knights right away and straight:
"Swiftly on your steeds, and off we shall ride!   8310
We shall burn and we shall kill all around Jerusalem!"
Off went the king and a huge army with him:
Through the land they started running and the towns they were
   burning.
This was noticed by those men who were living in Jerusalem,
Who then went against them, knights and serving men,
And fought against the king and by fighting overcame him,
And all his folk they slaughtered and King Agag they captured,
And so they conducted him up to King Saul.

And then Saul the king was more glad than anything;
The king asked his advisers about his course of action,   8320
Which would be the best thing: either execute or hang him.
     'Up then leaped Samuel, a prophet of Israel;
He was a very holy man, high in the Lord's favour:
No one in those days knew such a high man under God's law.
Samuel took King Agag captive to the market-place
And had him tied up very tightly to a strong stake which was
     there,
And took in his right hand a valuable brand,
And like this he called out to him, did Samuel the good man:
"You're known as Agag the king, but now you are sorrowing;
Now you must take your recompense for ruining Jerusalem,   8330
For having so greatly damaged this dear and noble city,
And slaughtering many a good man and depriving him of life-days.
As I await God's mercy you will not do this any more!"
Samuel raised the sword and struck down with it hard,
And cut in half the king in the market-place of Jerusalem,
And he scattered the pieces far and wide over the streets.
That's how Samuel acted and so you ought to treat Hengest.'
     This was heard by Aldolf, who was earl of Gloucester;
He leaped towards Hengest as if he were a lion.
And grabbed him by the hair, and after him he dragged him,   8340
And led him all around, and right round Conisbrough,
And outside the city he had him tied securely.
Aldolf drew his sword and struck off Hengest's head,   *Hengest's*
And the king took his corpse straight, as he was so   *Execution*
     brave a knight,
And placed him in the earth after the heathen practice,
And prayed for the soul (that no salvation should come to it!).
     And now Aurelius the king had men summon a hustings,
And had brass trumpets blown to bring together his force.
Marvellous was the crowd of folk, and they marched direct to
     York,
And there they besieged within it Octa and his men.   8350
The king got men to dig a ditch all around outside York city,
So that no one there at all could either come out or go in.
This Octa perceived and it caused him much grief,
And his heathen horde which he had in the city.
They gathered to consider what they ought to do;
And this said Octa, to his close friend Ebissa:

'Now I have decided what I'm going to do:
I and my own knights will now outright
In our bare breeches go out of this borough,
And wind round my neck a length of linked chains,   8360
And come to the king, his mercy begging.
Otherwise we'll all perish, if we don't follow this advice.'
   They all acted like this, just as Octa advised:
In deep concern, knights took off their clothes,
And out of the city went lords sick at heart,
All by twos together, twenty hundred of them.
   The noblest of kings, Aurelius, observed all of this:
He thought those naked knights a very strange sight.
Together came the army encamped about the country
And watched Octa coming, who was Hengest's son.   8370
He carried in his hand a long piece of chain;
He came up to the king in the presence of his soldiers;
He fell to the ground at the feet of the king,
And these words were spoken by Octa who was Hengest's son:
'Be merciful, my lord king, through the mild God himself,
For the love of God almighty, have mercy on my knights:
For all of our paganism has become paltry,
Our laws and our nation, since we're loathed by the Lord.
For we are failed all this time by Tervagant and Apollin,
By Woden and by Mercury, by Jupiter and Saturn,   8380
By Venus and Dido, by Frea and Mamilo,
And our beliefs are now loathsome to us,
But we want to believe in your beloved Lord,
For all the creed we've followed fails us all the time.
We are seeking for your grace, now and for all ages.
If you will make peace with me and will make a treaty with me,
We will be allied with you and become your loyal men,
Love your own people and preserve your laws.
If this you refuse, then do what you wish,
Whatever you want to do, whether execute or hang us!'   8390
   The king was compassionate and remained quiet;
He looked to his right hand, he looked to his left hand,
To see which of the wise men wished to speak first.[28]
All of them were silent and spoke not a sound;
There was no man so great who dared declare one word,

---

[28] This and the following speech by Aurelius (8422 ff.), and Tremorion's

And Octa went on lying at the feet of the king,
With all of his knights lying behind him.
Then the good Bishop Aldadus spoke up and said this:
'It has always been and for ever will be, and is now required of us
[That whoever] asks for mercy, mercy [he] must have;*   8400
He deserves mercy who begs for it deservingly.
And you yourself, lord king, are the leader of the nation:
Give your favour to Octa and his companions as well,
If they wish with true belief to receive the Christian faith;
For it may still come to pass in some country or other
That they may dutifully honour the Lord God.
Now all this kingdom stands entirely in your hands:
Donate them a location which you find convenient,
And take from them hostages such as you'd request,
And have them held firm in fetters of iron;   8410
Supply the hostages with clothes and food, supply them every
          comfort, every need,
And then you may well retain this race within your land;
And let them cultivate the land and live by their produce.
    'If it subsequently happens shortly afterwards
That they fail after a time to keep to the truce,
And grow lax in their labour and grow disloyal to you,
I'll now stipulate the sentence which at that stage you could give:
Get them run over by really savage riders,
And so have them destroyed, killed and also hanged.
This judgement I give you: may the just Lord give ear!'   8420
Then the king answered in keen and eager tones:
'I shall act exactly as you have made assessment!'
Then the king spoke like this: 'Get up now, Octa,
You are to act most virtuously by taking Christianity.'
    Then they baptised Octa and his bodyguard also
And all of his knights in that very place outright;
They selected their hostages and handed them to the king:
Fifty-three children they entrusted to the king,
And the king sent them straight in the direction of Scotland;
They swore solemn oaths that they would not betray him.   8430
The king gave into their hands sixty full hides of land,

advice and Aurelius's response (8476 ff., 8487) enhance the impression of rule
by consultation and shared decision-making, as is frequently the case with
Lawman's many additions in direct speech.

And on this they lived for the length of many years.
  The king was in York: a noble life he found it;
He took his couriers and sent them round his country
Ordering his bishops, his men of book-learning,
His earls and his landed men to come there to meet him,
To Aurelius the king, to a very great hustings.
In a very short time together they came:
The king greeted his people with most pleasing words:
He welcomed his earls, he welcomed his warriors,   8440
And all the bishops and the men of book-learning:
'I will declare to you quite undeniably
Why I have sent for you and for what purpose.
Here I present to each knight his property and his rights,
And to every single earl and to every single warrior;
What he may obtain, let him use that with pleasure.
And each man, on his own life, I command to love the peace;
I order you to design and to build up the churches,
To let the bells ring for God's praise to be sung,
For us with all our powers to honour our dear Lord.   8450
With all of his ability let each keep peace and amity!
See to cultivating land, now it all lies in my hand.'
  When this speech was uttered, they all liked this instruction.
The king gave them leave to go away from there:
Each journeyed homewards in the way he thought best.
For seven nights entirely the king stayed there quietly.
And then he took the long way down towards London,
To cheer all the citizens who had so often been concerned.
He had them strengthen the walls, he had them [erect] many
    halls,*
And put right all the earthworks which had formerly been
    broken,   8460
And he restored the law-code to them which existed in their elders'
    days.
There he appointed governors to control the people,
And from there he went directly to Winchester,
And there too he had constructed [halls and fine churches]*
Until he found it very pleasant there; then he moved on to
    Amesbury,
To the burial ground of his most beloved friends,
Whom Hengest with his knives had annihilated there.
He made enquiry there at once for masons skilled in carving stone,

And for every good artist skilled in working with the adze.
He intended to construct there a uniquely fine creation   8470
Which was to last for ever, as long as men shall live.
    There was in Caerleon a bishop called **Tremorion**;
He was a very wise man among the kingdoms of the world;
He was with the king, up there in the forest,
And there Tremorion, God's servant, spoke to the king like this:
'Now listen to me, Aurelius, to what I want to teach you,
And I will pronounce to you the best possible advice;
If you will approve of it, in turn it will appeal to you.
We have a prophet who is called Merlin:
If any one could discover him up on this high forest,   8480
And bring him in your presence by any manner of means,
If you were willing to submit to his wishes,
He would impart to you excellent secrets
Of how you might make this building sturdy and strong,
So that it could endure as long as men exist.'
Then the king replied (these words made him rejoice):
'Tremorion, dear friend, to this I shall attend.'
    The king sent his couriers over all his kingdom's area,
Asking every single man to enquire after Merlin,
And if anyone could find him, to bring him to the king;   8490
He would give him land, and both silver and gold,
And in this wide world he would perform his wish.
The messengers started riding, very far, and widely:
Some of them went due northwards and some of them went
        southwards,
Some of them went due east and some of them went due west;
Some went straightway along until they came to Alaban
(That is a spring which lies in Welsh lands);
That spring he loved and often in it bathed himself;
There the knights found him as he sat on its rim;
The moment they met him, politely did they greet him,   8500
And like this, very forthright, spoke to him those two knights:
'Health to you, Merlin, of all men the wisest!
Through us to you come greetings from one who is a good king:
Aurelius he is called, the most excellent of all kings;
All this great land stands in King Aurelius's hands.
Politely he requests that to him you should proceed,
And he will give you land, both silver and gold,
If in this state business you're willing to advise the king.'

Merlin gave an answer which depressed the knights there:
'I care nothing for his land, his silver nor his gold,   8510
Nor his clothes nor his horses: I myself have quite enough.'
Then he sat still for a very long space.
  Those knights were afraid that he would fly from them;
When at last his words broke they were good things which he
    spoke:
'You two are a pair of knights who have come here, directly:[29]
Yesterday before nones I knew that you would come,
And if I had not wished it, you never could have found me.
You bring me greetings from Aurelius the king:
I knew his nature before he came ashore,
And I knew the other, Uther his brother: 8520
I knew both of them, before they were even born,
Even though neither of them had I ever set eyes on.
But disaster, O disaster, that destiny is such
That the people's liege is not to live long.
Yet now I will accompany you and be your companion:
To the king I will proceed and perform all his wishes.'
  Off travelled Merlin and those knights with him
So long till they came to their liege and king;
This piece of good tidings came to the king:
Till then never in his life was the king so blithe   8530
For the coming of any man at all who ever came to him.
  Off to get his steed, and out the king rode,
And all his knights with him to give welcome to Merlin.
The king met up with him and splendidly greeted him:
He caught him in arms, he kissed him,
He called him his close friend;
Great was the rejoicing among the assembled retinue
All for Merlin's coming (who was the son of no man):
Alas that in the world there was no wise man
Who ever knew here whose son he could be   8540
(Except the Lord alone, whose knowledge is total).
The king led Merlin who was favoured off to his chamber:
He began at once to request with courteous expression

[29] Lawman adds Merlin's intuitive knowledge of why he has been sent for.
He has rearranged the material so that Merlin explains to the ordinary soldiers
(8620) that the stones were brought from Africa, rather than telling Aurelius at
the start, as in Wace.

That he should make him understand about the world's circuit,
And about all the years which were still to come here,
For it was his earnest wish that he should know of this.
　　Merlin answered then, and to the king he said this:
'O Aurelius the king, you ask me an unusual thing;
See to it that no more do you any such thing utter!
For [of baleful effect] is the spirit here within my breast,*   8550
And if among men I were to make any boasting
As entertainment, as an attraction, with amusing words,
My spirit will be roused and become silent,
And deprive me of my brains and stop up my wise words:
Then I would be dumb upon every decision.
But stop this kind of thing', said Merlin to the king,
'For whenever there comes trouble to any nation at all,
And people with humility wish to approach me,
If I by my own intent may remain silent,
Then I can pronounce on how things will come to pass.   8560
But I will advise you about your most pressing problem,
And tell you right here what you have in your heart:
There is a field beside Amesbury which is broad and very pretty,
Where by the knife your kin were deprived of life:
There was many a bold Briton betrayed to his death,
And you're intending to grace that place with great honour,
With marvellous buildings as memorial to the dead,
Which there will stand to the world's end.
But you haven't got a single man who knows anything about it,
Who could construct a building which would never collapse.   8570
But I shall instruct you in this difficulty,
For I know a structure surrounded with mystery,
And this structure stands within Ireland:
It is a most marvellous thing.
Its construction is of stone, apart from this one there is none:
As wide as the world's realm is, no other one resembles it.
When people are unwell, they journey to the stone,
And they wash the stone, and with that water bathe their bones.
Within a little while they're completely whole.   8580
But the stones are massive and immensely huge,
For there is no man ever born, in any borough whatever,
Who could by sheer strength bring the stones from there.'
　　Then replied the king: 'Merlin, you are saying strange things!
If no man ever born could bring them home from there,

Nor by any power could take them from their place,
How could I bring them away from there then?'
Then responded Merlin to the king speaking to him:
'O but yes, yes, my lord king! Long ago it was recorded
That cunning is better than any brute force, 8590
For with cunning one can achieve what force cannot compass.
But summon your army and advance to that country,
And be sure to take with you a force of good people,
And I shall go with you (this will enhance your honour).
Before you depart homewards you shall have your desire,
And you shall bring that structure with you to this land,
And so you shall convey it over to the cemetery,
And honour the location where your friends lie buried,
And you yourself are going to find rest for your bones in it:
When your life ends, there you shall rest.' 8600
   So spoke Merlin there, and afterwards sat silent,
Just as if he was going to depart from the world.
The king had him conducted into a handsome chamber,
There to be lodged in the way he liked.
   Aurelius the king had men announce a hustings
From all the lands which lay within his hands,
Asking counsel for himself in such case as this,
And they advised him sensibly, his senior nobles,
That he should follow the course which Merlin had proposed.
But they refused to lead the king out of this land: 8610
Instead they chose as leader Uther the good man,
And fifteen thousand knights, all with fine weapons,
Very brave Britons who were bound in that direction.
   When this force was all ready then they began to journey,
With all the best ships which were stationed by the sea,
And travelled so long that they came to Ireland, *Invasion*
And those knights most valiant took harbour there and *of*
   anchored. *Ireland*
They went up on the sea strand and gazed around at Ireland.
Then Merlin spoke and made speech with these words:
'Do you see now, bold men, that massive hill, 8620
The hill so very high that it comes close to the sky?
That is that amazing thing, which there is called "The Giants'
   Ring",
A thing quite unlike any other; it came from Africa.

Pitch all your tents across all these fields;
Here we shall rest for three whole days' space;
On the fourth day from here we shall depart,
And make towards that mount: there is what we want.
But first we must bathe ourselves and bring together our bold men,
Get our weapons ready for we shall really need them.'
So things were left, and there lay the army.   8630

     Then a king who was very strong owned all of Ireland:
He was called **Gillomaurus**, and great lord he was of men.
To him came the tidings that the Britons were on his land.
He had men summon his army through all Ireland's country,
And he began uttering threats that he would drive them out.
When the news came through of what the Britons were there to do,
Of how they came just for one thing, to fetch away the Stone Ring,
Then Gillomaurus gave vent to much mockery and scorn,
And said that they must be allies in stupidity,
Those who had travelled there across the broad sea   8640
Seeking there for stones as if in their own land were none!
And he swore by St Brendan: 'They'll not be taking one stone,
But for those stones they'll be getting the greatest of all troubles:
Their blood will come gushing out of their guts,
And that will larn 'em for looking for stones!
And then I'll be going off into Britain,
And tellin' King Aurelius I'll be fightin' for me stones,
And unless the king keeps quiet and does just what I want,
Then I'll be making a stand by fighting in his land,
Make waste places for him and many wildernesses   8650
And plenty of widows: their partners will all die!'
     So the foolish king played around with words,
But it turned out quite differently from what he expected.
His forces were ready, fell in and marched forwards,
So far, till they came to the British encampment.
Together they clashed and boldly attacked,
And fought very fiercely: the fated fell there.
The Irish were quite bare; the British wore their mail-coats:[30]
The Irishmen fell, and covered all the fields,
And the king Gillomaur set off to flee from there,   8660

_____

[30] Tatlock thinks Lawman must have been to Ireland to add the detail that
the Irish fought naked (_Legendary History_, pp. 416–17); in Wace they are
merely 'not well armed' (W 8113).

And fled away straight with twenty of his knights
Into a vast forest, quite bereft of honour:
His Irish folk had all been felled with steel.
So the king was ruined and his boasting at an end,
And so he went to the woods and left his folk falling.
   The British gazed round at the dead strewn over the ground:
Seven thousand lay there deprived of their life.
Across the fields the British advanced towards their tents,
And fittingly they saw to all their fine weapons,
And there they took rest as Merlin had instructed.   8670
On the fourth day they prepared to march forward,
Proceeded to the hill: they were all weaponed well.
   There stood that weird structure, massive and very strong.
Knights were striding up, knights were striding down,
Knights were going all around and earnestly observing:
They saw there on the land the amazing structure stand.
There were a thousand soldiers with weapons well supplied,
And all the others, in fact, were closely guarding their ships.
Then Merlin made a speech and spoke to the knights:
'You, knights, are strong: these stones are great and long;   8680
You have to go close to them and get a keen grasp on them;
You must stoutly twine them with strong sail-ropes;
Shove then and heave with very heavy force
Trees huge and long which are very strong,
And go up to one stone, all you who are clever
And come down on it with strength, to see if you can stir it.'*
Merlin knew quite well how things would work out.
The knights stepped over to it with a great show of strength:
They sweated and struggled but had no success
In managing to shift even one single stone.   8690
   Merlin looked at Uther, who was the king's brother,
And these were the words of Merlin the wise man:
'Uther, now pull back and call your knights to you,
And all stand around and watch very closely,
And be very quiet and keep very still,
Until I say to you directly how we're going to begin.'
Uther drew right back, and beckoned his knights
So he left behind no-one close up to the stone,
Just as far as a man might toss a small stone,
And Merlin went around and examined it closely;   8700
Three times he went round the ring, inside it and outside it,

And was moving his lips like a man saying prayers;
This Merlin went on doing there until he called to Uther:
'Uther, come quickly, and bring your knights with you,
And get hold of all the stones: you're not to leave a single one,
For now you can lift them like balls made of feathers*
And so by this expedient you can carry them aboard.'
   Just as Merlin instructed these stones were extracted,
And they stowed them on their ships and sailed off, in fact,
And so proceeded to travel over to this land,   8710
And conveyed them to a field which is amazingly wide:
Wide it is and very pretty, close to Amesbury,
Where Hengest betrayed the British with his Saxon knives.
Merlin began to erect them as they had stood earlier,
In a way no one besides him could have coped with or contrived,
Nor was there before that any man so clever born yet
As those stones to arrange and that structure to raise.
   That news came to the king in the north region   *Stonehenge*
Of Merlin's behaviour and of Uther his brother:
That they had safely come back to this land,   8720
And that that structure was complete and was standing upright.
Within the king's breast was a marvellous bliss,
And he had the hustings called as far and wide as his land spread,
So that all his people very merrily might come to Amesbury,
All his noble people, on the Whitsunday.
   To the place came Aurelius the king and all his folk with him;
There on the Whitsunday he called an assembly,
As I intend to describe to you in the story of this book:
Upon the plain there pavilions were pitched,
Over that broad field were nine thousand tents.   8730
All the Whitsunday on the field the king stayed,
[Wearing his crown there high upon his head]:*   8731a
He called for the spot called Stonehenge now to be consecrated.
Quiet for full three days did the king stay;
On the third day he gave high honour to his nobles:*
He appointed two bishops, both extremely good;
St **Dubricius** to Caerleon and to York went St **Samson**;
Both of them were holy and close to high God;
On the fourth day the doughty folk departed.
And so for some time things stood like this.
   Now there was still one wicked man, **Passent**, son of
     Vortigern;   8740

This same Passent had gone into Wales,   *Passent's*
And there at this same time he had become an outlaw,   *Rebellion*
Though he dared not long remain there because of Aurelius and
      Uther,
But he got ships which were good and travelled on the sea-flood;
Into Germany he journeyed with five hundred men,
And there he won many followers and made up a war-fleet,
And travelled for so long that he came to this land,
Into the Humber; there he did much harm.
But not for long did he dare to remain in that area:
The king was marching that way and Passent fled away,   8750
Along the sea-coast for so long that he came to Ireland;
There he at once found the king of that land:
His heart was very sore when he greeted King Gillomaur:
'Good health to you, Gillomaur, great chieftain of warriors![31]
To you I have come: I was Vortigern's son.
Of Britain was my father king: he loved you above all things,
And if on this occasion to go there you'd yourself be my
      companion,
The two of us would so arrange it that my father we'd well avenge,
And we'd well avenge your folk whom Uther killed here,
And your magic stone-work which they dragged away;   8760
And also I heard it said, as I travelled on the sea,
That King Aurelius has become very sick,
And lies within Winchester where he's bedridden;
You can trust me totally for this is absolutely true!'
Passent and Gillomaur made their agreement there;
Oaths they swore there, many and uncountable
That all of this land they two would place in their own hands;
The oaths indeed were deeply sworn, but then again they were
      broken.
   The king gathered his army far and wide through all his country;
To the sea coast went Gillomaur and Passent,   8770
Into the ships they slid and off they let them glide;
Off they went speedily until they came to Menevia,
Which was at that time a flourishing town

[31] Passent's speeches here and at 8778–84 are added by Lawman, who has
Passent egg on Gillomaur by supplying the information that Aurelius is ill (L
8762), whereas in Wace the narrator announces this after Paschent and Gilloman
reach Wales (W 8215).

Which now, to be specific, people call St David's.
There they took harbour in the greatest happiness:
Ships ran up on the strand: knights went up on the land.
Then said Passent (towards Gillomaur he went):
'Speak to me, King Gillomaur, now that we have come here:
Now I'm placing in your hands a half share of this kingdom,
For from Winchester there has come to me a certain knight's
    son   8780
And he tells me news of this kind: that Aurelius is going to die;
The disease lies under his ribs in such a way he can't live.
Here we two shall well avenge our associates and kinsmen,
Win for ourselves his dwellings, as will be best for us!'
   To the king that word came, inside Winchester,
That Passent and Gillomaur with an army had come over here.
The king called Uther, who was his dear brother:
'Uther, call up the army over all this country,
And march to our enemies and drive them from the country:
Either you must make them flee or you must fell them;   8790
I would go as well if I were not so ill,
But if I get better I'll come after you at once.'
Everything did Uther as the king said to him there;
And Passent at Saint David's was causing great distress,
And also King Gillomaur – much distress he made there.
They ran right through Britain, ravaging and burning,
While Uther in this country was gathering his army,
And it took a long time before he could move ahead,
And Passent set in his own hand all of the West Welsh land.
   Then it happened one day (his troops were very cheerful)   8800
That **Appas** there came faring (the fiends must have fetched him!)
And spoke to Passent like this: 'Come over here to us!
I will relate to you some really pleasant news.
I've just been in Winchester among your worst enemies
Where the king lies sickly and in a very sorry mood.
What will I get for it if I go that way riding
And give you the comfort of making him a corpse?'
As he went towards Appas, Passent's response was:
'I promise you today one hundred pounds (and I have got it)
If you "give me the comfort of making him a corpse"!'   8810
They made many promises to perform this treachery.
Appas went off in private to hatch out this plot;
He was a heathen person of Saxon derivation.

He put a monk's habit on and shaved his crown on top,
He took with him two supporters and then he set off
And went at once directly into Winchester,
Looking just like a holy man – the heathen devil!
   He went to the borough gate where the king lay in a bedroom
And greeted the porter by commending him to God   *Aurelius's*
And asked him in a hurry to go in to the king   *Death*
And to tell him in truth that Uther his brother   8821
Had sent to him there a splendid physician,
The very best doctor living in any land,
Who knew how to release every sick man from disease.
So this vile man lied to the people's very king,
For Uther had left and gone off with his forces,
Never had Uther set eyes upon him still less sent him there,
Yet the king thought it must be the truth and believed him well
     enough.
And who would have guessed that he was a traitor,
Since he was wearing chain-mail next to his bare skin,   8830
On top of that he had a horrible hairshirt
And then a monk's cowl made out of black cloth;
He had blackened his torso as if it were grimed with coal.
He knelt before the king; his words were very gentle:[32]
'May you recover health, Aurelius, most excellent of kings!
I was sent here by Uther, who is your own brother,
And entirely for the love of God I have come here to you,
Because I'm going to heal you and make you quite healthy
For the love of Christ, God's son (I don't care about reward,
Nor payment in land, nor in silver or gold,   8840
But for each sick one I do this for the love of my good Lord).'
   The king heard all this and it consoled him very much;
But where is there ever any man upon this earth of ours
Who would have guessed that he was a traitor?
He took his glass bottle at once and the king urinated in it;
A short time after that he took the glass bottle in hand
And held it up for inspection by all the king's knights,
And the heathen man Appas at once remarked thus:
'If you would believe me before tomorrow evening
This king will be completely well, recovered, if he wills it.'   8850
Then all those in the bedroom were blissfully happy.

[32] Lawman adds Appas's disguise and conversation with Aurelius.

Appas went off into a private room to hatch out that plot,
And used for it a poison which is called scamony,[33]
And came out straightaway among the chamber-knights*
And to the king he gave a dose of a good deal of cinnamon,
And ginger and licorice he handed over generously;
They all received that offering and he took them all in;
This con-man fell upon his knees before the nation's king
And in this way to him he spoke: 'My lord, now you must take
A dose of this liquor which will bring you health and vigour.' 8860
And the king drank it down: and there he drank in the poison;
As soon as he had drunk the doctor laid him down.
Appas gave these instructions to the knights in attendance:
'Now cover the king well so he works up a sweating.
Above all else, I'm telling you, our king will be quite well,
And I'll go to my lodging to discuss it with my men,
And around midnight I shall come right back,
With some other medication which will be pleasant for him.'
Off went the traitor; the king lay in slumber;
Appas went to his lodging and spoke to his men[34]   8870
In very secret whispers; then stole out of town.
    When it was midnight then the attendant knights
Sent six of their men to Appas's lodging;
They expected to find him and to lead him to the king.
But then he had fled (the fiends had ferried him off!).
The men came back again to where the king was staying,
And announced in the chamber Appas's departure.
Then could be seen copious grief:
Knights were falling down and longing for their deaths.
There was much lamenting, much heart-felt groaning;   8880
There was pitiful talking, there were men screaming!
They leaped over to the bed, and the king was [un]covered:*
He was still lying there asleep and in a terrific sweat;
With tears streaming down them, the knights awoke the king,
And they called to him with very soft voices:
'How are you, my lord? How is your [affliction]?*

[33] Scamony, an irritant purgative made of gum resin from the roots of
Convolvulus scammonia, is not lethal (Madden, III, 365 ff.).

[34] The whole scene of Aurelius's death – Appas sneaking off, grief at the
discovery of Aurelius's mortal sickness, his dying benediction on Uther, and
funeral directives – all derive from Lawman's imagination.

Now our doctor has departed without your permission!
He's slipped out of court and he's left us like idiots.'
    The king gave them a reply: 'I am completely swollen,
And there is no other help for it: soon now I shall be dead.   8890
And I'm asking you right now, you knights who are my own,
That you greet Uther, who is my own brother,
And invite him to hold my land in his control:
May God himself above all things let him be a good king!
And urge him to have courage and everywhere aright judge,
Be to the weak a father, to the destitute a consoler;
Then may he hold the land under control.
And now when I am dead today, all decide to act one way:
Let me arrive after my journey right there at Stonehenge;
There lie many of my kinsfolk, killed by the Saxons;   8900
And send off for bishops and men of book-learning;
My gold and my silver distribute for my soul,
And lay me in the east end right inside Stonehenge.'
There was no other help for it: there the king was dead,
And his men did exactly as the king had decreed.
    Of all this quite unaware, in the land of Wales was Uther;
Not by any cleverness could he know a thing about this,
However he had with him the prophet known as Merlin.
He returned to meet the army which had come to the country.
Uther was camped in Wales, in a wilderness,   8910
And was marching forward fast to fight against Passent.
Then in the evening time the moon began to shine
Almost just as brightly as if it were sunlight.
Then they saw from afar a very strange star: *The Comet*
It was broad, it was huge, it was quite immense:
From it came rays horrifyingly gleaming:
That star is called in Latin a 'comet'.
There came from the star a most grim-looking ray;
At the end of the ray there was a fine dragon,
And from the dragon's mouth came many rays spouting,   8920
But two of these were vast, quite unlike the others:
One drew towards France, the other towards Ireland;
The ray which drew towards France gave a bright enough
        radiance:
The uncanny symbol was seen above the Great Saint Bernard Pass;
The ray which stretched westwards was composed of seven beams.
This was seen by Uther: what it meant he'd no idea.

He felt sad at heart and strangely afraid,
And so was all that great assembly who were in the army.
    Uther called Merlin, and asked him to come to him,
And in this way spoke to him in very soft accents: 8930
'Merlin, Merlin, my dear friend, find it out yourself,
And tell us about this symbol which we have just seen,
For I do not know in all the world what will turn up from it;
Unless you direct us we shall have to ride back!'
    Merlin sat silent for a long space of time,
As if in a dream he were deeply disturbed;
They would say, those who witnessed it with their own eyesight,
That he kept on wriggling just as if he were a worm![35]
In the end he started waking, and then he started quaking,
And Merlin the prophet uttered these words: 8940
'O wretched time, O wretched time in this world's realm:
Great is the sorrow which has settled on the land!
Where are you, Uther? Sit in front of me now, here,
And I shall tell you of very many sorrows.
Dead is Aurelius, most excellent of kings!
So is the other, Constance your brother
Whom Vortigern betrayed with all his treachery.
Now Vortigern's descendant has destroyed Aurelius;
Now you alone remain out of all your family;
But don't hope for any ideas from those who are lying dead,   8950
But think of yourself: good fortune is granted you,
For seldom does he not succeed who takes thought for himself;
You are to be a good king and the lord of great men!
If just at midnight you arm all your knights,
So that in the morning light we may arrive all right
In front of St David's, there's where you'll fight;
Before you go from there you shall make a slaughter:
Both of them you'll slay there, Passent and Gillomaur,
And many thousands of the men who have come here with them.
That sign from the star which we could see so far,   8960
True it is, Uther my dear, it signified your brother's death.
    'In front of the star was that dragon, quite surpassing every snake;
That portent was on your account: that was you, Uther, yourself;

[35] Merlin's peculiar *awen*, his shaman-like behaviour here, and trance in 8979 are additions which Lawman could have taken from Giraldus Cambrensis's *Descriptio Cambriae*.

You are to have this land: your power will be great and strong.
Likewise the tokens are uncanny which came from the dragon's
    mouth;
Two beams went out, marvellously bright:
The first went far south out over France;
This is a powerful son who from your body is to come,
Who is to conquer by combat many a kingdom,
And eventually he shall rule many a people.   8970
The other beam which stretched to the west, marvellously bright,
That will be a daughter who will be very dear to you.
The beams then separated into seven lovely rays:
These are seven lovely sons who from your daughter are to come,
Who will amass many royal lands into their own hands:
They will be very strong, both at sea and on land.
Now that you have heard from me things which will help you
Speedily forthright advance to your fight!'
And Merlin started dozing as if about to sleep.

    Up rose Uther, now informed and aware,   8980
And ordered his knights 'to horse' right away,
And ordered them with speed to gallop to Menevia,
And to prepare all their effects: they were going to fight.
In the leading troop he put knights who were well proved:
Seven thousand knights, brave men and valiant;
In the mid-section knights who were attentive,
Another seven thousand splendid soldiers;
He had as rear-guard very brave knights,
Eighteen thousand very brave warriors,
And so many thousands were the foot soldiers   8990
That not with any numbers could one count them up.
    Off they went apace until they came to St David's.
There Gillomaur spotted the arrival of Uther,
And ordered his knights to their weapons then, straight,
And they fell to with speed and they all grabbed their knives,
And it was off with their breeches (odd was their appearance!)
And they grasped in their hands their very long spears,
They hung across their shoulders enormous battle-axes.
    Then Gillomaur the king said a most amazing thing:
'Here comes Uther, Aurelius's brother;   9000
He wants to sue for peace from me and not to fight against me.
The leading men are his servants: let us march against them,
You need not bother overmuch if you kill those wretches,

For if Uther son of Constantine wants to become my vassal,
And restore to Passent his father's realm,
Then I'll make a truce and allow him to live,
And lead him in shining fetters to my own territory.'
    The king spoke like this, whereas things turned out worse!
There Uther's knights were at the town in a trice:
They set fire to the town and were quickly fighting;   9010
With swords they rushed and struck them, and the Irish were all
        naked!
When the Irishmen perceived there was battle-ardour with the
        British,
They fought very fiercely, but nonetheless they all fell dead.
They challenged their king: 'Where are you, good for nothing?
Why won't you come this way, you're leaving us to be destroyed,
And your crony Passent, he can see us collapsing;
Come to our aid with full assistance!'
Gillomaur heard this and it caused him much distress;
With his Irish knights he entered the fight,
And Passent went ahead with him: both of them were fated!   9020
When Uther perceived that Gillomaur had arrived
He rode over to him and struck him in the side
So that the spear penetrated and pierced to the heart;   *Gillomaur's*
Hastily he turned around and overtook Passent,   *Death*
And these words were uttered by Uther the lucky:
'Passent, this is where you pause: here comes Uther on his horse!'
He struck him on his crown so that he fell down
And plunged the sword down his gullet – which wasn't to his
        palate! – [36]
So that the point of the sword stuck into the earth.
Then observed Uther: 'Passent, you stop there!   9030
So you've laid claim to Britain now as all your own: *Passent's*
As much is allowed you as the bit you're lying dead on!   *Death*
Here you must remain, you and Gillomaur your friend,
Get the best from Britain, for now I'm bestowing it on you both,
So that you two for many a year with us can stay right here,
And you'll never need to worry about your food supply!'
Those were Uther's words and he rode afterwards
Driving those Irishmen over stream and over fen,
And slaughtered all the force which with Passent came ashore.

[36] Lawman often indulges in black comedy in battle-scenes (cf. 9032).

Some dashed to the sea and leapt aboard ship: 9040
What with weather, what with water, there they came to grief.
That was how they got on there, Passent and Gillomaur.
   Now this fight was done and Uther came back home,
And straightaway went into Winchester.
On a broad paved street he chanced to meet
Three knights and their squires coming towards him.
As soon as they met him politely they greeted him:
'All health to you, Uther, these honours are your own;
Dead is Aurelius, most excellent of kings,
And he has placed in your hand all his royal land;   9050
He wished you every joy and to remember his soul!'
Then Uther cried extremely copiously.
   Uther went directly into Winchester:
There stood before him, outside the city
All of the citizens with very sad expressions;
As soon as they saw him like this they addressed him:
'Uther, be gracious now and in all ages!
Our king we have lost; at this we are distressed;
You were his brother and he did not have another,
Nor did he have a son who the king might become.   9060
But do you take the king's crown: it comes as your inheritance,
And we wish to help you and have you as our lord,
With our weapons and possessions and with all our might.'
   Uther listened to this: he was wise and well aware   UTHER
That there was no other course since his brother was now dead;
He received the crown, which became him really well,
And so with much honour he was made the king,
And maintained good laws and loved all his people.
   At the time he was made king and was choosing his ministers
Merlin departed (he had no idea where he'd gone to,[37]   9070
Nor in all the world's bounds what became of him).
The king was very sombre and so were all his soldiers,
And all his courtiers for this reason were depressed.
The king had people ride very far and wide:
He proffered gold and great wealth to each wayfaring man,

[37] Merlin's disappearance and Uther's resulting distress are supplied by
Lawman, and like his depression in 9169 and his obtuse behaviour in love
(9255) serve to demote the 'Pendragon', whose son appears correspondingly
more self-controlled.

To whomsoever could find Merlin in the land,
And he added much of value – but he heard nothing of him.
   Then Uther was pondering on what Merlin had been saying
On the armed expedition into Welsh land
Where they saw the dragon unmatched by every snake,   9080
And he thought of its significance, as Merlin instructed him.
The king was very dismal and felt very depressed,
For he'd never lost a dearer man since he'd been alive,
Never any other, not Aurelius his brother.
   The king had two images fashioned, two golden dragons,
All for love of Merlin, so much did he want him to come.
When the dragons were completed, the first was his companion,
Wherever in the country he would lead his army;
It was his army ensign in every single event;
The second he gave generously to the town of Winchester,   9090
To the bishop's throne which is situated there;
He gave his good spear in addition, so people could carry the
      dragon
When in procession the relics were borne round.
The Britons observed these dragons which in this way were
      constructed:
Ever after they called Uther, who bore the dragon as his ensign,
By the surname they attached, which was Uther Pendragon;
Pendragon in British is 'Dragonhead' in English.
   Now Uther was a good king, but of Merlin he [heard] nothing;*
This news came to Octa where he lived in the north,
And Ebissa his blood-brother, and **Osa** was another;[38]   9100
These Aurelius had sent there and established in his peace,
Placing into their hands sixty hides of his land.
Octa heard exactly how it had all occurred,
About Aurelius's death and about Uther's kingdom.
Octa called to him the closest members of his family;
They discussed between them their former deeds,
Saying, by their lives, they'd leave off Christianity;

[38] In *HRB* Octa arrives with a brother called Ebissa (Book VI, ch. 13, taken
from Nennius) but later his companion is called Eosa (Book VIII, ch. 6). Wace
provides a cousin called Ebissa until Aurelius' death, and then always refers to
Eosa (some *Roman de Brut* manuscripts have Eosa throughout). Lawman
assumes there are two people involved, and uses both names from here on,
sometimes spelling Osa as Ossa.

They held their hustings and became heathen.
Then from Hengest's kinsfolk there came together
Six thousand five hundred men who were heathen.   9110
   The news was known at once and announced around the land
That Octa son of Hengest had become a heathen,
And all of those very people whom Aurelius had pardoned.
Octa sent his messengers into Welsh territory
After the Irish who had run away from Uther,
And after the Germans who had just managed to escape,
Who had fled into the forests while Passent was being killed,
And hid themselves just anywhere while Gillomaur was being
      killed.
From the woods these people skulked and off to Scotland slunk;
More and more kept coming, moving towards Octa;   9120
When they had all got together there were thirty thousand of them,
(Not counting the women) of Hengest's kinsmen.
   They took their forces and proceeded to advance,
And seized into their hands all beyond Northumberland,
And the men who lived there; where they started marching
The host was extraordinary, and it went straight to York,
And on every side the city was surrounded,
And they besieged the borough, those heathen men,
And took into their hands all from there into Scotland;
All they set eyes on they treated as their own.   9130
   But Uther's own knights who were in the castle
Defended the town from within so that they could not get in;
Never was it heard of anywhere that a small band did as well as
      there.
The moment that Uther of these things was made aware
He summoned a strong force throughout all his kingdom
And very hurriedly he marched towards York city;
He marched at once and direct to where Octa was camped.
Octa and his host hastened towards them,
And they flung together with very fierce strength:
Hardily they hacked; helmets resounded;   9140
Fields grew fallow-hued with the blood of fated men,
And the heathen souls sank down to hell.
When the day's end came it had been so badly arranged
That the heathen hordes had the upper hand
And with outstanding force overwhelmed the British
And drove them to a mountain which was immensely huge;

And Uther with his men withdrew to the mountain,
Having lost in the fight his beloved knights,
At least seven hundred: his [numbers] were the less!*
    Uther was up the mountain which was known as Dinian;   9150
And the mountain was overgrown with a glorious wood.
The king was inside it with very many men
And day and night Octa besieged him, with his heathen men,
Besieged him all around; the Britons were in trouble!
It distressed King Uther that he wasn't aware earlier
That he did not have for his land a better understanding.
They frequently consulted about this special need,
As to how they could overcome Octa who was Hengest's son.
    There was an earl named **Gorlois**, a great man indeed he was,
He was an accomplished knight, a retainer of Uther's,   9160
Earl of Cornwall, known far and wide,
A most intelligent man, in all ways most able.
Uther said to him, in a sombre mood,
'I salute you, Gorlois, good leader of men!
You are my own man, and very much to you I'll grant:
You are an accomplished knight and a man of intellect;
All of my men I put in your judgement,
All these who are my men I submit to your command,
And we shall do exactly what you shall decide.'
Then King Uther Pendragon hung his head right down,
And stood completely silent and asked Gorlois his intention.   9170
    Then Gorlois answered him, indeed most deferentially:
'Tell me, Uther Pendragon, why do you hold your head right
    down?
You know God by himself is better than we are altogether?
To whomever he decides, he can distribute glory;
Let us promise him by our lives that to him we'll not be false,*
And let us consider all our misdeeds;
Let each man right now be absolved of all his sins,
Let each man absolve the other, as if he were his brother,
And let every good knight take upon himself great penance,
And we shall promise God to make atonement for our sins;   9180
And then just at midnight we'll get ready to fight!
These heathen hounds think we're totally bound;
Octa son of Hengest thinks he's got us all trapped:
They're lying on the fields here under their tent covering;
They being very weary, their weapons they've done carrying,

Now they're going to doze a bit and then fall fast asleep.
They're not worried a bit that we're going to attack 'em!
Exactly at midnight we shall move straight
In total silence down from this hill;
Let no knight be so mad as to utter a word,   9190
Nor any man whatever to blow his horn here.
But we shall step towards them as if we were going stealing:
Before they are aware of it we shall annihilate them;
Up to them we shall creep and tell them some secrets!
And let every valiant man stoutly set on them,
And so from this land we shall drive this alien band,
And by our Lord's might we shall reclaim our rights.'
    The whole army acted just as Gorlois had instructed;
Every man scrupulously made his confession,
Promising to do good and to abandon evil.   9200
Exactly at midnight the knights armed themselves
And in front of all descended Uther Pendragon,
And all his knights, in total silence,
And out upon the fields they struck among the tents,
And slaughtered the heathen with the utmost strength:
Their flaxen locks streaming, they fled down the fields;
For the men it was detestable: they were dragging their intestines;
In complete weakness they fell to the ground.
There at once was captured Octa son of Hengest,
His blood-brother Ebissa and his partner Osa.   9210
The king had them fastened with strong iron fetters,
And entrusted them to sixty knights who were expert fighters,
To hold them fast upon the open fields.
And he himself pushed on, producing a huge clamour,
And Gorlois the courteous from the other quarter,
And all their knights, ever right ahead,
Striking right down all they came near to.
Some crept towards the wood on their bare knees:
By the next morning they were most miserable people.
Octa was tied up and taken to London,   9220
So were Ebissa and Osa; they had never been so sad!
    This fight was finished and the king marched off
Into Northumberland in greatest triumph,
And then towards Scotland and set it all in his own hand.
He made truce, he made peace that each man might proceed by
From one land to another land, even carrying gold in his hand.

With his peace he did such things as never before could any king
Since the very time that the Britons travelled here.
    And then after a time he went back to London:
He was there at Easter with his excellent men.   9230
There was rejoicing in London town at Uther Pendragon!
He sent his messengers throughout all his kingdom:
He asked prominent men, he asked peasant folk,
He asked bishops, he asked book-learned men
That they should come to London, to Uther the king,
Into London town, to Uther Pendragon.
Swiftly the noblemen came up to London:
They brought wife, they brought child, as King Uther commanded.
With great devotion the king heard the Mass,
And Gorlois, earl of Cornwall and with him many knights: 9240
There was great rejoicing in the town with Uther Pendragon.
When the Mass was sung, to the hall they thronged:
Brass trumpets were blown, the trestle-tables laid;
All the company ate and drank, and were all making merry.
    There sat King Uther upon his high throne;[39]
Facing him was Gorlois – indeed the knight was courteous –
The earl of Cornwall with his gracious wife.
When the nobles were seated, all at their meal,
The king sent a server to **Igerne** the gracious,
The wife of Earl Gorlois, the most courtly of women.   9250
He kept on gazing at her, flashing glances with his eyes,
Kept on sending over attendants to her table,   *Uther*
Kept on grinning at her, giving her special looks;   *in love*
And she looked at him affectionately (but I couldn't say whether
        she loved him).
The king wasn't clever or quick-witted enough
To be able to conceal his intentions from his courtiers.
The king kept up this [folly] so long that Gorlois got annoyed,*
And was really enraged with the king about his wife.
    The earl and his knights stood up straightaway,
And those most affronted knights swept off with the wife.   9260

---

[39] This is the narrative juncture where Malory's *Le Morte Darthur* begins.
Lawman, as a priest, points to Uther's ingratitude to Gorlois, who rescued him
and turned imminent defeat into victory; by verbal parallels (9251-3; cf.
7166-7), he makes a grim comparison with Vortigern who also brought near
disaster on his kingdom by falling in love with a woman at a feast.

King Uther saw this and was upset about it,
And taking twelve wise knights to himself, straight
He sent after Gorlois, great leader of men,
And ordered him to come with haste to the king,
And give the king due reverence and admit publicly his fault
In disgracing the king by departing from his feasting,
He and his knights, without any right,
Just because the king was merry with him and was drinking to his
    wife;
And if he refused to come back to acknowledge his guilt,
The king would be after him with all his full force,   9270
Seizing all his land and his silver and his gold.
    Gorlois, great lord of men, got all this message
And delivered his reply, the most furious of earls:
'No, so help me the Lord, who made the daylight by his word!
Never will I come back again nor sue for peace with him,
Nor shall he ever in his life disgrace me with my wife.
Just you tell King Uther he can find me at Tintagel:
If he'd like to ride that way, there I'll be waiting for him,
And there I'll give him a hard game, and very much public shame.'
Off went the earl, anger in his heart;   9280
He was enraged against the king, amazingly greatly,
And threatened Uther the king and all his lords with him,
But then he didn't know what was to come soon after.
    The earl went at once down into Cornwall:
There he had two castles securely enclosed;   *Gorlois's*
These castles were excellent, acquired from his ancestors: *Rebellion*
He sent off to Tintagel his beloved who was amiable,
Igerne by name, most gracious of women,
And enclosed her securely inside the castle.
Igerne was sorry, and saddened at heart   9290
That for her sake so many men would come to destruction.
The earl sent messengers over all Britain's land,
Bidding every worthy man to make his way to him,
For gold and for silver and for other good gifts,
So that very quickly they should come to Tintagel;
And his own knights came straightaway.
When they were assembled, those splendid soldiers,
Then he had fully fifteen thousand of them,
And very securely they shut fast Tintagel.
    Tintagel stands right upon the sea-strand   9300

And is firmly enclosed by the sea-cliffs
So that it cannot be taken by any kind of men,
Unless perhaps hunger in there were to enter.
The earl marched from there with seven thousand warriors
And went to another castle, and fortified it firmly,
Leaving his wife inside Tintagel with ten thousand men,
Since there was no task for the knights by day or by night
Except for some to guard the castle gate and the rest without care
    to lie and sleep,
And the earl maintained the other and with him was his own
    brother.

Uther, that king most sturdy, came to hear of this,   9310
That his earl Gorlois had gathered his own force
And intended to make war with most extreme rage.
The king summoned his army through all this country
And through all the lands which he held in his command:
Peoples of many types travelled there together
And arrived in London, to the sovereign.
Out from London town went Uther Pendragon:
He and his knights went on straightaway
For so long a way that they came right into Cornwall,
And across that river they travelled which is called Tamar,[40]   9320
Right up to the castle where they knew Gorlois was.

With the greatest loathing for him they laid siege to the castle,
Often rushing upon them there with rigorous force;
United they dashed in: men fell there in death.
For seven whole nights the king with his knights
Lay in siege round the castle; his men there were stressed.
Against the earl he was not able to gain any advantage,
And for all those seven nights lasted that peculiar fight.
When King Uther realized that he had no success in this
He kept on musing thoughtfully what should be his policy,   9330
Since he loved Igerne every bit as much as his own life,
While Gorlois for him in all the land was the man he loathed most,

---

[40] Tintagel, where Arthur is conceived, is on the north coast of Cornwall and
the river name here should be Camel, which flows into the Bristol Channel. But,
like some manuscripts of Wace, O has *Tambre* here, and C has *Tambreis*, the
Tamar. Arthur's last battle is on the Tamar (14238), which, however, is located
at Camelford (14239), actually on the Camel, as Madden notes. Whichever is
Lawman's intended reading, in the extant text Arthur's life moves in an
inexorable circle back to its beginning. See also W n. 66).

And in every way he was oppressed with grief in the kingdom of
    this world
Because he could not be entitled to have his way at all.
    There was with the king an old man who was most useful;
He was a very rich subject and was sound in each decision;
His name was **Ulfin** (there was much common sense in him).
The king stuck out his chin and stared hard at Ulfin
(He was very distressed, his mind was disturbed);
Then Uther Pendragon addressed Ulfin the knight: 9340
'Ulfin, give me some advice, or I shall very quickly die;
I'm in such a state of deep desire that I simply can't exist,
For the lovely Igerne. Now keep these words secret,
For, Ulfin my dear man, your splendid instructions,
Aloud and in silence I shall now observe.'
    Then responded Ulfin to the king speaking to him:
'What I hear now is surprising for a king to say!
You're in love with Igerne and this is how you keep it dark!
The woman is too dear to you and her husband too detested;
You've been burning up his lands and making him a beggar,   9350
And threatening to kill him and destroy all of his kinsfolk.
Now do you think all that oppression will win over Igerne?
If it does then she acts differently from every other woman,
Finding love's sweetness in the midst of utter terror!
But if you love Igerne then you ought to keep it secret,
And straightaway send to her some silver and some gold,
And artfully love her with amorous promises.
Even then it's quite debatable whether you could get her,
Because Igerne is well behaved, a very loyal woman,
So was her mother and more of her family.   9360
It's the truth I'm telling you, dearest of all kings,
You must go about it another way if you want to win her over.
    'Now yesterday there came to me a very virtuous hermit,[41]
Who swore by his chin that he knew where Merlin
Each and every night seeks rest beneath the skies,
And he'd often spoken with him and had told him stories.

[41] Lawman adds an episode of seventy lines on the search for Merlin (who in
Wace is already present in the army). He may have taken the details of Merlin's
abode in the wilderness from Geoffrey's *Vita Merlini* (Le Saux, *Sources*,
p. 114–15). The episode proves Merlin's integrity (he again refuses payment)
and power of command.

So if we could coax Merlin into being in our scheme,
Then you would be able to get everything you want.'
   Then Uther Pendragon's mood was much calmer,
And he gave a ready answer: 'Ulfin, you've spoken well!   9370
I shall give into your hands thirty ploughs' worth of land.
If you get hold of Merlin and do just what I want.'
Ulfin went right through that army and sought through all the
    host,
And after a time that hermit he did find,
And in a hurry he brought him to the king,
Who would give him in hand seven ploughs of land
If only he could bring Merlin to the king.
   The hermit began to roam in the west region,
Into a wilderness, to a vast forest
Where he had been living for very many winters,   9380
And very often Merlin made his way in.
As soon as the hermit got in, then he encountered Merlin,
Standing under a tree, in strong anticipation.
He saw the hermit coming, which for some time had been his
    custom;
He ran towards him in greeting: they were both pleased to meet;
They hugged and they kissed and they chatted like friends.
Then Merlin remarked (he was really perceptive):
'Now tell me, my dear friend, why you didn't want to tell me
Not for any kind of thing, that you were going to the king!
But anyway I knew at once the moment that I missed you   9390
That you had come to Uther the king,
And what the king was saying to you, and offering you his lands
On condition you should bring me to Uther the king,
And Ulfin, who had sought you, to the king had brought you.
And Uther Pendragon, straightway at once,
Placed into his hands thirty ploughs' worth of lands,
And into your own hands seven ploughs' worth of lands.
   'So, Uther is passionate about the lovely Igerne,
Amazingly fiercely and for Gorlois's wife;
But for as long as for ever it will happen never   9400
That her he should win – except by my scheme –
For no woman is truer in the kingdom of this world.
Nevertheless he's going to have the beautiful Igerne,   *Merlin's*
And on her he'll beget one who'll be active far and wide; *Prophecy*
He shall beget upon her a most remarkable man;

For as long as will be for ever, death will come to him never;
All the time that this world stands, his reputation will endure,
And within Rome itself he shall rule the leaders.
All who live in Britain shall bow down to him;
Of him shall poets sing their splendid praises: 9410
From his own breast noble bards shall partake;
Great warriors shall upon his blood be drunk;
From his eyes shall fly glowing coals of fire,
Each finger on his hand a sharp sword of steel;
Ahead of him shall fall stone-constructed walls;
Warriors will tremble, battle-ensigns will fall;*
In this way for a long time he shall march across lands,
Conquer those who live there and impose his own laws.
These are the tokens of the son who will come from Uther
    Pendragon
And from Lady Igerne. This prophecy is very secret   9420
Since as yet it's known by neither Igerne nor Uther
That from Uther Pendragon shall arise such a son,
Since as yet he's unbegotten who will arouse all the nations.
  'But my lord', exclaimed Merlin, 'now it is your desire
That I shall hasten forth to the host of the king;
Your word I will listen to, and now I shall depart,
And for love of you I will travel, to Uther Pendragon,
So that you shall have the land which he placed in your hands.'
As they conversed like this the hermit began weeping;
Affectionately he kissed him; there they separated.   9430
Merlin travelled due south: he knew the land well enough;
Directly he hastened to the host of the king.
The moment Uther saw him, he moved over towards him,
And like this spoke Uther Pendragon: 'Merlin, you are welcome!
Here I place within your hands all the government of my lands,
And so that you may guide me in my pressing need.'
  Uther declared to him all he desired,
And how for him in all the nation Igerne was the dearest woman,
And Gorlois her husband the most detested of men –
'And unless I have your advice, very soon you'll see me dead   9440
[So desperately am I yearning for the wife of Earl Gorlois!']* 9440a
Then Merlin responded: 'Get Ulfin to come now,
And make him possessor of those thirty ploughlands,
And give to the hermit just what you promised.
But I don't want to own land, nor [silver, nor gold],*

Seeing that for giving good advice I'm quite the wealthiest man!
And if I wanted to own property my skills would grow the weaker.
  'But everything you want will turn out for you well,
For I know the kind of medicine, which you will find most
      pleasant,
So that all your [appearance] will become just like the earl's,*
Your voice, your gestures in the midst of that company,   9450
Your horse and your clothing; and just like that you'll ride off.
When Igerne is to see you, her reactions will be good.
She lies in Tintagel, securely locked in;
There is no knight however noble, elect of any nation,
Who by force could unbar the gates of Tintagel,
Unless they could be burst by hunger and by thirst.
This is the truth which I wish to tell you:
In all respects you'll appear as if you were the earl,
And I will be in precise detail like the man **Britael**
Who is a very stern knight and is the earl's steward;   9460
Jordan is his chamberlain (he's a very splendid man):
Instantly I'll transform Ulfin to be the same as Jordan;
So you'll be the lord, I'll be Britael your steward,
And Ulfin, Jordan your chamberlain; and this very night we're
      going in:
You are to go as I instruct, wherever I shall direct.
During this very night a full fifty knights
With their spears and their shields must surround your pavilions,
So that no living man can come anywhere near there,
And should any man at all come there, he must be instantly
      beheaded,
For those knights shall say (those splendid men of yours)   9470
That you have had blood-letting and are resting in your bed.'
  These things were immediately arranged just like this;
Off went the king – no one knew a thing –
And there went along with him Ulfin and Merlin;
They took the direct way that down to Tintagel lay.
They approached the castle gate and called out like
      acquaintances:[42]
'Undo the bars on this gate: the earl's arrived here,
Gorlois the lord and Britael his steward,
And Jordan the chamberlain; all night we've been travelling!'

[42] The domestic details here are all Lawman's addition to the scene.

The porter proclaimed it all around and knights ran up on the
    battlements
And exchanged words with Gorlois, and identified him for   9481
    sure.
The knights were very prompt and opened up the castle gate,
And allowed him to come inside (they were not at all concerned
    that time:
They thought they were quite certain to have a celebration).
    So then by his magic they had Merlin inside there,
And in their command [were holding] no less than Uther himself,
    the king,*
And were conducting there with him his loyal servant, Ulfin!
This news travelled quickly indoors to the lady,
That her husband had come, and with him his three men.*
Out came Igerne, out to meet the 'earl',   9490
Speaking these words, with loving expression:
'Welcome, my lord, whom I love best of men,
And welcome Jordan, and Britael, you are too.
Did you escape from the king without any harm?'
Then Uther spoke with confidence (just as if he were Gorlois):
'Enormous is the throng which is with Uther Pendragon,
And I have in the night stolen away from the fight
Because I was longing for you: of all women I love you best!
Move into the bedroom and have my bed made up,
And I shall take my rest for this whole night's space,   9500
And all day tomorrow, so I can entertain my men.'
Igerne moved to the bedroom and had a bed made for him:
That most regal bed with royal cloth was spread.
The king looked at it closely and got into his bed,
And Igerne lay down beside Uther Pendragon!
    Now Igerne was confident that this man was Gorlois,[43]
From no kind of hint of anything did she recognize Uther the king.
The king turned to her as man is bound to do to his mate,
And had his own way with the dearest of women,
And on her he begot a remarkable man   9510
Most courageous of all kings who ever came to men,
And **Arthur** he was known as, here on this earth.

---

[43] Twice Lawman asserts that Igerne did not know that this man was not her
husband (see also 9513), and in another addition (9598–9) has Igerne refusing
to believe Uther's claim. Igerne is raped (Morris, *Character of Arthur*, p. 28).

Igerne had no idea who was lying in her arms;
All the time she was confident that this man was the Earl Gorlois.
    There was no longer time than the arrival of daybreak
When all at once and rightly the knights there realized
That the king had travelled off away from his troops.
Then the knights declared (though it was not at all the case)
That the king had fled away, quite prostrated by panic
(But they were all lying when they said that of the king);   9520
On this they held much discussion about Uther Pendragon.
Then the earls remarked, and the men of highest rank:
'Now that Gorlois is aware how everything goes here,
That our king has departed and has deserted his host,
He will instantly arm his infantry,
And out he'll come to fight and fell us to the ground,
Making huge slaughter with his savage leaders;
Then it would be better for us if we never had been born!
But let us blow brass trumpets and bring our host together,
And **Cador** the courageous shall carry the king's standard,   9530
Raising high the dragon at the head of this detachment,
And march to the castle with our courageous men;
And the Earl Aldolf shall be our commander,
And we shall obey him as if he were the king;
And so we shall rightly against Gorlois fight;
And should he wish to speak with us and request this king's peace,
Establish a settlement with true and sober oaths,
Then we may with full honour make our way from here;
Then our inferiors can't make any reproaches
That out of rank terror we ran away from here.'   9540
All the inhabitants approved of this notion.
    Brass trumpets they blew, brought the host together,
Up they raised the dragon, unique among all standards.
There many a strong fellow slung his shield over his shoulder,
Many a brave captain; and marched to the castle.
Gorlois was inside, with his brave men:
He had brass trumpets blown and brought his host together:
Leaping on steeds, the knights began riding.
The knights were very alert and sallied forth from the gate.
They encountered at once; steadfastly they struck: 9550
Fated men fell, sank down on the field:
There was much bloodshed, a bad time for the folk;

In the fighting, true it is, someone slew the Earl Gorlois.   *Gorlois's*
Then his men started fleeing and the others were pursuing;   *Death*
They came to the castle and inside it they pushed:
Soon there came inside it both the two armies.
There they continued the fight as long as there was light;
Before the daylight had dispersed the castle was quite conquered.
No slave there so mean who was not an excellent leader.

Swiftly came those tidings into Tintagel,   9560
Straight into the castle which Uther was in,
That he was slain, true it was, the earl, their lord Gorlois,
And all his men at arms, and his castle captured.
This was heard by the king as he lay there love-making,
And he leapt from the bedroom as if he had been a lion.
Then declared King Uther (of this information quite aware):
'Silence, silence now, you knights in the hall!
Here I am, no doubt of it, your own lord, Gorlois,
And Jordan my chamberlain and Britael my steward.
Myself and these two knights slipped off from the fight,   9570
And we made our way here and have not been killed there!
But now I shall hasten and assemble my host,
And myself and all my knights entirely by night
Shall march to a town and meet Uther Pendragon,
And unless he speaks of atonement I will avenge myself with
      honour.
And you will block up this castle extremely securely,
And encourage Igerne not to be too anxious;
Now I'm going off straightaway, so I bid you all goodnight!'
In front of him went Merlin and the lord Ulfin,
And Uther Pendragon next, out of Tintagel fortress;   9580
They kept on going all night, until it was broad daylight,
When he came to the place where his army was stationed.
Merlin had by then replaced, in every detail, the king's face,
And then the knights recognized their own king and lord.
There many a fine Briton was filled with relief!
Then there was in Britain rejoicing in plenty:
Horns were sounding, musicians' songs resounding,
Glad knights, each and every one dressed in all his finery.
There for three days the king continued his stay,
And on the fourth day to Tintagel he marched.   9590
He sent into the castle his especially good lords,
To salute Igerne, the most noble of women,

And send her as a token what in bed they had spoken.
He ordered her to surrender the castle with speed:
No other course could be adopted, since her husband now was
    dead.
Igerne was still assuming that it was the case
That the dead earl had come to visit his household,
And would have believed that it must be a lie
That this king, Uther, could ever have come there.

    Knights went to take counsel, knights went to commune;   9600
They decided that they would not hold the castle any longer,
So letting their drawbridge down, they surrendered to Uther
    Pendragon.
Then all this royal land once more stood in Uther's hand.

    There Uther the king took Igerne as queen;
Igerne was pregnant by Uther the king,
All through Merlin's magic, before they were married.
The time arrived when it was destined that Arthur should
    be born.   *Arthur's*
The moment he came on earth, fairies received him:[44]   *Birth*
They enchanted the child with a very strong spell:
They gave him the power to be the greatest of all soldiers;   9610
They gave him a second thing: that he would be a noble king;
They gave him a third thing: that he should live long.
They gave to him, the royal heir, the most excellent gifts:
That he was the most generous of all living men.
These the elves bestowed on him, and so the child throve.

    After Arthur there was born the gracious lady –
She was called **Anna**, the graceful young girl –
And afterwards she married **Lot**, the ruler of Lothian;
In the land of Lothian she was the liegemen's lady.

    Long years lived Uther with great happiness here,   9620
In great peace, in great quiet, liberal in his kingdom.
When he was an old man, then a disease came upon him;
The disease knocked him down: sick lay Uther Pendragon;
In this sickness he lay here for fully seven years.
Then the British became very badly depraved:*
They frequently committed crimes, fearing no reprisals.

---

[44] The 'fairies' are an addition to Wace, perhaps taken from French romances
like *Lancelot du Lake* or, if Lawman was writing well after 1200, from *Ogier le
Danois* (Madden).

All this time in London, lying fettered in prison
Was Octa son of Hengest who had been captured in York,
And his companion Ebissa and the other one was Osa.
They were guarded by twelve knights both by day and
    by night,   9630
Who were thoroughly bored with lolling round in London!
Octa heard information about the king's illness,
And chatted to the warders who were supposed to watch him:
'Pay attention now, you knights, to what I want to announce:
We are lying here in London, firmly trussed in prison,
And for many a long day now you've been in command of us;
It would be better for us by far to be living in Saxony,
Surrounded with great riches, than wretched like this here.
And if you were to change sides, and to do what I want,
I would give you land, much silver and much gold,   9640
So that, rich for ever more, you'd be rulers in that land,
And live out your lives as you'd most of all like to,
Seeing you can't expect to get good gifts out of your King Uther,
Since any minute now he'll be dead and his troops quite deserted;
Then you won't have either the one thing or the other.
But you work it out, you good chaps, and direct your charity at us,
And bear in mind what you'd prefer if you were lying bound like
    this,
When you could live in comfort in your own country.'
    Again and again did Octa talk like this with those knights.
Knights started discussing; knights started deciding: 9650
To Octa they said softly: 'We'll do just what you want!'
They swore solemn oaths that they would not betray them.   *Octa's*
Then there came a night when the wind was blowing   *Rebellion*
    right;
Off went the knights in the middle of the night,
Leading out Octa and Ebissa and Osa;
Along the Thames they took their way out on to the sea,
Off they sailed into Saxon lands.
Their kinsfolk came to meet them in enormous crowds;
They progressed throughout that people where they most
    preferred:
They were donated lands, they were given silver and gold.   9660
Octa thought carefully what could be his policy;
He intended to come here and avenge his father's wounds.
They acquired an army of innumerable folk

And travelled to the sea with tremendous menace:
[Off they set immediately] till they arrived in Scotland.*
At once they got quickly to land and they attacked it with fire!
The Saxons were cruel: they slaughtered the Scots,
With fire they destroyed three thousand farmsteads;
Many Scots they slaughtered, quite beyond reckoning.
    These bad tidings came to Uther the king: 9670
Uther grieved terribly and was dreadfully depressed
And sent into Lothian for his beloved friends,
And greeted Lot, his son-in-law, wishing him all health,[45]
And instructing him to take in hand all his royal lands,
His knights and his freemen and freely to govern them,
And lead them in an army as the laws stood for the country,
And he instructed his beloved knights to be loyal to Lot,
With gestures of affection, as if he were the nation's king.
Because Lot was a very good knight, and had conducted many a
        fight,
And was very generous to every single man,   9680
He handed him the regency of this entire country.
    Octa caused much warfare and Lot fought him often,
And often he gained the advantage and often he lost it;
The British were high-spirited and excessively haughty,
And were quite without respect because of the king's age,
And behaved most contemptuously to the earl Lot,
And all his instructions they performed most inadequately,
Were all in two minds – they had more trouble for that reason!
This was soon reported to the sick monarch,
That his great men despised Lot totally.   9690
    Now I shall recount to you, in this same chronicle,
How King Uther then organized himself.
He said that he would himself travel to his army,
And with his own eyes observe who was doing well there.
There he had constructed a fine horse-litter,
And had forces summoned for defence throughout all his kingdom,

---

[45] Lot seems to be already married to Anna although her elder brother Arthur
is still barely fifteen. His kingdom, which has become 'Lothian' in Malory, is
spelled: *Loeneis* C 9619, *Loæines* C 9672, *Leones* C 9618, *Leoneis* O 9617/8,
9619 and *Leoneys* O 9672. P. J. C. Field recommends reading *Lyonesse* here
(review of B&W, *N&Q* (1991), 97) but Geoffrey reads *ad consulatum Lodone-
sie . . . remisit* (*First Variant*, ed. Wright, p. 145) which Wace renders *Loeneis*.

So that each man on pain of death must come to him at once,
To avenge the king's disgrace, or pay with lives and with limbs:
'And should there be any man who will not swiftly come,
I shall as swiftly execute him: either behead him or hang
    him!'[46]   9700
All of them immediately came to the court:
There they did not remain, not the fat ones nor the thin.
The king straightaway took all of his knights,
And journeyed at once to the town of Verulam.
   Uther Pendragon surrounded Verulamium town;
Octa was inside it with all of his men.
In those days Verulamium was a very regal domain:
There St **Alban** was martyred and deprived of his life's days,
After which the town was laid waste and many people slain.
Uther was outside and Octa was inside;   9710
Uther's army advanced to the walls.
The proud men angrily made an assault:
Not one stone of the walls could they make fall,
And with no amount of force could they damage the wall:
Very pleased with himself was Hengest's son Octa
When he saw the British backing off from the walls,
And mournfully returning to their own tents.
Then Octa remarked to his companion Ebissa:
'Uther the crippled man came here to Verulam,
And wants a battle with us here lying on his stretcher!   9720
He's intending to use his crutches to give us a fatal thrust!
But tomorrow when it's daylight, the troops must all arise
And open up our fortress gates: we'll get a hold on all those great
    men;
We're not going to lurk in here just because of one lame man!
Out we shall gallop mounted on our noble steeds
And rush upon Uther and rout all his retainers:
All those who've ridden this way are all of them fated!
And then let's seize the cripple and shove him in our fetters[47]
And keep the pathetic thing until he perishes,
And that's how his handicapped limbs will get healed,   9730
And his arthritic bones: with agonizing rods of steel!'*

---

[46] Uther's self-assertion, characterized by his speech here and at 9743 ff., is more notable than in Wace.
[47] The savage humour of Octa's boast is Lawman's own.

That was Octa's conversation with his comrade Ebissa,
But it all turned out quite other than what they expected.
    In the morning when the dawn came they unfastened the doors;
Up rose Octa, Ebissa and Osa
And ordered their knights to get ready to fight,
To undo their broad gates and unbar the fortress.
Octa rode out and after him went a great crowd;
With his valiant warriors he encountered disaster!
Uther had realised Octa was coming towards them,   9740
Intending to fell his force to the ground.
Then shouted Uther with a vigorous voice there:
'Where are you British, my brave commanders?
Now has arrived that very day when the Lord may give us aid;
Octa shall discover that, for threatening to fetter me!
Remember now your ancestors, how good they were at fighting;
Remember the reputation which I have handed on to you:
Don't you ever let these heathens have use of your homes,
These same rabid dogs get control of your lands;
And to the Lord I shall pray who made the light of day   9750
And to all of the saints who are seated high in heaven
That on this field of battle [I] may have their succour.*
Now march speedily to them; the Lord give [us] his support,*
The all-powerful God give protection to my men!'
    Knights began riding, spears began gliding,
Broad spears were breaking, shields were splitting,
Helmets were shattering, soldiers collapsing.
The British were bold and active in the battle,
While the heathen hounds were falling to the ground:
There were killed Octa, Ebissa and Osa!   9760
Seventeen thousand there tumbled into hell;
Many escaped from there towards the north area.
All during daylight Uther's own knights
Killed and captured all they came near;
When it was evening the battle was all won.   *Victory*
    Then the men in the army sang with full force,
And these were the words of their joyful songs:
'Here comes Uther Pendragon,
To Verulam he's come;   9768
He's been a-dubbing new knights:
Sir Octa, Sir Ebissa
And old Sir Osa too.   9769

He's cuffed them pretty soundly
To show they've joined the Order,   9770
To give men tales of them to tell
Among their tribe at home,   9771
And give men songs of them to sing
Throughout all Saxony.'   9772
    Then Uther was happy and greatly relieved,
And addressed his troops, whom he held in much esteem,
And Uther the aged uttered these words:
'The Saxon men considered me merely contemptible,
They mocked at my infirmity with their scornful words
Because I was carried here on a horse-litter,
And said that I was dead and my troops were in a trance;
Yet now a great miracle is manifested in this realm   9780
When this dead king has now killed off the living,
And has set some fleeing off on the wind.
Now this has occurred by the will of the Lord.'
    The Saxon men fled exceedingly fast,
Those who from the sides had escaped from the fight;
Off they went striding away into Scotland,
And chose as their king **Colgrim** the handsome;   *Colgrim*
He was Hengest's kinsman and dearest of men to him,   *the*
And Octa had loved him all the time he was alive.   *Leader*
Those Saxon men were severely disheartened,   9790
And strode off together straight into Scotland,
And Colgrim the handsome they appointed as king,
And assembled an army far and wide around the country,
And said they were going, through their hostile arts
In Winchester town to kill Uther Pendragon.[48]
O tragedy, that things like this should ever happen!
    Now the Saxon men said, in their secret consultations:
'Let us take six knights, clever men and agile,   *Saxon*
Cunning as spies, and let's send them to court.   *Conspiracy*
Make them move along in the guise of almsmen,   9800
And stay at the court with the great king,
And every single day travel through all the assembly,
And go to get the royal dole, as if they were infirm,
And listen very keenly among those unfortunates
To learn if by a trick one might, by daytime or by night

---

[48] Winchester is an error for Verulam (9768).

Within Winchester town get at Uther Pendragon,
And with murderous intent kill that same king.'
(Then would all their wishes be entirely achieved,
And they would be unconcerned about Constantine's kin.)
    Now off went the knights, all in broad daylight,[49]   9810
In the clothing of almsmen (most accursed knights)
To the king's court: there they caused havoc;
They went to the dole as if they were not hale,
And listened eagerly for news of the king's illness:
How someone might contrive to bring about the king's death.
Then they met a certain knight coming from the king direct,
A relation of Uther's and his favourite retainer.
These traitors, as they were sitting all along the street,
Called out to the knight with kindly expressions:
'Lord, we are feeble men in the kingdom of this world;   9820
A while ago we were accounted great men in this country
Until the Saxon men displaced us to the depths
And deprived us of everything, taking from us our property.
Now we're reciting prayers for Uther our king;
For this each day in just one meal we have food in exchange:
Not at all do meat or fish come into our begging-dish,*
Nor any kind of liquor except for gulps of water,
Nothing but water drinks: that's why we're so thin.'
    The knight heard this lament and straight back he went,
And came to the king, as he lay in his bedroom,   9830
And said to the king: 'Good health to you, my lord!
Outside here are sitting six men similar in bearing,
All of them are companions and all are dressed in hessian.
Formerly they were, in the kingdom of this world,
Virtuous leaders, with goods well endowed;
Now to the depths the Saxon men have sent them
So that in this world they are reckoned worthless,
They can't get hold of any food except just for bread
Nor of any liquor except for gulps of water;
That's how they lead their lives within your own land,   9840
And they're praying their prayers that God will let you live long.'
Then said King Uther: 'Get them to come in here;

[49] The plotting of Uther's murder is entirely Lawman's, and shocks the reader
because he has omitted at 9783 Wace's sombre reference to Uther's growing
sickness and the disbanding of the army.

I want to clothe them, I want to feed them,
For the love of my Lord all the time I'm alive.'
There came into the bedroom those traitorous men;
The king had them clothed, the king had them fed,
And at night he would lay each of them in his bed;
And each for his part paid eager attention
To how they might kill the king with foul murder.
But not at all, not for anything could they kill Uther the king   9850
Nor by any scheming could succeed in getting at him.

   Then it happened at one time when the rain was pouring down,
That a doctor who was there called out from the bedroom
To one of the attendant knights and told him straightaway
To run to the well which was just outside the hall
And set there a good serving-man to protect it from the rain:
'Since the king can't endure any draught in the world
Except cold well water, in which he takes pleasure:
It's the finest of drinks for the disease that he has.'
Immediately those six knights heard that conversation: 9860
They were prompt in doing harm, and went out then in the dark
Straight to the well and there they did their harm.
They instantly drew out six shining phials
Brimful of poison, the most bitter of all liquids:
Six entire phials they poured into the well;
Then immediately all the well was affected by the poison.
Then the traitors were most blithe that they were alive
And off they went away: they did not dare to remain there.

   Then right away arrived two attendant knights
Carrying in their hands two goblets of gold.   9870
They approached the well; their goblets they filled
And went back again at once to where King Uther was,
Straight into the bedroom where he lay on his bed:
'Greetings to you, Uther! Now we have come here
And have brought for you what you have been asking for:
Cold well water; take it and enjoy it!'
Up got the sick king and sat on his bed,
And drank some of the water; at once he started sweating,
His heart-beat grew weaker, his face grew ever blacker,[50]
His belly started swelling: the king was really dying!   9880

---

[50] The verb *blakien* can mean 'become pale' or 'grow black' but Wace's 'darkened' suggests that the latter is the sense here.

There could be no help for it: there King Uther lay dead,   *Uther's*
And everybody died if they had drunk from that water.   *Death*
   When the courtiers saw the tragic state of the king,
And of the king's attendants who had been destroyed by the
      poison,
Then out to the well ran those knights who were nimble
And blocked up the well with strenuous labour,
With earth and with stones they made a steep mound.
   Then the household detachment took the dead king's body –
A tremendous procession – and carried him out,
Stern-minded men, into Stonehenge,   9890
And there it was they buried him, beside his dear brother:
Side by side together both of them lie there.
   Then all together came those who were highest in the land,
Leaders and warriors and educated men,
They all came to London to a very crowded hustings.
The powerful leaders adopted as their policy
That they would send messengers over the sea
Into Brittany for the best of all the youth
That there was in those days in the kingdom of this world,
Arthur he was called, the best of all knights,   9900
And announce that he must come at once to his own kingdom,
Because Uther now had died just like Aurelius before him,
And Uther Pendragon had no other son
Who after his own days could govern the British,
Could rule them with honour and take the kingdom over,
Since there were still in this land some Saxons left behind:
Colgrim the courageous and many thousand confederates
Who often brought vile injuries to our own British men.
   Speedily the British selected three bishops
And seven mounted men mighty in wisdom;   9910
Off they began to move right into Brittany[51]
And very swiftly to Arthur they came:
'Good health to you, Arthur, most noble of knights!
Uther sent you greeting when about to depart

[51] Only Lawman has Arthur brought from Brittany (where Aurelius and
Uther had been kept in protection in childhood), and he adds the official greeting
(9913–22) and Arthur's response (9928–9). A strong claimant to the throne of
England in 1199 was Arthur of Brittany, whom King John probably strangled
with his own hand (see n. 108 below).

And requested that in Britain you should yourself
Hold to the just laws and help your own people
And defend [your own] kingdom as a good king should do,*
Put to flight your enemies and drive them from the land,
And to God's gentle son he prayed, to come to your aid
That you might succeed and receive the land from God,   9920
For dead is Uther Pendragon and you are Arthur, his son,
And dead is the other, Aurelius his brother.'
   So they finished talking, and Arthur sat without speaking:
One moment he was pallid, and in colour very blanched,
Next moment he was red and his emotions much aroused.
When at last his words broke, they were good things which he
    spoke,
Up he spoke like this, piously, that noble knight Arthur:
'Lord Christ, God's own son, now come to our aid,
So that all my whole life I may keep the laws of God.'
Arthur was fifteen years old when this message he was told   9930
And all those years were well employed for he had grown up very
    well.
   Arthur immediately summoned his knights
And ordered every single man to collect up his weapons
And get their horses saddled in most extreme haste,
For he intended to be on his way to this other Britain.
To the sea proceeded splendid leaders
At St Michael's Mount with a very massive army:
The sea sent them up on to that shore; at Southampton they came
    ashore.
Arthur the great began to ride off,
Directly to Silchester which seemed to him best.   9940
There the British troops were boldly assembled;
Great was the celebration when Arthur came to the city:
There was the blast of trumpets, and very triumphant men.
There Arthur the young was raised to the throne.   ARTHUR
   When Arthur was made king – now hear a strange thing:
He was generous with food to every man alive,
A knight of the very best, of amazing courage;
To the young he was a father, to the old folk a consoler,
And he was with the foolish amazingly strict;
Wrong he found really disgusting and justice always dear;   9950
Each of his cupbearers and chamber attendants
And all of his footmen carried gold in their hands,

On their backs and on their bed they had cloth of fine weave;
Every single cook he had was also a splendid champion,
Every single knight's squire was also a bold fighter.
    The king kept all his court in the greatest content,
And with such qualities he surpassed all kings:
In vigorous strength and in great wealth,
And such was his character that all people knew of it.
Now Arthur was a good king, and his courtiers loved him,   9960
What concerned his kingdom was widely known all round.
    The king held in London a very crowded hustings;
To it were invited all his feudal knights,
The great men and the humble, to honour the king.
When they had all come, an immense throng,
Up stood King Arthur the noblest of kings,
And had brought before him the most special relics;
To these did the king kneel some three times:
His warriors could not guess what he would decree.
Arthur held up his right hand: there he swore on oath   9970
That never in his life, not at any man's direction,   *Coronation*
Would the Saxons be contented in the land of Britain,   *Oath*
Would not be honoured with land nor enjoy any favours,
But he would expel them because they were his enemies,
Slew Uther Pendragon who was Constantine's son,
As they had done the other, Aurelius his brother,
For which in his land they were more loathed than all people.
    Arthur straightaway took his wise knights:
Like it or loathe it, they must all swear the oath
That they would remain for ever loyally with Arthur   9980
And avenge King Uther, whom the Saxons had killed here.
Arthur sent written messages far and wide throughout his land
To seek out all the knights whom he might acquire,
So that at once to the king they might come,
And he would in his land with affection maintain them,
Supplying them with land, with silver and with gold.
    Off the king went with an immense force of men;
He led amazing numbers and advanced direct to York;
There he lay for one night; in the morning he went right on
To where he knew were Colgrim and his confederates with
        him.   9990
Since Octa had been slain and deprived of his life's days
(He who was Hengest's son, who out of Saxony had come)

Colgrim was the leading man who came out of Saxon
      lands   *Campaign*
Following Hengest and Horsa his brother   *Against*
And Octa and Osa and their companion Ebissa.   *Colgrim*
Colgrim held jurisdiction in those days over the Saxons,
He led them and he guided them with stern authority:
Many were the supporters who were marching with Colgrim.
   Colgrim heard the tidings about Arthur the king,
How he was coming towards him and wished to do him
      harm.   10000
Colgrim thought carefully what might be his policy,
And assembled his army all through the north country.
To there proceeded in unity all the Scottish people:
Picts then and Saxons joined forces together,
And men of many origins accompanied Colgrim.
Onward he was marching with an immense contingent
To oppose Arthur, most admirable king;
He proposed to kill the king within his own land
And fell all his followers, thrown to the ground,
And set all this kingdom in his own hands,   10010
Felling Arthur the young right to the ground.
   Off then went Colgrim and his army with him,
And went with his army till he reached a stretch of water;
The water is called the Douglas, the destroyer of people.
There Arthur encountered him, ready with his forces;
At a broad ford the forces engaged:
Their vigorous champions strongly attacked,
Those fated fell there, thrown to the ground;
There was very much bloodshed, misery was rife;
Spear-shafts shattered; soldiers fell down there.   10020
Arthur noticed that; his mind was disconcerted;
Arthur thought carefully what could be his policy,
And withdrew to the rear into a more open field;
His enemies assumed he was about to escape:
That delighted Colgrim and all his army with him!
They assumed that Arthur must be filled with cowardice
And rushed over the water as if they were raging mad.
   When Arthur noticed that Colgrim had come very close to him
And that they were both of them on one side of the water,
Arthur noblest of kings announced these words: 10030
'Do you see, my Britons, right here beside us,

Our avowed enemies (may Christ exterminate them!)
Colgrim the savage, out of Saxon lands?
In this land his kindred slaughtered our ancestors,
But now the day's arrived which the Almighty has appointed
When he must forfeit his life and his friends will all be lost,
Or we ourselves must die: we cannot see him left alive.
The men of the Saxons are to suffer sorrow,
And we're to revenge honourably the dear men of our retinue.'

 Arthur caught up his shield, covering his breast, 10040
And began rampaging like the rime-grey wolf,*[52]
When it comes loping from the snow-laden woodlands
Intending to savage such creatures as it fancies.
Then Arthur called out to his beloved knights:
'Forward and quickly, my valiant warriors,
All of us together at them! We shall all have victory
And they will heel over like the high wood
When the wild wind weighs into it with force!'
There flew across the fields thirty thousand shields
And struck into Colgrim's knights so that the earth
  reverberated; 10050
Broad spears smashed; shields were clattering;*
The Saxon men fell, thrown to the ground.
Colgrim was watching this: he was distressed about it,
He the most able man to come out of Saxon lands.

 Colgrim began to flee, fast and furiously,
And his steed carried him with superb power
Over the deep water, and protected him from death.
The Saxons started sinking: disaster was their lot.
Arthur turned his spear's point against them and stopped them
  getting to the ford:
There the Saxons drowned, at least seven thousand; 10060
Some started floundering as the wild crane does
In the moorland fens when its flighting is impaired
And the speeding hawks are bearing down upon it,
Hounds in the reedbeds pounce on the wretched bird;
Then nothing does it any good, neither land nor water:

---

[52] This is the first of seven 'long-tailed similes' (see also 10047–8, 10061–7, 10398–413, 10609–710, 10629–36, 10647–50) and one metaphor (10639–45). Lawman may derive this stylistic technique from Latin epic or its twelfth-century imitations (*E&I*, pp. 63–6).

Hawks are striking at it, dogs are biting at it;
Then the regal bird has reached its death hour.*
   Over the fields Colgrim fled with speed
Until to York he came, riding most remarkably;
He dashed into the city and firmly shut the gates: 10070
Inside there with him he had ten thousand men,
They were splendid citizens who were on his side.
Arthur came in pursuit with thirty thousand men
And marched direct to York with a record band of troops,
And besieged Colgrim who defended it against him.
   Seven nights before there had gone marching southwards
Baldulf the great, the brother of Colgrim,   *Baldulf*
Encamped beside the sea's edge waiting for **Childric**.
Now Childric at that time was an emperor in firm command
Within Germany – which land he inherited as his own.   10080
Then Baldulf heard as he was camped beside the sea
That Arthur had Colgrim trapped inside York city.
Baldulf had assembled seven thousand men,
Very brave warriors who were camped by the sea.
They came to a decision that they'd ride back again,
Abandoning Childric, and march back towards York,
And fight against Arthur and annihilate his troops.
Baldulf swore in his rage that he'd put Arthur in his grave,
And be lord of all this realm with his brother Colgrim;
Baldulf would not wait for the emperor Childric   10090
But there and then he set forth and betook himself due north
From one day to the next with ever more determined troops
Until he came into a wood in a waste area,
A full seven miles from Arthur's forces.
With seven thousand knights, he had intended in the night
To ride down upon Arthur before the king was aware
And lay low his people and put Arthur to death.
   But it all turned out quite other than he had expected,
For Baldulf had in his bodyguard a certain British knight,
A kinsman of Arthur's who was known as **Maurin**.[53]   10100
Maurin slipped away to the woods on the sly,
Through woodland and through fields till he came to Arthur's tents,

---

[53] Lawman supplies Maurin and Patrick (10155) and the speeches of the
Britons (10179-81) to show the loyalty of Arthur's men and to enhance his
prestige as a leader.

And straightaway said this to Arthur the king:
'Greetings to you Arthur, most admired of kings!
I have arrived here: I'm one of your relatives,
And Baldulf has arrived here with a troop of tough soldiers,
And this very night intends to kill you and your knights
To avenge his brother who has lost all his vigour.
But God is to prevent him by means of his great powers!
So now send out Cador, who is the earl of Cornwall,   10110
And with him some fine knights, good and brave fighters,
A full seven hundred of the better leaders,
And those I shall instruct, and those I shall direct,
As to how to kill Baldulf just as if he were a wolf.'

Off went Cador and all of those knights
Until they came near the spot where Baldulf lay under canvas.
They made an assault on them from every side:
They killed and they captured all whom they came close to;
Those killed there amounted to nine hundred all counted.

Baldulf had slipped away to save his own life   10120
And fled through the wild places with furious speed,
Having reluctantly left his own loyal men,
And fled so far northwards that he advanced forwards
To where Arthur lay on the uplands with his vast army
All around York city: that king was most amazing.
Colgrim was inside, with his Saxon men:
Baldulf thought carefully about what should be his policy,
By what kind of trick he could get inside quick,
Into the borough, to Colgrim his brother,
Who of all men alive was to him most beloved.   10130
Down to his bare skin Baldulf had himself stripped
Of the beard on his chin; he made himself a spectacle:
He had half his head shorn, and took a harp in his hand –
[He'd learned to play the harp well during his
          childhood]* –   10133a
And with his harp he made his way to the king's army
And there began to play and sing and provide much entertainment:
People kept on hitting him hard with sappy sticks;
People kept on cuffing him the way they do an idiot;
Everyone who met him contemptuously treated him
So that no one had any notion of Baldulf's true position,   10140
Thinking he was a mere idiot who had just come into court.
So long did he go up this way, so long did he go down that way

That those who were inside the town eventually got wind of it
That this was really Baldulf, brother of Colgrim.
They threw out a rope which Baldulf firmly grasped
And hauled Baldulf up until he heaved himself inside:
By a device of that kind did Baldulf get inside.
  Then rejoiced Colgrim and all his knights with him
And severely started menacing Arthur the king.
Arthur was close beside and could see all this mockery   10150
And he worked himself up into an amazing rage
And instantly ordered all his splendid folk to arm:
He intended to conquer the city by force.
Just as Arthur was about to make assault on the walls
There arrived on horseback the aristocrat **Patrick**,
A nobleman from Scotland, very well set up in lands,
Who started to call out at once to the king:
'Greetings to you, Arthur, most admired of Britons!
I wish to announce to you a fresh piece of news,
Concerning Emperor Childric, the powerful and frantic,   10160
The strong and also brave: he is in Scotland,
Has anchored in a harbour and is burning down the homes
And controls all our land under his own cruel hand;
He has a force which is notable, made up of all the power of
    Rome;
He declares in his boasting when his bowl is filled with wine
That not in any place do you dare await his onslaughts,
Not on field nor in the woodland nor in any [place] at all,*
And if you were to wait for him, he would put fetters on you,
Slaughter your people and possess your land.'
  Often Arthur had been sad, but not till then were things so bad,
And he withdrew to the rear at one side of the city,   10171
Calling his knights to emergency council:
Warriors and leaders and the holy bishops,
Requesting them to advise him how he might, in his realm,
Maintain his dignity with his force of men
And fight against Childric the powerful and strong
Who intended to march that way to give aid to Colgrim.
The Britons there beside him then gave him this answer:
'Let's travel straight to London, and let him march right behind,
And if he comes riding past he'll have to take his
    punishment: 10180
He himself and his army are destined to be doomed.'

Arthur wholly approved of what his people advised him:
He set off travelling until he came to London;
Colgrim was in York and was there expecting Childric:
Childric proceeded to advance through northern parts[54]
And seized into his hands a great deal of land:
The entire Scottish region he gave to one of his retainers
And the whole of Northumberland he placed in his brother's
        hands;
Galloway and Orkney he gave to an earl of his;
He himself took the land from the Humber down to
        London;   10190
He did not intend to show to Arthur any clemency whatever
Unless Arthur, Uther's son, were willing to become his vassal.

Arthur was in London with all the British leaders;
He summoned his army throughout all this country:
Every single man who bore him good will
Must rapidly and at once come up to London.
Then all the land of England was filled with misery:
Here there was weeping and lamenting and immeasurable grief,
Much hunger and distress at the gate of each and every man.*

Arthur sent across the sea two excellent knights   10200
To Howel his cousin, dearest to him of all creatures,
A knight among the best, who commanded Brittany,
Asking him to come over here at once,
To come to the country to help his kindred people,
As Childric had in his hands a great deal of this land   *Childric*
And Colgrim and Baldulf had become his allies
And intended to drive King Arthur out of his native land,
Depriving him of his birthright and of his noble realm:
Then all his family would be tainted with the terror of his disgrace,
Their reputation lost in the realm of this world;   10210
Then it would be better if the king had not been born at all.

Howel, highest man in Brittany heard all of this,
And proceeded at once to call up his best knights,
And ordered them to horse in very great haste,

[54] Lawman amplifies the defeat of Childric, already expanded by Wace from
HRB, IX, chs 2–5, by supplying specific details, inserting narrative strands, citing
speeches, by poetic heightening and by developing the impression of place. From
Wace's presentation of Arthur's growing political control, the episode becomes
a study in the interplay of personalities.

To travel to France to the other free knights
And say to them that they must come very soon and quickly
To Saint Michael's Mount with very many forces,
(All those who wanted silver and gold
And wanted to win honour in the kingdom of this world).
To Poitou he sent off his excellent soldiers,   10220
And some towards Flanders furiously quickly,
And two there went off into Touraine,
And sent into Gascony knights who were also good,
Motioning them in force towards St Michael's Mount,
And promising them splendid gifts before they went to sea
So that they would the readier relinquish their own land
And with Howel the gracious come across to this land
To give aid to Arthur, most admirable of kings.
    Thirteen days had gone by since the dispatch had reached there
When they surged towards the sea as hail does from the sky; 10230
Two hundred ships were there, very well captained:
They were all filled with people and put out to sea:
The wind and the weather stayed just as they wanted
And at Southampton they sailed into land.
Up from the ships leaped enraged soldiers
Carrying ashore their helmets and corslets:
With spears and with shields they covered all the fields.
Many a bold Briton was present; there was boasting uttered:
They swore with great boasts, by their own very lives
That they themselves would treat Childric known as great,   10240
The [aggressive] emperor with much injury there,*
And if he refused to flee away and be off to Germany
And wished instead on land in a fight to make his stand,
And with his bold warriors wait here for their [harm];*
Here they would have to leave what they liked the most:
Their heads and their hands and their gleaming helms,
And in that way they would on land be lost to all their friends;
The vile heathen hounds would hurtle into hell.
    Arthur was in London, most admired of kings,
And heard being spoken most assured speeches   10250
That Howel the mighty had come to this land,   *Howel*
To Southampton directly with thirty thousand knights   *Arrives*
And with countless folk who were followers of the king.
Arthur turned towards him with tremendous joy,
With an enormous crowd of men towards his own cousin.

Together they came (there was delight in the court):
They kissed and embraced and spoke with affection,
And immediately assembled their knights right away.
     And so there were combined two excellent armies:
Howel was to command thirty thousand knights,   10260
While Arthur had in his land forty thousand in hand.
Directly they travelled towards the north district,
Towards Lincoln where Emperor Childric held siege,
But so far he had not been able to take it
Since there were inside it seven thousand good men,
Brave men they were, all day and all night.
     With his army Arthur advanced upon the town,
And Arthur urged his men sternly that all day and all night*
They must travel silently as if they were going stealing,
Travel across the country and relinquish loud noise: 10270
Their horns and their bugles must all be abandoned.
Arthur took a knight who was a good man and brave in fight
And sent him into Lincoln, to his well-loved men,
And as a certainty he must say volubly
That Arthur was coming, most admired of kings
Exactly at midnight and with him many a good knight: –
'And you inside here, at that time must be alert
That when you hear the uproar, then the gates you must unbar,
And dash out of the city and destroy your enemies,
And hit out at Childric, the strong and the mighty,   10280
And then we shall larn 'em some good British yarns!'
     It was exactly midnight: from due south the moon was shining;
Arthur with his army swept down upon the city:
The men were just as silent as if they were going stealing;
They strode on till they could see a full view of Lincoln,
When Arthur the courageous like this began to call:
'Where are you, my knights, my champions in battle?
Can you see the tents where Childric lodges in the fields,
With Colgrim and Baldulf with all their brute force,
The people from Germany who have brought us tragedy,   10290
And the men from Saxony who promise us calamity,
Who have eliminated utterly the noblest in my family,
Constance and Constantine and Uther who was my father,
And Aurelius Ambrosius who was my father's brother,
And many thousand men of my own exalted kin?
Let us march over to them and lay them to the earth

And avenge honourably our family and realm.
And now each and every good knight all together ride on straight!'
   Arthur started riding, the army was stampeding
As if the whole earth were eaten up with flames;*   10300
In among Childric's tents they swooped down in the fields,
And the man who was the first there to start the battle cry
Was Arthur the great warrior, the son of King Uther,
Who shouted loudly and with courage, as comes best from a king:
'Now may Mary aid us, the meek mother of our God,
And I am praying to her Son that he be our assistance!'
   At these very words they took aim with their spears,
Stabbing and striking all those they came close to,
And knights from the city strode out towards them.
If they fled back to the city, there they would perish,   10310
If they fled to the woodland they would be destroyed there:*
Let them go where they could, they would still be attacked.*
It's not recorded in a book that there was ever any fight
Within this realm of Britain where destruction was so rife,
For they were the most wretched of all races who have come here!
There was a deal of bloodshed: there was destruction among men;
Death there was rife and the earth was resounding.
Childric the emperor had a single castle there
On the plain of Lincoln – he was lying up inside it –
Which was recently constructed and really well defended,   10320
And also in there with him were Baldulf and Colgrim,
Who saw that their army was undergoing huge fatalities,
And right away at once it was on with the mail-coats
And they fled from the castle, bereft of all their courage,
And fled right away at once to the wood of Calidon.[55]
They had as their companions seven thousand riders,
And behind them they left slain and deprived of their life's days
A full forty thousand who were felled to the ground:
Men who came from Germany all of them damned in misery,
And all the Saxon men levelled to the ground.   10330
   Then Arthur was aware, the most admirable of kings,
That Childric had fled, into Caledonia he'd sped,
And Colgrim and Baldulf, both had made off with him,
Into the high wood, into the high hurst.

[55] *Calidon* is probably meant to be in Scotland (cf. 10332 *Caledonia*) but see
Wace, n. 21; Robert Mannyng, *Chronicle* (1338) places it in Lincolnshire.

And Arthur went on their track with sixty thousand knights:
The soldiers of Britain surrounded all the wood,
And on one side they felled it for a seven mile extent,
One tree on another, and 'truly' they worked fast!
On the other side he laid siege to it with his levied army
For three days and three nights: it put them in tremendous plight.
   Then Colgrim realized as he was holed up in it   10341
(Who was there without food, in sharp hunger and distress)
That not for them nor their horses was there any help at all.
And in this way Colgrim called to the emperor:
'Tell me, my lord Childric, in words which are truthful,
Can there be any reason why we are lurking here like this?
Why don't we sally forth and summon up our armies,
And start up the fighting against Arthur and his knights?
It's better for us to be laid out on the land but with our honour
Than like this in here to perish with hunger.   10350
It's tormenting us terribly and our men are held in contempt;
Or else let's send straight out to him, and seek a truce from
    Arthur,*
And plead for his mercy and pass hostages to him
And create an alliance with the noble king.'
   Childric was listening as he sheltered in the fort,
And he gave his reply in a really sad voice:
'If Baldulf your own brother wants this and agrees,
And more of our confederates who are here with us inside,
That we should sue for peace from Arthur and set up a treaty with
    him,
Then just as you want, that's what I'll do,   10360
Since in the realm this Arthur is reckoned a most noble man,
Beloved among his followers and a man of royal stock;
Entirely from kings he comes: he was King Uther's son,
And often it does come to pass in many kinds of peoples,
Where valiant knights embark on fierce fight,
That what they win at first they will lose again at last;
And for us right here and now it's turning out like that,
But if only we can live, then for us things will improve.'
   There came an instant and forthright response from the knights:
'We all approve of this proposal, for you have put it well.'   10370
They selected twelve knights and sent them off straight
To where he was in his pavilion by the edges of the wood.
One of them began to shout at once in a sturdy voice:

'Lord Arthur, your safe-conduct: with you we wish to speak!
Childric, styled the emperor, has sent us over here,
As did Colgrim and Baldulf, both of them together;
Now and for all eternity they request your clemency:
They will become your vassals and your renown they will advance,
And they will hand over to you hostages in plenty,
And regard you as their lord, as you will like most of all,   10380
If only they may leave and go from here alive
Into their own land and take there the loathed report;
For here we have experienced many kinds of evils:
At Lincoln we left behind our most beloved kinsmen,
Sixty thousand men who are lying there slain,
And if it might be the wish of your heart
That we across the sea may travel under sail,
Then never any more shall we come back here,
For here we have lost for good our own loved relations;
As long as will be for ever here shall we come back never!'   10390
   Then Arthur laughed, and with a loud voice:
'May thanks be given to God who governs all decisions
That Childric the strong has had sufficient of my land!
He divided up my land among all his doughty knights,
Me myself he had planned to drive from my native land,
To regard me as a wretch and to retain all my realm,
And to have destroyed all my family and condemned all my folk.*
But things have turned out for him as they do with the fox:
When he is most brazen, up in the forest,
And has his freedom for playing and has fowls a-plenty,   10400
In his wild sport he climbs and he seeks out the crags;
Out in the wild places he excavates dens:
Let him roam wherever he wishes, he never has any distress,
And thinks he is in valour the finest of all creatures,
When towards him up the mountains here come men climbing,
With horns and with hounds, and with hallooing voices;
There hunters are yelling; there foxhounds are belling,
Driving the fox on across dales and over downland:
He dashes to the high-wood and seeks out his den;
At the nearest point he presses down into the hole.   10410
Then the bold fox is quite bereft of bliss,
And men are digging down to him upon every side;
Then he there becomes the saddest who of all beasts was the
    proudest.

'That's how it was with Childric, the powerful and mighty:
All my kingdom he intended to get into his clutches,
But now I have driven him to the very edge of death,
Which of the two I decide to do, to behead or hang him.
Now I decide to give him peace and allow him speech with me;
I shall neither behead nor hang him but will accede to his request:
I wish to take hostages from his highest-ranking men,   10420
Horses and their weapons, before they go from here,
And so they are to travel like wretches to their ships,
To sail across the sea to their splendid land,
And dwell there dutifully within their realm,
And announce the tidings of Arthur the king,
Of how I have set them free for my father's soul's sake,
And from my own generosity have dealt gently with the wretches.'
   In this affair King Arthur was short of all good judgement,
There was no man who was quite so rash as to dare to put him right;
This he regretted bitterly a very short time after.*   10430
Childric came from under cover to Arthur who was king,
And he became his vassal there with each one of his knights.
Fully twenty-four hostages Childric handed over there:
They were all selected specially and born in the nobility.
They gave up their horses and their fine mail-coats,
Their spears and their shields and the long swords of theirs:
Everything they had there they then left behind;
They started their journey till they came to the sea
Where their fine ships were standing by the sea.
   They had the wind they wanted, and very pleasant
          weather: 10440
They pushed out from the shore ships massive and long;
They all left behind the land and laid course along the waves
Until they could not see any sight of land at all.
The water was still, which suited their will;
They set their sails gliding right alongside,
Plank against plank; people spoke to one another,
Deciding that they wanted to come back to this land
And avenge with honour their own loved relations,
And lay waste King Arthur's land and kill those who lived here,
And conquer the castles and do acts of wild delight.   10450
So they travelled on the sea for such a long time
That they arrived midway between England and Normandy;
They went about on their luff and laid course towards land,

Till they came (no doubt of this) to Dartmouth reach at Totnes;
In the very greatest joy they jumped down ashore.   *Childric's*
   As soon as they came to land they slaughtered the   *Return*
     people:
They put to flight the peasants who were ploughing the soil;
They hanged all the knights who had command of the lands;
All the dutiful wives they stabbed to death with knives,
All the young girls they gang-raped to death,   10460
And the men of learning they laid out on hot coals;
All the serving-men at court they killed by clubbing them;
They demolished the castles, they laid waste the land,
They burned down the churches; there was distress in the land!
The babies at the breast they drowned in the waters;
The livestock which they seized they slaughtered completely,
To their quarters dragged it and stewed it up and roasted it;
Everything they grabbed which they could get close to.
All day long they were singing about Arthur the great king,
Claiming they had won for themselves homes   10470
Which were going to be their holdings in their own control,
And there they would be staying in winter and in summer,
And if Arthur had such courage that he wanted to come
To fight against Childric the powerful and mighty,
'[We]'ll make a bridge, really fine, from the bits of his spine*
And pick out all the bones from the admirable king,
And join them together with links of gold chain,
And lay them in the hall doorway which each man has to go
     through
In tribute to Childric, the mighty and the rich!'
   All this was just how they played, to King Arthur's
     disgrace,   10480
But all happened quite another way very shortly after:
Their boasts and their games turned to their own shame,
As it does almost everywhere when a man behaves like that.
   The Emperor Childric conquered everything he looked at:
He took Somerset, and he took Dorset,
And all Devonshire's people he entirely destroyed,
And he treated Wiltshire with the utmost wickedness;
He seized all the lands down to the sea sands;
Then ultimately he ordered men to start blowing
Horns and brass trumpets, and his host to assemble,   10490
And he wanted to be off and completely besiege Bath,

And also to blockade Bristol round about the coastline;
Such was their boasting before they came to Bath.
  To Bath came the emperor and besieged the castle there,
And the men inside it with valour proceeded
To mount upon the stone walls, well supplied with weapons,
And they defended the place against the mighty Childric.
There encamped the emperor and Colgrim his companion,
And Baldulf his brother and very many others.
  Arthur was in the north, and knew nothing of this;   10500
He travelled all through Scotland and set it all into his own hand:
Orkney and Galloway, the Isle of Man and Moray,
And all of the territories which were their tributaries.
Arthur assumed that it was a certain thing
That Childric had laid course back to his own land,
And that never again would he ever come back here.
  Then to Arthur the king there came the tidings
That Childric the emperor had come to the country
And in the south region was wreaking great chaos.
Then Arthur announced (most admired of kings):   10510
'I am deeply sorry that I spared my enemy,
That in the hilltop wood I did not [kill him off] with hunger,*
Or did not slice him right up with slashes from my sword!
Now this is how he pays me back for my good deed!
But so help me the Lord who made the light of day
For this he shall endure the most extreme of all agonies,
Harshest contests; I shall be his killer,
And both Colgrim and Baldulf I myself shall kill,
And all of their supporters shall suffer death.
If the Ruler of heaven wishes to grant this,   10520
I shall honourably avenge all his evil deeds;
If the life in my breast is able to last in me,
And if he who created moon and sun is willing to grant me this,
Then Childric will never cheat me again!'
  Now the call went from Arthur, the most admired of kings:
'Where are you, my knights, brave men and valiant?
To horse, to horse, worthy warriors,
And swiftly towards Bath we shall now be on our way.
Get men to erect really high gibbets
And bring here the hostages in front of our knights,   10530
And they shall be hanged there upon the high trees.'

There he had executed all twenty-four children,[56]
From the German race, of very noble families.
Then came the tidings to Arthur the king
That his cousin Howel was sick (and this news made him sad)
Lodged in Dumbarton by the Clyde; and there then he had to leave
    him.
With exceeding haste he started making off
Until beside Bath he moved on to a plain,   *Siege*
And there he dismounted, and all of his knights,   *of Bath*
And on with their mail-coats, those stern men of war,   10540
And he divided his forces into five sections.

When he had stationed them all and all were surveyed
Then he put on his mail-coat fashioned from steel mesh[57]
Which an elvish smith had made with his excellent skill:
It was called **Wygar**, which **Wiseman** had smithied.
His thighs he covered up with cuisses of steel;
Caliburn his sword he strapped by his side –
It was made in Avalon and endowed with magic powers;
His helmet he set on his head, high and made of steel:
On it was many a gem and it was all bound with gold –   10550
It had once belonged to the noble King Uther –

[56] The twenty-four noble children (a detail added by Lawman) recall Belinus'
killing of Roman hostages (2655, 2849).

[57] To Wace's version of the common motif of the arming of the leader,
Lawman adds the name of the helm, Goosewhite (10552). Line 10545 is
problematic: ME *he* may refer to the smith (he) or the byrny (it); hence Wygar,
which Pilch derives from OW *gwydd-gar* ('lover of wisdom'), could be the
smith's name, and *witeʒe* ('witty/skilful') an epithet describing him: 'he was
called Wygar the skilful artificer' (so the second edition of Barron and Weinberg's *Laʒamon's Arthur*, based on Madden 21131-4), or *Witeʒe* is the mail-
coat's name: 'he who made Witeʒe was called Wygar'; the interpretation offered
in the first edition of B&W is, however: 'he who made Wygar was called
Witeʒe'; using this last nomenclature but reinterpreting the syntax, Burrow and
Turville-Petre offer a third reading: 'it was called Wygar, which Witeʒe wrought'
(with *wygar* perhaps derived from OE *wig-heard* ('battle-hard')) as in Brook's
Selections (p. 124), and this is the reading offered here: *Witeʒe* ('Wiseman') is
the smith, a name which may ultimately derive from *Widia/Wudga*, who was
not himself a smith but son of the legendary Wayland the Smith (Brook, who
cites A. C. L. Brown's article, 1 *MP*, (1903), 99 n. 4: in this footnote, G. L.
Kittredge rejects Madden's translation, and his attempt to derive *Wygar* from
Wayland, and translates: 'It (the coat of mail) was named Wygar which Witeʒe
wrought', suggesting also the derivation from *wig-heard*).

It was known as **Goosewhite**, among all others quite unique.
He hung about his neck a shield which was precious:
Its name in British was entitled **Pridwen**;
Inside it was engraved with red gold stencilling
A most precious image of the mother of our Lord;
In his hand he took his spear which bore the name of **Ron**.
When he had donned all his armour, then he leaped on his charger;
Then the bystanders were able to behold
The most handsome knight who ever led forth host: 10560
Never did any man see a more splendid knight
Than was this Arthur who was most aristocratic.
    Then Arthur called out in a loud voice:
'Look here now, ahead of us, those heathen hounds
Who slaughtered our ancestors with their evil tricks,
And who for us in the land are the most loathsome of all things.
Now let us charge towards them and fiercely set upon them
And avenge with acclaim our race and our realm,
And avenge the great disgrace by which they have debased us
When over the billows they came to Dartmouth sound.   10570
And they are all utterly forsworn and they are all utterly cast
    down:
They are all doomed, with the Lord's divine aid.
Now let us hasten forward in combined formation
Every bit as gently as if we had no harsh intentions,
And when we come up to them, I myself will start:
Among the very foremost I shall begin the fighting.
Now we shall ride and across the land we'll glide
And no man for his very life must move at all loudly,
But travel with all speed. Now the Lord give us support!'
    Then Arthur the great man set off at a gallop,   10580
Headed over the plain and was making for Bath.
The tidings came to Childric, the powerful and mighty,
That Arthur with his forces was coming all prepared for fight.
Childric and his bold men leaped upon their horses,
Firmly grasped their weapons, knowing Arthur was their enemy.
Arthur, most admired king, noticed this thing;
He noticed one heathen earl making straight for him
With seven hundred knights all prepared for fight,
The earl himself advancing in front of his contingent;
And Arthur himself was riding at the head of all his army.   10590
Arthur the resolute took Ron in his hand,

He steadied the sturdy shaft, that stout-hearted king,
He set his horse galloping so that the earth resounded,
And raised his shield before his breast: the king was enraged!
He struck the earl Borel straight through the chest
So that his heart was split; and the king called out at once:
'The first one is fated! Now may the Lord afford us aid,
And the heavenly Queen who gave birth to the Lord.'
   Arthur, most admired of kings, called out again:
'Now at them, now at them! the first deed was well done!'   10600
The British set upon them as must be done with scoundrels:
They gave savage slashes with axes and with swords.
From Childric's men there fell fully two thousand,
While Arthur did not lose a single one of his!
There the Saxon men were the most abject of people,
And the men of Germany the most mournful of all nations.
Arthur with his sword sent many to their doom:
Everything he struck with it was instantly done for.
The king was every bit as enraged as the wild boar is
When among the oakmast he meets many [pigs].*   10610
   Childric was aware of this and began to turn away,
And he set off across the Avon to find safety for himself,
And Arthur leaped into pursuit just like a lion
And flushed them into the water: many there were fated;
To the depths sank there two thousand five hundred,
And all the River Avon was spanned with a bridge of steel.
Childric fled across the water with fifteen hundred knights,
Intending to slip off and pass across the sea.
Arthur spotted Colgrim climbing to the mountains,
Making a break towards the hills which look down on Bath, 10620
And Baldulf made off after him, with seven thousand knights,
Supposing that up in the hills they could make a noble stand,
Defend themselves with weapons and wound Arthur's force.
   Then Arthur noted, that most admired king,
Where Colgrim offered resistance and made his stand too;
Then the king called out, loudly and with courage:
'My bold-hearted warriors, march to the hills!
For yesterday Colgrim was of all men most courageous,
Now he's just like the goat holding guard on its hill:
High on the hillside it fights with its horns;   10630
Then the wild wolf comes, on its way up towards them;
Even though the wolf's alone, without any pack,

If there were in one pen a full five hundred goats,
The wolf would get to them and would bite them all.
In just that way today I shall quite destroy Colgrim:
I'm the wolf and he's the goat: that guy is going to be doomed!'
    Once again Arthur called out, most admired of kings:
'Yesterday Baldulf was of all knights the boldest;
Now he's standing on the hill and staring at the Avon,
Sees lying in the stream fishes made of steel,   10640
They're girded with swords but their swimming is all spoiled;
Their scales are fluttering like shields adorned with gold;
Their spines are floating just as if they were spears.*
These are remarkable sights to see in this land:
Such beasts on the hill, such fish in the spring;
Yesterday the emperor was the most audacious monarch,
Now he's become a hunter and horns are his accompaniment,
He's dashing over the broad plain and his dogs are barking;
There beside Bath he has abandoned his hunting:
He's in flight from his own quarry, so we'll be the ones to stop it
And so bring to nothing those brazen boasts of his,   10651
And in this way we'll regain true rights of ownership.'
    And with those very words which the king was speaking
He raised high his shield in front of his chest,
Grasped his long spear and set spurs to his horse;
Almost as fast as a bird in its flight
There went following the king twenty-five thousand,
Of valiant men in wild rage, armed with their weapons.
They made towards the mountains with very mighty force
And into Colgrim they struck with most savage whacks.   10660
And Colgrim took them on and felled the British to the ground,
Fully five hundred in the first onrush.
This Arthur noted, that most admired king,
And marvellously and mightily he became maddened,
And in this way started shouting Arthur the great man:
'Where are you, my British, my bold and brave soldiers?
Here ahead of us are standing all our noted enemies!
Unharmed let us go and let us grind them to the ground!'
    Arthur grasped his sword in his right and he struck a Saxon
      knight,
And the sword (it was so splendid) sliced till at his teeth it ended!
And then he struck another who was the first knight's
      brother   10671

So his helm and the head with it fell upon the ground;
At once he gave a third blow and he cut one knight in two.
Then the British men were strongly emboldened
And imposed upon the Saxons some most severe contusions
With their spears which were long and with their swords which
    were strong.
There the Saxons fell in their last fatal hour,
In hundreds upon hundreds they fell in heaps upon the ground,
In thousands upon thousands they went on falling on the ground.

    Then spotted Colgrim that Arthur was coming to him: 10680
Because of all the corpses Colgrim couldn't slip aside;
Baldulf was fighting there right beside his brother.
Then Arthur called out in challenging tones:
'Here I come, Colgrim! we two are reaching for this country
And now we're going to share this land in a way you'll find least
    pleasing!'
After these words which the king was uttering
He lifted high his broad sword and heavily struck down
Striking Colgrim on the helmet and carving down the centre,[58]
And through the coif on his mail-coat, till it stuck in
    the man's chest,   *Colgrim and*
And he reached out to Baldulf with his right hand   *Baldulf*
And swiped his head right off together with his helmet.   *Die*

    Then noble King Arthur gave a great laugh,   10692
And began to recite these words of rejoicing:
'Lie there now, Colgrim: you certainly climbed high,
And your brother Baldulf who is lying by your side,
Now's the time I invest all this realm in your possession,
The dales and the downland and all my doughty men!
You climbed up this hill marvellously high
As if you were on your way to heaven; now you've got to go to
    hell;
There you will recognise a good many of your tribe.   10700
Give my regards to Hengest who was the most handsome knight,
Ebissa and Octa and from your tribe lots more,
And ask them to stay there all winter and all summer;
Then in this land we shall live in joy,
And pray for your souls – that they will never have salvation! –

---

[58] Lawman's Arthur kills his enemies with his own hands to a mocking funeral oration (10694).

And your bones shall lie here, right beside Bath.'
   Arthur the king called Cador the courageous
(He was the earl of Cornwall and a most courageous knight):
'Listen to me, Cador, you come from my own family;
Childric has now run off and has gone away from here;   10710
He thinks that he'll be safe to come travelling back again.*
But take from my forces five thousand men,
And travel directly, by day and by night,
Until you arrive at the sea in advance of Childric,
And everything you can conquer, enjoy that with pleasure,
And if you manage to kill the emperor with the greatest cruelty,*
I'll give you as reward all of Dorsetshire.'
   As soon as the noble king had spoken these words
Cador sprang to horse as a spark does from the fire;
A full seven thousand accompanied the earl.   10720
Cador the courageous and many of his kindred
Went across the wolds and over the wild places,
Over dales and over downlands, over deep waters;
Cador knew the way which towards his own lands lay:
Westwards he went, this is the case, right on to Totnes,
By day and by night; he got there directly,
So that Childric never discovered the least detail of his coming.
Cador came to his country in advance of Childric
And had all folk in the area marshalled in front of him,
Vigorous peasants with enormous clubs   10730
With spears and great cudgels collected for that very purpose,
And he put every single one of them into the ships' bilges,
Ordered them to keep well hidden so that Childric wasn't aware of
    them,
And when his men arrived and were trying to climb in
They were to grab their cudgels and vigorously thump them,
And with their staves and with their spears to slaughter Childric's
    adherents.
   The peasants did exactly as Cador had instructed:
Off to the ships went the peasants in grim fury;
In each of the ships there were a hundred and fifty,
And Cador the courageous moved towards a high wood   10740
Five miles from the spot where the ships were stationed,
And hid his men as he desired in the utmost silence.
   Childric came soon after marching on the plain,
Intending to rush to the ships and run away from the land.

As soon as Earl Cador, a man of courage, could clearly see
That Childric was on the plain between him and the peasants
Then Cador called out in a clear voice:
'Where are you, my knights, my good, valiant fighters?'[59]
Remember what Arthur, our admirable king
Commanded us at Bath before we left the company!   10750
Now see Childric flying, trying to flee from the land
And making for Germany where his ancestors lie
Where he'll collect up an army and come back here again
And invade our interior, intending to avenge that Colgrim
And Baldulf his brother, who lie dead beside Bath.
But may he never survive to see that hour! He will not if we have
    the power!'
Upon concluding that speech the great earl had spoken
In a mood of harsh anger he rode at their head;
The valiant soldiers strode out of the wood-shaw
And went after Childric, the powerful and mighty.   10760
Childric's knights looked back behind them:
Saw battle standards proceeding across the plain,
And five thousand shields gliding across the fields.
Then Childric became most distressed in his emotions,
And the mighty emperor ventured these words:
'This is King Arthur and he wants to eliminate us all!
Let's run off now quickly and rush into the ships
And get away from here by water and not bother about where we
    go to!'
    When the Emperor Childric had uttered these remarks
He set off in flight fearfully quickly   10770
With Cador the courageous coming after him at once.
Childric and his knights came to their ships straightaway
Intending to shove off those sturdy ships from land.
The peasants were hiding, with their cudgels, inside them:
They raised up their cudgels and brought them down hard;
By their clubs many knights there were instantly slain,
And stabbed by their pitchforks and pinned to the ground.
Cador and his knights attacked them from behind.
    Then Childric realized they were facing disaster
When all his great force fell in heaps on the ground!   10780

[59] Cador addresses his men in the style of his leader; his humour (10790) is
similar too.

Now he spotted to one side a very lofty hill;
That river flows beneath it which is termed the Teign
And the hill is called Teignwick: that's the way Childric fled
As quickly as he could manage with twenty-four knight
    companions.
Cador was aware how things were going there,
That the emperor was in flight and heading for the heights,
And Cador went after him with as much speed as he could,
And gained on him steadily and caught up with him.
Then announced Cador, the most courageous earl,
'Wait, Childric, wait; I want to give you Teignwick!'   10790
Cador raised his sword and struck and killed Childric.   *Childric's*
Many who were fleeing made for the water: *Death*
In the waters of the Teign there they met their end:
Cador killed everyone whom he found alive,
And some crawled into the woodland and he destroyed all these
    there.
  When Cador had conquered all of them and had seized all that
    land as well
He imposed a very firm peace which remained a long time after:
Even were a man wearing gold rings upon his arms
No man whatever would dare to treat another man with
    wrong.   10799
  Arthur had travelled on out into Scotland   *Scottish*
For Howel lay firmly enclosed in Dumbarton beside   *Campaign*
    Clyde:
The Scots had besieged him through their base deception,
And if Arthur had not come very soon Howel would have been
    captured
And all his people slain and deprived of their life's days.
But Arthur arrived speedily with superior strength
And the Scots started fleeing far from that area
Off into Moray with much manpower.
And Cador came to Scotland where he found Arthur:
Arthur and Cador marched into Dumbarton
And there discovered Howel with great joy, in health: 10810
From all his former sickness he had now recovered;
Great was the rejoicing held in the fortress.
  The Scots were in Moray and intended to remain there,
And with their brazen words they uttered their boasts,
Claiming that they wanted to take charge of the realm

And await Arthur there with their bold force,
Since never would Arthur ever dare, for his life's sake, to come
    there!
Arthur, quite devoid of fear, then came to hear
Of what the Scots had been saying in their words of scorn.
Then announced Arthur, most admired of kings: 10820
'Where are you, Howel, highest of my kindred,
And Cador the courageous, you who come from Cornwall?
Have brass trumpets blown and assemble our forces:
Exactly at midnight we shall march off directly
Towards Moray, there to prove our honour;
If the Lord who made the light of day should so desire it
We shall be telling them some mournful stories,
Bring down their boasting and themselves be killing.'
    Exactly at midnight Arthur arose directly:
Horns began blowing with resounding noise,   10830
Knights began getting up and speaking words of anger.
With great manpower onwards into Moray,
Thirteen thousand men [forced] their way onwards:*
In the first company, men especially courageous;
Then came Cador, the earl of Cornwall,
With seventeen thousand splendid combatants:
Then came Howel with his champions, to fight well
With twenty-one thousand most outstanding champions:
Then came Arthur, most admired of kings,
With twenty-seven thousand, striding after them.   10840
Shields there were gleaming as the dawn light began.
    News came to the Scots where they were now living
That King Arthur was coming towards their own land,
Fantastically quickly with an enormous force.
Then those were in most terror who before had been most bold
And took off in flight amazingly fast
Into that water where there are very many marvels.
    This is an uncanny mere set upon middle earth,[60]   *Loch*
With marshland and reeds and the water is very broad,   *Lomond*
With fish and with water fowl, with fiendish creatures!   10850
The water cannot be measured; vast sea-monsters swim round
    within it;

---

[60] The sea-monsters and elvish creatures (10848–52) are an addition to the
account in Wace and resemble Old English traditional motifs.

There are elvish creatures playing in the terrible pool;
There are sixty islands stretching down the long water:
On each of the islands is a rock both high and strong
Where eagles make their nests and other huge birds;
The eagles have a certain custom in the reign of every king
Whenever any invading force comes flocking to the country:
Then all of the birds fly far up into the air,
Many hundred thousands of them and create a huge contention;
Then the people know without doubt that a great trial is to come
     to them
From some kind of people who propose to visit that land.   10861
For two or three days this sign occurs in this way
Until unknown men journey to that land.
There is still one more marvel to mention concerning that water:
There flow [into] that mere on many a side*
From dales and from downlands and from deep valleys
Sixty different streams, all gathered together,
Yet out of that mere no man has ever found one
Which flows outwards there, except at one end
A normal sized brook which discharges from the mere   10870
And trickles very tranquilly down to the sea.

     The Scots were scattered and in much distress
Over the many mountains situated in the water;
Arthur commandeered ships and proceeded towards them
And slew them without number, many and in plenty,
And many thousands there had died for total lack of bread.
Arthur the admirable was on the east side;
Howel the good was in the south part
And Cador the courageous was on guard in the north,
And his lesser people he placed on the west side;   10880
Then all the Scots seemed very foolish men,
Lurking there among the crags entirely encircled;
Of these, sixty thousand came to a sad end.

     By then the king of Ireland had arrived in the harbour,
Twelve miles from where Arthur was encamped with his force,
Having come to help the Scots to bring down Howel.
Arthur, most admired king, came to hear of this,
And took his one main force and hastened there with speed,
And found King Gillomaur who had come ashore just there:
Arthur fought against him and refused him any truce,   10890
And felled the Irish men with great fierceness to the ground,

And with twelve ships Gillomaur took flight from the shore
And travelled to Ireland with very great trouble,
While Arthur on the land slew all whom he found,
And then returned to the lake where he had left his kinsman,
Howel the courteous, highest-ranking in Britain
(Not counting Arthur, most noble of kings).
Arthur met Howel where he was stationed by the harbour,
Beside the broad loch where he had been waiting;
Then the men in the army were extremely happy   10900
About Arthur's arrival and his noble achievements.

   There Arthur remained for two days and two nights;
The Scots were lying on the crags, many thousands of them dead,
Perishing with hunger – the most abject of peoples.
On the third day the dawn brought in good weather,
There came approaching the army all those who bore the tonsure,
And three intelligent bishops well instructed in the Bible,
And many priests and monks who could not be counted,
Canons were coming there, many most distinguished men,
With all of the relics most respected in the land,   10910
And they all craved peace with Arthur, and his compassion.

   To that place came the women who were living in that land:
They were carrying in their arms their unfortunate children;
They were crying in Arthur's presence amazingly bitterly,
And tossing their lovely tresses down to the earth,
Cutting off their locks and laying them down there
At the king's feet in front of all of his soldiers,
[Dragging] their nails down their faces and leaving them bleeding;*
They were nearly all of them practically naked.
In great distress they started calling out to King Arthur,   10920
And some of them spoke like this in their [affliction]:*
'King, we are upon this earth the most abject of all people!
We beg for your compassion, for the sake of God's care.
In this country you have slaughtered our own compatriots
With hunger and distress and with many kinds of harm,
With weapons and with water and with many misfortunes,
Have made our children fatherless, bereft of every comfort.
You are a Christian man: we ourselves are Christian too;
The Saxon men are merely heathen hounds:
They came to this land and these folk here they killed;   10930
If we gave them allegiance it was to avoid trouble,
For we had no man at all who might reconcile us with them.

They caused us great disaster, and you are doing just the same:
The heathen men hate us and the Christians give us grief;
What will become of us?' cried the women to the king.
'Give us back those men still living lying on the crags there,
And if you show compassion to those human creatures
Then your honour will be greater, both now and hereafter!
Lord Arthur, our king, loosen our fetters;
All this land you have captured and all this people
        overcome: 10940
We lie beneath your feet; with you lies our entire release.'
    All this heard Arthur, most admired of kings,
This weeping and this lamenting and untold desolations.
Then he gave it consideration, and he felt compassion;
As he deliberated he found he could do as they asked:
He gave them life, he gave them limb and their own lands to
        manage.[61]
He had brass trumpets blown and summoned the Scots
And down from their crags they came to the ships;
From each and every side they sidled towards land:
They were very badly harmed by the sharp pangs of hunger. 10950
Oaths they then swore that they would never be traitors,
And then they handed over hostages to the king,
And all of them immediately became the king's men,
And then they hurried off; the hosts separated there,
Each man to the area where he had his homestead,
And Arthur established a peace there, good among the best.
    'Where are you, my cousin Howel, the man I love the most?*
Are you looking at this enormous mere where the Scots have been
        so harmed?
Can you see these lofty trees, can you see the eagles soaring?
Within this vast fen there are fish beyond counting: 10960
Are you looking at the islands which are lying in the water?'
The whole vista seemed to Howel uncannily strange,
And standing by the surging water he was extremely surprised,
And like this responded Howel of noble rank:
'Since I was born a male child lying at my mother's breast
I have never seen in any land such surprising things
As before me right now with my eyes I behold.'

    [61] The term 'gave them limb' means he did not remove hands, genitals or
ears.

The Britons were exceedingly surprised and amazed.
Then Arthur called out, most admired of kings:
'Howel, my own cousin, the man I love the most,   10970
Listen to my words, about a most famous marvel
Which to you I will recount by my own true account:
At this mere's end where this water leaves
Is a little tiny pool which people wonder at:
It is in its length sixty-four handbreadths,
Measured in its width it is twenty-five feet;
It is but five feet deep; it was dug out by elves;
It possesses four corners and there are four kinds of fish in it,
And each fish is in its area, where it finds its species,
Nor can any reach the others except for those which match its
    type;
No man was ever created who was in any skill so far
    advanced,   10981
No matter how long he might live, who might ever understand
What it is that stops one fish from floating off to the others
Since there is nothing between except just pure water.'
    Then Arthur, most admired king, once again continued:
'Howel, at the limit of this land, close to the sea shore,
Is a loch extremely vast; its waters are unpleasant,
And when the sea is surging as if madly raging
And spills over into the loch in huge quantities,
Even so there is no more water added in the mere;   10990
But when the sea gushes out, and the earth shines with moisture,
And it's gone back in, into its former gulf,
Then the mere swells up and the waves grow dusky,
Waves are spilling out there, enormously huge ones,
Flowing out on the land so people instantly get fearful;
If any man comes by there not knowing anything about it,
To see the strange sight beside the sea-shore,
If he turns his face towards the mere there,
No matter how low born he is, he'll be very well protected,
The water will slip by him and the man will stay there
    gently,   11000
According to his desire he remains there very quiet,
So he's not any way damaged by the action of the water.'
    Then remarked Howel, high-ranking in Britain:
'Now I hear described wonderful accounts,
And wonderful is the Lord who established it all!'

Then called out Arthur, most admired of kings:
'Blow all my horns with resounding echo,
And announce to my knights that I shall travel straightaway.'
Brass trumpets were blowing, horns there were sounding:
There was acclamation in the army beside the active king   11010
For each was reassured and was marching to his region,
And the king made proclamation, by their pure existence,
That no man in the world should become so insane,
Nor any soldier so stupid as to break his truce,[62]
And if any man did this, he must endure the punishment.

   After these words the army advanced:
Men there were singing unfamiliar songs*
About this King Arthur and about his warriors,
And they said in their songs that while this world lasted
There would never again be such a king as Arthur was in
    everything,   11020
No other king nor kaiser in any country whatever.

   Arthur went off to York with an amazingly large force
And stayed there for six weeks in supreme delight;
The walls of the city were broken down and crumbling
Where Childric had burned them up, with the halls, completely.
Then the king summoned a famous priest called **Piram**;
He was a very wise man and very well versed in books:
'Piram, you are my own priest, so the easier will you find things.'
The king took a true cross relic, potent and authentic,
And [placed] it in Piram's hand and with it extensive tracts of
    land,*
And the archbishop's crozier he handed to Piram there;   11031
Piram had been a good priest; now he was an archbishop.
Then he was instructed by Arthur, most admired of kings,
That he should erect churches and restore the ritual
And protect God's people and in fairness instruct them;
And he ordered all the knights to give just decisions,
And the tillers of the soil to betake themselves to toil,
And every single man to greet every other;
And whichever man acted worse than the king had given orders,
He would have him hurried off to burn at the stake,   11040
Or if he were of lowly birth then he must hang for it.*

---

[62] Arthur's threat of punishment for truce-breaking (see also 11040, 11048) marks him as a good king.

Then once more called Arthur, most admired of kings,
Instructing that each man who had forfeited his land
No matter what the penalty which had driven him away,
He should now return, rapidly and soon,
Whether great or mean, and have his own again,
Unless he were so ill disposed as to be traitor to his lord,
Or a perjurer against his lord – such a man the king condemned.
  Three brothers arrived there, who were of royal descent,
Lot, Angel and **Urien,** a splendid trio of men!   11050
These three chieftains came towards the king there,
And went down upon their knees in the emperor's presence:
'All health to you, Arthur, most admired of kings!
And your warriors with you: may they ever flourish!
We are three brothers, from kings we're descended;
All our rightful land has gone out of our hands
For the heathen men have made us most abject,
And laid waste for us Lothian, Scotland and Moray,
And we beg you, for the love of God, that you give us assistance
And for your own reputation that you be gentle with us.   11060
Give us back our rightful land and we shall always love you,
Regard you as our lord in every way a subject should.'
  Arthur, most admired of kings, was listening to this,
To how these three knights made a courteous request,
He felt pity in his heart and he proceeded to speak,
And these words were said by the most supreme of kings:
'Urien, become my man: you're to return again to Moray;
In it you shall be called the king of that land,
And be exalted in my army with those who owe you allegiance.
And in Angel's hand I place all of Scotland now at once: 11070
Take it now into your hand and be king of all that land;
From the father to the son, down the line my men you'll all
     become.
And you, Lot, my beloved friend, may God be gracious to you,
You have my sister as your wife: you will fare the better for it!
I am giving you Lothian, which is a lovely country,
And I will add to it lands which are excellent
Alongside the Humber, worth a hundred pounds,
For my father Uther, in the time that he was king here
Had great love for his daughter who shared his very thoughts,[63]

---

[63] An insoluble crux. This may be a corrupted reference to Anna's training

And she is my sister, and she has two sons herself,   11080
Who in this land are to me the most beloved of children!'
In this way King Arthur spoke; **Gawain** was then a little child,
And so was the other, **Modred**, his brother –
That Modred was born was a pity: he was cause of much tragedy!
   Arthur went to London and his liegemen with him;
In his own land he held a very great assembly
And reinstated all the laws which were in statute in his forebears'
    days,
All the good laws formerly extant here;
He established peace and plenty and all liberties.
Then he went to Cornwall to Cador's own kingdom.   11090
Here he encountered a girl unsurpassed in beauty:
This young girl's mother came from the Roman people,
A relation of Cador's, who gave that girl in wardship to him,
And he took her in tenderly and delicately fed her;
Her family was noble from among the Roman people;
Not in any country was there any girl so courtly
In her speech and her behaviour, nor of such gracious manners.
She was called **Guinevere**, most gracious of women;
Arthur took her as his wife, and loved her very dearly;
This maiden did he wed, and he took her to his bed.   11100
   Arthur was there in Cornwall throughout all that winter,
And all for the love of Guinevere, whom he loved most of women.
When the winter was over, and quickly it was summer,
Arthur considered carefully his next activity,   *International*
That his good people should not lie in idleness.   *Reputation*
He marched off to Exeter at the midsummer festival
And there held an assembly of the aristocrats,
Announcing he intended to go into Ireland,
To transfer all that kingdom into his own hand,
Unless its king, **Gillomaur**, came first and very soon to him   11110
And spoke to him graciously and requested Arthur's mercy,
Then he would lay waste his land and handle him harshly
With fire and with steel play a very strict game there,

---

in etiquette; if C *wes his bæd iþohte* is emended to *wes in ibere ituhte* the sense
is 'was instructed in deportment' (cf. *OED* s.v. *tight*[1], 3: 'to instruct'). O
sophisticates to *þorh alle cunnes þinge*. Another possible emendation is *þe wes
him dære biþoht* ('who loved him dearly') (*MED* s.v. *bithinken* v., 6: *wel ben b.*
'be well-disposed to sb.')

And slaughter the inhabitants who wished to oppose him.
In response to the words which the king had been speaking
The assembled folk answered the king very fairly:
'Lord king, keep your promise, we are all prepared
To march and to ride everywhere as you require!'
   Many bold Britons there looked like the angry bear:
They had lowering brows and battle-fury in their brains;   11120
Off to their quarters marched the knights and their squires,
Rocked their mail-coats free of rust and burnished their helmets,[64]
Rubbed down their precious horses with pieces of linen,
Horses well-shorn and shod: a superb cavalry turn-out!
Some trimmed horn, some trimmed bone and some prepared steel
    arrows,
Some made leather thongs, fine and very strong,
Some prepared spears and got ready the shields.*
   Arthur sent a summons throughout all his kingdom
That every good knight should come to him straight
And every fine man should come straightway at once,   11130
And each man who would not take part would have his private
    parts removed,
But whoever came willingly, he would become rich.
Seven nights after Easter, when men had finished fasting,
Then to the ships straightaway came all of the knights:
The wind stayed on their side and sped them to Ireland. *(i) Conquest*
Arthur went on land and harried those who lived there: *of Ireland*
He slaughtered many people and plundered cattle in great numbers
But kept on pressing every man to respect church property.
   The message came to the king who was overlord in the land
Of the arrival there of Arthur who was wreaking untold harm
    there;   11140
He summoned all his people throughout all his kingdom,
And his Irish forces marched forward to the fight
As opponents of Arthur the admirable king.
Arthur and his knights armed themselves straight
And marched forth against them, an enormous force.
Arthur's followers were all protected with armour;
The Irish men were almost entirely naked,
With spears and battle-axes and with very sharp knives.

---

[64] Chain-mail rusts within hours and was cleaned by placing the armour in a
sand-filled rotating cylinder (*MED* s.v. *rokken* v., 2 [c]).

Arthur's men sent flying countless feathered arrows,
And massacred the Irish, sending many of them tumbling: 11150
They were unable to endure in any way whatever,
But fled away fast in very many thousands,
And Gillomaur the king fled, taking himself off,
With Arthur coming after him. He captured the king,
And so had within his hands the king of that land.

 Arthur the mighty went to set up headquarters;
In his mind he felt all the more relieved that Gillomaur was so
  close by.
Arthur, most admired of kings, was now displaying
In the presence of his people plentiful friendship:
He had the king well dressed in every kind of splendour,   11160
Who even sat beside Arthur, alongside him even ate,
With Arthur he drank wine, which he did not think so fine,
Nonetheless when he perceived that Arthur was delighted,
Then exclaimed Gillomaur (in his heart he felt most sore):
'Lord Arthur, be reconciled! don't mutilate or murder me!
Your vassal I'll become and deliver to you my three sons
(My own beloved sons) to perform all your desire.
I'll do something still more, if you wish to show me favour:
I will deliver to you some very high-born hostages,
Some sixty children of very powerful noblemen.   11170
I'll do something still more, if you wish to show me favour:
Seven thousand pounds every year from my own land
I will send off to your land, with sixty marks in gold.
I'll do something still more if you will show me favour:
All of the horses with all of their trappings,
The hawks and the hounds and my finest treasures
I shall place into your hands from all of my lands;
And when all this is completed I shall take a sacred relic
From Saint Columkille who performed God's own will,[65]
And the head of Saint Brendan which God himself made
  sacred,   11180
And the right foot of Saint Bridget, most holy and effective,
And plenty of sacred relics which have come here from Rome,

---

[65] Columkille (Columba) (b. *c.* 521, d. Iona 597) preached in Ireland and
then evangelized the Picts in Scotland; Bridget (b. *c.* 450, d. 523) founded the
first Irish religious community for women in Kildare; the discovery of their relics
in the late twelfth century promoted a popular cult.

And I'll swear to you in truth that I shall never betray you,
But instead I shall love you and regard you as my lord,
And regard you as the high king and myself as your mere
    underling.'
  Arthur was listening, most admired king,
And he began laughing with a loud bellow,
And gave him an answer with most gracious words:
'Cheer up, now, Gillomaur, don't let your feelings be so sore,
Since you have been sensible, things will turn out well for
    you,   11190
For people who are intelligent merit sympathetic treatment;
You shall not suffer any more, because of your common sense:
You have offered me a lot; for that you shall be better off!
On this spot, outright, in the presence of all my knights,
Let there be restored to you the larger part of that half measure
Of gold and of treasury; but you must become my vassal,
And send half that tribute each year into my country.
Half of the horses, and half of the trappings,
Half of the hawks and half of the hounds
Which you were offering me, I will leave to you,   11200
But the children I will take with me who come from your nobility,
Those whom they love best of all – then I can trust them the better!
And so you'll remain in your self respect,
In your own kingdom, in your rightful inheritance:
To you I shall give this so that no king shall do wrong to you
Without atoning for it on his bare back!'
So spoke Arthur, most admired of kings.
  Then he had within his hand the whole region of Ireland
And its king who had become his man and had bestowed his three
    sons on him.
  Then Arthur spoke out to his own superb knights: 11210
'Let's go off to Iceland and take it into our own hands!'
The army advanced there and came quickly to Iceland: *Conquest*
Alcus the king was called, chieftain of that area,   *of*
He listened to the tidings of Arthur the king,   *Iceland*
And acted like a wise man and went towards him at once,
At once and straightaway with sixteen knights in envoy,
Carrying in his hand a massive bar of gold.
As soon as he saw Arthur he bowed down upon his knees
And the terrified king uttered these words to him:
'Welcome, Sir Arthur, welcome my lord!   11220

Here I place within your hands the whole region of Iceland:
You are to be my high king, and I shall be your underling;
I shall owe you such obedience as one ought his overlord,
And your vassal I'll become and deliver to you my beloved son
Whose name is **Esscol**, and you are to do him the honour
Of dubbing him as knight in your own retinue;
His mother, whom I married, is daughter of the King of Russia.
And also, every year, I shall give you money:
Seven thousand pounds in silver and in gold,
And for every proposal I'll be ready at your need.   11230
This I shall now swear to you upon my own sword here:
The sacred relic in its hilt is the highest in this land;
Whether I like it or I don't, I shall never be your betrayer!'
     Arthur heard all this, most admired of kings
(Arthur was agreeable where he got what he was after,
And savage as a man possessed with his opponents),
Arthur heard the placating words from the king of the people,
All that he requested, all this he granted:
Hostages and oaths and all that he promised.
     Then a message was reported with reliable words   11240
To the king of Orkney who was extremely brave –
He was called **Gonwais**, a heathen champion –
That King Arthur intended to come to his land:
With a vast navy he was hurrying to his nation.
Gonwais marched to meet him with his wise leaders
And delivered into Arthur's hands all of Orkney land,
And thirty-two islands which are part of it,
And did homage to him with the greatest reverence,
And he made him a promise in the presence of his courtiers
That each year he would furnish a full sixty ships: 11250
At his own expense he would convey them to London
Loaded, to be specific, with splendid sea-fish.
And this covenant he confirmed and hostages he found,
And firm oaths he swore that he would never be a traitor,
And then he took leave, and began to travel away:
'Lord, I bid you a very good day; I shall come whenever I may,
For you are my lord, and most beloved of all kings.'
     When Arthur had completed this, he wished to accept still more:
He instructed his good scribes and sent off to Jutland,
With greetings to King **Doldanim**, with orders to come at once to
     him,

And to become his own liegeman and to bring to him his
    two sons: 11261
'And if you should refuse to do what I propose
Then I shall send you all of sixteen thousand
Brave battle warriors to your grave disadvantage;
They will lay your land waste and slaughter your people,
And dispose of that land as seems most suitable to them,
And fetter you yourself and bring you here to me!'
  The king heard this threat coming from the emperor,
And instantly seized his own splendid garments,
His hawks and his hounds and his fine horses,   11270
Much silver and much gold and his two sons in his hands,
And off he went marching to Arthur the great king
And Doldanim the good made this declaration:
'All health to you, Arthur, most admired of kings,
Here I'm bringing the two, both of these here are my sons:
Their mother is a king's offspring; she is my own queen,
I won her in my plundering in the land of Russia;*   11278
I deliver to you my beloved sons; I myself will become your own
    man,   11277
And I shall send tribute from my own land
Every single year as items of tribute:*   11280
I shall send to you in London seven thousand pounds' worth;
This I shall swear: that I shall never be a traitor,
But rather I shall become your vassal; this will enhance your
    honour.
You shall I never betray, not to the very last day!'
  Arthur selected messengers and sent off to Wendland,[66]
To **Rumareth** the king, with instructions to inform him with speed
That he had within his grasp both Britain and Scotland,
Jutland and Ireland, Orkney and Iceland;
He directed Rumareth to come and bring him his eldest son,
And if he refused to, he'd drive him from his lands,   11290
And if he could catch him he would execute or hang him,
And destroy all his land and condemn all his liegemen.
  The message came to Rumareth, the rich king of Wendland;
He too was very frightened as the others had been earlier:
Most unwelcome were the tidings from Arthur the king!

---

[66] Lawman seems to locate 'Wendland' between the Elbe and the Vistula, but
see Wace, n. 33.

Nonetheless King Rumareth listened to advice:
He took his eldest son and twelve excellent earls
And went off to Arthur the admirable king,
And went down at his feet and decorously greeted him:
'All health to you, Arthur, most admired of Britons!   11300
I am called Rumareth, I am the king of Wendland;
I have heard a good deal described concerning your courage,
And that you're famous far and wide, king of greatest valour!
You have in many lands conquered realms by your own hands;
There is no king of any land who could ever you withstand,
Neither king nor kaiser, in no combat whatever;
In every project you begin you act according to your whim.
Here I have come to you and have brought you my eldest son;
Here I place within your hands my own self, my royal lands,
And my own beloved son, and my liegemen every one,   11310
My wife, my jewelled garments and all my joys together,
On condition you secure me against your savage attacks;
And do you now be my high king and I shall be your underling,
And deliver into your hands five hundred pounds of gold;
Such gifts I shall find for you every single year.'
    Arthur granted everything which the king requested,
And then he held secret council with his best leaders
And declared that he wanted to return to this land
And to see Guinevere the most gracious queen.
He had brass trumpets blown to summon his host   11320
And off to ship they marched, soldiers marvellously pleased.
The wind blew as they wished, the weather was as they wanted,
They were all delighted at it; they landed up at Grimsby.
    The nobles of this land heard of this at once,
And to the queen came tidings of Arthur the king,
That he had come safe and sound with his men in good spirits.
    Then here in Britain there was great celebration:
There were songs sung to fiddles and harping as well,
Pipes and brass trumpets merrily played there;
Poets sang in praise of Arthur the king   11330
And of the great reputation which he had earned for himself.
People came to his court from many different countries;
In every direction the people were contented.
Everything that Arthur gazed at paid homage to him:
The rich and the poor, as thick as hail falling;
The most wretched of the Britons was greatly enriched.

On this topic one may read concerning King Arthur
That for twelve years after this he went on living here
In peace and in plenty, in total tranquillity:
No man contended with him, nor did he create any contests, 11340
Nor could any man whatever imagine any pleasures
In any other country in more measure than in this,
Nor could any man experience half as much enjoyment
As there was with Arthur and with his folk here.

    I can describe how things turned out, amazing though it's bound
      to seem:[67]
It happened one Christmas day, when Arthur was lodged in
      London,   *Yuletide*
People had come to him from each of his dependencies: *Fight*
From Britain's land, from Scotland, from Ireland and from Iceland
And from all the other lands which Arthur held in hand,
All the greatest leaders with their horses and their squires: 11350
There were seven sons of kings with seven hundred knights who'd
      come,
Not counting the courtiers paying service to Arthur.
Each of them was feeling proudly exultant,
Giving out that he himself was better than his fellows;
The folk came from many realms: there was much rivalry,
Since if one would count himself so high, the second would much
      higher.

    Then the brass trumpets were blown and the trestle-tables
      covered:
Fine golden bowls were carried out to the hall floor,
And with them soft towels, all made of white silk;
Then Arthur sat down, and beside him Queen Guinevere,   11360
Then all the earls were seated, and after them the barons,
Then next the knights, as they were assigned;

---

[67] The 'fight in the hall' is Lawman's most famous addition to Wace; it is a virtual parody of a common theme in Celtic and Germanic tales (for example, the close of the Norse *Hrólfs saga Kráka* and the Old English *Finnsburh Fragment*). Lawman reinterprets Wace's Round Table, a cosmopolitan centre for culture and fashion, and stresses instead the explosively competitive racial admix resulting from Arthur's extension of Empire (11347 ff. and 11476–90). The Wendish prince Rummareth saves his lord, another Germanic motif found in the Anglo-Saxon Chronicle s.a. 755, 'Cynewulf and Cyneheard', where a British hostage is wounded defending Cynewulf, and in *The Battle of Maldon* 265–72, where a Northumbrian is killed avenging Byrhtnoth.

The nobly connected then brought in the food,
Exactly in decorum, first to the knights,
Then to the foot soldiers and then to the squires,
Then to the baggage-men, right down the tables.
    The company became aroused: blows were freely given;
First they started throwing loaves, as long as there were some left,
And then the silver goblets which were filled with wine,
And after that, clutching palms quickly caught up throats!   11370
    Then a young man jumped forward who'd come there from
        Wendland;
He'd been given to Arthur to be held as hostage;
He was the son of Rumareth who was king of the Wends;
In this way the knight spoke there to Arthur the king:
'Lord Arthur, be off quickly, into your bedroom,
And your queen with you, and your close relations,
And we'll decide this conflict between these foreign combatants!'
Having spoken these words he leaped up to the trestle-boards
Where carving knives were lying in front of the lord king:
Three knives he caught up and with one quickly struck   11380
Into the neck of the knight who first began that very fight
So that down to the hall floor his head went crashing;
Fast he slew another, this same fighter's brother:
Before the swords came out he had finished off seven.
There was a huge fight there: every man struck the other;
There was enormous bloodshed, consternation in the court!
    Then the king emerged from out of his chamber;
With him a hundred courtiers, with helmets and with corslets,
Each carrying in his right hand a broadsword of bright steel.
Then shouted Arthur, most admired of kings: 11390
'Sit down, sit down at once, all of you, or you will lose your lives!
Anyone who refuses to sit will be condemned to death.
Seize and bring me the actual man who first started this fight,
Clap a noose around his neck and drag him to the marshes,
And fling him in a deep bog and there let him lie,
And seize all his closest relatives whom you can discover,
And strike off their heads with your broad swords;
From the women you can discover among his closest relations
Carve off the noses and let their beauty be destroyed;
In that way I'll quite obliterate the tribe from which he
        came,   11400
And if ever any more I subsequently hear

That any of my courtiers, whether great or humble,
From this same slaughter should [seek] revenge after,*
Then no compensation from gold or treasure will atone,
Neither strong steed nor war gear, to buy him off from death
Or from being drawn apart by horses, which is the punishment for
    traitors.
Bring here the sacred relics and I shall swear upon them,
As shall all you knights who were present at this fight,
You earls and barons, that you will never break it.'
    The first to swear was Arthur, most admired of kings,   11410
Then the earls took the oath, and then the barons took the oath,
Then the landholders took the oath, then the servitors took the
    oath,
That they would never again instigate a brawl.
The dead were all taken up and carried to their resting-place,
And then brass trumpets were blown with very rousing sound:
Whether they liked it or loathed it, each one took water and a
    cloth,
And then, reconciled, they sat down at the table,
All in awe of Arthur, most admired of kings.
Cup-bearers were jostling, minstrels were singing,
Harps gave out joyful sounds: courtiers were jubilant.   11420
For a whole week like this the court was employed.

    Next, it says in the story, the king went to Cornwall;
There a man came quickly to him who was a skilled craftsman,
And he encountered the king and gave courteous greeting:
'All health to you, Arthur, most admired of kings!
I am your own vassal; many a land I have traversed;
I know a marvellous number of the skills of woodworking.
I heard tell beyond the sea such novel tidings
About your own knights who at your table started fighting
At the midwinter feast; many fell there.   11430
In their mighty arrogance they were acting games of murder,
And because of their high connexions each must sit near top-table.
But I shall make for you a most suitable table   *The*
Where sixteen hundred and more can easily be seated,   *Round*
Each in turn all round so that no one gets left out,   *Table*
No inclusion and exclusion, just one man opposite another.
When you want to ride you can carry it alongside,
And set it up wherever you want, according to your fancy,
And you need never again be afraid in all the wide world

That ever any proud knight would at your table start a fight, 11440
Since the important there must be equal with the simple.'
 Timber was obtained and the table was begun:
In the space of four weeks the work was completed.
On a certain festival the court was assembled,
And Arthur himself turned quickly to the table,
And ordered all his knights to the table straightaway.
When all those knights were seated at their food
Then each was chatting to the other just as if he were his brother;
They were all seated around it and none was excluded;
Every single kind of knight was very well placed there; 11450
Each was seated equally, the important and the simple,
And no one there could boast about a different kind of toast
Than the drink of his companions who were sitting at the table.

 This was the very table which the Britons boast about,
And they tell many kinds of fiction about Arthur who was king,
But so does every man who has great love for another:
If he loves that man too much then he is bound to lie,
And in his fine praise he'll say more than he deserves;
However bad a man he is, his friend will back him up still;
On the other hand if strife should arise in the community, 11460
On any occasion between two individuals,
Lies will be invented about the one who isn't liked:
Even if he were the best man who ever ate bread at table
The man who found him hateful would invent some vices for him;
It's not all true, it's not all false which poets are proclaiming,
But this is true fact about Arthur the king:
There has never been a king so valiant in everything;
It's found as fact in the annals just as it actually was,
From the start to the end, concerning Arthur the king,
No more and no less, just as his deeds were recorded, 11470
But the Britons loved him greatly and often lie about him
And recount many a thing about Arthur the king
Which never really happened in the whole of this world!
A man can say enough, if he just tells the truth,
Of outstanding things about Arthur the king.

 Arthur was then very great, his court very glorious,
So that no knight was valued nor his actions reckoned valiant,
– Not in Wales, nor in England, in Scotland nor in Ireland,
In Normandy nor in France, in Flanders nor in Denmark,

Nor in any land whatever which lies on this side of the
    Alps –   11480
No knight (as I said) would be thought good, nor his deeds
    reckoned bold
Unless, concerning Arthur and his outstanding court –
His weapons and his garments and also his war-mounts –
He was able to tell in song about Arthur the young
And about his knightly courtiers and about their great prowess,
And about their magnificence and how well it suited them;
Then he would be welcome anywhere in this world's span,
Wherever he might come to, even if he were in Rome.

    All those who heard the stories told about Arthur
Found accounts of the good king very extraordinary;   11490
And so it had been prophesied before he was even born,[68]
So the famous prophet Merlin had foretold about him,
Saying that a king would come from Uther Pendragon
Such that minstrels should make a board for food from the king's
    own breast
And at it would be seated really splendid poets,
Who would eat their fill before they fared away;
And they would draw draughts of wine from the king's tongue
And be drinking and delighting by day and by night;
This sport was to endure for them as long as this world lasts.

    In addition Merlin stated that more was to come: 11500
That everything he looked at was to bow down at his feet;
In addition Merlin stated a marvel which was greater:
That there would be immoderate sorrow at this king's departure,
And as to this king's end – no Briton would believe it,
Unless one means the final death at the last great Judgment
When our Lord God is to judge all the nations;
Otherwise we can't determine as to Arthur's death
Because he himself said to his splendid Britons,

[68] Wace refused to translate the *Prophetiae Merlini* in *HRB* (see Wace, n. 9), and Lawman consequently does not include the prophecies in the Vortigern episode, but he must have had access to Geoffrey's Latin text (which also circulated separately from *HRB*) or to an Anglo-Norman translation, since this is one of seven passages alluding to Merlin's prophecy of Arthur (8965–76, 9404–23, 11493–504, 13530–8, 13964–5, 14200–2, 14295–7; Arthur himself refers to Sibylline prophecies at 12547: see Le Saux, *Sources*, 117; on Merlin, see Kelley M. Wickham-Crowley, 'Narrative innovations', in Le Saux, *Text and Tradition*, pp. 207–19).

Down south in Cornwall where Gawain had been killed
And he himself was badly wounded, grievously severely,   11510
That he was to voyage into Avalon,
Into the island, to **Argante** the gracious,[69]
Because with health-giving lotions she would heal his wounds,
And when he was entirely healed he would instantly come to them.
The Britons believ[e] this: that he will come like this,*
And they are always looking for his coming to his land,
Just as he promised them before he went away.

   In this world Arthur was a wise king and powerful,
A good man and peaceful; his subjects all adored him.
He possessed knights both proud and exalted in spirit   11520
Who reported to the king of remarkable things;
In this way the courtiers called upon the high king:
'Lord Arthur, let us voyage to the realm of France
And reduce all that land into your own hand,
Put to flight all the French and fell their monarch,
Get control of all the castles and put British guards in them,
And rule over their realm with robust force.'

   Arthur then responded, most admired of kings: *International*
'I shall perform your wishes, but first I wish to go to   *Reputation*
   Norway,
And with me I wish to take Lot, who is my brother-in-law: 11530
He is the father of Gawain whom I love so dearly,
For there has come from Norway some new
      information   *(ii) Conquests*
That King **Sichelin** is dead there, his courtiers deserted,   *in*
And he has bequeathed all his kingdom already to Lot *Scandinavia*
   here,
For the king's entirely lacking either sons or daughters,
And Lot is his sister's son: for that reason he's preferred.
So as a new king in Norway I intend to invest him,
And well I shall instruct him to direct his people well.
And when I have done this, I shall afterwards come home,
And prepare my forces and voyage across to France,   11540
And if the king opposes me, refusing to sue for peace,
Then I shall fight against him and fell him to the ground!'

---

   [69] *Argante* may be a corruption of Morgan, who in Geoffrey of Monmouth's
Vita Merlini (918-23) is a healer and magician and one of nine sisters on a
blessed isle (see Le Saux, *Sources*, p. 114).

Arthur had horns blown and also brass trumpets
And had his very bold Britons mustered at the seaside;
Fine ships he possessed beside the sea waves:
Fifteen hundred of them hastened from the land
And went winging across the sea as if they could fly,
And turned towards Norway with terrific force.   *Conquest*
As soon as they arrived they went into harbour,   *in*
With their full power they stepped on the realm's shore.   *Norway*
Arthur sent his messengers far throughout that country   11551
Ordering them to come at once and take Lot as their king,
And if they refused to, he would slaughter them all!
     Then the Norwegian earls took their ambassadors
And sent them to the king with request that he depart:
'And if you refuse to return you will have sorrow and misery,
For as long as is for ever it will not happen ever
That we shall choose as king a man who is a foreigner;
For if Sichelin has departed there are others here as talented
Whom we can by our own decision choose to be king,   11560
And this is a fact and there is no other!
Either take yourselves off now and go straight back home,
Or in one week from today we'll give you a great battle!'
     Next the Norwegian earls came to the conclusion
That they would have a king who came from their own race,
For all the words of Sichelin they reckoned were stupid.
'And as long as shall be for ever this shall happen never!
But we shall take **Riculf**, a rich and powerful earl
And elect him as our king: this we find agreeable,
And shall summon our army throughout all this country   11570
And advance towards Arthur and rout him in battle
And we shall get Lot running and rout him from the land,
Or else by fighting we'll cause him to fall.'
     They elected Riculf who was an earl of Norway,
And raised him to the throne (though not by right of succession)
And summoned their army through all Norway's country:
And Arthur for his part began to march through that land;
He traversed that land; its towns he burned down,
A good deal did he plunder, many people did he slaughter,
And Riculf started riding towards Arthur right away: 11580
Together they clashed and battle commenced;
The Britons turned towards them; there was trouble in full;
They snatched from the scabbard swords of great length;

Heads flew on the battlefield; faces were blanched;
Man against man set shaft into breast;
Byrnies were broken; the British were busy;
Shields bristled with shafts; soldiers were falling,
And all through the daylight lasted this great fight.
If they shifted east, if they shifted west, the Norwegians got the
worst;
If they shifted south, if they shifted north: the Norwegians were
falling.
The British were bold: the Norwegians were killed.   11591
Of the Norwegians there fell twenty-five thousand,
And King Riculf was killed there and deprived of his life-days;
Few were left on their feet from the folk who had lived there;
Those whose wretched lives remained to them begged for Arthur's
mercy.
    Arthur gazed at Lot whom he loved very much
And Arthur the great man began to call to him:
'Lot, come over here to me: you are my dear kinsman;
Herewith I bestow all this kingdom upon you;
You are to hold it of me and have me as your guardian.'   11600
    Now Lot's eldest son, Gawain, had come there from Rome
From the court of the Pope who was called **Sulpicius**,
Who long had been training him and who dubbed him as knight;
Things were very well ordained that Gawain was created
Because Gawain was most high-minded, and excelled in every
virtue:
He was generous with food and a knight among the best.
All Arthur's courtiers were greatly enlivened
By the coming to court of Gawain the courageous,
And by his father Lot, who had been elected a king.
Then Arthur spoke with him, bidding him to keep a binding truce
And bidding him to love those of his people who stayed peaceful,
And to eliminate entirely those who would not keep the peace.
    Then Arthur, most admired of kings, cried out again:
'Where are you, my Britons? now get marching at once!
At the sea's edge prepare my good ships!'
The knights did exactly as Arthur commanded:
When the ships were ready, Arthur set off for the sea,
Taking with him his knights, his Norwegian leaders,
And his bold British men; and he launched off on the waves,
And the undaunted king came into Denmark.   11620

He had his tents erected: out across the fields they spread;
Brass trumpets he had blown, his arrival to make known.

    Now there was then in Denmark a very mighty king,   *Denmark*
Aescil he was called, chieftain of the Danes;   *Invaded*
He could see that Arthur conquered everything he wanted;
King Aescil thought carefully what might be his policy:
He was loth to lose the land he so loved
And could see that by power he could not hope to prevail
Against Arthur's force in any combat at all.

    He sent his good wishes to Arthur the king,   11630
Some hounds and some hawks and some very good horses,
Silver and red gold, with really [prudent] words.*
And Aescil the famous did one thing further:
He sent to the most excellent in Arthur's entourage,
Asking them to intercede for him with the noble King
So that he could become his vassal and give up his son as a hostage
And send him every year a certain tribute from his land,
A boat solidly filled from gunwale to bilge
With gold and great treasure and with gorgeous garments,
And then he would swear that he would never be a traitor.   11640

    News came to Arthur, most admired of kings,
That Aescil, the Danish king, wished to become his underling
Without any fighting – he and all his knights.
Then Arthur the great was in very good spirits,
And answered like this, with unassuming words:
'Good luck to the man who with very good sense
Gains peace and goodwill and lasting friendship for himself;
When he can see how he'll be bound by sheer force
On the verge of losing all of his beloved realm,
Then with forethought he may loosen the fetters he so loathes.' 11650

    Arthur told the king to come and to bring his eldest son,
And the king of Denmark did so at once:
He quickly fulfilled what Arthur had willed;
They came to a conference and were accorded.
Then Arthur cried again, that most admired of kings:
'Now I wish to go to France with my enormous force:
I desire to have from Norway nine thousand knights,
And out of Denmark I shall conduct nine thousand of the
      countrymen,
And from the Orkneys eleven hundred,
And out of Moray three thousand men,   11660

And out of Galloway five thousand of the people,
And out of Ireland eleven thousand.
And out of Britain from my own bold knights
There shall throng past me thirty thousand,
And from Jutland I shall lead ten thousand of the people,
And out of Friesland five thousand men,
And from Brittany Howel the brave,
And with such folk I shall invade France.
And as I trust in God's grace still more shall I promise:
That from all of the lands which lie within my hands   11670
I shall order out every worthy man who knows how to wield his
     weapons,
As he wants to live, and to retain his limbs,
That he must come with me to fight against **Frollo**
Who is the king of France – he must meet his fate –
In Rome city he was born and comes of a Roman clan.'

    Arthur moved forwards till he came to Flanders;   *International*
He conquered that land and settled it with his men,   *Reputation*
And then he turned from there towards [Boulogne]*
And took [all of] Boulogne's lands into his own hands*
And then he took the route which led towards France.   11680
Then he issued his instructions to all in his service:
Wherever they advanced they were not to take plunder
Unless [they] were able in strict fairness to obtain it,*
By fair exchange in the king's entourage.

    Frollo heard information where he was, in France,[70]   *(iii) France*
Of Arthur's success and all his attainments   *Invaded*
And how he won everything which he had looked at,
And everything he set his eyes on gave allegiance to him.
Then was King Frollo horribly frightened!
In that same age when this was occurring   11690
All the land of France then was known as Gaul,
And from Rome into France had Frollo advanced,
And every year he was to send tribute from that land
Ten hundred pounds' worth in silver and in gold.
Now as chieftain of France Frollo received information
Of the country-wide chaos Arthur caused in the land.

---

[70] Lawman considerably extends this fight with Frollo, qualifying Wace's
approval of Frollo's courage (W 10069, echoed in L 11764, 11825) by
suggesting his terror at 11689 and 11824.

He sent messengers at once quickly towards Rome,
And urged the Roman people to make right consultations
About how many thousand knights they wanted to send there.
So that with ease he might against Arthur fight,   11700
And send Arthur the strong flying from the land.
   Knights began riding out of Roman territory,
Twenty-five thousand of them advanced upon France.
Frollo heard of this in his enormous force,
That the Roman forces were riding to his country;
Frollo and his folk advanced then to meet them,
And they came together, men of courage and valour,
An immeasurable army from all parts of the earth.
   This news came to Arthur, most admired of kings,
Who summoned his army and moved off towards them.   11710
There has never yet been a king alive on this earth
Who ever in the world before commanded such an army,
For from all of the kingdoms which Arthur had in his control
He led off with him all the bravest men,
Until he had no idea at all how many thousand there were.
   As soon as Arthur and Frollo had encountered in combat
Fiercely they attacked all those whom they met.
Knights of great strength grasped spears of great length
And rushed at each other with furious force.
All through that day there were very many blows;   11720
Folk fell to the ground in their fated final moments;
Grieving soldiers sought a couch in the grass;
Helmets were ringing, warriors howling;
Shields were shattered, soldiers were slumping.
Arthur, most admired of kings, called aloud then:
'Where are you, my Britons, my very bold fighters?
The day is drawing on, and this army is defying us;
Let us send flying to them sufficient sharp spears,
And teach them to ride the road back towards Rome!'
   After those words which Arthur was speaking   11730
He sprang forward on his steed as a spark does from the fire;
Following him there were fifty thousand men,
Hardened battle-champions hurried to the fight,
Struck down on Frollo where he was in the throng
And forced him to flee with many of his folk.
There Arthur slaughtered countless numbers of folk.
Then Frollo the great fled into Paris

And barred up the gates in very deep gloom,
And these words he spoke, in sorrowing mood:
'I wish very much that I had never been born!'   11740
Inside Paris then there were pathetic tales indeed,
Gestures of despair; citizens shivered in terror;
The walls they were repairing, the gates fortifying,
Food they were seizing, everything they got hold of;
From every quarter to the city they hurried;
All those who held with Frollo travelled there fast.
Arthur, most admired of kings, heard this,
That Frollo was hiding in Paris with an enormous force,
Declaring he intended to resist Arthur.

    Arthur went to Paris, quite unfaint-hearted,   11750
And surrounded the walls and erected his tents;
Round it on four sides he lay for four weeks and a day.
The people who were inside there were absolutely terrified;
The city was packed with people inside it
Who quickly ate the food which had been collected.
When four full weeks had elapsed since Arthur had taken his stand
      there,
There was in the city immeasurable sadness
Among the wretched people who were lying there starving:
There was weeping, there was wailing and tremendous distress.
They cried out to Frollo and begged him to come to terms,   11760
To become Arthur's vassal and enjoy his favour,
And hold the kingdom now from Arthur the courageous,
And not permit the abject folk to perish quite from hunger.

    Then Frollo replied – he had a fine spirit!
'No, so help me God, who controls all destinies!
Never shall I become his man, nor he become my liege lord;
I myself shall fight; on God's side lies the right!'
Once more exclaimed Frollo, a fine man in spirit:
'No, so help me the Lord who made the light of day!
Never shall I at all beg Arthur for mercy,   11770
But I intend to fight without any single knight,
Body against body, in the presence of my people,
Hand against hand, with that King Arthur.
Whichever of us two will prove the weaker, straight he'll be the
      lesser,
Whichever of us two is able to survive, by his friends he'll be the
      more esteemed.

And whichever of us two can get the better of the other,
Is to have all the other's lands delivered into his own hands.
   'This I shall request, if Arthur wishes to grant it,
And this I shall swear upon my own sword,
And I shall find hostages, the sons of three kings,   11780
To prove that I shall surely keep to this promise
And will not renege on it, by my very life;
Because I prefer to lie dead before my own people
Than to see them on the ground perishing from hunger.
After all, we have destroyed our knights in the fighting,
Full fifty thousand soldiers are fallen
And many a good housewife has been made a grieving widow.
Many a child fatherless and bereft of comfort,
And now these folk are fearfully harmed by sheer hunger.
Therefore it is better that just between us two   11790
We deal and dispose of this kingdom by fight;
May the better man have it and enjoy possessing it!'
   Frollo took twelve knights straight after speaking these thoughts
And sent them with speed to Arthur the king,
And enquired if he wished to accept this agreement
And through his own hands to lay claim to the kingdom;
Or to reject it to his own people's ruin;
And if he obtained it, let him possess it with power.
   The message came to Arthur, most admired of kings,
Who had never been so blithe before in his life: 11800
He was pleased by the tidings from Frollo their king,
And Arthur the lucky made this declaration:
'King Frollo of France has spoken most aptly:
It is better that the two of us decide for this realm
Than that our stalwart lords should be slaughtered there.
I approve of this arrangement in my people's assembly,
To do what he proposes on an appointed day;
This is to be tomorrow, in front of both sets of men,
When we shall each of us fight the other, and may the less plucky
      man fall!
And whichever of us two retreats and wants to give up this fight,
Let him in each land be cursed as a coward.   11811
Then songs can be sung of such a king as that
Who gave his solemn promise and then forsook his knighthood!'
   Frollo king of France heard this reported,
That Arthur wished to fight in person without any other knights.

Frollo was a strong man and stern in his emotions,
And he had made his promise in the presence of his whole
    household
And he could not without great disgrace bring shame upon himself
By going back on the bold bragging he had uttered in the city.
When he said what he said, he had certainly believed   11820
That Arthur would decline it and would not accept the challenge,
For if Frollo had known, as the king within France,
That Arthur would allow him what he had asked for,
He would not have been so bold for a ship full of gold!
But just the same, Frollo was a very brave fighter,
A tall knight and a strong man and full of great spirit,
And he said he would keep to the day they'd agreed,
'On the island which is encompassed by water:
The island lies – be sure of this – within the city of Paris;
There I will in fight determine my own rights,   11830
With a shield, and garbed as a knight.
Tomorrow now will be the day; let it go to him who win may!'
    So came the tidings to Arthur the king
That Frollo was willing to contest France by fighting;
He had never been so blithe before in his life,
And started to laugh in a really loud voice,
And these were the words of Arthur the brave:
'Now I know that Frollo is willing to fight with me,
Tomorrow at daybreak, as he himself determined,
Upon the island which water has surrounded,   11840
For it befits a king that his word can be relied on.
Have the brass trumpets blown and bid my men assemble,
So that every good man may tonight be keeping vigil
And praying to our Lord, who controls the lot of all,
That he may protect me against Frollo the furious,
And with his right hand may preserve me from shame.
And if I succeed in winning this kingdom to my own command,
Then every single poor man will be provided for,
And I shall perform Almighty God's will.
Now may he give me assistance who can do all things well;   11850
May the high, heavenly King support me with his aid,
For I intend to love him as long as I have life!'
    All through the long night there were hymns by candle-light:
Devoutly clerics were intoning holy psalms to God.
When daylight came next morning the attendants started stirring;

Arthur the mighty took his weapons in his hands;[71]
He threw on his back a most precious mantle,
A shirt of soft linen and a tunic made of velvet,
A very choice mail-coat of interlocking steel;
On his head he set an excellent helmet,   11860
By his side he buckled his sword Caliburn;
His legs he protected with mail leggings of steel,
And fastened on his feet very fine spurs.
Equipped in this way the king leapt on his steed;
Then he was passed a really splendid shield
Which was made entirely of elephant ivory.
Then he was handed a stout ash shaft
At the end of which was a very fine spearhead
Forged in Carmarthen by a smith whose name was Griffin;
This had belonged to Uther, the previous king here.   11870
    When the fierce man was armed, he prepared to move off.
Then anyone who had been about would have observed
The regal champion riding off vigorously:
Since this world's creation it has been nowhere narrated
That any man so handsome ever moved on horseback
As was King Arthur, son of King Uther.
    There rode behind the king brave army commanders,
Forty hundred of them in the first contingent,
Noble army leaders arrayed all in steel,
Bravest Britons, ready with their weapons;   11880
After them hastened fully fifty hundred
Whom Gawain headed: a champion who was deadly.
Afterwards there surged out sixty thousand men,
Very brave Britons bringing up the rearguard.
    King Angel was there; Lot was there and Urien,
And Urien's son was there, whose name was **Ywain**;
Kay was there and **Bedivere**, supervizing the army there;
Howel was present, leading man in Brittany;
Cador was there too, most courageous in the throng;
From Ireland there came Gillomaur the mighty;   11890
King Gonwais was present, Orkney's favourite;
Doldanim the brave was there, who'd come from Jutland,

[71] To focus attention on Arthur, Lawman repeats the arming topos from
10543–57, and adds specific prayers (11922–5) which are an attempt to deal
with the problem of Christian knights attacking fellow-Christians.

[And Rumareth the strong who'd come from Wendland];*   11892a
King Aescil was there, Denmark's favourite.
Of folk on foot there were so many thousand men
That no man in this world's region has ever been so clever
In any number system as to total up the thousands,
Unless he naturally had the wisdom of the Lord,
Or unless he had within him the same brain as Merlin.

    Arthur moved forward with innumerable folk   11899
Until he came completely inside Paris city,   *The*
On the west bank of the river, with his vast company.   *Fight with*
On the east bank stood Frollo with a huge force too,   *Frollo*
Ready for the fight in front of all his knights.
Arthur took charge of a good boat and embarked in it
With his shield and his steed and all his war-gear
And he shoved that sturdy boat off from the shore
And strode up on the island, leading his steed in hand.
His men who brought him there by the king's order
There on the waves left the boat, freely floating.

    Frollo got into his boat – this king was regretting   11910
That he'd ever had the idea of fighting with Arthur;
He crossed to the isle with his splendid armour,
Up on to the isle he stepped, dragging his steed after;
The men who brought him there by the king's order
There on the waves left the boat, swiftly floating,
And the two kings remained there alone.

    Then people who had been about would have observed
Folk on the banks who were fearsomely afraid;
They scrambled up on halls, they scrambled up on walls,
They scrambled up on bowers, they scrambled up on towers 11920
So they could see the contest between the two kings.
Arthur's men prayed, with very much devotion,
To the good God and to his holy mother
That their own lord might have victory there;
And the others likewise prayed for their king.

    Arthur set foot in stirrup and leaped on his charger,
And Frollo in his war-gear leaped on his steed
The one at his own end upon that island,[72]
And the other at his end in that island.

---

[72] Judicial combat was often held on an island to ensure fair play; it was replaced by the Grand Assize in 1179 under Henry II's legal reforms.

Those royal knights brandished their spears   11930
And reined in their steeds; they were experienced knights.
The man could not be found in any land whatever
Who had sufficient foresight to be able to foretell
Which one of the two kings would lie there defeated,
For both of them were brave knights, worthy men and valiant,
Men powerful in vigour and of very mighty strength.
They spurred on their steeds and were riding to make impact,
Furiously galloping, sending sparks flying after them:
Arthur struck Frollo with furious force
High up on his shield;   11940
And the trusty steed jumped out in mid stream.
Arthur's sword came out: destruction was in its point!
And he pitched into Frollo where he was, there in the water:
Very soon their contest might have come to a finish!
But Frollo gripped in his hand his lengthy spear,
And made a counter-attack on Arthur as he came at him, *
And struck the brave steed right in the breast
So that the spear went right in and Arthur tumbled off.
    Then a roar arose which the earth again re-echoed:
The skies were resounding with the people's shouting.   11950
The Britons there were on the point of crossing the water
But Arthur started up at once unharmed in full strength,
And gripped his good shield decorated with gold,
And against Frollo, with expressions of hostility;
He flung over his chest his fine, broad shield.
And Frollo flung himself at him in a fierce attack
And lifting his sword up struck it down hard
And smashed into Arthur's shield – it fell on to the field;
His helmet on his head and his battle-coif of mail
Suddenly failed on the front of his head   11960
And he received a wound which was four inches long;
It did not pain him badly because it was not too big,
But the blood spurted down all over his chest.
Arthur was deeply enraged in his feelings
And his sword Caliburn he swung with full strength
And struck Frollo right on his helmet so that it split in two,
Sliced through the mail-coif till it stopped at his breast.
Then Frollo fell on the earth of the field:
On that grass bed he gave up his spirit.
The Britons rejoiced with a roar of acclaim   11970

And the (other) folk fled exceedingly fast.
  Arthur the mighty came to the shore,
And the most admired of kings shouted out like this:
'Where are you, Gawain, my favourite man?
Order all these Roman citizens to leave here in peace:
Let each man have his home, as God permits him.
Command each man to keep the peace, on pain of life and limb,
And I shall confirm it just a week from today.
Order these people then to travel together
And come to me in person; they shall prosper because of it. 11980
They are to give to me homage with due honour,
And I shall maintain them within my control
And impose on the land very just laws,
For now the Roman law code must fall in abeyance,
Which formerly applied here in the reign of Frollo
Who lies slain on the island and deprived of his life's days.
After this very soon his kinsfolk in Rome
Shall be hearing tidings from Arthur the king,
For with them I wish to speak and Rome's walls I shall break
And remind them how King Belin there led his Britons in, 11990
And conquered all the lands which belong to Rome.'
  Arthur turned to the gate in the front of the city;
Discerning men arrived, who directed the city,
And allowed Arthur in with all of his men,
Delivered to him the halls, delivered to him the castles,
Delivered to him (most surely) the whole city of Paris.
There was much rejoicing among the British forces!
  That day arrived in the city which Arthur had appointed
And all the male inhabitants came, and became his vassals.
Arthur took his army and divided it in two, 12000
And handed over half of it into Howel's charge,
And instructed him to go at once with that great army,
With the British men, territories to win.
Howel then acted just as Arthur had instructed:
He conquered Berry and all the lands near by,
Anjou and Touraine, Auvergne and Gascony   *Conquest*
And all of the ports which belong to those parts.   *of France*
  The Duke who ruled Poitou bore the name **Guitard**:
He refused to obey Howel and remained always opposed to him,
Refused to seek a truce; but Howel fought against him; 12010
Frequently he felled men, frequently he made them flee:

Howel devastated all that land and destroyed the people.
It was obvious to Guitard, who was overlord in Poitou,
That all those who lived there were being lost to him;
He made peace with Howel, along with all his followers,
And became the vassal of the valiant King Arthur.
Arthur was gracious to him, loved him very greatly,
And allowed him to retain his lands because he did him homage.
And so Howel had made a handsome beginning!

    Arthur governed France by a generous arrangement: 12020
Taking his army he traversed all that country;
To Burgundy he travelled and brought it under his control,
And then he laid his course into Lorraine
And all of its lands he took into his own hands.
All that Arthur set his eyes on gave allegiance to him,
And he returned after this home again to Paris.

    When Arthur had established France by a sound truce,
Ratified and reconciled so the country could relax,
Then he directed the veteran knights whom he'd retained for a
    long time
To come before the king and to receive their reward,   12030
Because for many years now they had been his partners;
To some he gave lands and to some silver and gold,
To some he gave castles, to some men he gave clothes;
He bade them depart in joy, atone for their wrongdoing,
And forbade them to bear weapons now that age had come upon
    them,
And told them in this life to have great love for God
So that at its finish He would surely give them paradise,
Which they might enjoy with the angels in delight.
All the veteran knights travelled off to their lands,
While the young remained with their beloved king.   12040

    For all of nine years Arthur remained there:[73]
Nine years liberally he held France in his control.
And then no longer afterwards did he rule that land,
But all the time that kingdom remained in Arthur's hands
Remarkable things occurred in the region:
Many a haughty man Arthur made humble

---

[73] Within these nine years of peace in France, Mannyng locates the adventures
of the thirteenth-century French prose romances (*Chronicle of England*
10961–78); see also Putter, 'Finding time for romance', pp. 7, 8).

And many an arrogant man he brought underfoot.
   It happened one Easter when men had finished fasting
That Arthur on Easter Day had assembled his nobles,
All the greatest people who belonged to France   12050
And to all the territories tributary to her.
There he confirmed his knights in all their own rights:
To each he gave such property as he had deserved.
   In this way spoke Arthur, most admired of kings:
'Kay, look in this direction! You are to be my   *Governorships*
      seneschal;
Here I donate you Anjou because you've acted well,
And all the privileges which appertain to it.
Kneel to me, Bedivere: you are my senior butler here:
As long as I'm alive I shall have love for you;
Here I give you Neustria, neighbour to my own realm.'   12060
(In those days Neustria was what is now called Normandy);
That same couple of earls were Arthur's favoured men
In council and in consultation on every occasion.
Then once again said Arthur, most admired of kings:
'Come here, **Howeldin**, you're my subject and my kin,[74]
You take Boulogne and possess it with pleasure.
Draw nearer, **Borel**, you're a wise knight and sensible:
Here I donate to you Le Mans with much respect:
Possess it with pleasure because you've acted well.'
So did King Arthur deal out his illustrious lands,   12070
According to their deeds because he deemed them worthy.
Then there were happy tales in King Arthur's halls:
There were harping and singing and pleasures all the time.
   When Easter was over and April went from homes
And grass was growing everywhere and water was calm   *The*
And men told each other that May had arrived,   *Crown-Wearing*
Arthur took his splendid folk and travelled to the sea
And assembled his ships which excelled among the best

---

[74] Howeldin (distinct from Arthur's cousin Howel) is Wace's Holdin, who
receives Flanders, while Boulogne goes to Ligier, and Puntif to Richier; a line
was probably lost here from Lawman's copy of Wace: see Wace, n. 36; Richier
is present in the ambush episode (L 13208), and *Laeyer* (probably Ligier) is earl
of Boulogne in L 12171–2 but is re-spelled *Leir* of Boulogne (MS O: *Leayr*) in
13808; this Borel (also in Wace) is clearly not the man killed by Arthur at
10595, an incident only found in Lawman, who is somewhat economical with
names.

And journeyed to this country and came ashore in London;
He came ashore in London to the joy of those who lived
     here: 12080
Everyone who set their eyes on him was full of delight
And at once started singing about Arthur the king
And about the splendid triumphs which he had achieved.
There father kissed son and wished the boy welcome,
Daughter her mother and brother another,
Sister kissed sister (their feelings were more tender).
In many hundred places there stood by the wayside
People who were asking about many kinds of things,
And knights who were informing them about their achievements
And bragging a good deal about great acquisitions. 12090
No man could describe, however dextrous his style,
One half of the happiness there was among the British.
Each man moved as he required freely in this kingdom,
From one town to the next with considerable ease,
And so for a short time things stayed just like this:
There was content among the British while their brave king was
    there.
   When Easter had gone and summer came to the land
Arthur consulted with his chief counsellors
About how in Caerleon he'd wear his crown ceremonially
And upon Whitsunday his people there he'd summon. 12100
   At that particular time it was the general opinion
That there was not in any land a city as lovely,
Nor as widely renowned as Caerleon-upon-Usk,
Except for the noble city which is called Rome.
Even so with the king there was many a man in the land
Who declared the city of Caerleon more resplendent than Rome,
And said that the Usk was the sweetest of all rivers.
There were extensive meadows all around the city;
There were fish, there were birds, and it was very beautiful;
There was timber, and wild animals in wonderful profusion; 12110
There was all the pleasure any man could imagine,
Yet never since Arthur's visit has the town ever flourished,
Nor is it ever going to between now and Doomsday.
Some books declare as certainty that the city was bewitched,[75]

---

[75] Lawman follows Wace in repeating Geoffrey's lavish account of the crown-wearing at Caerleon, but adds a note on its 'bewitched' state, of which nothing

And it is very obvious that this is quite likely.
    In that city stood two very glorious minsters:
One dedicated to Saint Aaron – it had many relics in it –
The other to Saint Julian the Martyr, who is favoured by the Lord.
There were most devout nuns, many of them noblewomen;
The bishop's chair was at Saint Aaron; there was many a good
        man.   12120
Canons were there, who were known far and wide;
There was many a good scholar, well-steeped in learning:
They were most advanced in the skills of surveying the heavens,
Of looking at the stars, both the near ones and the far;
This art is labelled 'Astronomy'.
Frequently they told the king about very many things:
They informed him in words what would happen to him here.
    Such was the city of Caerleon: there was great wealth in it,
There was much excitement around the active king.
The king took his messengers and sent them through his
        country   12130
Ordering the earls to come, ordering the barons,
Ordering the kings to come, and also the warlords,
Ordering the bishops to come, ordering the knights to come,
Ordering all the freemen who were in the land at all:
On their very lives ordered them, to be at Caerleon on
        Whitsunday.
    Knights began riding very great distances,
Riding towards Caerleon from many kinds of lands.
On Whitsunday there arrived King Angel,
King of Scotland with his splendid folk;
Many was the handsome man who accompanied that king.   12140
From Moray King Urien and his handsome son Ywain;
Stater king of South Wales and **Cadwathlan** king of North Wales,
Cador, Earl of Cornwall, whom the king was fond of;
Morvith of Gloucester, **Maurin** of Winchester,[76]

else is known, though this may be a reference to the *Vita Merlini* which says
that Caerleon will fall into the Severn (Le Saux, *Sources*, p. 112); from 1211 it
was the seat of the Welsh prince 'King' Morgan ap Hywel, who claimed that the
English had annexed his territory.
    [76] Lawman has garbled Wace's names in this list (see Wace 10269 ff.). In
Geoffrey the earl of Oxford is *Boso*, Wace's *Bos*. In the Otho MS of Lawman's
Brut he is *Beofs*, but in the Caligula MS usually *Beof* (though at 13602 he is
Bos); perhaps the scribe of the common ancestor of both manuscripts connected

Gurguint, Earl of Hereford, and Beof, Earl of Oxford;
Gursal the brave from Bath came riding there;
Urgent of Chester, Jonathas of Dorchester,
Arnold of Salisbury, and Kinmarc of Canterbury,
Balien of Silchester, Wigein of Leicester,
Argal, earl of Warwick, with outstanding followers;   12150
Dunwale, son of Apries, and Kegein, son of Elauth,
Kineus who was Coitt's son, and Cradoc son of Catell;
Aedlin, son of Cledauke, Grimarc, son of Kinmark,
Run Margoitt, and Netan Clofard, Kincar and Aikan,
Kerin Neton and Peredur, Madoc, Traher and Elidur:
All of these were Arthur's admirable earls,
And the highest born and worthiest leaders in all this land,
Except for the barons who ate at Arthur's table.
   No one could identify or name all those people.
There were three archbishops within this nation: 12160
In London, and at York, and St Dubric in Caerleon,
Who was a very holy man, accomplished in everything.
In London stood the archbishop's see which later moved to
      Canterbury,
After the English won this island for themselves.
   It would be quite impossible to count the folk at Caerleon:
Gillomaur the king was there, favourite of the Irish,
Malverus, king of Iceland, King Doldanim of Jutland,
King Kailin of Frisia, Aescil, king of Denmark;
Lot was there, the courageous, who was king in Norway,*
And Gonwais, king of Orkney, beloved of the outlaws,   12170
The man of fury came, the Earl of Boulogne:
Laeyer was his name and his men came with him;
From Flanders the Earl Howeldin, from Chartres the Earl Gerin:
These two conducted with them all the men of France;
Twelve fierce earls came, who were ruling men in France:
Including Guitard, earl of Poitou, Kay the earl of Anjou,
Bedivere, earl of Normandy (the land was then called Neustria),

the name with *Bevis* (ME *Boeve*), hero of the Anglo-Norman romance of about
1200. Geoffrey took the names which Lawman corrupts at 12151–5 from Welsh
genealogies (see Wace, n. 40). Such lists in chronicles and romances reflect the
growing importance of chivalry in the twelfth and thirteenth centuries: identity,
paternity and place of origin were very serious matters and even in the fifteenth
century Malory retains such details.

From Le Mans came the Earl Borel, from Brittany the Earl
    Howel –
Earl Howel was a grand man and gorgeous was his apparel,
And all those folk from France were clothed very finely,   12180
All armed appropriately with horses in good condition.
There were in addition fifteen bishops.
There was no knight and no squire, nor leader one would admire,
From the ports of Spain to the towns of Almaigne
Who had not arrived there if he had been invited,
All out of their respect for Arthur's noble rank.
    When all this assembly had arrived, each king with his retainers,
Then anyone who had been about could have beheld
Many an unknown man who had made his way to the city,
And many kinds of new things around Arthur the king: 12190
There were many unusual clothes, there were many stern knights;
There the lodgings were luxuriously adorned,
There the quarters were forcefully appropriated;
On the fields there were many thousand tents,
And huge supplies of bacon and oats and [wheat];*
No one could make an estimate of the wine and of the ale there;
Hay was supplied, and grass, and good things in quantities.
    When these people were assembled with the splendid king,
Then Whitsunday arrived as the Lord had appointed it;
Then the bishops all came in the presence of their king,   12200
And the three archbishops, into Arthur's presence,
And took up the royal crown which was right and proper for him
And placed it upon his head amid great celebration,
And so they conducted him wholly under God's direction;
Saint Dubricius walked in front – he was Christ's elect –
The archbishop of London walked at his right side,
And by his left side the archbishop of York,
Fifteen bishops preceding, selected from many places,
All of them there were vested in very resplendent copes
Which were embroidered all over with bright-burnished
    gold.   12210
    Four kings walked there ahead of the kaiser,
Bearing aloft in their hands four swords made of gold;
The first, a very valiant man, was named as follows:
This was Cador the king, Arthur's protégé,
The second, carrying sword in hand, came from Scotland,
Then the king of North Wales, and the king of South Wales,

And so they conducted the king to the cathedral.
The bishops were entoning as they conveyed the people's king;
Brass trumpets were blowing, the bells there were ringing,
Knights came riding past, ladies came gliding past.   12220
Truly it has been declared and proved to be a fact
That nobody has ever before seen among mortal men here
Half such exalted pomp in any convocation
As there was with Arthur of noble lineage.
    Into church proceeded Arthur the magnificent.
Archbishop Dubricius, to whom the Lord was gracious,
(He was the papal legate and in parliament a prelate)
Sang the holy Mass in the presence of the king.
There accompanied the queen most attractive women,
The wives of all the prominent men living in the country,   12230
And the daughters of the great men had come to the queen,
Just as the queen had instructed, on pain of her full censure.
    In the south transept of the church sat King Arthur in person
While on the north side sat Guinevere the queen.
There came in ahead of her four eminent queens,
Each wearing on her left hand a ring of red gold,
And with three snow-white doves sitting on her shoulders;
Now these four queens were the consorts of those four lords
Who were carrying in their hands the four golden swords
In front of Arthur, the most admired of kings.   12240
Many little girls were there with the lovely queen,
There were many gorgeous robes on those handsome people;
There was also much rivalry among so many nations,
For each thought themselves to be better than the others.
    Many knights at once arrived at the church,
Some to pick a fight, some to see the king,
Some to stand and stare at the outstanding women.
There were songs of rejoicing which lasted a long time:[77]
I reckon if it lasted seven long years
Then those who were there would still be wanting more.   12250
When the Mass was over they crowded out of church:
The king with his attendants went to the feast
Among his great retinue: there was revelry in the court!

[77] Lawman omits Wace's details of the gorgeous clothing and reduces the
account of glorious liturgical music to one line, probably indicating his lower-
status audience.

The queen on the other side went to her seating;
She had an amazing number of her own attendant women.
When the king was seated with his followers at the feast,
To the king came Saint Dubricius, his Bishop so virtuous,
Who removed from his head his high royal crown –
Because the gold was so heavy the king was disinclined to wear
    it –
And placed on the king's head a much lighter crown,   12260
And then he put a similar one on the Queen as well.
These were the customary ways in Troy, in their ancestors' days,
From whom the Britons in their great renown were all descended:
All the men who could bear weapons were seated at their feasts
Apart in one place; they reckoned this good manners;
And likewise the women had their location.
When the king was seated with all his courtiers at the feast,
The earls and the barons at the king's high table,
The seneschal stepped forward; this was Kay,
Most exalted knight in all the land after the king,   12270
In the whole crowd of those at Arthur's court;
Kay instructed those attending on him, many men of high
    standing –
There were a thousand brave knights, of extremely high fame,
Who waited on the king, and on his bodyguard.
Each knight wore crimson cloth and ornaments of gold
And on all their fingers were clusters of gold rings:*
These men carried the food courses from the kitchen to the king.
On the other side was Bedivere, the chief butler to the king;
With him were the sons of earls, born of noble lineage,
And the sons of the highest-ranking knights who had arrived there,
And the sons of seven kings who were serving with him.   12281
Bedevere walked ahead with a golden mazer,
After him a thousand more thronged towards the courtiers
With every kind of beverage which one could imagine;
And the queen on her side, most gracious lady,
Had a thousand men in attendance, noble men and prominent,
To serve the queen and those who were with her.*
No person in existence, however great his prominence,
Learned man or layman, living in any nation,
Could ever know how to describe in any kind of archive   12290
One half of the magnificence there was in Caerleon,
In the silver, and the gold, and resplendent clothes

On the men of noble status who were present in the court,
In the horses and the fine hawks, in hounds for the hunt,
And in the rich garments which there were on the courtiers;
And of all the peoples who were living in the world there,
The people of this land were accounted most attractive,
And the women also most lovely in complexion
And most splendidly dressed and most accomplished of all.
For they had all promised one thing, by their very persons,   12300
That they would all wear outfits in one colour scheme:
Some wore white, some wore red, and some wore vivid green,
And every kind of homespun tweed they found most disagreeable,
And each discourtesy they reckoned unworthy.

   The country of England then enjoyed its greatest fame,
And the inhabitants were also most esteemed by the king.
The upper-class women who were living in this land
Had all declared, in their undisputed words,
That in the whole of this nation none would take a husband,
Not one single knight, however noble his rank,   12310
Unless he had been tested three times in combat,
And given proof of his valour and made trial of himself.
In confidence then he might seek himself a bride.
Because of these high standards the knights were valorous,
And the women most virtuous and better provided for.

   In Britain during those days were many delights.
When the king had feasted, with all his company,   *Sports*
Then the very brave warriors turned out from the town,
All the kings and their commanders,
All the bishops and all the clerics,   12320
All the earls and all the barons,
All the leaders, all the servers,
In their best clothes went down the fields.
Some began horse-racing, some began foot-racing,
Some began vaulting, some began shooting,
Some were wrestling and holding competitions;
Some on the tilting field were dodging behind shields;
Some were hurling balls far across the fields –
A multitude of sports they were playing at there,
And whoever managed to win the first prize in his sport   12330
Was escorted with singing in front of the king,
And for his victory in sport the king gave him good prizes.

   All of the queens had come to that place,

And all the ladies were leaning over the walls
To watch the contestants and the people playing.
These games and competitions continued for three days;[78]
Then on the fourth day the king made a speech,
And awarded his fine knights all their just deserts:
He gave silver, he gave gold, he gave horses, he gave lands,
Castles and suits of clothes: he made his men contented;   12340
There was many a bold Briton before Arthur's throne.

   Now novel tidings came to the king:[79]
Arthur the great king was sitting at a table;   *Roman*
In front of him were sitting kings, and many war-leaders,   *Campaign*
Bishops and clerics and very valiant knights.
There arrived in the hall some amazing information:
There arrived twelve valiant lords clothed in rich cloth,
Exalted war-leaders, great men in their armour,
Each holding in his hand a massive gold ring,
And round the head of each man a golden band was
    encircled.   12350
They advanced together, two by two in pairs,
Each by the hand clasping his partner,
And paced across the hall floor into Arthur's presence,
Until eventually they arrived before the throne of King Arthur.

   They saluted Arthur immediately with deferential   *(i) Challenge*
    words:
'Good health to you, King Arthur, beloved of the Britons,
And good health to your attendants and all your gracious people.
We are twelve knights who have come here with a purpose,
Powerful and important: we are from Rome.
We have come to this place from our emperor   12360
Who is called **Lucius**; he commands the Roman people.
He instructed us to come here to Arthur the king,
And commands us to greet you with his grim message,
Saying that he is amazed to an extreme degree
Where on this globe you discovered such conceit
As to dare to decline any order from Rome

[78] Most tournaments lasted three days, and concluded with a prize-giving. Lawman has used a Wace manuscript which did not include the list of musical instruments and the dice-playing (see Wace, n. 47).

[79] This is the point where the early fifteenth-century alliterative *Morte Arthure* begins.

Or to level your gaze at the face of our forebears,
And who it was dared to teach you to turn so assertive
That you dare to threaten the issuer of decrees,
Lucius the emperor, most supreme of all men living.   12370
You have control of all your kingdom under your own rule
And you refuse to pay homage to the kaiser for your land,
For that same land which Julius had in his hands,
When in days gone by he conquered it by fighting.
And you have been holding it under your control;
With your bold knights you deprive us of our rights!
But tell us, Arthur, quickly, and send reply to Rome –
We shall bear your message to Lucius our emperor –
If you will acknowledge that he is the king over you,
And if you will become his subject and acknowledge him
          as lord,   12380
And make amends to the kaiser for Frollo the king
Whom you wrongfully did put to death in Paris,
And now you're holding all his lands, unjustly, in your own hands.
If within the next twelve weeks you turn to just ways
And are willing to submit to all Rome's jurisdiction,
Then you might continue living with your countrymen.
And if you refuse to do this, you will receive much worse:
The kaiser will come here, as a king does to what is his own,
– A king most courageous – and seize you by force,
Lead you fettered in triumph before the people of Rome;   12390
Then you'll have to endure what previously you scorned!'
     As these words were said the Britons leapt from the table:
All Arthur's court there was considerably enraged
And swore a mighty oath by our Almighty Lord
That all those who brought this message must be put to death,
To be drawn apart by horses was the death they must endure.
The deeply roused Britons rushed there to them,
Latched on to their hair and laid them out on the ground;
There the Roman men would have been wretchedly maltreated
If Arthur had not leapt across as if he were a lion   12400
And as the wisest of the Britons spoken these words:
'Stop it, stop at once! Let these knights live!
Here in my own court they are not to come to any harm!
They have ridden here from the territory of Rome
As Lucius who is their lord had given them instruction:
Each man must travel where his lord tells him to go;

No man ought to condemn a messenger to death,
Unless he has behaved so wickedly as to be traitor to his lord.
But now, sit down quietly, you knights in this hall,
And I shall make my own decision in this extremity   12410
What message they are to take back to Lucius the emperor.'
    Those warriors on their benches then all sat down,
And the disturbance died away in the presence of the king.
Then Arthur arose, the most admired of kings,
And he summoned to him seven sons of kings,
The earls and the barons and the bravest soldiers,
And all the most intelligent of the country's inhabitants;
They went into a structure which was firmly secured,
An old fort made of stone: stout men had fashioned it.
There his wise counsellors began to hold council   12420
As to what answer he would give to Lucius the emperor.
When all the barons had been seated on benches,
Then all within the hall went utterly silent:
So great was their awe of the glorious king
That no one there dared to speak in case the king would punish
    them.
    Then Cador stood up there, the most senior earl present,
And uttered these words in the great king's presence:
'I give thanks to my Lord, who made the light of day,
That I have lived to see this day which has dawned in the court,
And these same tidings which have now come before our
    king,   12430
So that we need not any longer lie lolling around here!
For idleness is hateful in every nation,
For idleness makes a man lose all his manhood!
Idleness makes a knight abandon all his duties,
Idleness encourages many wicked actions;
Idleness brings to grief many thousand men;
In an easy life few men make great achievements;
For ages we've been lying quiet: it's diminished our renown.
But now I give thanks to the Lord who made the light of day
That the Roman people have turned out so aggressive,   12440
And are making boasts about coming to our boroughs
And tying up our king and carrying him to Rome.
But if what is being said is true, as some men are telling,
That the Roman people have turned out so aggressive,
And are so hard-headed and so full of hatred

That they now want to come into our country,
Then we shall draw up for them some dire messages:
Their savagery shall turn out to be their own sorrow.
Well, I've never for very long liked peace in my land:
Peace holds us in its tether till we're practically in torpor.'   12450
   Gawain, who was Arthur's nephew, was listening to this,
And grew very annoyed with Cador for making known these
    words,
And Gawain the good answered in this way:
'Cador, you may be a great man, but your advice is not much
    good!
Peace is good, and quiet is good when people agree to it freely,
And God himself created it through his own divinity,
For peace makes a good man perform actions which are good;
Because things go better for each man, the land is the happier.'
   Arthur was listening to these earls disputing,
And the noble man spoke like this to his angry men: 12460
'Sit down, all of you, straightaway, my knights,
And each, on pain of death, hear my decree!'
Everyone in the hall sat completely silent;
Then the bold king spoke to his great people:
'My earls, my barons, my bold battle-leaders,
My valiant men, my beloved friends,
Through you I have won, beneath the path of the sun,
Gains which make me a great man and ferocious with my foes:
I have gold and great treasure, I am a ruler of good men;
Alone I did not conquer; no, we did it all together!   12470
To many a fight I've led you, and always [you] arranged things
    well*
So that many kings' realms are under my control;
You are good knights, valiant, courageous;
This I have put to proof in very many lands!'
   Arthur, most admired of kings, then continued speaking;
'Now you have heard, you highest of my leaders,
What the Roman men between them have all been arranging,
And what message they have sent us here into our own land,
In writing and by word of mouth and with much venom;
Now we must consider how we can defend,   12480
As right demands, our nation, and our own reputation
Against this powerful race, against this Roman people,
And send them a reply in our regal words,

How with true wisdom we can send our note to Rome
And demand of the emperor for what reason he despises us,
For what reason he is treating us with threats and with scorn.
I am severely angered and extremely ashamed
That he reproaches us for losses which in past days we incurred:
They say that Julius Caesar won by combat on the field;
In battle and by force men commit great injustice,   12490
For Caesar attacked Britain simply by brute strength
And against him the Britons could not defend their land,
But with force of arms [he] went at once, and took from them all
        their lands,*
And immediately after, they all became his subjects;
Some of our race they had slaughtered and some had torn apart
        with horses,
Some they led in chains out of this our land,
And they conquered this land unjustly by transgression,
And, as if by right, now they demand tribute from this land!
We can just as easily, if we agree to it,
Make just claim on them through our King Belinus,   12500
And through Brennus, his brother, the duke of Burgundy:
These were our ancestors from whom we are descended;
These men besieged Rome and conquered all the realm,
And in front of mighty Rome they hanged their hostages,
And after that they took the entire land and placed it in their own
        hands;
And so we ought by right to ride away to Rome!
    'Now I'll speak no more of Belin and say no more of Brennus,
But discuss the emperor, Constantine the mighty:
He was the son of Helena, from British stock descended;
He conquered Rome and ruled over the realm.   12510
    'Let's set aside Constantine, who gained himself all Rome that
        time,
And speak about Maximian who was a very strong man:
He was the king of Britain who conquered all France;
Maximian the strong took charge of all Rome,
And he conquered Germany with tremendously great power,
And everything from Romagna in Italy to Normandy.
    'And these were my ancestors, my esteemed predecessors,
And they owned all the territories which were tributary to Rome,
And through such example, I ought to possess Rome.
They want me to hand over tribute from my lands,   12520

I'm going to do the same, if I get the chance, to Rome!
I desire to rule all Rome at my own discretion!
And he wants to bind me up securely here in Britain,
And slaughter my British with his assaults in battle.
But if it's granted by the Almighty, who created days and nights
    here,
He must bitterly atone for all his brazen boasts,
And his Roman people will perish because of it,
And I shall be savage where he now holds sway.
   'All stay quiet now; I want to announce my intention –
No one is going to act otherwise, but it will be so
    performed!   12530
He wants it all, I want it all, which we two both have;
Let the one who can win it with ease have it now and always!
And now we shall discover who God will favour with it!'
  So spoke the bold man who had the Britons in his command,
Who was Arthur the king, the Britons' own darling!
His champions were seated: to his speeches they listened;
Some of them sat silent a long space of time;
Some of them whispered many words secretly between them:
Some of them found it really fine; for some of them it troubled the
    mind.
  When for a long time they'd been listening to the king,   12540
Then spoke Howel the gracious, greatest of Brittany,
And uttered his speeches in the stern king's presence:
'Lord king, hear me out, as I have now done you!
You have spoken the sober truth, and may salvation be yours!
Long ago was announced what we are now to determine,
In former years what is now found here:
Sibyl spoke of it – her statements were true,
And she set it down in a book to be a guide for people –
That three kings would come from the land of the Britons
Who were to conquer Rome and the entire realm,   12550
And all the lands which lie adjacent to it;
The first of these was Belinus, who was a British king;
The second was Constantine, who was king here in Britain;
You are to be the third who is to possess Rome,
And if you want to begin this you're going to win it,
And I will assist in it with my utmost ability:
I'll send across the sea to my own splendid soldiers,
To my brave men of Brittany, and we'll then fare much better;

I shall give notice to all the noblemen of Brittany,
Throughout all my lands, on pain of losing life and limb,   12560
That they must at once be ready to march with you to Rome;
I shall place all my land in pledge for silver coin,
And all the property of my lands, for silver and for gold,
And so we'll march to Rome and slay the emperor Lucius,
And restore your own rights. I'll convey you ten thousand knights.'
    So ran the speech of Howel, the highest man in Brittany.
When Howel had spoken what seemed to him appropriate,
Then spoke Angel the king, Scotland's own darling,
As he stood upon a bench, with both of his brothers,
Namely Urien and Lot, two very able men.   12570
This was how King Angel spoke, to Arthur the courageous:
'My lord Arthur, I declare to you with true observations
That to those same things Howel has spoken none shall take any
        exception,
But we shall perform it by our very lives!
And, mighty lord Arthur, listen to me for a space:
Call to give you counsel your powerful earls
And all the greatest men there are in your court
And invite them to tell you in their truthful declaration
What they will do to aid you to destroy your enemies.
I shall convey you the knights of my people,   12580
Three thousand warriors, all selected for their worth,
Ten thousand men on foot, most efficient fighters,
And let us march on Rome and conquer the realm.
Very deeply may we be ashamed and very greatly angered
That they should send messengers seeking tribute from our land,
But, so help us the Lord who made the light of day,
They shall atone for this with their very lives,
For when we have Rome and all of that realm,
We shall take the territories which are tributaries to it:
Apulia and Germany, Lombardy and Brittany,   12590
France next and Normandy' (it was then called Neustria),[80]
'And so we shall moderate their unmitigated pride!'
    When this king had spoken then all of them responded:
'Disgraced be the very man who refuses his assistance

[80] Since Brittany and Normandy are under the command of Howel and
Bedivere, and could not form part of the prizes of battle, this must be a mistake;
Wace's Angusel only mentions Lorraine and Germany.

With goods and with weapons and with all his strength of arms!'
  So all at Arthur's court were strongly aroused there:
Knights were incensed until they trembled with fury.
When Arthur had listened to the clamour of his courtiers,
He called out sharply (the king was really angry):
'Sit down quietly, you knights in this assembly!   12600
And I shall describe to you what I intend to do:
I shall have my missives prepared and carefully composed,
And send the emperor heart-sorrow and a fine supply of grief,
And I shall march immediately down upon Rome;
I shall not carry tribute there, but instead I'll bind the emperor,
And after that I will hang him, and I'll lay waste all that land
And put all the knights to death who have opposed me in the
    fighting.'
  Arthur took hold of his document with its defiant declaration
And handed it to the men who had brought him the message,
And then he had them robed in ultimate splendour,   12610
In the most superior robes he had in his chamber,
And ordered them to leave at once for Lucius in Rome,
And he would come after them as fast as he was able.
These twelve went on their way towards their own land;
[There were not in any land] in such silver and such gold*
Knights so well robed, nor in all respects so well treated
[As] Arthur treated these, [for all] the words they brought!*
These twelve knights voyaged till they arrived in Rome:
They saluted their emperor, their sovereign lord:
'All health to you, Lucius, you are our high master!   12620
We have been with the stern man, with Arthur the king;
We have brought you in writing very proud words;
Arthur is the boldest man whom we have ever gazed on,
And he has supreme power, and his soldiers are brave;
Every mere [serving-boy] acts like a knight there;*
Every mere squire acts like a mighty warrior there;
There the knights act as if they were kings.
Food comes forth abundantly and men are very confident,
And the women the most lovely of those now alive,
And Arthur himself, the valiant, is above all the most
    resplendent.   12630
  'Through us he sends word to you that he intends to come to
    this land;
He refuses to bring tribute, but in person wants to fetter you,

And then he wants to hang you, and lay waste all this land,
And Germany, and Lombardy, Burgundy and France, and also
    Normandy,
And just as he slew Frollo, his foe, so will he do us all,
And possess himself solely of everything we own.
He will conduct here kings, earls and commanders;
And we hold here in our hands the documents he sends
Which spell out to you what he will do when he invades us here!'
    When the message was delivered the kaiser was a desperate
    man,   12640
And all the Romans were excited by a most extreme rage;
They kept on conferring, they kept on consulting,
Before they could agree what action they should take,
But all the same, eventually they found a solution
By means of the senators who conduct the senate:
They advised the kaiser that he should write closed letters
And send out his summons through many kings' realms,
And command them to come quickly, all of them to Rome,
Out of every single land which bore [him] allegiance,*
And all those who were keen to gain land or goods by
    fighting.   12650
People soon arrived in the city of Rome,
No one had ever assembled so many there before.
They declared they'd decided to cross by Great St Bernard Pass
And to make an assault upon Arthur wherever they came upon
    him –
Killing Arthur in battle or hanging him, and annihilating his
    army –
And appropriate for the emperor the realms of King Arthur.
    The first king who arrived there was a very courageous man,
Epistrod, king of Greece; also **Ethion**, duke of Boeotia;
With a great fighting-force came **Irtac**, king of Turkey;
Pandras, king of Egypt, from Crete King **Hippolytus**,   12660
From Syria, King **Evander**, from Phrygia Duke **Teucer**,
Maeptisas from Babylon, from Spain the Emperor **Meodras**
From Media King **Boccus**, from Lybia King **Sextorius**,
From Bithynia **Polydeuces**, from Ituria King **Sexes**,
Ofustesar, king of Africa – no king bore him resemblance – :
With him came many an African, from Ethiopia he brought the
    black men.
The Roman people themselves marched to the mustering,

Those who lived closest to mightiest Rome:
Marcus, Lucius and Catullus, Cocta, Gaius and Metellius:
These were the six who supervized the whole Senate.   12670
  When this force was assembled from many kinds of places
Then the kaiser had people count up all the army:
There were counted aright there a sum of eager fighters,
It came to four hundred thousand, the knights in that throng,[81]
With their arms and their mounts, the equipment of a knight.
That man has never been born, not in any borough at all,
Who could have counted the masses who marched there on foot.
Before August the first they moved off on their march,[82]
Always directly on the path which lay towards St Bernard pass.
  Now for a time let us leave these forces,[83]   12680
And let us speak of Arthur, that most admired of kings:
When he had sought out his excellent soldiers
And each of them had gone home to where he had land
And the knights had come back again swiftly to the court
With arms well appointed to their utmost ability
From Scotland, from Ireland, from Jutland, from Iceland,
From Norway, from Denmark, from Orkney, from the Isle of
    Man,
From those same lands there were a hundred thousand
Valiant champions in armour in the style of their own homelands:
These men were not knights nor in knightly guise attired   12690
But they were the most courageous men who have ever been
    acknowledged,
With massive battle-axes, with long two-edged swords.
From Normandy, from Anjou, from Brittany and Poitou,
From Flanders, from Boulogne, from Lorraine and from Louvain
There came one hundred thousand to the royal army,
Knights among the very best, fully tried under arms.
There came the Twelve Companions whom France was to obey,
They brought along with them twelve thousand knights;
And from this land of ours Arthur took in his charge

[81] The numbers here and at 12700 are corrupted in Lawman and his sources
and do not tally.
[82] Lawman says 'Harvest Day' which probably means Lammas, 1 August,
matching Geoffrey's 'Kalends of August' and Wace's 'the beginning of August'.
The muster has taken only three months since the challenge was issued at
Caerleon at Whitsun.
[83] This transition formula derives from romance narratives.

Fifty thousand valiant knights and brave men in the fight;   12700
Howel of Brittany from his native people
Led ten whole thousand, knights among the best.
The soldiers on foot, as they moved off,
No one knew how to count in any number system.
    Then Arthur gave command, that most admired of kings,
At an appointed time that the army should assemble
(On pain of losing life itself) at Barfleur harbour,
And there he would muster his glorious troops.
He entrusted this land to a remarkable knight,
He was Gawain's brother – as regent there was no other;   12710
Modred he was called, the most dishonourable man:
He never kept a promise to any man at all,
(He was related to Arthur, from his illustrious race)
Yet he was a knight supremely brave and he had tremendous spirit,
Arthur's sister's son. For the queen he harboured passion
(That was wicked behaviour; to his uncle he was traitor!)
But it was all kept very quiet in the parliament and at court,
Because nobody realized this could be really going on,
But people assumed him honest, since Gawain was his brother,
And the most loyal of all the men who ever came to court;   12720
Because of Gawain, all the more was Modred popular with people,
And the valiant Arthur made him very satisfied:
He took his entire kingdom and placed it into Modred's hands,
With Guinevere his queen, most respected of the women
Who among this people have been living in the land;
Arthur donated everything he owned
To Modred and the queen; this made them most contented.
It was a very bad thing that they were ever born:
They betrayed this country with unmeasured miseries,
And in the end the Evil One brought them to destruction   12730
In which they forfeited their lives and their souls
And have ever since been loathed in every single country,
So that nobody ever wanted to proffer a good prayer for their
        souls,
Because of the treason that man did to Arthur his uncle.
    All that Arthur had he made over to Modred,
His land and those who lived there, and his beloved queen,
And then he took his army of very fine soldiers
And then marched immediately towards Southampton.
At once there came sailing across the wide sea

Innumerable ships to the king's people.   12740
The king dispatched the folk over all the long ships:
Thousands and thousands of them thronged to the ships:
Father wept for his son, sister for her brother,
Mother for her daughter, when the host departed.
They had very fine weather with a following fresh breeze:
Exceedingly excited were men to enter open sea; *Roman Campaign*
They hauled up the anchors; the army started cheering;
Onwards the ships were surging, the minstrels were   *(ii) Departure*
     singing;
They hauled up the sails, they tautened the rigging;
With the most serene weather and the sea slumbering,   12750
Lulled by this calmness, Arthur fell asleep.

   As the king slept, he experienced a dream,   *Arthur's*
The dream itself was fearsome and it frightened the king;   *Dream*
When the king awoke he was extremely disturbed
And began to moan in quite a loud voice.
There was no knight so venturesome in the whole of Christendom
Who dared enquire of the king about his condition
Before the king himself spoke, and conversed with his barons there,
And so Arthur stated, when he woke up from his sleep:
'Christ, my Lord and Master, controller of what comes to
     us,   12760
Guardian of this good world, comforter of men
By your gracious will, O commander of the angels,
Do you permit my vision to turn to my advantage!'
   Then Angel the king spoke, the beloved of the Scots,
'My Lord, describe to us your dream, and may our destiny be
     fortunate!'
'Gladly', said the king, 'may good things come of it!
As I lay dozing, I drifted into sleep:
It seemed to me that in the sky a mysterious beast appeared,
In the clouds to the east, ugly in appearance,
With lightning and thunder, menacingly it advanced;   12770
There is no bear so hideous in any land on earth.
Then there came from the west, whisking through the clouds,
A dragon all burning which engulfed boroughs;*
With its fire it set alight all this land's realm:
It seemed to me as I stared that the very sea caught alight
With lightning and the fire which the dragon carried by.
This dragon and bear, both from opposite directions,

With intense speed were approaching each other,
They crashed into each other with furious impact:
Their eyes were flaring as if they were firebrands;   12780
Time and again the dragon was winning, and then again it was
     losing,
But all the same eventually it managed to fly up
And flew down instantly with a furious assault
And struck at the bear which then tumbled to the earth,
And there he killed the bear and tore it limb from limb.
When the battle was finished the dragon flew away.
This was the dream I had when I was lying there asleep!'
     The bishops listened to this, and men who'd learned from books;
Earls listened to it; barons listened to it;
Each from his understanding spoke intelligently: 12790
They interpreted this dream [as they thought appropriate];*
No knight there had the courage to interpret it unfavourably
Lest he would be made to lose those parts he specially loved!
     On they were speeding, eastwards and quickly:
They had a favourable wind and the most serene weather;
They had everything necessary; they came to land at Barfleur.
At Barfleur in Côtentin many men came pouring in
From all of the lands in which Arthur held command.
As soon as they were able they disembarked from the ships;
The king instructed his retainers to go and seek for shelter,   12800
And the king wished to relax before his men arrived.
     After just one single night there came to him a courteous knight
Who came to tell tidings to Arthur the king:
He said that a monster had made its way to the place
From the west side of Spain, a really bloody fiend,*   *The Giant*
And within Brittany it was actively doing harm: *of*
Along the coastlands it had devastated widely;   *Mont Saint Michel*
In what is now Mont Saint Michel it destroyed the land
     everywhere.*
'My lord king', said the knight, 'I'll tell you truly right away:[84]
He has seized a relative of yours with hideous force,   12810
A lady of noble birth, Howel's precious daughter,
Elaine was her name, most exquisite of maidens;

---

[84] Lawman's invention of a knight who reports the giant's atrocities from his
own experience heightens the emotional tension.

He has dragged off to the mountain that most exquisite of
    maidens,
And this fiend for a full fortnight has held her captive in that
    plight;
We have no idea at all whether he has mated her;
The males whom he seizes he makes into his meals,
With cattle, sheep and horses, goats and pigs as well;
This whole land he'll bring to ruin unless you remove our grief,
The land and those who live here: we depend on you entirely!'
The knight continued speaking to the people's king: 12820
'My lord, can you see the mountain, and the enormous forest?
That's where the monster lives which is preying on the people.
We have tried to attack him a great many times,
From the sea and on the land: he has crushed his attackers,
Has sunk all our ships and drowned all the mariners,
Has laid lifeless those who were fighting him on land.
We've endured it all so long that now we leave him alone,
To do what he wants according to his fancy;
The knights in this district dare not fight him any more.'
    Arthur was listening, most admired of all kings;   12830
He called Earl Kay, his seneschal and kinsman, over to him,
Bedivere he also called on, he was the king's butler.
He instructed them precisely to be all prepared at midnight,
With their full armour, to go adventuring with the king,
As long as no man in Christendom knew about their movements
Except for King Arthur and those two knights going with him,
And their six squires – fine men and courageous;
And the knight who told the king about it was to be their guide.
    Exactly at midnight when men were all asleep
Arthur made his way, most admired of all kings;   12840
Ahead of them rode their [local] knight, until it was daylight;*
Then they dismounted from their steeds and arranged their armour.
Not far away they could see a massive fire smoking
On top of a hillside surrounded by the sea-tides
And there was a second very high hill there, which the sea flowed
    up close to;
On the top of it they could see a fire which was large and very
    fierce.
The knights there were doubtful as to which way they should go
So the giant wouldn't be alerted to the king's arrival.
    Then Arthur the determined came to a decision

That they should move together very close to the first fire   12850
And if they found him there they should put him straight to death.
The king moved forward until he came close:
He couldn't find anything save a huge fire there, blazing.
Arthur walked round it, with his knights by his side
And they couldn't find anything on the hill which was living,
Only that huge fire and a great heap of bones,
At a guess they would estimate thirty cartloads' worth!
Then Arthur couldn't think of any useful plan,
And began to converse with his earl, Bedivere:
'Bedivere, go quickly down from this hill,   12860
Make your way across the deep water, wearing your full armour,
And being very cautious approach the other fire,
And walk all around it and look about attentively
To see if you discover any trace of the ogre.
And if you get wind of him in any way whatever,
Go down quietly till you come to the water,
And say to me speedily what it is you've seen;
And if it should happen that you get up to the fire
And the ogre gets wind of you and makes a lunge at you,
Then take up my good horn which is bound round with
        gold   12870
And blow it with all your strength as one must in emergency,
And fling yourself at the fiend and begin to fight him,
And we shall come rushing as quick as we can get there;
And if you find him there close beside the fire
And you can get back again without being noticed,
Then I utterly forbid you, as you value your own life,
To start any fighting whatsoever against the demon.'
   Bedivere attended to what his lord said to him:
He buckled on his weapons and made his way forward
And ascended the mountain, which is very lofty;   12880
He was carrying in his hands a very sturdy spear,
With a shield on his back all garnished with gold,*
High helmet on his head all made of steel,
His body encased in a fine gleaming corslet,
He bore by his side a blade made of steel,
And on he went striding, that sternly strong earl,
Until he soon came close beside the fire,
And underneath a tree he began to pause.
Then he heard sobbing, desperately strong,

Sobbing and wailing and miserable crying;   12890
Then the knight assumed that it must be the giant,
And he broke into a fury as if he were a wild boar,
And instantly forgot what his lord had said to him;
He threw his shield before his breast, gripped his spear firmly
And rushed forward closer towards the great fire,
Expecting to discover the fearsome devil
So that he could fight it out and give proof of his prowess.
    What he found there was a noblewoman, her head all a-tremble,
A white-haired woman weeping in her anguish,
Cursing the bad luck that left her still alive   12900
And sitting by the fire with pitiful crying,
Sitting and staring, all the time, at a recent grave
And giving vent to her expression in a voice of misery:
'Alas, Elaine, alas dear girl!
Alas that I fed you, that I fostered you,
Alas that the death-demon has destroyed you like this here,
Alas that I was ever born: he has smashed my limbs as well!'
Then the woman looked around her to see if the giant was returning,
And saw Earl Bedivere who had arrived there;
Then the white-haired woman spoke, as she sat beside the
      fire:*   12910
'What are you, radiant creature? Are you an angel or a warrior?
Is your coating of feathers all fastened with gold?
If you come from Heaven you might go from here safely,
But if you are a mortal knight you'll be destitute immediately
Because now the monster's coming and he'll tear all your limbs apart;
Even if you wear steel all over he'll master you entirely.
   'He went into Brittany, to the noblest of all dwellings,
To the castle of Howel, the chieftain of Brittany:
He smashed all the gates and squeezed himself inside,
He grabbed the curtain wall and hurled it to the ground,   12920
He tossed down the chamber door and it shattered in five pieces;
He found inside the chamber the loveliest of all young women,
Elaine was her name, of most exalted lineage,
The daughter of Howel, chief man in Brittany,
Relative of Arthur, of the royal line itself.
I was her foster-mother, and delicately reared her.
There the giant dragged the two of us off away with him
[And carried us, in a short time] the length of fifteen miles*
Into this wild desolate wood here to this very place;

A week ago this same day he did all this to us.   12930
As soon as he came here, he grabbed hold of that virgin,
He wanted to have intercourse with the innocent girl:
She wasn't any older than a mere fifteen years
And being a virgin she couldn't endure his intimacy:
The moment he laid her she lost her life immediately,
And here is where he buried her, that most gentle of all ladies,
Elaine, my own foster child, Howel's own daughter.
When he had finished doing that, he grabbed me the same way,
Threw me on the floor and laid me as well;
Now he has painfully broken all my bones,   12940
My limbs are all out of joint; my very life is joyless.
    'So, now I've told you how it was we were got here,
Fly from here fast in case he should find you,
Because if he comes in rage with his evil attacks
The man has not been born who could stand as your protector!'
    At these very words which the woman was saying
Bedivere began to reassure her with most respectful words:
'My dear madam, I am human, and a knight of some repute,
And I wish to declare to you the clear explanation
That no warrior has yet been born of any kind of woman   12950
Who could not with sheer strength be made to stoop down low.
And I honour you, old woman; your strength is very weak now,*
But now I bid you good day, and I'll be off on my way!'
    Down clambered Bedivere, back towards his liege lord
And told him about his concern and all of his adventure
And what the ancient woman had told him of the maiden,
And how every day the ogre raped the aged woman.
Then the three of them together held whispered consultation
Of how they could embark on the monster's destruction.
    Meanwhile the giant came striding, moving swiftly to his fireside:
He was carrying on his shoulders an enormous load   12961
Of twelve pigs together, all tied in a bundle
With very thick twine which was twisted together.
He tossed down the dead swine and squatted beside them,
Stoking up his fire by piling on to it huge trees;
As he tore apart six pigs at the woman he kept grinning,[85]

---

[85] Lawman increases the nurse's role, with her momentary illusion that
Bedivere is an angel (12911) and her rape by the giant. In the alliterative *Morte
Arthure* the giant is eating babies.

And after a few minutes he flung himself upon her,
But he had no expectation of what came from his copulation:*
He raked out his ashes and started grilling his rashers
And he gulped those six pigs down before he got up from his
    seat,   12970
All smothered in ashes – it was a quite disgusting dish!
And then he shuffled off and started to stretch*
And sank down beside the fire spreading out his limbs.
   Now let us leave the giant there and consider the king:
Arthur at the water's edge gripped his weapons in his hands,
With the brave earl, Sir Bedivere, both prudent and wary,
The third man being Kay, the king's steward and his kinsman.
Across the stream they came, resplendent in their armour
And went climbing up the hill as hard as they could
And finished up striding close alongside the fire   12980
Where the giant sprawled and slept as the woman sat and wept.
Arthur stepped back beside his companions,
Forbidding them on pain of losing life and limb together
That neither of them should presume to proceed any further
Unless [they] should see that there was dire need.*
Bedivere halted there and Kay kept him company;
Arthur strode ahead, a warrior stern of spirit,
Until he came to the hearth where the demon lay unconscious.
Arthur was utterly devoid of all timidity –
This was quite apparent, amazing though it seems,   12990
For Arthur there and then could have easily hacked the ogre,
Struck down the demon as he lay there sound asleep;
Yet Arthur refused absolutely to attack him in his sleep,[86]
Lest at some future date he might hear himself reproved.
   Then at once Arthur called out, that most admired of kings:
'On your feet, you fiendish brute, and face your final moments!
Now we two shall hold debate on the death of my kinswoman!'
Before the king had finished saying all these words
The giant started up and seized his mighty club
Intending with the blow to pound Arthur all to pieces;   13000
But Arthur raised aloft his shield high above his helmet
And the giant struck it from above so it was entirely shattered
And Arthur swiftly struck at him a blow with his sword

---

[86] Arthur demonstrates an early instance of British fair-play by refusing to
attack the giant asleep.

Swiping off his chin along with all his jawbone,
And slipped behind a tree which was standing alongside,
And the giant's swift return blow did not hit him at all,
Instead he struck the tree so his club splintered to shreds,
And Arthur at once ran right round the tree,
And like this Arthur and the giant ran all around it three times.
Now the giant was very heavy, so Arthur ran much faster,   13010
And overtook the giant and raising his fine blade
Sliced him off at the thigh – and the giant collapsed,
And Arthur stood watching as the demon started speaking:
'Lord, lord, spare me now! Who is it I am fighting with?
I never guessed that any man in the great realm of this world
Could ever have so easily defeated me in battle
Unless it had been Arthur, the most admired of all the British,
And anyway I've never been all that afraid of Arthur.'
    Then to him spoke Arthur, most admired of kings:
'I'm King Arthur myself, favourite of the Britons!   13020
Tell me about your own tribe and where they are located,
And who it was in the world who were counted as your parents
And from which country you have sneaked in here,
And why with violent death you have murdered my kinswoman.'
Then the devil responded, lying helpless, gazing on:
'All this I shall do, and I'll be reconciled with you,
If you'll only let me live and get my limbs all healed.'
    Arthur lost his temper, in a total fury,
And called out for Bedivere, his brave champion:
'Move quickly, Bedivere, and chop his head off right here,   13030
And carry it away with you down from this mountain!'
Bedivere came quickly and chopped his head off neatly,
And so they went away from there down to their comrades.
[Then finally the king sat down] and had a chance to rest,*
And these were the words of the plucky Arthur:
'I have not fought a fight before within this fine country
(Except when I killed King **Riun** on the mountain of Ravinity).'[87]
    Then they walked onwards and came to the army;
When [they] saw that head they found it very strange,*
Wondering who beneath the heavens might lay claim to such
        a head.*   13040

---

[87] The mountain of Ravinity (MS O: *Rauin*; Wace: *d'Araive*; HRB: *Aravius*)
is probably an error for Mons Eryri, i.e. Snowdon.

Howel of Brittany came towards the king,
And the king told him all about the girl.
Then Howel was distressed and grieved deeply about it,
And took all his friends and found his way to the mountain
Where the girl from Brittany lay buried in the earth.
There he soon had erected a most elegant church,
Dedicated to Saint Mary, the mother of Our Lord,
And then he gave that hill a name before he went away,
And called it 'Elaine's Tumulus'; now they call it Mont Saint
    Michel.
   Then Arthur's army was assembled in their glory,   13050
From Ireland and from Scotland people had by then arrived.
Then the king gave the command to blow brass trumpets in the
    army,
And off marched from Brittany brave and active men,
All throughout Normandy (which then was known as Neustria),
Through all of France they marched, and folk flocked to join them,
They moved out from France and into Burgundy.
There his informers came and halted his companions,*
And made known to the king there in that country
That **Lucius** the emperor and all his Roman army
Were coming to that place, away from their terrain,   13060
Intending to forge ahead in towards France
And conquer it all, and then move on to this land here,
And slaughter all the Britons whom they found there still alive,
And lead Arthur the courageous in chains off to Rome.
   Then the bravest of all kings was furiously angry
And gave orders that his tents should be pitched across the plains,
And there he would encamp until he knew the facts
Of where he might with confidence intercept the kaiser;*
Where the brave king was stationed was a river called the Aube.
A cautious knight came riding to the king's encampment   13070
Who was very badly wounded and his army sadly battered:
The men who came from Rome had robbed him of all his land.
He revealed to the king unknown information
Where the emperor was in camp, with all his Roman force,
And where he might [encounter] him if he wanted to attack him*
Or to make a treaty with the men of Rome:
'But, sir Arthur', said the knight, 'I shall declare to you outright
That [making peace] will do you more good than going to fight
    [against him],*

Because for every two of yours, they can count on twelve,
So many of them kings, so many of them commanders;   13080
There is not in any territory anyone who could inform you
Of the total of the folk who are following that king,
Excluding the Roman people from his own population
And excluding the peoples who from him seek peace.'
  When the reports were all recorded and Arthur had assessed
     them
Then the king called immediately for his closest knights
And they decided among themselves on constructing a fort
Next to the river which was known as the Aube.   *Roman*
In a most convenient spot it was speedily constructed: *Campaign*
Many men had a hand in it and in all haste it was complete; 13090
For if Arthur had misfortune when he came to fight,
Or his folk were to fall, or started to flee,
Then he intended to stand firm, in his strongly-built fort.
  Then he called to him two earls, dignified and wise,
Born in the aristocracy: the king held them in affection;
The first came from Chartres and was called Gerin: there was
     much common sense in him;
The second one was Beof of Oxford: far and wide spread that
     earl's fame;
In addition the king called Gawain, the kinsman he held
     most dear,   *(iii) Gawain's*
Because Gawain knew Latin; Gawain knew Celtic too: *Embassy*
He had been raised in Rome for very many years.   13100
The king took these three courteous knights and sent them off to
     the kaiser,
Ordering him to take his army and be off back to Rome
And never again into France lead any force whatever:
'And if you should go there leading in your own army,
You shall be captured and condemned to death!
For France is my own, and I won it fairly in fight,
And if you refuse to give up the idea of going there
Then let us prepare for battle and let the worse man perish!
And let's leave the poor people to live their lives in peace.
There was a time when Romans did conquer that nation,   13110
But since then they have lost that nation in battle,
And I conquered it in fight and by fighting will retain it!'
  Off went the knights, splendid warriors,
Namely Gerin and the gracious Beof and Gawain the doughty,

Corsleted and helmeted on their lofty steeds,
Each one carried on his shoulder a very fine shield;
They held in their hands very strong spears.
Off they set on horseback, proud men from the host;
Many of those tried warriors who were staying with Arthur
Accompanied Gawain and requested him humbly   13120
To raise up some contention among the Roman people
'So that we can prove ourselves in the press of battle,
For it's many years now since their threats arrived here,
And boasts they keep making that they are going to behead us.
Now it's a great disgrace to our race if it will all be put aside
Unless there can be some strife before we sign the truce:
Some spear-shafts shattered, mail-coats shredded,
Shields smashed to bits, soldiers hacked about,
Swords deeply plunged into crimson blood!'
    The earls forced their way through a vast tract of forest   13130
And marked out a course which lay across the mountains
Until they soon arrived at the Roman army:
Admirably armed and advancing on their horses.
There anyone who happened to be on the spot might see
Men by many thousands thronging from their tents
Just to get a glimpse of those three gallant knights,
And to gaze at their horses and to gaze at their equipment
And to listen to the tidings from Arthur the king.
And first of all, right away, they questioned the knights,
Asking if the king had sent them to the emperor   13140
To consult with the kaiser and plead for his peace.
But not for any conversation would those three noble earls
Pause and wait before they arrived on horseback
Before the door of the tent in which the emperor was.
    There they dismounted and handed over their horses
And so in full armour they entered the tent,[xx]
Into the presence of the emperor, Lucius by name;
As he sat on his couch they announced their message to him:
Each spoke his piece as seemed appropriate to him,
Telling him to travel back to his country,   13150
And never in hostility ever visit France again.

[xx] Entering the royal presence without leaving weapons outside was both a
threat and an insult; Beowulf and his men leave their arms outside Hrothgar's
hall (*Beowulf* 325, 333).

All the time those three earls were announcing their message
The emperor went on sitting there just like a moron,
And no response whatever did he return to these earls,
But he was listening intently, malevolence in his mind.
    Then Gawain was as outraged as an angry noble can be,
And this was the outburst of Gawain the brave:
'Lucius the great, you are the emperor of Rome;
We are the men of Arthur, most admired of the British:
He sends you his instructions without any greetings,   13160
Commanding you to go to Rome, the realm which is your own,
Leaving him to rule in France, which he conquered by fighting,
While you rule your realm and your Roman citizens.
In the past your ancestors made invasion in France,
In battle they acquired immeasurable goods;
And so for a time they lived there, and subsequently lost it:
Arthur won it in fair fight and now he wants to keep it;
He is our liege lord, we are his feudal knights:
He ordered us to tell the true facts to your person;
If you refuse to turn back, he will be your killer,   13170
And if you persist in not returning, but pursue your own purpose,
If your aim for that kingdom is to clutch it in your hands,
Then tomorrow is the very day: if you can catch it, keep it!'
    Then the emperor did reply, in a towering rage:
'I refuse to go back again, and I will conquer France;
My ancestors held it, and I intend to have it.
But if he's willing to be my vassal and acknowledge me as lord,
And pay me loyal allegiance and look up to me as leader,
Then I shall make a truce with him and all his trusty men,
And concede the regency of Britain, which Julius had at his
        command,
And many other countries, which Julius also had command
        of,   13181
Those realms which he controls to which he has no right at all;
And these he's going to lose unless he lets a peace be made.'
    Then answered Gawain who was Arthur's nephew
'Belinus and Brennes, both those two brothers
Were rulers in Britain and by conquest won France,
And then they turned swiftly and took charge of Rome,
And there they stayed afterwards for very many years.
When all this was happening, Brennes was your emperor
And ruled the Roman people and all her tributaries.   13190

And so Rome is our inheritance, and you've got it in your grasp,
And we intend to get it or we'll die in the attempt,
Unless you're willing to admit that King Arthur is your liege,
And send him every year the tribute from your lands;
And if you go to him in peace, then you can live the easier!'
   Now there was sitting by the emperor a knight of his close
     family:
Quencelin was his name, an important man in Rome;
This knight responded, in the emperor's presence,
And like this he spoke (he was a most unlucky man):
'Knights, go back again and give this message to your king: 13200
[The British may be daring] but they're thought to be worth
    nothing*
Because for all that they keep bragging, their prowess is very
    small.'
He was about to say more when Gawain drew his sword
And struck him on the head – and so he split in half!
And Gawain with all speed made straight for his steed,
And all of them mounted with murderous expressions,
And Gawain the plucky spoke these words in parting:
'So help me the Lord himself who created the daylight
If anyone at all among you men is so courageous
As to come in pursuit of us, I shall cut him down: 13210
He shall be sliced in pieces by my broad-bladed sword!'
   After this very speech the emperor exclaimed:
'Stop them, stop them! They're all going to swing
High on the gallows, or else be drawn apart by horses!'
After this outburst coming from the emperor
The earls galloped off and set spurs to their steeds.   *The Pursuit*
In their hands they were brandishing very strong spears,
Carrying before their chests their wide covering shields.
Immediately in a rage earls started riding after
And all the time the emperor was shrieking aloud: 13220
'Seize them, kill them! They have disgraced us all!'
There anyone who happened to be on the spot might hear
The shouting of thousands of men of that nation:
'To arms, to arms here! Let's be getting after them;
Fetch our shields here: the scoundrels are escaping!'
Fully armed champions at once set off after them,
Six here, seven there, eight here and nine over there.
And meanwhile those earls were galloping madly

And every now and then they would have a look behind,
And all the time the Roman knights were coming after quickly,
                                                                    13230
And one who galloped fastest was coming very close,
Shouting out all the time in a really savage way:
'Turn back, you knights, and defend yourselves by fighting!
You disgrace yourselves badly by wanting to sneak off!'
    Gawain understood the shouting from the Roman soldier
And turning his steed, started riding over to him,
And ran him through with the spear so that he was spitted on it,
And drew the spear towards him: the fellow died at once,
And Gawain the courageous called out these words:
'Knight, you ride too quickly; you'd be better off in Rome!'   13240
The knight's name was **Marcel**, one of the nobility.
When Gawain noticed him collapsing to the ground
He instantly drew out his sword and struck off Marcel's head,
And Gawain the plucky expressed this opinion:
'Marcel, go to hell, and tell them your tittle-tattle,
And stay there a long spell with Quencelin your pal,
And hold secret meetings there: you'd've done best to stay in
        Rome;
And like this we'll teach you how to speak our British tongue!'
    Gerin saw how things were going, saw there the Roman lying,
And urged on his horse and encountered another one,   13250
And struck him through with his spear and gave expression to
        these words:
'Keep on riding, Roman, and roll down into Hell,
And so if God will aid us, we shall bring [you] down to earth;*
Threatening doesn't do much good unless there are some deeds
        too!'
Beof who was a brave man saw what his comrades had done,
And wheeled his horse round with terrific speed
And made for a knight with all the force he could find,
Striking him above the shield so his fine corslet collapsed
And so right through his neck; [he] died on the spot.*
And so this earl gave a shout of inspiration for his friends: 13260
'The British will pour scorn on us if we get away from here
Unless we get things going better before we go away!'
After that challenge which the earl had issued,
They all turned round immediately, tremendously fast,
Each drawing his sword swiftly, and each one slew his Roman,

And then they turned their horses and continued on their track,
With the troops of the Romans always riding behind them:
These kept on striking blows at them, kept on shouting names at
    them,
Kept on screaming out to them, 'You are all going to perish!'
But they did not succeed at all in making even just one of them fall,
Nor in doing any harm to them in those hostile assaults;   13271
But every so often the earls wheeled around again,
And before the two sides parted, the Romans had come off the
    worse.
So they continued for fifteen whole miles
Until they came to a position below a splendid woodland
Close beside the fortress where Arthur was enclosed;
Three miles away from it there came thronging to the wood
A force of nine thousand whom Arthur had sent,
From the brave Bretons, who knew the land best:
They were anxious to get news of brave Gawain's progress,   13280
And of his companions, what had become of them,
Whether they were still alive [or] lying by the roadside.*
    These knights slipped through the woodland in utter silence
To the top of the hill, and gazed round expectantly.
They made all the horsemen dismount in the woodland
And prepared all their arms and all of their armour,
Except for a hundred men who were to keep watch
In case they could by any chance catch sight of anything.
Then they spotted in the distance on a spreading plain[89]
Three knights galloping as fast as they could go;   13290
After those three knights there were coming thirty;
Behind that thirty they could see three thousand;
Behind those were thronging another thirty thousand!
They were Roman soldiers, all arrayed in armour,
And the earls in front of them were galloping fast,
Exactly on the right road which led towards the wood
Where their companions were lying well concealed.
    The earls rode right into the woods, with the Romans in pursuit;
The British made a rush at them on their rested steeds
And struck them from the front, [felling] one hundred at
    once.*   13300

---

[89] The shift of perspective is most effective, from the dramatic pursuit seen at
close quarters, to the Bretons on the hilltop scanning the plain below.

Then the Roman forces thought that Arthur was arriving,
And they [fled] in frightful panic, with the British in pursuit*
Who slaughtered fifteen hundred of the Roman force.
Then there arrived to their assistance from their own armed force
Sixteen thousand soldiers whom Arthur had sent to them,
Very bold Britons clad in coats of mail.
There arrived on horseback an earl of great repute,
Petreius by name, a nobleman from Rome,
With six thousand warriors to give aid to the Romans,
Who with tremendous force hurled themselves at the British, 13310
Taking very few of them captive there, but killing very many.*
The British made for the wood, with the other men behind them,
And the British, now on foot, made a firm stand against them,
While the forces of the Romans fought from their horses,
And the British set upon them and slaughtered their [horses]*
And seizing many captives dragged them into the woods.
Then Petreius grew enraged about his men getting the worst of it
And along with his forces he withdrew from the wood,
While the British rushed upon them and struck them from the rear.
    When the British, clear of the woodland, came out on the plain
The Romans resisted them, repulsing them fiercely.   13321
Then in earnest began the fighting: earls were falling, and many a
    fine knight:
In just one day fifteen thousand fell there,
Excellent men, before it was evening.
There a man might discover if he wanted to try his might,
Arm against arm, strong man against strong man,
Shield against shield; soldiers kept on falling.
The roadways were running with thick streams of blood;
Across the fields were scattered gold-adorned shields.
All the day long they kept on fighting strongly.   13330
Petreius on his side kept his people together,
With the result that very soon the British got the worst of it.
    The great earl of Oxford realized at once –
(Beof was his name, a noble British man)
That in no way whatever was it likely to happen
That the British could avoid a rout, unless they had direction.
Then the earl called together the excellent knights
From the very best men of all the British forces
And from the most stalwart of those still surviving,

And making his way out on the field, close up to their
       forces, 13340
(Much disturbed by deep emotion) he made a speech like this:
'Knights, now listen to me: may the Lord aid us!
We have come to this place and embarked on this battle
Without Arthur's advice, and yet he is our leader:
If things go well for us, we shall please him all the more,
And if things go badly for us, he will simply hate us.
But if you want my advice, then let's advance in high hopes!
We are three hundred knights, all warriors in helmets,
Valiant men and brave and of very highest rank.
Make known your nobility: we come from one nation! 13350
Ride in when I ride, and follow as I guide;
All of you charge on the knight that I choose;
Don't seize any chargers, nor any knightly armour,
Just let every brave knight strike always on target!'
   After the words addressed by the earl of Oxford
To his comrades at his side, then he started to ride,
With just as much speed as the hound drives the deer,
With his comrades behind him with their utmost power;
Right through the thick of the fighting sped the band of knights,
Galloping their steeds, killing people as they went – 13360
Tragedy overtook those who were on their path ahead of them
Because they trampled everything on their horses and their
       chargers
And so they came close and captured Petreius:
Beof rode up to him and got his arms round him
And dragged him off his horse and knocked him to the ground
Knowing that his bold knights were right at his side;
The Britons struck out and dragged Petreius off
And the Roman army fought resolutely back
Till in the end no one recognised who it was they were fighting,
They were so coated with gore there was confusion in the combat!
   Then Gawain caught sight of them from his position in the
      battle:
With seven hundred knights he made his way in that
      direction, 13372
Killing everything in his path which he came across there
And at the gallop he grabbed Petreius on his good horse's back
And took Petreius off with him, though he was troubled by it,
Until they came into the woodland, where they were confident

That they could guard securely the leader of the Romans,
And then back out on to the field they went, and again began
    fighting.
   There was to be seen a great deal of distress:
Shields shattering, soldiers falling,   13380
Helmets caving in, great men perishing,
Blood on the fields and faces bloodless.
The British made an assault and the Roman forces fled:
The British struck them down and seized many alive,
And then by the day's end the Romans were in trouble [there].*
Men were firmly trussing the Roman champions,
Marching them to the woodlands in front of Gawain:
All night they were watched there by two thousand knights.
The next day, as dawn broke, the detachment started moving,
Onwards they marched to meet their liege lord,   13390
Bringing him such booty as he rejoiced to accept.
Then Arthur spoke as follows: 'Welcome to you, Petreius!
Now I'll give you a lesson in the Celtic language:
In the presence of the kaiser you boasted you would kill me,
Seize hold of all my castles, and my kingdom as well,
And much joy will you get from what you wanted to grab!
Certainly I'll give you my castle in Paris,
And there you will be living – but not in the style you'd like –
And nor will you ever get out of there again alive!'
   Arthur took the knights who had been captured there,   13400
And three hundred horsemen he also took at once,
All from one contingent,
Very brave knights and valiant men in fight
And told them next day to rise with determination
And fasten the Roman men with very strong chain fetters
And conduct Petreius to the city of Paris.
Four earls he detailed to escort them as they went:
Cador, Borel, Bedivere and Richer;
He told them to keep close so that they would be safe
And return immediately to their sovereign lord.   13410
This was all discussed; but it was soon discovered:
There were informers moving through the king's army
And they heard rumours of an accurate report
Of where Arthur was dispatching the knights he held as captives,
And the spies very promptly made off into the night
And came very quickly to the Roman kaiser

And recited their entire report: how those four earls were to travel,
Conducting Petreius to the city of Paris,
And they outlined the complete route which conveyed them to
   Paris
And where they could be intercepted in a narrow deep
     ravine   13420
And relieved of their possession of the important man, Petreius,
And the four earls could be overcome and tied up securely.
   The emperor of Rome, Lucius, listened to all this
And leapt for his arms as if he were a lion,   *Roman*
Giving orders to ten thousand sturdy campaigners   *Campaign*
To arm and to mount and to move ahead with speed.
He summoned **Sextorius**, duke of Turkey, king of Libya,
He sent for **Evander**, who from Babylon had come there,
He summoned the senators **Bal Catel** and **Carrius**
(All these were of royal blood, and all of them were
     excellent)   13430
To ride on the instant and rescue Petreius.
   As soon as it was evening they began advancing,
With twelve local people to act as their guides
Who were very cautious and knew the routes thoroughly.
As the Roman party rode out, their mail-coats were ringing,
Their helmet plumes tossing, high on their heads,
And shields at their shoulders: they were tough Roman soldiers.
They travelled all night, eagerly spurring   *(iv) The*
Until they reached the track which led towards Paris.   *Ambush*
They had got there first: the British hadn't come yet – [90]   13440
O alas! courageous Cador knew nothing about this:
That the Roman forces had ridden in front of them there.
They arrived in a forest in a really pretty setting,
In a deep valley with no view on either side.
They made the arrangement to take up positions there.
There they lay in silence for just a little space,

---

[90] Despite Lawman's censure by critics as savage and bloodthirsty, he is not
deeply engaged by this ambush episode or by the battle of 'Saussy' (13570), the
second episode in this, the most densely written section of Geoffrey's narrative.
Lawman adds little, cuts the battle formation here (W 12130–72) and omits
Borel's death-throes and the names of the other British slain – in Wace there are
four of these, not three (13481).

And day began breaking and the wild creatures started waking.[91]
  Then Arthur's men arrived, jogging down the road,
Along the very way where the other army lay.[92]
They rode along singing: the soldiers were exultant.   13450
Just the same, Cador was present, very clever and alert:
He and the good Earl Borel were riding abreast there
And leading between them five hundred knights
And moved on ahead then, fully armed soldiers;
Richer and Bedivere moved to their rear there
Conveying the knights whom they had taken captive,
Petreius and his comrades, who had been conquered.
  So they came riding right into the Romans,
And the Romans rushed upon them with really savage force,
Slashing at the British with very severe blows;*   13460
They broke the British line: disaster hit the men;
The woods began re-echoing; warriors were falling;
The British stood up to them, defended themselves stalwartly.
  Richer heard the turmoil, as did Bedivere the earl,
As their comrades up front were fighting it out;
They seized hold of Petreius and all of their captives
And with three hundred squires sent them into the woods,
While they themselves hastened towards their companions,
Striking at the Romans with redoubled strength:
Many blows were inflicted; many men there were
    slaughtered.   13470
Then Evander realised – the heathen king was very clever –
That their own folk were doing better and the British getting
    weaker
And, his most superior knights moving in unison,
Fell on the British as if about to devour them:
The British collapsed then and came off the worst.
They were slaughtering and capturing all they came near to;
The British were in trouble without King Arthur there:
They had too little support there in their supreme need.*

  [91] The stirring of the animals at dawn supplies narrative density, as do the
nodding of the Roman plumes (13436) and the singing of the marching British
soldiers (13450).
  [92] Whereas Geoffrey and Wace have Arthur moving to Ostum (Autun),
Lawman seems to mean either Aouste (in the Ardennes) or Oust on the Somme
(see B-H).

There Borel was slain, deprived of life's days:
King Evander killed him, with his evil tricks,   13480
Along with three Britons who were noble men born.
There in the slaughter were three hundred of their supporters,
And many captured alive: they were chained up closely.
They knew of no useful plan; they all expected to perish,
But all the same they fought on as bravely as they could.
    Now there had gone out on reconnaissance from Arthur's army
The king of Poitou, a veteran of fame,*
Guitard he was called, and Gascony he ruled;
He had as his companions five hundred riders
And three hundred bowmen, valiant in battle,   13490
And seven hundred footmen eager to inflict great harm:
They had gone into the countryside to collect provisions,
Both fodder and food to carry back to the forces.
They heard all the clamour coming from the Romans
And abandoned their activity and advanced in that direction,
Stern-minded men, and speedy, they were not at all slow,
And so quickly they came up level with the fighting.
Guitard and his knights instantly and tightly
Gripped hold of their shields (they were very brave knights)
And all their archers too pressed ahead beside them,   13500
And the foot-soldiers moved ahead fast,
And all together they struck in a savage onslaught:
At the first onrush the Roman troops fell,
Fifteen hundred of them in heaps on the ground;
There Evander was killed, he who had been so cruel;
Catullus of Rome there forgot all his decrees;
Those who had been keeping stationary started off in flight.
The Romans turned their backs and took off and fled,
The British made off after them and attacked them savagely,
Taking so many captive, killing so many more there   13510
That the British force could not slaughter any more,
And the men of the Romans who were able to escape
Rushed away instantly off to the emperor
And gave him these tidings about Arthur the king,
Because they thought for a fact that it was Arthur who had come!
    The emperor and his force were terribly afraid.
When the Britons had been slaughtering to their own satisfaction
They turned back again then, boldly with their booty,
Returning to the place where the battle had occurred,

They buried the dead and carried off the living,   13520
And sent for Petreius whom they had previously captured
And for his companions who had been captured too,
And sent them all, no doubt of this, into the city of Paris,
Filling three castles with them, and firmly locked them in,
At Arthur's instructions, most admired of kings.
   All the British people felt affection for Arthur,
All who lived in the land felt very much in awe of him,
As indeed did the emperor: Arthur made him feel most anxious!
And all the Roman people were afraid of King Arthur.
So what Merlin had prophesied was proved to be true,   13530
That Rome would [feel fear] because of King Arthur
And the stone walls around it would tremble and fall;
This same symbol would signify Lucius the emperor,
And those of his senators who came with him from Rome,
And concerning the very manner in which they would collapse;
What Merlin in former years had said, they found it happen there,
As they had done already and did subsequently everywhere:
Before Arthur was born Merlin had predicted all of it!
   The emperor heard reports, accurately recorded,
Of how his men were captured and his soldiers also slain.   13540
Then in all his army there was uncontrolled sorrow:
Some were mourning their friends, some were cursing their foes,
Some were calling for weapons: they were all in confusion!
Then Lucius realised how bad his luck had become,
For every day he was losing people from his lands,
But the sorrow he felt most was the loss of his nobles.
He then became terrified to a tremendous degree,
And accepted advice and secret opinions
That he should go to Aust with all his armed forces:
On past Langres he would travel – he was in terror of King Arthur!
Arthur had his informers in the army of the emperor   13551
Who quickly let him know which way he was to go.
Arthur very quickly had his army assembled,
Secretly by night, with his very best knights,
And off the king went with his splendid army.
He left Langres behind him lying on his right hand,
And marched in front on the road which Lucius was to march on.
When he came to a valley under a hillside
The most courageous of kings came to a halt;

By its correct title, the valley is called Sosie.[93]   13560
There Arthur dismounted and commanded all his veterans
[With very great speed to (make ready) their weapons]*   13561a
And prepare themselves for fighting in the way that brave knights
    should,
So that when the Roman people came riding along there
They could take vengeance on them, as brave knights should also
    do.
All the young squires and the warriors who were unwell,
And very many thousands of the inferior ranks,
The king positioned on a hillside along with many standards: *Battle*
He did this as a trick intending to talk much of it,   *of*
As indeed happened subsequently, just a short time later.   *Saussy*
    Arthur took ten thousand of his noble knights,   13570
And sent them out to the right, well clad in their armour;
Another ten thousand he kept on his left side,
Ten thousand to the fore, and ten thousand to the rear;
With himself he retained just sixteen thousand;
He dispatched at a distance, in a wood nearby there,
Seventeen thousand superior knights,
Men with good war-gear, who were to guard the woodland
So they could all withdraw there if the need arose.
    There was in Gloucester city an earl among the best of them,
Morvith was his name, a man who was most brave: 13580
To him Arthur entrusted the wood and the detachment:
'And if it should happen, as immortal God may arrange,
That they are overwhelmed and start to make a run,
Then set off in pursuit, with all the strength you have,
And deprive of life at once all those you can overtake,
The fat ones and the thin, the rich ones and the poor,
For in no [nation] anywhere nor among any people*
Are there any knights as excellent as those I have myself,
Knights as fierce, knights as fine,
Knights as strong there are not in any land: 13590
You are the most courageous knights in the whole of Christendom,

---

[93] *Sosie* could be Val Suzon, Dijon (see articles by Matthews and Keller in *Speculum*, 49 (1974), 680–6, 687–98) or high ground at Saussy (Tatlock, *Legendary History*, pp. 102–3; Thorpe, *Geoffrey of Monmouth*, p. 127 n. 1) but see Wace, n. 60, where the valley of the Suize, a tributary of the Marne, is intended; Langres (L 13550) is in Upper Marne.

And I am the most powerful king after God himself!
Let us perform this action well. May God give us success!'
    The knights replied softly, out in the open air:
'We shall all do our best and we shall all make an effort;
May the knight who does not show his strength be ever counted
        craven!'
Then he sent out on both flanks all the foot-soldiers,
Then had the dragon banner raised, unique among standards
And entrusted it to a king who knew well how to hold on to it.
Angel, king of Scotland, held the first battalion in his command;
Cador, the earl of Cornwall held the next contingent;   13601
Beof, earl of Oxford, he had one as well,
And Gerin, earl of Chester held the fourth one himself;
Aescil, the Danish king, controlled the forces which were on the
        downs;
Lot held another one: he was much loved by the king;
Howel of Brittany held yet another one,
And Gawain the courageous stood beside the king;
Kay who was the king's high steward was in charge of one
        division,
The king's butler, Bedivere, he had another;
Howeldin, earl of Flanders, had a company under him;   13610
Guitard, king of the land of Gascony, had a great force;
Wigein, earl of Leicester, and **Jonathas**, earl of Dorchester,
These controlled two detachments which were on foot there;
Curselin, earl of Chester, and the earl of Bath, called **Urgein**,
Were both controlling the detachments which were on foot there
Which on the two flanks were to move forward to the battle;
In these two earls, who were valiant knights,
Arthur had confidence: they were trustworthy earls.
    When all the battalions were positioned as Arthur thought
        appropriate,
Then the king of Britain called over to him   13620
All his advisers, who made incisive decisions,
And Arthur said immediately to his admirable men:
'Now pay attention to me, my very dear friends:
You have made two attacks on the men of the Romans,
And twice they have been conquered and slaughtered and captured
Because with great injustice they coveted our land,
And, my heart is telling me, through our Lord on high,

Once again they shall be conquered, both slaughtered and
    captured.
You have conquered Norway, you have conquered Denmark,
Scotland and Ireland you've brought under your control,   13630
Normandy and France you have conquered in battle:
Thirty-three kingdoms I hold in my own possession
Which for me you have won in this world beneath the sun;
And these are the most accursed men of all men now alive,
A race of heathens – to God they are loathsome:
They abandon our Lord God and give allegiance to Mahound,
And the emperor Lucius has no concern for God at all;
Heathen hounds he has as his companions,
God's antagonists; we shall overmaster them,
Fell them to the ground and ourselves stay safe and sound,   13640
By the goodwill of the Lord, who governs all actions!'
    Then the earls who were there replied: 'We are all ready*
To live or to lie dead beside our beloved king!'
When the army was quite ready it was by then daylight.
Lucius turned off at Langres, with all his Roman liegemen;
He got his men to blow his fine golden trumpets
To summon his army: he wished to ride onwards
From Langres to Aust, as his direct route lay.
The troops of the Romans started riding off,
Until they had arrived one mile away from Arthur.   13650
Then the Roman forces heard really dire reports:
They could see all the valleys, all the downlands,
All the hillsides, quite covered with helmets:
Soaring battle-standards, supported by soldiers,
Sixty thousand of them, tossing in the wind,
Shields were glinting, mail-coats shimmering,
Gold-coloured surcoats; very grim soldiers;
Steeds were prancing; the earth seemed to shudder.
    The kaiser saw the king striding along beside the wood edge;
Then Lucius remarked (and he was lord of all Rome),   13660
Addressing his men with echoing tones:
'What are those outlaws who are obstructing our road here?
Let's seize our arms and against them advance!
They must be destroyed; some must be flayed alive;
They have all got to die, to perish in dire torments!'
When these words were said, they all seized their weapons.
    When they were equipped with their splendid weapons,

Lucius the lord of Rome made a speech at once:
'Let's quickly up and at 'em; we're all bound to do well!'
There had travelled with him twenty-five kings,   13670
All heathen people, who held their lands from Rome,
Earls and dukes as well, from the eastern world:
'Masters', Lucius spoke again, 'may Mahound show you his
      favour;[94]
You are powerful rulers and yet subject to Rome;
Rome is mine by right, the most resplendent of all cities,
So I ought to be the greatest of all men who are alive.
You see here upon the field those who are our foes;
They intend to rule in dominance over our realm,
To treat us as menials and themselves be triumphant.
But we shall prevent them by forceful resistance,   13680
For our race was dominant over all mortal men
And conquered all the lands which they once looked upon,
And Julius the conqueror journeyed into Britain
And gained by his conquests very many kingdoms.
Now it's the ambition of our underlings to be over us as kings!
But they are going to pay for it on their naked backs!
They shall never again travel back to Britain!'
    As soon as he had spoken, the army started off;
By thousands together they thronged in a convoy:
Each king formed a platoon from his own people.   13690
When it was all positioned and the armies in place,
Then there were, if counted accurately, fully fifteen contingents!
Two kings in every section worked in co-operation;
Four earls and a duke formed a joint detachment,
And the emperor alone, along with ten thousand warriors.
When that host started marching the earth began resounding;
Trumpets were blowing to summon the forces;
Horns were re-echoing with uplifting tones:
Sixty thousand of them were blowing in unison;
From Arthur's companies responded even more   13700
Than sixty thousand soldiers blowing at the horn;
The very heavens echoed; the earth began to quake.
    Together they charged as if the sky would crash down:

---

[94] Arthur's self-justification (L 13637) in attacking Lucius, a fellow-Christian, is endorsed by Lucius's speech here (not in Wace) deferring to his pagan auxiliaries as 'masters' (*lauerdinges*).

First they sent flying over, tremendously fast,
Arrows as thick as the snow falling down;
Then they sent stone-balls crashing their way savagely;
After that spears were cracking, and shields were splitting,
Helmets were caving in, and great men falling;
Coats of mail were shattering, blood gushing out;
The fields were discoloured; their standards tottered;   13710
All through that wood went wandering wounded knights
          everywhere,
Six thousand there were who were trampled by steeds;
Men lay expiring, blood was pouring [out] there;*
Bloody streams went tumbling along all the tracks;
There was turmoil in the host; the tragedy was immense.
According to what the writings say which wise men have
          composed
That was the third greatest conflict to occur in this world.
Then in the end no combatant knew
Whom he was supposed to strike and whom he ought to spare,
Since men could not recognise each other as there was too much
          blood.
  Then the battle moved ground from where they had been
          fighting   13721
And they began across a wider area to assault each other,
And began a new contest, bodies closely pressing;
The Roman soldiers were being roughly handled there!
Then three kings arrived there who came from heathen lands:
The first was Ethiopian, the second was an African,
The third came from Libya, which is a heathen land.
They entered the battle-line from the east end of it,
Breaking the shield-wall which the British were holding there,[95]
And instantly felled fifteen hundred men,   13730
Very brave fighters from King Arthur's forces;
Then at once the British turned their backs on the battle.
  Then there rode upon the scene two courageous earls,

[95] The shield-wall (sceld-trume; cf. Beowulf 3118: scild weall) was a 'hedge-
formation' (see The Battle of Maldon, ed. D. R. Scragg (Manchester, 1981),
note to 102 wihagan; and cf. Maldon 242 scyldburh, 277 bordwall). It was a
defensive wall of overlapping shields as in the Bayeux Tapestry (London, 1973,
plates 65, 66) quite different in operation from the Roman testudo, where
shields formed both a wall in front and a roof above as those within a phalanx
raised them over their heads.

Namely Bedivere and Kay, Arthur's butler and his cousin;
They saw their British soldiers being hacked down by blades
And those very fierce earls, growing furiously angry,
With ten thousand knights moved straight into the fighting,
Into the midst of the throng where it was thickest,
And struck down the Roman soldiers remorselessly,
Moving through the skirmish exactly as they wished.   13740
In this they were too daring, protecting themselves feebly:
O woe, alas, woe alas that they were not cautious then!
That they could not defend themselves against their opponents,
But they were too foolhardy and too presumptuous,[96]
Fighting too strongly and going too far in
And moving too far apart in that far-spread fighting.
    Then the king of the Medes arrived, a massive and well built
        man,
A heathen warrior, who caused great harm there;
He led in his contingent thirty thousand horsemen
And was holding in his hand a very sturdy javelin: 13750
He stabbed with the javelin with his forceful strength,
And struck Earl Bedivere from the front on his chest,
Which shattered the mailcoat both behind and in front:
His chest was laid wide open: warm blood came gushing out.
Instantly Bedivere fell down, stark dead upon the ground.
There was anguish, grief in plenty;
Kay found Bedivere lying stretched out dead there
And wanted to carry away the corpse by himself
So he surrounded it with two thousand knights,
Fighting very fiercely and felling the Romans   13760
And slaughtering many hundreds of the Median men.
The fighting was extremely keen and they stayed there too long!
    Then there came passing by a most unpleasant king,
With sixty thousand superior men from his own lands;
It was Se[x]tor[ius] the valiant who came out from Libya;*
There the stalwart king started fighting against Kay
And wounded him severely in the savage contest
To death itself: the action was tragic!

[96] Kay's and Bedivere's foolhardy presumptuousness (they are *trop talentif* ('hot-headed') in Wace), the reference to Bedivere's sister's son (simply 'nephew' in Wace), and especially line 13802 are reminiscent, perhaps not fortuitously, of *The Battle of Maldon*.

Immediately his knights carried him out of the fighting:
With immense force they plunged through the press.   13770
King Arthur grieved bitterly when he heard the news.
    The great leader called **Ridwathelan** noticed this fact then –
He was Bedivere's sister's son, descended from high-ranking
        Britons –
That with his sturdy javelin **Boccus** had stabbed Bedivere;
He was mortally dismayed [to see] his uncle's death*
For of all the men there he had loved him most;
He called for the best knights from his own kindred,
From those whom he loved the most and knew were living still:
Five hundred by the count hurried together.
Then spoke Ridwathelan, the nobleman of Britain: 13780
'Sirs, you come from my family: come over here to me
And let's avenge my uncle Bedivere, who was the best of our clan,
Whom Boccus has stabbed to death here with his stout spear;
Let's all rush together and beat down our enemies!'
Uttering those words, he galloped away
Instantly accompanied by his admirable comrades,
And spotted King Boccus in the centre of the combat
By his spear and his shield; many a king had he killed!
Ridwathelan drew his sword at once and struck a blow at him
And struck the king on the helm so that it split in half,   13790
And the coif underneath it too, and then it stopped at the teeth!
And the heathen king collapsed to the ground,
And his foul soul sank down into hell.
Then Ridwathelan spoke (he was revengeful in mood):
'Now Boccus you have paid for Bedivere's slaying,
And for all eternity your soul will keep the Devil company!'
After these words, as fast as the wind blows
He hurled himself into the fight like the whirlwind over fields
When up on high it piles the dust from the earth;
In just that way Ridwathelan rushed upon his foes.   13800
Everything they came close to they slaughtered right there
For as long as they could wield their glorious weapons;
In all that great fight there were no better knights
For as long as the life in their breasts lasted within them.
King Boccus they had slaughtered, and a thousand of his warriors:
So Bedivere was avenged in truly fitting fashion!
    There was a valiant earl from a noble line

Whose name was Laeyer; he was the lord of Boulogne;[97]
In the battle he caught sight of an enemy approaching
Who was an emir: he was governor of Babylon;   13810
He was felling many people flat upon the ground,
And the earl discerned that: it made him feel most distressed;
He pulled across his breast a very broad shield
And grasped in his hand a spear which was very strong,
And spurred on his horse with all the strength he had
And he hit the emir hard then with a penetrating blow
Underneath the breast-bone so that the corslet shattered
And the spear went right through him and came out behind
To the space of six full feet; the foe fell upon the ground.
The son of this emir soon spotted this;   13820
Gecron he was called; he gripped his spear at once
And struck the earl Laeyer sharply on the left side
And straight through the heart; the earl sank to the earth.
Gawain noticed that from where he was in the fight
And he grew extremely strongly enraged;
Howel, high ruler of Brittany, saw it as well
And he moved in that direction with fifteen hundred men,
Seasoned soldiers in battle they sped there with Howel,
And Gawain along with them, a very valiant-hearted man,
And he had as his followers two thousand five hundred   13830
Very brave Britons; then they began the battle.

The Roman soldiers were being roughly handled there:
Howel was attacking them, Gawain was assaulting them;
There were hideous horrors: the heavens resounded;
The earth began to tremble; the very stones split;
Torrents of blood gushed from tormented people;
The carnage was tremendous. The British were exhausted.
Kinard, the earl of Striguil went away from King Howel[98]

[97] Laeyer was *Læ3er* at 12172 (see n. 74 above) where he is called the *wilde eorl of Builuine* but MS C spells the name *Leir* here. This expanded episode develops his 'fury', and Gecron is invented as a fittingly noble slayer, but there is compensatory omission of the following lines of Wace (12748 ff.).

[98] In Wace he is *Kimar, count of Triguel*. Either the scribe of the manuscript from which both C (*eorle of Strugul*) and O (*eorl of Strogoylle*) ultimately derive, or (more likely) Lawman himself associated this character with the famous earl of Pembroke, William Marshal, who was regent from 1216 to his death in 1219 during Henry III's minority. William, who rose to prominence through success in battle and tournament and as an adviser of kings, became

And took with him **Labius, Rimarc** and **Boclovius**:
These were the men of greatest courage that any king
    commanded, 13840
These among mere mortals were earls strong and mighty;
In their magnificent spirit they refused to follow Howel the good
But by themselves they slaughtered everyone whom they came
    close to.
    A man who was important among the Roman forces
Saw Kinard the courageous killing their countrymen
And the knight dismounted from his precious steed
And seized in his hand a spear with tip of steel,
Which he plunged into blood, and then went to one side
Until he came in the end where stout Kinard was fighting:
He lifted Kinard's corslet and there struck the earl dead. 13850
All the Roman legions gave a loud cry then
And bearing down upon the Britons they broke up their ranks,
And their standards were flattened; folk slid to the ground;*
Shields split apart there; soldiers were falling;
There fell to the earth fifteen thousand men,
Very bold Britons; disaster was everywhere.
That contest was so severe it lasted a long time there.
    Gawain began proceeding through that prodigious carnage,
Summoning all his knights as he found them in the fighting.
Close by there came riding Howel the mighty: 13860
They combined the men they both had and began to march off in
    haste,
Riding up to the Roman folk in fierce raging anger,
And turning on them vigorously broke the French ranks,
And Gawain immediately there discovered
Lucius the emperor lurking under his shield*
And Gawain struck a blow at him with his sword made of steel,
And the emperor at him; it was a savage sport,*
Shield against shield – splinters flew about –
Sword against sword struck blow after blow:

Lord of Striguil on his marriage to the Giffard heiress in 1189; Striguil is
Chepstow, at the southern end of the Welsh March. Lawman must have known
of William Marshal, who held Gloucester Castle and sheriffdom in the 1190s
and was popularly and erroneously known as 'earl of Striguil'. William became
earl of Pembroke in 1199 on John's accession (see David Crouch, *William
Marshal* (London, 1990) pp. 61–9, 77–8).

Sparks sprang from the steel; the foes were mad with fury.   13870
There was a most vicious conflict: all the army was aroused;
The emperor was trying to destroy Gawain
So that on a later day he could boast about the deed,
But the British crowded in on him in terrific choler
While the Roman soldiers rescued their emperor
And they clashed together as if the skies were crashing down.
    All through the daylight they continued with that fight.
Then just a short time before the sun's decline
Arthur, most admired of kings, let out a cry:
'Now all of us at 'em, my valiant knights,   13880
And may God himself assist us to topple our enemies!'
When Arthur had spoken brass trumpets were blown:
Fifteen thousand men crowded there to blow
Horns and trumpets; the earth began to tremble
At the tremendous blast. Because of the huge threat*
The Romans turned round, away from the fighting,
Their standards fell flat, their great men expired;
Those who could took flight; the fated fell there;
There was massive slaughter: [massive grief, massive dread];*
No one could recount, [in annals or in oral tales]*   13889a
How many hundred men were hacked to death there   13890
In the tremendous press, in the great slaughter.
    The emperor was slain in a very strange way,
So that no one knew afterwards how to give an explanation
In any country anywhere, of who killed the kaiser,
But when the fighting was all finished, and all the folk rejoicing
Someone found the emperor stabbed to death there by a spear.
Word came to Arthur as he sat in his tent
That the emperor was slain and deprived of his life's days.
Arthur had a tent pitched in the middle of a wide field
And had Emperor Lucius's body carried there on a bier,   13900
And there had him shrouded with a gold-embroidered pall,
Setting men to keep watch there for three entire days,
While he ordered the construction of a magnificent object,
A lengthy coffin, and had it all coated in gold,
And had the body placed in it of Lucius of Rome,
A very formidable man for all the length of his lifetime.
    Arthur did even more, that most exalted of all Britons:
He ordered a search made of all the nobility,
The kings and the earls and all the greatest soldiers,

Who had been slain in the battle and deprived of their lives' days;
He had them all buried with very great ceremony.   13911
But three kings he got to bear Lucius the emperor,
And had biers fashioned which were rich and most resplendent,
And had them speedily sent off to Rome
And greeted all the Roman citizens with really great derision,
Saying that he was sending them this tribute from his lands
And that he would send them more salutations of this kind again,
If they were eager to gain King Arthur's gold,
'And very shortly afterwards [I]'ll be riding into Rome*
And first-hand news [I]'ll give [you] about the king of Britain,
And repair the walls of Rome which have long since been ruined:
And so I shall overmaster the untamed men of Rome!'   13922
All this vaunting was done in vain, because it turned out quite
        otherwise;
Quite differently things went; he turned away from that people,
All through Modred his [kinsman] – that most wicked of all men!*
    In the great battle those knights lost to Arthur
Were twenty-five thousand men, hacked to pieces on the earth,
Very brave Britons, bereft of their lives.
Kay was very gravely wounded, grievously badly;
He was carried into Kinon and shortly afterwards he died.   13930
There he was buried, just beside the castle,
In the hermitage. He was a splendid man!
Kay was the earl's name, and they called the castle Kinon;
Arthur had given him the town, and that's where he had his tomb,
And the name there was altered, taken from his own,
Because of Kay's death: Caen, Arthur called it,
And now and for all time so the name there will remain.
After Bedivere was slain and deprived of his life's days
Arthur had him borne off to his castle Bayeux,
And there he was buried inside the borough limits: 13940
Just beyond the south gate he was placed in the earth.
Howeldin was ferried across the foam to Flanders,
And all his best knights were ferried directly,
Off to the earldoms from which they had come.
And all of their dead were laid in the earth:
In Thérouanne they are lying, every one of them.
The Earl Laeyer was led away into Boulogne.
    And Arthur subsequently stayed in a district,
In Burgundy it was, where it best pleased him.

He took control of all that land and commissioned all the
    castles,   13950
Announcing his intention of annexing that land.
And then he made a declaration that in the summer he'd decided
To travel down to Rome and take possession of all the realm,
And himself be the emperor where Lucius used to live;
And many of the Roman citizens wanted things to go that way,
Because they were so terrified out of their very lives
That many had taken flight from there and abandoned their castles,
And many sent messages to Arthur the mighty,
And many sought audience, and entreated Arthur's favour,
But some there were who wanted to hold out against
    Arthur,   13960
To hold Rome against him and defend all the realm,
But all the same, so afraid were they of meeting misfortune,
That they could not in the name of Christ adopt a useful course of
    action.
Then came to pass what Merlin spoke of long before,
That the walls of Rome would fall down before Arthur;
This had already happened there in relation to the emperor
Who had fallen in the fighting with fifty thousand men:
That's when Rome with her power was pushed to the ground.
    And so Arthur really expected to possess all of Rome,
And the most mighty of kings remained there in Burgundy.   13970
    Now there arrived at this time a bold man on horseback;
News he was bringing for Arthur the king   *Arthur's*
From Modred, his sister's son: to Arthur he was welcome,   *Downfall*
For he thought that he was bringing very pleasant tidings.
Arthur lay there all that long night, talking with the young knight,
Who simply did not like to tell him the truth of what had
    happened.
The next day, as dawn broke, the household started moving,
And then Arthur got up, and, stretching his arms,
He stood up, and sat down again, as if he felt very sick.
Then a good knight questioned him: 'My lord, how did you get on
    last night?'
Arthur responded (his heart was very heavy):   13981
'Tonight as I was sleeping, where I was lying in my
    chamber,"[99]   *Dream*

    [99] To Wace's account Lawman has added Arthur's dream, a negative counter-

There came to me a dream which has made me most depressed:
I dreamed someone had lifted me right on top of some hall
And I was sitting on the hall, astride, as if I was going riding;
All the lands which I possess, all of them I was surveying,
And Gawain sat in front of me, holding in his hands my sword.
Then Modred came marching there with a countless host of men,
Carrying in his hand a massive battle-axe.
He started to hew, with horrible force,   13990
And hacked down all the posts which were holding up the hall.
I saw Guinevere there as well, the woman I love best of all:
The whole roof of that enormous hall with her hands she was
        pulling down;
The hall started tottering, and I tumbled to the ground,
And broke my right arm, at which Modred said, "Take that!"
Down then fell the hall and Gawain fell as well,
Falling on the ground where both his arms were broken,
So with my left hand I clutched my beloved sword
And struck off Modred's head and it went rolling over the ground,
And I sliced the queen in pieces with my beloved sword,   14000
And after that I dropped her into a dingy pit.
And all my fine subjects set off in flight,
And what in Christendom became of them I had no idea,
Except that I was standing by myself in a vast plain,
And then I started roaming all around across the moors;
There I could see griffins and really gruesome birds.
    'Then a golden lioness came gliding over the downs,
As really lovely a beast as any Our Lord has made.
The lioness ran up to me and put her jaws around my waist,[100]
And off she set, moving away towards the sea,   14010
And I could see the waves, tossing in the sea;
And taking me with her, the lioness plunged into the water.
When we two were in the sea, the waves swept her away from me;

balance to the propitious dream on the outward journey to France (12767 ff.).
He also adds the messenger and his politic tact (14022 ff.), and the incensed
reaction of the courtiers. He may have invented these details, or taken them
from another tradition (Madden). Le Saux thinks the source is Geoffrey's *Vita
Merlini* or perhaps the Welsh poems which were Geoffrey's own sources
(*Sources*, pp. 113–14).

[100] MS C has the masculine form *leo* here, but the feminine pronoun *hire* in
the next line; if this is a lioness, it may stand for Argante, who will come to take
him after his last battle.

Then a fish came swimming by and ferried me ashore.
Then I was all wet and weary, [and I was sick with sorrow].*
And upon waking, I started quaking,
And then I started to shudder as if burning up with fire,
And so all night I've been preoccupied with my disturbing dream,
For I know of a certainty this is the end of my felicity,
And all the rest of my life I must suffer grief.   14020
O alas that I do not have here my queen with me, my Guinevere!'
    Then the knight responded: 'My Lord, you are mistaken;
Dreams should never be interpreted as harbingers of sorrow!
You are the most mighty prince who has rule in any land,
And the most intelligent of all inhabitants on the earth.
If it should have happened – as may Our Lord not allow it –
That your sister's son, Lord Modred, your own queen might have
        wedded,
And all your royal domains might have annexed in his own name,
Those which you entrusted to him when you intended going to
        Rome,
And if he should have done all this by his treacherous deeds, 14030
Even then you might avenge yourself honourably with arms,
And once again possess your lands and rule over your people,
And destroy your enemies who wish you so much evil,*
And slay them, every one alive, so that there is none who survives!'
    Then Arthur answered him, most excellent of all kings:
'For as long as is for ever, I have no fear whatever,
That Modred who is my relative [the man whom I love best]*
Would betray all my trust, not for all of my realm,
Nor would Guinevere, my queen, weaken in her allegiance,
She will not begin to, for any man in the world!'   14040
Immediately after these words, the knight gave his answer:
'I am telling you the truth, dear king, for I am merely your
        underling:
Modred has done these things: he has adopted your queen,
And has placed in his own hands your lovely land;
He is king and she is queen; they don't expect your return,
For they don't believe it will be the case that you'll ever come back
        from Rome.
I am your loyal liegeman, and I did see this treason,
And so I have come to you in person to tell you the truth.
Let my head be as pledge of what I have told you,
The truth and no lie, about your beloved queen,   14050

And about Modred, your sister's son, and how he has snatched
    Britain from you.'
  Then everything went still in King Arthur's hall;
There was great unhappiness for the excellent king,
And because of it the British men were utterly depressed;
Then after a while came the sound of a voice;
All over could be heard the reactions of the British
As they started to discuss in many kinds of expression
How they wished to condemn Modred and the queen
And destroy all the population who had supported Modred.
Most courteous of all Britons, Arthur then called out aloud, 14060
'Sit down quietly, my knights in this assembly,
And then I shall tell you some very strange tales.
Now tomorrow when daylight is sent by our Lord to us,
I wish to be on my way towards entering Britain,
And there I shall kill Modred and burn the queen to death,[101]
And I shall destroy all of them who gave assent to the treason.
And here I shall leave behind my most beloved man,
Howel my dear kinsman, the highest in my family,
And half of my army I shall leave in this country,
To hold all this kingdom which I hold in my command; 14070
And when this matter is all done, then I shall go back to Rome,
And entrust my glorious kingdom to Gawain, who is my kinsman,
And then I shall fulfil my vow, upon my very life:
All of my foes will make a miserable end!'*
  Up stood Gawain then, who was Arthur's nephew
And uttered this speech (the earl was enraged):
'Almighty Lord God, controller of our lot,
Protector of all this planet, why has it happened
That my brother Modred has devised this murderous plot?
But today I renounce him here, in front of this assembly, 14080
And I'll condemn him to death, with the Lord's consent;
I want to hang him myself, the highest of all criminals,
And following canon law I shall have the queen drawn apart by
    horses,
For I shall never have any happiness as long as they're alive
And until I have avenged my uncle in the most appropriate way!'

---

[101] Arthur promises to execute Modred and Guinevere for treason, not out of
vindictiveness. Gawain, Modred's brother, claims the right to judge Modred as
his peer (14083): hanging, drawing and quartering is the punishment for traitors.

The Britons then answered him with very bold voices:
'All our weapons are prepared; so tomorrow we shall leave!'
    In the morning when daylight was sent by the Lord to them
Arthur began marching with his noble followers:
Half his army he left behind and half he led off with him: 14090
Off he went through that land until he came to Wissant;
Rapidly he assembled ships, many and well supplied,
But for a whole fortnight the force had to stay there,
Awaiting the right weather, deprived of every wind.
    Now there was a wicked soldier in King Arthur's army
Who, as soon as he heard discussion about Modred's death,
Took his squire at once and sent him to this land,
With a warning to Guinevere of what had been happening,
And how Arthur was travelling with numerous troops,
And what he was proposing to do and exactly how he would
        act.   14100
The queen came to Modred, whom she loved best of all men
And told him the tidings of Arthur the king,
What he was proposing to do and exactly how he would act.
Modred took his messenger and sent off to Saxony
For **Childric** the second, who was a very powerful king,
Inviting him to come to Britain: he could share it if he did so.
Modred asked Childric, the mighty and the powerful one,
To send messengers far to the four corners of Saxony
And ask all the knights whom they were able to acquire
That they should come quickly here to this kingdom,   14110
And he would give Childric a share of his realm –
Everything beyond the Humber – in return for helping him
To fight against his uncle, who was King Arthur.
Childric turned instantly in towards Britain.
    When Modred had stocked up his army with men
The full total of them came to sixty thousand,
Hardened battle-heroes who came from heathen races,
And who had come over here in order to harm Arthur
To give aid to Modred, most accursed of men.
When the army was assembled from every human race,   14120
When they were there in mass they made up a hundred thousand,
Heathens and Christians, all with 'King' Modred.
    Arthur waited at Wissant: a fortnight seemed too long to him,
While Modred knew everything which Arthur planned there:
Messengers came to him daily from King Arthur's court.

Then on one occasion heavy rain began to fall,
And then the wind began to shift: it was now blowing from the east,
And Arthur rushed aboard along with all his army,
Giving orders to the mariners to bring him in to Romney,
Where he intended to gain entry into this country.   14130
But when he came to the haven, there was Modred facing him:
As the dawn was breaking, they started fighting;
And went on all that long day: many a man there lay dead.
Some were fighting on the land, and some down on the sands;
Some sent sharp spears flying from on board the ships.
   Gawain pressed ahead and was clearing a passage,
And very swiftly struck down eleven leaders there:
He struck down Childric's son, who with his father there had come.
The sun went to rest; for men there was distress!
There Gawain was slain, and deprived of his life's days   14140
By some Saxon earl: may his soul suffer for it!
Arthur was dismayed and grieved deeply about it,
And the greatest of all Britons gave vent to these words:
'Now I have lost my own beloved liegemen!
I knew from my strange vision that sorrows would befall me:
Slain now is King Angel, who to me was very special,
And Gawain my own sister's son: I despair that I was ever born!
Up now, from the ships, my valiant soldiers, quick now!'
At these words there went to battle
Sixty thousand on the instant, very splendid men,   14150
And broke Modred's battle-line, and he himself was very nearly caught!
   Modred took to flight and his men followed suit:
They fled in full panic: even the fields were shaking!
The rocks were set [running] with the streams of blood.*
That battle would have been quite finished, but the night came
    down too fast:
If the night had not come they would all have been killed!
The night came down between them out in hollows and on
    downland,
And Modred got so far that he arrived in London.
The citizens had heard how everything had gone*
And denied him entry, along with all his army.   14160
Then Modred made off from there towards Winchester
Where they took him in along with all his men,
And Arthur went in pursuit with all the power he had,
Until he came to Winchester with a very large force,

And encircled all the city, while Modred stayed inside it.
When Modred realized that Arthur was so close to him
He kept on thinking frantically what could be his policy;
Then on that very night he ordered all his knights
Fully armed to make a sortie from that city,
Announcing that he wished, by means of battle, to resist.   14170
He promised to the citizens their full freedom for ever
On condition they would help him in his dire need.
When it was daybreak, all their strength was ready.
Arthur was watching it: the king was in a fury;
He had shrill trumpets sounded to summon men to battle.
Ordering all his leaders and his noble knights
To begin battle together and beat down his opponents,
And destroy the whole city and hang those citizens.
They advanced to the attack and made a fierce assault;
Then Modred mused on what he might do,   14180
And he did again there just as he'd done elsewhere:
It was the basest kind of treachery, since he always acted vilely:
He betrayed his own comrades outside Winchester,
And had fetched to his presence his favoured knights, on the instant,
And all his dearest favourites from his entire force,
And crept away from the conflict – may the Devil get him! –
And left those good people to perish there completely.
All day they fought on: their lord was with them, they thought,
And must be alongside them in their extreme need.
Meanwhile he took the route which led into Southampton,   14190
And pressed on towards the port – that most accursed of men! –
And seized all the ships there which were of any use,
And all the steersmen he needed for the ships,
And the most evil king alive then sailed off to Cornwall!
Meanwhile Arthur was forcibly setting siege to Winchester,
And all its inhabitants he executed: there was mourning in excess!
The young and the aged, all of them he slaughtered.
When the people were all dead, and the town entirely burned,
He had the walls absolutely dismantled then completely.
Then had come to pass there what Merlin once predicted: 14200
'You shall be wretched, Winchester, for the earth shall engulf
     you!'[102]

---

[102] See n. 68 above. From Geoffrey's *Prophetiae Merlini* (*HRB*, VII, chs 3, 4):
'Say to Winchester: "The Earth shall swallow you!".'

So spoke Merlin, the most trustworthy prophet.

   The queen was lodged in York; she had never felt such horror;
This was Queen Guinevere: most unhappy of women.
She had the report, reliably expressed,
Of how often Modred had fled, and how Arthur had besieged him;
She hated the very time that she was still alive.
She stole out of York when it was dark
And made off towards Caerleon as fast as she could manage,
[Because she did not wish to see Arthur again for all the world
      around,   14209a
She came to Caerleon by night, with two of her knights],*   14210
And she had her head covered with a holy veil,
And she was there as a nun: the most troubled of women.
No one knew about the queen, about where she had gone then,
Not for many years afterwards was it known for sure
[How she had met her] death [and where she departed],*
Any more than if she herself had been plunged in the sea.[103]

   Modred was in Cornwall and had summoned many knights;
To Ireland he sent off his messengers at great speed,
To Saxony he sent off his messengers at great speed,
To Scotland he sent off his messengers at great speed: 14220
He ordered to come immediately all those who desired to have
      lands,
Or silver, or gold: either money or land;
In every respect he protected himself;
That's what any wise man does when necessity compels it.

   Arthur (the angriest of kings) heard about this,
That Modred was in Cornwall with a massive following of men
And intended to remain there till Arthur arrived.
Arthur sent out couriers throughout all his kingdom
Ordering all in the land still alive to attend
If they were fit for fighting and carrying arms,   14230
[Excluding any traitor who was loyal to Modred,   14230a
Those he refused to have, though they might well want to
      come];*   14230b
And whoever ignored what the king demanded
The king would burn alive upon the spot where he was standing!

---

[103] Lawman is almost certainly not referring to a tradition otherwise unknown
in which Guinevere was drowned, but is using an expression, similar to our
'sunk without trace', which he had used earlier in the *Brut* (5659).

There came flocking to the army a tremendous force,
On horseback and on foot, thick as hoarfrost falling.*
    Arthur went to Cornwall with his enormous army.
Modred heard of this and moved up against him
With an enormous host: many there were fated.
Upon the River Tamar they approached together:[104]   *Battle of*
The place is called Camelford – may that name last for   *Camelford*
    ever!
And at Camelford sixty thousand were assembled,   14240
And many thousand in addition; their leader was Modred.
    Then Arthur the powerful rode to the place
With an enormous host; however, it was doomed!
Upon the River Tamar they encountered each other,
Raised their battle-standards, rushed together there,
Drew their long swords, laid into helmets:
Sparks started out, spears were clattering,
Shields were shattering, shafts were splintering:
In all parts of that vast host all the men were engaged:
The River Tamar was in flood with a great tide of blood.   14250
No one in that battle could recognize any warrior,
Nor see who did less well, nor who better, so confused was the
    conflict,*
For each man struck forcibly, whether he was knight or squire.
    Modred was there slain and deprived of his life-days,
[And all of his knights were slain] in the fight;*
There were slain all the sprightly
Courtiers of Arthur, the high [and the low],*
And all of the Britons of Arthur's Round Table,
And all those whom he fostered from numerous kingdoms.
And Arthur was badly wounded with a broad halberd;   14260
Fifteen appalling wounds he had on him:[105]
Into the very least of them two gloves could be thrust!
Then there were no more who survived the battle,
Out of two hundred thousand men who lay there hacked apart,

---

[104] MS C here has *Tanbre* (which must have been the reading of Lawman's
copy of Wace, for *Camble*, with a misreading of *t* for *c*) and Lawman must
understand by this the Tamar, though Camelford (14239) is on the River Camel,
traditionally identified as the *Camlann* of the *Annales Cambriae*. See Wace,
n. 66, and n. 40 above.

[105] Wace does not mention these terrible wounds, which must come from
another tradition.

Save King Arthur alone, and of his knights just two.[106]

Arthur was mortally wounded, grievously badly; *Arthur's*
To him there came a young lad who was from his clan, *Death*
He was Cador the earl of Cornwall's son;
The boy was called **Constantine**; the king loved him very much.
Arthur gazed up at him, as he lay there on the ground, 14270
And uttered these words with a sorrowing heart:
'Welcome, Constantine; you were Cador's son;
Here I bequeath to you all of my kingdom,
And guard well my Britons all the days of your life
And retain for them all the laws which have been extant in my days
And all the good laws which there were in Uther's days.
And I shall voyage to Avalon, to the fairest of all maidens,
To the Queen Argante, a very radiant elf,[107]
And she will make quite sound every one of my wounds,
Will make me completely whole with her health-giving
    potions. 14280
And then I shall come back to my own kingdom
And dwell among the Britons with surpassing delight.'
    After these words there came gliding from the sea
What seemed a short boat, moving, propelled along by the tide
And in it were two women in remarkable attire,
Who took Arthur up at once and immediately carried him
And gently laid him down and began to move off.
And so it had happened, as Merlin said before:
That the grief would be incalculable at the passing of King Arthur.
The Britons even now believe that he is alive 14290
And living in Avalon with the fairest of the elf-folk,
And the Britons are still always looking for when Arthur comes
    returning.
The man has not been born of any favoured lady,

---

[106] There are no survivors mentioned in Wace, though the thirteenth-century *Mort Artu* has Girflet and Lucan attending the dying Arthur.

[107] Gerald of Wales says that Arthur's sister took his body to Avalon (*Speculum Ecclesiae*, c. 1216) but Geoffrey and his derivatives give her name as Anna, while *Argante* looks like a corruption of Morgan, his sister and healer in other early traditions. Only Lawman, who introduced fairies (*aluen*) as well-wishers to the infant Arthur (9608), describes her as an 'elf' or fairy. Wace mentions Avalon but no boat or women. Departure of the dead or dying in a boat is a Norse tradition: Sinfjøtli is carried away by boat in *Vølsunga saga*, ch. 10.

Who knows how to say any more about the truth concerning Arthur.
Yet once there was a prophet and his name was Merlin:
He spoke his predictions, and his sayings were the truth,
Of how an Arthur once again would come to aid the English.[108]

[108] 'An Arthur' may mean Arthur of Brittany in whose murder in 1203 King
John was implicated. While Wace cites Merlin as saying that Arthur's death
would be 'doubtful', explaining that people still doubt whether he is dead or
alive, Lawman claims Merlin as an authority for Arthur's return, which is more
obliquely suggested in Wace. By 'the English' (*Anglen*) Lawman probably means
'England's inhabitants' generally, as he does in his Preface, line 7 *Engle*.
However, O here reads *Bruttes* ('the Celtic races').

EMENDATIONS TO THE
CALIGULA MS OF LAWMAN

6510 *elders: ælde* C; *alle Bruttes* O; Madden suggests (III, 486) that *ældre* is correct.

6579 *in their command*: Madden's edition reads (*hæfden*) *on anwolde* for C, as in O; B&L omit the last two words in their edition.

6581 *from . . . land*: Madden's edition reads *of þissen londe.* for C, the same reading as O; B&L omit *londe.* in their edition.

6672-3 *all . . . castles and: al Brutlo[n]des erþe.alle þe castels and* O; *al þat lond.* (only) C.

6675 *then: suþþe* O; *swa* C.

6686 *fulfil . . . desires: don oure wille* O; om C. B&L emend C to *don eore wille.*

6810 *begin to understand: noht hit onderstonde* O; *nænne ræd luuien* C. O presents a typical half-rhyme and is probably correct.

6810a *Nor . . . advice: ne non of dedes: don after reade* O; at 6810 C reads *ah nalde he at þan ende; nænne ræd luuien* indicating that *ræd* is probably correct and C has conflated two half-lines.

6829 *stationed: wonede* O; *weoren* C.

6870 *who was: þat was* O; *þene* C.

6923 *lot: lot* O; *beoð* (= beod) 'order' C.

6926 *things go on: hit fareþ* O; *we uerden* ('we travelled') C.

6927 *heavens: luste* ('will, desire') C; Madden, B&L emend to *lufte*; om O.

6950-4 *we/us/our: we* O; *heo/heom/heore* C: the emendations in C are based on the abbreviated version of the passage in O, which uses first-person pronouns.

6954 *give: ʒeuen* ('gave') C; om O.

6958 *beliefs: ileuen* C, interlined in later hand over *ilauerd*, which is struck out; *bilefues* O in 6957.

6976 *ancestors': aldene* C; Madden emends to *aldrene*; om O.

6987 *they've laid flat: iuæld* C: supplying *habbeð*, as suggested by Madden (III, 487); *falleþ* O.

7040 *country: lond* interlined in later hand, C; *þat þou dedest to deaþe* O.

7046 *both*: *beoren* crossed through, *beyne* added in later hand in margin, C; line om O.

7109 *events*: *gomen* C; Madden translates 'event' (Errata, vol. II), as in *MED* s.v. *game* n., 1: 'action, course of events'; line om O.

7146 *ever*: *euere* O; *ær* ('before') C.

7169 *such*: *soche* O; *ælche* C.

7178 *agreeable*: *icweme* O; om C; B&L emend C by O.

7331 *Epiford*: O; *Epif* in margin in later hand, C, *ord* in body of text.

7381 *young*: Madden says 'read *ʒunge king*' because O reads *ʒonge king*, but the original may have had an absolute adjective in the form *ʒinge* (cf. *King Horn* 129 *ʒinge: tiþinge*), and O has probably sophisticated.

7414a Line from O, with *hi* supplied; line om C.

7417 *Who*: *þat* O; *&* C.

7447a–7448 From O; C omits one-and-a-half lines.

7475 *this*: *þes* O; *þus* C.

7592 *he could hide*: *he hit habbe mihte* O (M, B&L); *hit hit habben hælr* C.

7600 *deceived*: *bi-swac* O (M III, 488]; *bispac* C (wynn/þ confusion).

7618 *instantly*: *sone* O (B&L); om C.

7637 *his steed*: *his stede* O; *ane ste* C.

7657 *pavilions*: *coine lan* (altered from *coine lond*) C; B&L emend C to *comelan*; om O.

7727 *the work*: *þis worck* O; om C.

7767 *blows*: *dunt* O; *dūdes* C; B&L emend to *duntes*.

7781 *listen*: *lust* O; *ʒerden* (? = *yherden*) C; Brook reads *ʒernden* and glosses 'made enquiries'.

7855 *veil*: *huʒe* C; om O. Brook glosses 'composed her features' (i.e. he reads C as = *hewe*). I emend to *huue*, *houve* ('headdress'; OE *hufe* ('headcovering')).

7927 *falling ... ground-level*: *uolden to grunde* C; om O. MED associates Lawman's frequently used expression *folden to grunde* with *fellen* 'collapse' (cf. 13819 *feol to grunde*). However, the use seems closer to MED s.v. *folden* v.(2), 3(a): 'lay (someone) low', and 3(b) *folden to grounde* 'collapse, fall in battle; fell, kill'. As *falleð* occurs earlier in line 7927, Madden (III, 490) interprets *uolden* here as adverbial (= 'down to the ground').

7957 *And ... fighting*: from O; om C: B&L emend C by O.

8040 *court*: *hirede* C, altered by the scribe to *herede*; O sophisticates. Madden reads *hirede* and trans 'all together'.

8054 *covered*: *wræc* C; om O. Madden's suggested emendation to *wræh* is adopted by B&L.

8130a Line from O; line om C.

8138 *forces*: *hælp* C; *heop* O. A crux. Brook accepts *hælp* C and trans 'when the head (i.e. king) is worthless he is unable to provide help for his subjects in their misfortunes'; Madden emends to *hæp* ('lot'); I emend to *heap* ('crowd, bulk, or strength'), hence 'forces' (*MED* s.v. *hep* ('strength')). Madden cites Wace: 'Rien ne valt *li gent* que on amine/Qui a faible et fol chavetaine', (from Paris, Bibliothèque Nationale, MS fonds français 1450, used as copy-text by Le Roux de Lincy, the edition used by Madden) which would support the sense 'crowd of men'; but Arnold prints 'Petit fait a criendre *compaigne*/Ki ad fieble e fol chevetaine/De malvaise gent senz seinnur/Ne deit l'um mie aveir poür' (W 7693 ff.), which cannot have been in Lawman's copy of Wace. *Heap* ('crowd') occurs several times in Lawman's *Brut* (e.g., 2051, 2948, 9149), usually occasioning some scribal confusion, especially in C, and it seems likely that this was the original reading here.

8186 *fiercely*: *fastliche* O; *feondliche* C; probably attraction to preceding line.

8215 *field*: *feld* O; *wald* C (? = 'plain').

8258 *perpetrated*: following the emendation *iuræmmed* (M and B&L for *iuræinned* ('sought, asked') C; O sophisticates.

8300 *And*: *and* O; *þe* ('who') C.

8400 *That whoever*: *þat wo* O; *þene we* C.   *he*: *he* O; *we* C.

8459 *erect*: *arere* O; *bulden* C.

8464 *halls . . . churches*: from O (B&L); om C.

8550 *of . . . effect*: *bæli wis* C (M); B&L print as *bæl iwis*; Hall emends to *bælwes* ('of malignity').

8686 *come down on*: translating *cumeþ* C; Hall emends to *scuueþ* ('push'); om O.

8706 O reads *ase feþerbeddes*.

8731a Line from O; line om C.

8734 *gave high honour*: *heʒe wurþede* C (B&L); line om O. Madden reads (unconvincingly) *he ʒewurðede* ('he honoured') (which would appear in Lawman's language as *he iwurðede*); Hall emends to *hæʒe wurþede he*.

8854 *chamber-knights*: emending *þe burh-cnihtes* C to *þa bur-cnihtes*; *his cnihtes* O.

8882 *uncovered*: emending *hedden* C to *un-hedden*; om O.

8886 *affliction*: *beonste* or *beouste* C, with marginal cross: emended by Madden and B&L to *beorste*; line om O.

9098 *heard nothing*: *ne horde* O; *nefde* C

9149 *numbers*: *heap* O; *hælp* C; Madden (III, 494) thinks the meaning here is 'hap, luck'; Brook says 'help, means of assistance' is possible here; *MED* s.v. *hēp*, 1(d) glosses this occurrence as 'military strength, numbers'.

9175 *we'll not be false*: *nulleð liʒe* C (= *MED* s.v. *līen*, 2(a): 'be false to, betray'); *loueie wolleþ* ('will praise') O.

9257 *this folly*: *game* O (Brook); *him* C. O seems to be rationalizing a difficult term; I suggest *blame* (*MED* s.v. *blame*, 2(b): 'offence, blunder'), for which O's reading is a homoeograph and C's a misreading based on *b/h* confusion.

9416 *battle-ensigns*: *heore mærken* C; *hire marke* O; Madden proposes emending to *here-merken* (III, 494).

9440a Line from O; line om C.

9444 *silver ... gold*: om C, O; B&L read *neouðer seoluer na gold*, based on 9986 etc. The line would be better metred with a reading **na seoluer neouðer gold*.

9449 *appearance*: *cheres* O; *gareres* C (B&L).

9486 *were holding*: *heo Vðer* C; *Vther* O; B&L emend to *heolden*; Madden and B&W delete *heo*, but Madden adds 'or read *æc*' ('also').

9489 *three*: *þreo* C, O. In fact Uther has two men with him but the error is presumably either archetypal or authorial; if the latter, it may be a confused attempt to echo the Old English construction *he þreora sum*: 'he with two companions'.

9625 *depraved*: *onbalded* O; B&L emend to *unbalded*; *balded* C: B&W read *ibalded* ('emboldened') as in 10674, but Madden gl *vnstrong* as 'bad, wicked' in 3039 and 3537 and this seems to be a similar pejorative use of the prefix *un-*. In 5223 *vnstrong* is a translation of *de bas parage* in Wace (*infimus* ('basest') Bede).

9665 *Off ... immediately*: *forþ hii wende sone þat* O; om C.

9731 *agonizing*: retaining *bitele* ('sharp') C (B&W) rather than emending to *bitere* (B&L); line om O.

9752 *I*: *ich* O (B&L); om C.

9753 *us*: *vs* O; *eou* ('you') C.

9826 *Not at all*: reading *na no fisc* as in Madden's text and B&W, rather than B&L *ma no fisc*; *noþer fles noþer fisce* O.

9917 *your own*: *þine* O; *þisne* ('this') C.

10041 *rime-grey*: *runie* C (so B&L); *wode* ('maddened') O. Brook reads *rimie* (as in 744); Madden derives *rimie* from OE *hremig* ('wild'), but *MED* gl. 10041 with 744 s.v. *rimie* as 'rimy'; B&W read *runie* and gl 'savage'.

10051 *clattering*: *brustleden* C, or 'shattering'; om O. D&W gl 'bristled', B&W 'clashed'.

10067 *death hour*: reading *on his fæie-sið* for *fæie on his siðe* C; *adrad on eche side* O; see also 14074; the word seems to have caused difficulties for scribes.

10133a Line from O; line om C.

10167 *place*: *stude* O (B&L); *hude* C.

10199 *distress*: *hæte* C; *hate* O. Cf. 10342 *hete* C, *hate* O; 10925 *hete* C, *hate* O (also 2017, 4365, 15912). In most instances the word seems to be OE *hete* ('malice') (cf. OE *hetol* ('fierce'), rather than OE *hǣtu* ('heat')); B&W suggest 'drought, thirst'.

10241 *aggressive*: *bolde* O; om C: B&L emend C to *balde*.

10244 *harm*: *beorkes* C; om O. 'Bark' is interpreted by B&W as 'barking of dogs', i.e. antagonism. 'Bark' however seems to be an error. *Barque* ('vessel') is not attested before 15c, and Brook emends to *beornen* ('soldiers, men'). I emend to *beorstes* ('harms') (*MED* s.v. *brest* n.(2), 2(b): 'injury' from OE *byrst*). Alternatively the form in C could be a metathesized form of *brek(k)e* ('predicament, difficulty') (*MED* s.v. *brike* n.(2) from ONF *brike* ('trap'); cf. *Cursor Mundi* 6344: *wiþ-outen any brek or brest*).

10268 *urged ... sternly*: *for-bæd* C; *for-bed* O. Madden trans 'fore-ordered', which is unparalleled before 17c instance of *for-bode*. B&W suggest *MED* s.v. *for-bede* v., 1(c): 'restrain, control'. I assume the prefix *for-* has intensive rather than adversative or temporal sense and translate 'command strongly' (see Jaček Fisiak, *A Short Grammar of Middle English*, I (1966), p. 114 (7)).

10300 *eaten up with flames*: *for-bærnen* C; om O. Hall emends to *forwurþe* ('would perish') (as in 10310).

10311 *they would be destroyed*: *me heom for-dude* ('one would destroy them') O; *hi heom forduden* ('they would destroy them') C.

10312 *they ... attacked*: *me hii slowe* O; *heo heom sloȝen* C. Hall reads *me heom* (= passive, see 10311), correcting O.

10352 *send straight*: following Hall's interpretation of *wið and wið* C as = *wið þet* ('at the same time'); O reads *him wiþ* ('send to him').

10397 *all ... folk*: reading *cun al* with Madden, Brook and B&W, rather than *cun ai* (B&L).

10430 *he regretted*: *him ofþuhte* C, O; or trans 'they suffered for' (Hall).

10475 *We*: *we* O; *heo* C.

10512 *kill ... off*: *a-cwelled* O; *adefed* ('made deaf') C is emended to *adrefed* ('driven off') by B&L, Brook, B&S; B&W suggest *adeded* ('deadened') (*MED s.v. adēden* v., [b]). I propose *aderfed ('tortured to death'); cf. *MED* s.v. *derfen* v., (a): 'afflict, harass, torment, torture', as in 4354 *hunger him derfde*. But *MED* gl. 10512 (unconvincingly) s.v. *?adēven* v., (2) 'subdue or annihilate' (deriving the putative form either from OE *adȳfan* ('immerse') (whence 'drown', 'kill') or from *adēafian* ('deafen') (whence 'stun', 'kill')). Neither *MED* s.v. *?adēven* nor my proposal *aderfen is attested elsewhere.

10610 *pigs*: *swyn* O (B&L); om C.

10643 *floating*: reading *wleoteð* C as a spelling for *fleoteð*, assuming that a form *uleoteð* with *u-* as a spelling for voiced *f-* was misinterpreted by scribe as *w-*; line om O. Burrow suggests a derivation from *wlitigian* ('shine, gleam') (*N&Q*, 225 (1980), 2–3), cited in B&W, who translate C as 'gleam'.

10711 *come ... again*: *aȝen cumen liðen* C; *aȝein hider wende* O. B&W trans 'hoping to sail home in safety'; Madden trans 'with safety again to come', noting *hider* O. But *aȝen* means 'back' and in 10753 Cador interpreting Arthur's instruction is anxious that Childric will return: *and æft cumen hidere*; *hider* in O 10711 and C 10753 is probably an error for ⟨*æft/aȝen cumen*⟩ *liðen*.

10716 Taking *ufele* C as adv., 'harmfully, injuriously', as elsewhere in Lawman, rather than as adj. agreeing with 'Childric' (B&W).

10833 *forced*: *þreaste* O (M); *wræsten* C.

10865 *flow into*: *falleþ in* ('flows into') O (M, D&W, B&W, and suggested by Brook but not in B&L); *walleþ of* ('flows from') C.

10918 *Dragging*: *sette to* O; *to* C.

10921 *affliction*: *on sið* C; om O. B&W interpret *sið* as '(in) distress'; Madden suggests 'in affliction?' or 'on journey'. See *MED* s.v. *sith*, 2(b): 'misfortune, afflicton', though Lawman may have written *on site* ('in care, grief, trouble') (*MED* s.v. *sit(e* n.(1), (a): 'anguish' (b): 'affliction' but chiefly in Northern texts).

10957 *Where are you*: the archetype of C and O must have omitted a line here, probably because of the similarity between 10957 and 10970, and Field (*N&Q* 236 (1991), 97) suggests it may have closely resembled 10969, 10985, 11006. If so, it would have read: *Þa cleopede Arður, æðelest kingen* ('Then Arthur called out, most admired of kings').

11017 *singing*: *songen* O (M, B&L); *suggen* ('said') C.

11030 *placed*: *bi-toc* O (B&L); om C.

11041 *lowly*: reading *læȝ* ('low') for *læð* ('odious') C; om O.

11127 *prepared*: *beouweden* C, altered by later hand to *beoveden* by interlining and crossing through; *beoude* O, in line 11125. Brook follows C's uncorrected form; B&L read *beoveden*; B&W suggest *bounen* ('get ready'), but this is pleonastic as *bounen* is almost identical in sense with *b(e)onnenden* following.

11278 The line is displaced in C; om O. I follow the emendation of B&W.

11280 *items ... tribute*: *giueles* C; O sophisticates to *soue* ('seven') *þousend poundes*; Madden emends to *gaueles*, but *gauel* also occurs in 11279 C, O.

11403 *seek*: *are* C (B&L, Hall, B&W read *arere* ('stir up')); om O.

11515 *believe*: *ileueþ* O; *ilefde* (past tense) C.

11632 *prudent*: *red-folle* O; *ræh-fulle* C. B&W read with C and trans 'brave'.

11678 *Boulogne*: *Boloyne* O (B&L); om C.

11679 *all of*: *and al* O (B&L); om C.

11683 *they*: *hii* O; *he* C.

11892a Line from O; line om C.

11946 *made a counter-attack*: *kept* C; *kepte* O. Madden corrects his trans 'observed' in the text to 'intercepted' (III, 503); B&W trans 'fended off' (*MED* s.v. *kepen* v. 3b (b)), but in fact he seems to be attacking (see *MED* s.v. *kepen* v., 7: 'meet in resistance', and 18: 'assault'). In *MED*, 11946 is glossed under *kepen* v., 17: 'await the arrival of'.

12169 *in Norway*: *bi Norþe* C, O, perhaps for *bi Norþe* with wynn/ thorn confusion.

12195 *wheat*: *wete* O; *water* C; B&W read with C.

12276 *were*: C reads either *iriuen* or, as Madden would read, *irinen* ('adorned') from OE *gehrinan* (III, 503), though his text, and that of B&L, reads *iriuen*; *MED* treats *iriuen* as an error for *irinen*; B&W read *iriuen* and trans 'adorned'.

12287 *those*: *þaie* O; *þan* C; B&L read *þai*, which means that the female attendants also serve the queen (though the 3 pers. pl. pron. is usually *heo* or *hii* in Lawman). But presumably the sense is actually that the maidens were also served by the 1000 serving-men, and therefore the pronoun should be in an oblique form, not nom.; B&W read *þan* with C, which they identify as the dative pl. of the demonstrative pron. *þat* (see Millar, 'Ambiguity in ending and form' (1995)), and remark that *þæinen* ('serve') takes the dative in 12274, as in Old English.

12471 *you*: *ʒe* O; *ʒet* C (? = *ʒit* ('the two of you'), but Arthur is addressing all his men).

12493 *he: he* O; *heo* C, which reads *ah mid stre(n)ðe heo eoden an hond; and bitahten him al heore lond*, which Brook trans 'but they resisted *him* with force and *yet* they had to hand over all their land to him'. O has *ac mid strengþe he* (Caesar) *ʒeode and hond; and binam ʒam hire lond*. Madden says that O is right, the C scribe having in error taken *eoden an hond* in the sense 'submit' and supplied a pl. subject (III, 504).

12615 *There . . . land*: from O; om C.

12617 *As: ase* O; *þus* C   *for all: al for* C; om O, which sophisticates.

12625 *serving-boy: cnaue* O; *swein* C, by attraction to 12626.

12649 *him: he* ('which he loved') O; *heom* ('who loved them (?)') C.

12773 *which . . . boroughs*: from O; only *bur* and *suel* in C, the rest, written by second hand in margin, was trimmed 'by the rascally binder' (Madden, III, 505).

12791 *as . . . appropriate: ase heom best þoht* O; om C.

12805 *bloody: reordi* C; *lopliche* O. *rerden/reordien* v. means 'speak'. Angart (*English Studies*, 36 (1955), 3) suggests *dreori* (cf. *MED* s.v. *dreri*, 2(b): 'causing fear', and (c): 'cruel'; B&W trans 'cruel'. But cf. *MED* s.v. *dreri*, 3(a): '?bloody', but not citing Lawman.

12808 *destroyed: he hit wasteþ* O; *þat lond ewelde* C. Madden emends *ewelde* to *awalt* as in 12016.

12841 *local: lod-cniht* C, O. B&L emend to *lond-cniht*; B&W keep C and trans 'guide' (*MED* s.v. *lodes-man* n., (b)).

12882 *garnished: irust* C; O damaged: *. . . st*. B&W adopt C and trans 'encrusted with gold'; *MED* gl this instance 'ornamented', s.v. *irust*, from OE *gehyrstan* ('adorn'), with metathesis; Madden emends to *ibrusted* (III, 506) (cf. *MED* s.v. *ibrusted*, gl 'studded', citing three other instances in Lawman).

12910 *white-haired: (ore)* O (damaged); *here* C, presumably for *hore*.

12928 *And . . . time: and hire bar a lutel wile* O; om C. I have emended O to *us bar*.

12952 *honour: hire* C; om O. Madden gl 'serve', B&W trans 'and so aid you', from *MED* s.v. *heren* v., 6 (a); I read *here* (*MED* s.v. *heren*, 6 (a): 'obey, follow the advice of', or 4(a): 'listen to').

12968 *copulation: wif-þing* C; *wisinge* O (? = *wishing* ('concupiscence')). B&W trans C as 'woman', but *wif-þing* must mean 'sexual congress' (cf. Madden, III, 505).

12972 *shuffled . . . stretch: gon ræmien . . . raxlede* C; *gan remi . . . leyde him* O, which sophisticates. It is not clear what happens here: Madden gl 'roar . . . stretch'; B&W have 'yawned and stretched'; *MED* gl *ræmien* s.v. *remen* ('stretch oneself, yawn') and gl *raxlien* similarly: (a) 'stretch, stretch arms'; (c) 'exhale?, yawn'. Does the giant stretch and yawn or yawn and stretch? These verbs form a traditional collocation: a similar instance occurs in *Piers Plowman* B, v. 391: *raxed and [remed]* (ed. Kane and Donaldson, 1975) where thirteen manucripts read *rored* for *remed*; here *MED* gl *remed* s.v. *ramen* ('cry, shout'). The two verbs *remen* and *ramen* must have been often confused. The giant may have been stretching and yawning or roaring, or any combination of these; since he has just been eating and is now getting sleepy he may be belching rather than yawning, and stretching.

12985 *they: hii* O; *he* C.

13034 *Then . . . down: þo sat þe king adun* O (B&L); om C.

13039 *they: þo hii* O; *þa þe* C.

13040 *lay claim to: were ikenned* O; *hafed ikenned* ('had engendered') C.

13057 *halted: heolden* C; O sophisticates. B&W trans 'and joined his company'; Madden treats *heolden* as sp. for adj. *holden* 'loyal': 'and his faithful companions'.

13068 *might:* B&L print *minte*. Madden and B&W read *mihte*.

13075 *encounter: finde* O; *iwinde* (? = *ifinde*) C. C has *hine* twice, superfluously in second half-line.

13078 *making peace: set* (? = *sette*) . . . *grið* O (damaged); *freondscipe to habben* C.　　*fight . . . him: fihte him wiþ* O; *for to fihten* C.

13201 *The . . . daring: Bruttus beoð bolde* O (B&L); om C.

13253 *bring . . . earth: grundien* C; *ʒou sarui* O. *MED* gl *grundien* s.v. *grounden* v., 6 (b): 'strike to ground, overcome sb., defeat', but cites the emendation *we scullen [eou] grundien* and two 15c instances as the only transitive uses; *MED* follows Madden, who gives as the literal sense 'fell you to the ground' (III, 508) and reads 'sink you' in his translated text; Hall gl 'bring you to the ground'. But C as it stands has no direct object, and B&W gl 'triumph' and interpret 'prove ourselves worthy', deriving this from *grundien* in the sense 'lay a foundation'. A similar verb occurs at 15289 *folc unimete grunden an uolde*, which appears to mean: 'disembarked'. The simplest emendation at 13253 would be *ʒe* for *we*: 'you will fall down, descend' (*MED* s.v. *grounden* v., 6 (a), assuming that the error *we* stood in the common ancestor of C, O, which O has tried to rationalize by adding the object *ʒou* and substituting *sarui* ('treat').

13259 *he:þe* C; the full line in O reads *þat þe spere deore; rof þorh þon swere*. The line may originally have read *& þurh þene sweore wælt;*

þat he ful sone swælt ('(and) went through the neck so that he died at once').

13282 *or*: *oþer* O; *þa* C.

13300 *felling*: *fuld* O; *feollen* C. Madden emends to *feolden* (pret.).

13302 *fled*: *torned þe rugges* O; *afered* C. I emend to *aflemed* ('driven away'), as in 4222.

13311 *taking ... captive there*: reading *lut þer of-nomen* ('captured few there') (M and B&W) rather than *lut þer-of nomen* ('took few of them') (B&L).

13315 *horses*: *hors* O (rewritten as 13315–16); *hors* added in margin, later hand, C.

13385 *there*: *wa wes Rom-leoden wa* C; O damaged. B&L emend second *wa* to *þa*. Line perhaps originally read *þa wes Rom-leoden wa*.

13460 *severe*: reading *bitele* C (B&W) rather than *bitere* O; B&L emend C to *bite[r]e*.

13478 *support*: Madden reads *hele* (III, 75) and B&L read *helþ* in their text, but *help* in the footnote; B&W read *hele* and gl 'strength' (*MED* s.v. *hēle* n., (1)).

13487 *veteran of fame*: *har mon iblowen* C; ... *man iblowe* O. Madden emends *har* C to *hard*; I assume that *har* is 'grey, old' (*MED* s.v. *hōr* adj., 2(a): 'white or gray-haired', and 2(c): 'an old man') (cf. *Battle of Maldon* 169; *Beowulf* 1307); B&W read *har* and gl 'doughty'.

13561a Line om C; O (damaged) reads *þat hii an hiȝeng ... en hire wepne*. I conjecture *nimen hire wepne*; B&W omit.

13587 *nation*: *leode* C (B&W); *londe* O. For *þeode* (M), C has *leode* at the end of the line as well; end of line is damaged in O.

13642 *replied*: Madden prints *answarede* (B&W); B&L print *answatede*.

13713 *out*: *vt hurnen* O; *at urnen* C (M).

13765 *Sextorius*: *Setor* C; O damaged, space for five letters. He is *Sexstorius* in 12663 and *Sextorius* in 13427. Madden would read *Sertor* (cf. Wace: *Sertorius*) or *Sextor*. B&W read *Setor* in the Middle English text and *Seftor* in their translation.

13775 *to see ... death*: *þe he i-seh Beduer deaȝe* O; *þa his æm wes an deðe* C. My translation follows emendation to *þa he i-seh his æm wes an deðe*.

13853 *flattened*: Madden's translation reads 'they felled the standards' (III, 108), which he later modified to 'the standards fell', taking *feollen* C as an intransitive verb (III, 509); B&W trans 'banners fell'.

13865 *lurking*: *leouien* C; om O. B&W read with C and gl 'actively defending himself'. Probably C should read *leonien* (MED s.v. *lēnen* v. (1), 3: 'crouch, lie in hiding' (from OE *hleonian*; MED cites forms *leonen* and *leonie*; cf. 5375 *leonede* ('leaned over')).

13867 *it was a savage sport*: *com wes swi sturne* C; *gome was wel kene* ('(that) man warrior was very brave') O. Madden suggests '? read *gome*' (III, 108) and translates 'who was man exceeding stern'. B&W emend C to *comp* ('contest') (MED s.v. *camp* n.: 'battle, fight, war'), observing that a sense 'man' would be syntactically difficult in relation to the following matter (C spells the word *gume* in fact). Emending O to *gomen* ('game, sport') (MED s.v. *game* n., 3(a): 'tournament or battle') achieves the same sense.

13885 *threat*: *ibeote* C; *drede* O.

13889 *massive . . . dread*: *moche . . . moche care* O (damaged). C presents the first half of 13889 in place of the off-verse of 13888. I have supplied 'dread' as the probable missing noun in O.

13889a The first half-line occurs in 13888 C; O (damaged) reads *ne may no . . . telle ine boke ne in spelle*.

13919–20 *I*: *ich* O (M); om C. C thus has only 13922 in direct speech, while O reads *ʒou* (*heom* C) in 13920 and continues the message in direct speech from 13919 to 13922.

13925 *kinsman*: *Modred his may* O; *Modred his mæin* ('Modred's strength, military might') C (and B&W trans thus).

14015 *and . . . sorrow*: reading *and of sorʒen seoc* (Hall) for *of sorʒen and seoc* C; *and swipe seak* O.

14033 *wish . . . evil*: *þe þe ufel unnen* C; *sleane to grunde* O (sophisticates); Hall emends to *. . . on uuele unnen* to restore the Middle English idiom.

14037 *the . . . best*: *þat man his me leouest* O; om C.

14074 *miserable end*: *wæi-sið makeʒe* C: B&W gl 'meet a fearful end' as if from *wa*, *wæi* ('sorrow'); *þis swikedom . . . (g)e* O (damaged). Probably origiⁿal read *fæisið (makien)* = 'die' (MED s.v. *fei(e-sīth)*) and cf. 14367 *fæi-sið makede* and 1863 *faeisiðe makede*, both referring to kings' deaths; cf. emendation proposed for 10067 above.

14154 *running with*: *ʒurren* C; om O. The verb *ʒurren* denotes the chattering of people and the whirring of ships' ropes in a storm. Emerson gl '(the stones) babbled (with streams of blood)'. Brandl and Zippel gl 'rattled'. B&W (following Madden) gl 'jarred'. I suggest reading *hurnen* (cf. O 676), *vrnen* (cf. 5976) ('ran') (MED s.v. *rennen* v., (1)).

14159 *everything . . . gone*: *al ifaren* C, so printed in Madden, Brook, B&W, but B&L print *il ifaren* ('had gone wrong'); *ifaren* O.

14209a–14210 Both lines taken from O; the first is not in C. C reads 14210 as *þider heo brohten bi nihte; of hire cnihten tweiӡe.*

14215 *How ... death: in woch wise ӡeo was dead* O; *whaðer heo weore on deðe* C.   *and ... departed: and ӡeo hinne ... ende* O; om C. Emerson reads *and hu heo henne wende* ('how she departed'), emending O. I emend *whiðer heo iwende;* cf. the similar form in the first half of C 14215, which has *whaðer* ('whether'), perhaps a homoeograph error. In 14216 Emerson assumes that the construction continues with a second *whaðer* and emends *þa* C: 'or whether she had been (submerged in water)', and Brook follows; B&W read with C and trans 'whether she was dead ... when she was herself submerged in water', assuming a lacuna. Line 1416 is not in O. The expression 'any more than if he/they were lost in/plunged in the sea' seems to be idiomatic, meaning 'no knowledge at all of' (cf. 5659, and see note to line 14216).

14230a, b Both lines from O; om C.

14234 *hoarfrost: rim* C; *ren* ('rain') O. Madden suggests *rein* ('rain'), which Emerson adopts.

14252 *conflict: wiðe* C; *weder* O. Bennett emends to *wiðer* ('hostility'); B&W read with C and trans 'mêlée'; D&W treat *wiðe* as adv. and gl 'whoever was joined in battle with one another'.

14255 *And ... slain: and alle his cnihtes islaӡe* O; om C.

14257 *and ... low: and Loӡe* O (B&L); om C.

SELECT BIBLIOGRAPHY
FOR WACE'S *ROMAN DE BRUT*

Complete Editions of Wace

Le Roman de Brut, ed. Le Roux de Lincy, 2 vols. (Rouen, 1836–8)
Le Roman de Brut de Wace, ed. Ivor Arnold, 2 vols., SATF (Paris, 1938, 1940)

Selections

La Partie arthurienne du Roman de Brut, ed. I. D. O. Arnold and M. M. Pelan (Paris, 1962) (using BN MS fr.794)
La Geste du Roi Arthur, ed. and trans. E. Baumgartner and I. Short, (Paris 1993), pp. 28–259 (using Durham Cathedral MS C.iv.27)

Translations

Wace and Layamon: Arthurian Chronicles, trans. Eugene Mason, Everyman's Library (London: J. M. Dent, 1912, repr. 1962)
La Geste du Roi Arthur: see above (into Modern French)

Other Works by Wace

La Vie de Sainte Marguerite, ed. E. A. Francis, FFMA (Paris, 1932) and H–E. Keller (Tübingen, 1990)
La Conception de Notre Dame, ed. W. R. Ashford (Chicago, Ill., 1933)
La Vie de Saint Nicolas, ed. E. Ronsjö (Lund, 1942)
Le Roman de Rou, ed. A. J. Holden, SATF, 3 vols (Paris, 1973).

Manuscripts

Fahlin, C., 'Quelques remarques sur l'édition du *Roman de Brut* de Wace publiée par Ivor Arnold', *SN* 11 (1938–9), 85–100
Draak, M., 'The Hague manuscript of Wace's *Brut*', in *Amor Librorum*:

Bibliographic and other Essays: A Tribute to Abraham Horodisch (Amsterdam 1958), pp. 23–7

Wace's Source and Other Earlier Chronicles

Geoffrey of Monmouth: 'Historia Regum Britanniae', ed. Neil Wright, I: 'Vulgate' Version (Cambridge, 1984); II: First Variant Version (Cambridge, 1988)

Geoffrey of Monmouth: A Variant Version, ed. Jacob Hammer (Cambridge, Mass., 1951)

Geoffrey of Monmouth: 'The History of the Kings of Britain', trans. Lewis Thorpe (Harmondsworth, 1966)

Annales Cambriae, in Nennius, British History (see below)

Bede: 'Historia Ecclesiastica', ed. B. Colgrave and R. A. B. Mynors (Oxford, 1969)

Bede: 'Ecclesiastical History of the English People', trans. Leo Sherley-Price, rev. E. Latham (Harmondsworth, 1990)

Gildas, De Excidio Britonum, ed. and trans. Michael Winterbottom (London and Chichester, 1978)

Nennius, British History and the Welsh Annals, ed. and trans. John Morris (London, 1980)

The Historia Brittonum 3: The 'Vatican' Recension ed. D. N. Dumville (Woodbridge, 1985)

On HRB

Gillingham, John, 'The context and purposes of Geoffrey of Monmouth's History of the Kings of Britain', Anglo-Norman Studies, 13 (1990), 99–118

Hanning, Robert W., The Vision of History in Early Britain (New York, 1960)

Piggott, Stuart, 'The sources of Geoffrey of Monmouth', Antiquity, 15 (1941), 266–86

Roberts, Brynley F., 'Geoffrey of Monmouth and Welsh historical tradition', Nottingham Medieval Studies, 20 (1976), 29–40

—— 'Geoffrey of Monmouth, HRB and Brut y Brenhinedd', in AOW, pp. 97–116

On HB

Dumville, D. 'The historical value of the Historia Brittonum', Arthurian Literature, 6 (1986), 1–26

Other Twelfth-Century Chronicles

Geffrei Gaimar, *Estoire des Engleis*, ed. A. Bell, Anglo-Norman Texts 14–16 (Oxford, 1960)

Henry of Huntingdon, *Historia Anglorum*, trans. Thomas Forester (Llanerch, 1991)

William of Malmesbury, *De Gestis Regum Anglorum*, trans. Joseph Stephenson (Llanerch, 1989)

Wace's Language

Keller, H–E., *Etude descriptive sur le vocabulaire de Wace* (Berlin, 1953)

Background and Reference

Culhwch and Olwen, ed. Rachel Bromwich and D. Simon Evans (Cardiff, 1992)

Le Jeu de Saint Nicolas, ed. F. J. Warne (Oxford, 1972)

Morte Arthure, ed. John Finlayson, York Medieval Texts (London, 1967)

Ackerman, R. W., 'The English rimed and prose romances', in *ALMA*, pp. 480–519

Bromwich, Rachel, A. O. H. Jarman and Brynley F. Roberts, eds., *The Arthur of the Welsh* (Cardiff, 1991)

Charles-Edwards, Thomas, 'The Arthur of history', in *AOW*, pp. 15–32

Blair, Hunter P., *An Introduction to Anglo-Saxon England* (Cambridge, repr. 1974)

Jarman, A. O. H., 'The Merlin legend and the Welsh tradition of prophecy', in *AOW*, pp. 117–45

Loomis, Roger Sherman, ed., *Arthurian Literature in the Middle Ages* (Oxford, 1959)

—— 'The oral diffusion of the Arthurian legend', in *ALMA*, pp. 52–63

—— 'The Legend of Arthur's survival', in *ALMA*, pp. 64–71

Lovecy, Ian, '*Historia Peredur*' in *AOW*, pp. 171–82

Morris, Rosemary, 'The *Gesta Regum Britanniae* of William of Rennes: an Arthurian epic?', *Arthurian Literature*, 6 (1986), 60–125

Page, Christopher, *Voices and Instruments of the Middle Ages* (London, 1987)

Roberts, Brynley, '*Culwch and Olwen*, the Triads, saints' lives', in *AOW*, pp. 73–95

Rychner, J., *La Chanson de Geste* (Geneva, 1955)

Sims-Williams, Patrick, 'The early Welsh Arthurian poems' in *AOW*, pp. 33–71

Tatlock, J. S. P., *The Legendary History of Britain* (New York, repr. 1974)

Thomson, R. L., '*Owain*', in *AOW*, pp. 159–69

Weiss, Judith, *The Birth of Romance*, Everyman's Library (London, 1992)

Literary and Source Studies

Barron, W. R. J., and Françoise Le Saux, 'Two aspects of Laȝamon's narrative art', *Arthurian Literature*, 9 (1989), 25–56

Foulon, C., 'Wace', in *ALMA*, pp. 94–103

Houck, M., *Sources of the 'Roman de Brut' of Wace* (Berkeley, 1941)

Keller, H–E., 'De l'amour dans le *Brut*', in *Continuations: Essays on Medieval French Literature and Language in Honor of John L. Grigsby*, ed. Norris J. Lacy and Gloria Torrini-Roblin (Birmingham, Ala., 1989), pp. 63–81

Pelan, M. M., *L'Influence du Brut de Wace sur les premiers romanciers* (Paris, 1931)

Schmolke-Hasselmann, Beate, 'The Round Table: ideal, fiction, reality', *Arthurian Literature*, 2 (1982), 41–75

Wulf, Charlotte A. T., 'A comparative study of Wace's Guenevere in the twelfth century', in *Arthurian Romance and Gender*, ed. Friedrich Wolfzettl (Amsterdam and Atlanta, 1995), pp. 66–78

SELECT BIBLIOGRAPHY
FOR LAWMAN'S *BRUT*

Complete Editions of Lawman's Brut

Madden, Sir Frederic, ed., *Laȝamon's 'Brut', or Chronicle of Britain: A Poetical Semi-Saxon Paraphrase of 'The Brut of Wace'*, 2nd edn, 3 vols. (1847; Osnabrück, 1967)

Brook, G. L., and R. F. Leslie, eds., *Laȝamon: 'Brut', edited from British Museum MS. Cotton Caligula A. ix and British Museum MS. Cotton Otho C. xiii*, 2 vols., EETS OS 250, 277 (London, 1963, 1978)

Selections

Barron, W. R. J., and S. C. Weinberg, eds., *Laȝamon's Arthur: The Arthurian Section of Laȝamon's 'Brut'* (Harlow, 1989). (Lines 9229–14297, with facing-page translation, introduction and notes)

——*Laȝamon 'Brut': or Hystoria Brutonum: Edition and Translation with Textual Notes and Commentary* (Harlow, 1995). (Whole poem, with facing-page translation)

Brook, G. L., ed., *Selections from Laȝamon's 'Brut'* (Oxford, 1963), rev. John Levitt, 2nd edn (Exeter, 1983). (Arthur's Begetting; Early Reign; Origin of Roman War; The Morte. Notes, Glossary, Introduction by C. S. Lewis]

Hall, J., ed., *Laȝamon's 'Brut': Selections* (Oxford, 1924). (Prologue; Leir; Brennes and Belin; Conquest of Rome; Merlin and Stonehenge; Arthur and Childric; The Round Table; Arthur's Dream; Gurmund; Brian; Cadwalader. With notes and glossary)

Extracts included in Anthologies

Alexander, Michael, and Felicity Riddy, eds., *The Middle Ages (700–1550)* Macmillan Anthologies of English Literature, 1 (London, 1989), pp. 121–9. (Arthur's Death, taken from Brook's *Selections*)

Bennett, J. A. W., and G. V. Smithers, eds., *Early Middle English Verse and Prose* (Oxford, 1966). (Arthur's Dream. With notes and glossary)

Brandl, A., and O. Zippel, *Middle English Reader* (Berlin, 1916). (Prologue; Modred's Treason; Arthur's Last Battle: MS C, with variants from O, and relevant passages of Wace and Geoffrey)

Burrow, J. A., and Thorlac Turville-Petre, *A Book of Middle English*, 2nd edn (Oxford, 1996), pp. 96–105. (Battle of Bath, lines 20534–21706)

Dickins, B., and R. M. Wilson, eds., *Early Middle English Texts* (London, 1951). (245 lines: Prologue (from MSS C and O), and five short extracts from the Arthurian section. With notes and glossary)

Emerson, O. F., ed., *A Middle English Reader* (London, 1929). (Arthur's Last Battle: Glossary, some notes)

Hall, Joseph, ed., *Selections from Middle English 1130–1250*, 2 vols. (Oxford, 1920). (Vortigern and Rowena. Notes)

—*Layamon's 'Brut': Selections* (Oxford, 1924)

Garbáty, T. J., ed., *Medieval English Literature* (Lexington, Ky, 1984). (Prologue; Murder of Gracien; Birth of Arthur, Fairy Gifts; Plot against Uther; Arthur Battles the Forces of Colgrim; Childric; Battle of Bath; Round Table; Giant of Brittany; Lucius; Arthur's Dream; Last Battle. Marginal glossing)

Kaiser, R., ed., *Medieval English*, 3rd edn (Berlin, 1958), pp. 332–40. (Prologue; Brutus; Bladud and Leir; Godlac; Round Table; Arthur's Death; Conclusion. Some readings from O)

Mätzner, E., *Altenglische Sprachproben*, 2 vols. (Berlin, 1867), vol. I, pp. 19–39.

Morris, R., and W. W. Skeat, eds., *Specimens of Early English*, 2nd edn (Oxford, 1898), pp. 64–86. (Hengest and Horsa. Notes)

Translations

Layamon's 'Brut': A History of the Britons, trans. Donald G. Bzdyl, Medieval and Renaissance Texts and Studies 65 (Binghamton, NY, 1989)

Wace and Layamon: Arthurian Chronicles, trans. Eugene Mason, introd. Gwyn Jones, 2nd edn, Everyman's Library (London, 1962). (Translation of MS C of *Brut* lines 6388–14297, taken largely from Madden's foot-of-page literal translation)

Willhelm, James J., 'Layamon's *Brut*: "The Death of Arthur"', in *The*

Romance of Arthur, II, ed. James J. Wilhelm (New York, 1986), pp. 19–28

Manuscripts

Brook, G. L., 'A piece of evidence for the study of Middle English spelling', *NM*, 73 (1972), 25–8

Bryan, Elizabeth, 'The two manuscripts of Laȝamon's *Brut*': some readers in the margins', in *Text and Tradition*, ed. Le Saux, pp. 89–102

—— 'Sir Frederic Madden's annotations on Laȝamon's *Brut*', in *Orality and Literacy*, ed. Pilch, pp. 21–69

Le Saux, Françoise, 'Listening to the manuscript: editing Laȝamon's *Brut*', in *Orality and Literacy*, ed. Pilch, pp. 11–20

Roberts, Jane, 'A preliminary note on British Library, Cotton MS Caligula A. ix', in *Text and Tradition*, ed. Le Saux, pp. 1–14

Stroud, J. A., 'Scribal editing in Lawman's *Brut*', *JEGP*, 51, (1952), 42–8

Weinberg, Carole, 'The Latin marginal glosses in the Caligula manuscript of Laȝamon's *Brut*', in *Text and Tradition*, ed. Le Saux, pp. 103–20

Lawman's Sources and Other Chronicles

Wace

Le Roman de Brut de Wace, ed. Ivor Arnold, 2 vols., SATF (Paris, 1938, 1940)

Geoffrey of Monmouth

Geoffrey of Monmouth: The History of the Kings of Britain, trans. Lewis Thorpe (Harmondsworth, 1966)

The Historia Regum Britanniae of Geoffrey of Monmouth, vol. I: *Bern Burgerbibliothek, MS 568*; vol II: *First Variant Version: A Critical Edition*, ed. Neil Wright, 2 vols. (Cambridge, 1985, 1988)

Hanning, Robert W., *The Vision of History in Early Britain from Gildas to Geoffrey* (New York, 1960)

Anglo-Saxon

Bede: A History of the English Church and People, trans. Leo Sherley-Price, rev. E. Latham, 2nd edn (Harmondsworth, 1968)

The Anglo-Saxon Chronicle, trans. G. N. Garmonsway, Everyman's Library, 2nd edn (London, 1972)

Middle English
The Chronicle of Robert Manning of Brunne, 1338, ed. F. J. Furnivall,
  2 vols. (London, 1887)

Lawman's Language and Metre

Amodio, Mark C., 'Laȝamon's Anglo-Saxon lexicon and diction',
  Poetica, 28 (1988), 48–59
—'Some notes on Laȝamon's use of the synthetic genitive', *SN*, 59
  (1987), 187–94
Blake, Norman, 'Rhythmical alliteration', *MP*, 67 (1969), 118–24
Brehe, S. K., 'Rhythmical alliteration: Ælfric's prose and the origins of
  Laȝamon's metre', in *Text and Tradition*, ed. Le Saux, pp. 65–87
Cannon, Christopher, 'The style and authorship of the Otho-revision
  of Laȝamon's *Brut*', *MÆ*, 62 (1993), 187–209
Cable, Thomas, *The English Alliterative Tradition* (Philadelphia, 1991),
  pp. 2–3, 58–63, 66, 157
—'Lawman's *Brut* and the misreading of Old English meter', in
  *Language and Civilisation: A Concerted Profusion of Essays and
  Studies in Honor of Otto Hietsch*, ed. Claudia Blank and P. S. Selim
  (Frankfurt, 1992)
Friedlander, Carolynn van Dyke, 'Early Middle English accentual
  verse', *MP*, 76 (1979), 219–30
Glowka, A. W., 'Prosodic decorum in Laȝamon's *Brut*', *Poetica*
  (Tokyo), 18 (1984), 40–53
—'The poetics of Laȝamon's *Brut*' in *Text and Tradition*, ed. Le
  Saux, pp. 57–64
Grant, Marshal S., and Douglas Moffat, 'Laȝamon's archaic use of the
  verbal prefix *to*-', in *Text and Tradition*, ed. Le Saux, pp. 15–28
Iwasaki, Haruo, 'A few notes on the vocabulary of Laȝamon's *Brut*',
  Poetica (Tokyo), 24 (1986), 1–15
—'Case and rhyme in Laȝamon's *Brut*', in *Linguistics Across Histor-
  ical and Geographical Boundaries: In Honor of Jaček Fisiak on the
  Occasion of his Fiftieth Birthday*, ed. Dieter Kastovský and Aleksan-
  der Szwedek, 2 vols. (Berlin, 1986)
Iyeri, Yoko, 'Negation in the *Brut*', in *Text and Tradition*, ed. Le Saux,
  pp. 29–46
Jack, George, 'Relative pronouns in Laȝamon's *Brut*', *LeedsSE*, n.s. 19
  (1988), 31–66
McIntosh, Angus, 'Early Middle English alliterative verse', in *Middle*

English Alliterative Poetry and its Literary Background, ed. David Lawton (Cambridge, 1982), pp. 20–33

Millar, Robert, 'Ambiguity in function: Old English *pæt* and the demonstrative systems of Laȝamon's *Brut*', NM, 94 (1994), 415–32

—— 'Ambiguity in ending and form: reinterpretation in the demonstrative systems of Laȝamon's *Brut*', NM 96 (1995), 145–68

Moffat, Douglas, 'The intonational basis of Laȝamon's verse', in *Prosody and Poetics in the Early Middle Ages*, ed. M. J. Toswell (Toronto and London, 1995), pp. 133–46

Mustanoja, Tauno, 'Some reflections on Lawman's poetical syntax', in *So Meny Peple Longages and Tonges: Philological Essays in Scots and Medieval English Presented to Angus McIntosh*, ed. Michael Benskin and M. L. Samuels (Edinburgh, 1981), pp. 335–40

Noble, James, 'Variation in Laȝamon's *Brut*', NM, 85 (1984), 92–4

—— 'The four-stress hemistich in Laȝamon's *Brut*', NM, 87 (1986), 545–9

—— 'The larger rhetorical patterns in Laȝamon's *Brut*', *English Studies in Canada*, 11 (1985) 263–72

Ogura, Michiko, 'Periphrases with Old English and Middle English verbs', *Chiba Review*, 13 (1991), 37–70

Sauer, Hans, 'Laȝamon's compound nouns and their morphology', in *Historical Semantics, Historical Word-Formation*, ed. Jaček Fisiak, Trends in Linguistic Studies and Monographs (Berlin, 1985), pp. 483–532

Serjeantson, Mary, *A History of Foreign Words in English* (London, 1935)

Shrader, Richard J., *Old English Poetry and the Genealogy of Events*. Medieval Texts and Studies 12 (East Lansing, 1993), pp. 155–83

Stanley, E. G., 'Laȝamon's un-Anglo-Saxon syntax', in *Text and Tradition*, ed. Le Saux, pp. 47–56

Tatlock, J. S. P., 'Epic formulas, especially in Laȝamon', PMLA, 38 (1923), 494–529

—— 'Layamon's poetic style and its relations', in *The Manly Anniversary Studies in Language and Literature* (Chicago, 1923), pp. 3–11

Van Gelderen, Elly, 'Tense and *to* (as a preposition) in Layamon', *Folia Linguistica Historica*, 13 (1993), 133–42

Wyld, H. C., 'Studies in the diction of Layamon's *Brut*', *Language*, 6 (1930), 1–24; 9 (1933), 47–71, 171–91; 10 (1934), 149–201; 13 (1937), 29–59, 194–237

Background and Reference

Alcock, L., *Arthur's Britain* (Harmondsworth, 1971)

Blenner-Hassett, R., *A Study of the Place-Names in Lawman's 'Brut'*, Stanford University Publications: Language and Literature 9:1 (Stanford, Calif., 1950)

Clanchy, M. T., *From Memory to Written Record*, 2nd edn (Oxford, and Cambridge, Mass., 1993), p. 125

Collier, Wendy, '"Englishness" and the Worcester Tremulous Hand', *LeedsSE*, n.s. 26 (1995), 35–47

Ekwall, E., *The Concise Dictionary of English Place-Names*, 4th edn (Oxford, 1990)

Harding, Alan, *England in the Thirteenth Century*, Cambridge Medieval Textbooks (Cambridge, 1993)

Norgate, Kate, *England under the Angevin Kings*, 2 vols. (London, 1887), esp. vol. II, p. 491

Poole, A. L., *From Domesday Book to Magna Carta, 1087–1216*, Oxford History of England, 2nd edn (Oxford, 1955).

Literary and Source Studies

Alamichel, Marie-Françoise, 'King Arthur's dual personality in Laȝamon's *Brut*', *Neophilologus*, 77 (1992), 303–19

——'Le roi Arthur dans le *Brut* de Lawamon: le moi et l'autre', in *L'Alterité dans la littérature et la culture du monde anglophone*, Actes du Colloque Le Mans 1991 (Publications de l'Université du Maine, 1993).

——'The function and activities of women in Laȝamon's *Brut*', in *A Wyf Ther Was: Essays in Honour of Paule Mertens-Fonck*, ed. Juliette Dor (Liège, 1992), pp. 11–22

——'Space in the *Brut*: Laȝamon's vision of the world', in *Text and Tradition*, ed. Le Saux, pp. 183–92

Allen, Rosamund, 'Female perspectives in romance and history', in *Romance in Medieval England*, ed. Maldwyn Mills *et al.* (Cambridge, 1991), pp. 133–47

——'"Long is Ever": the Cassibellaunus episode in three versions of the *Brut*', *New Comparison*, 12 (1991), 71–88

——'The implied audience of Laȝamon's *Brut*', in *Text and Tradition*, ed. Le Saux, pp. 121–39

——'Counting time and time for recounting: narrative sections in Laȝamon's *Brut*', in *Orality and Literacy*, ed. Pilch, pp. 71–91

Anderson, Judith H., 'Arthur, Argante and the ideal vision', in *The Passing of Arthur*, ed. Baswell and Sharpe, pp. 193–206

Barron, W. R. J., *English Medieval Romance*, Longman Literature in English Series (London, 1987), pp. 134–7

Barron, W. R. J., and Françoise Le Saux, 'Two aspects of Laȝamon's narrative art', *Arthurian Literature*, 9 (1989) 25–56

Baswell, Christopher, and William Sharpe, *The Passing of Arthur: New Essays in Arthurian Tradition* (New York, 1988)

Bennett, J. A. W., *Middle English Literature*, ed. and completed by Douglas Gray (Oxford, 1986), pp. 68–89

Borges, Jorge Luis, 'The Innocence of Layamon', in *Other Inquisitions*, trans. Ruth L. C. Simms (New York, 1966), pp. 158–62

Brewer, Derek, *English Gothic Literature*, Macmillan History of Literature (London, 1983), pp. 9–14

——'The paradox of the archaic and the modern in Laȝamon's *Brut*', in *From Anglo-Saxon to Early Middle English: Studies Presented to E. G. Stanley*, ed. Malcolm Godden, Douglas Gray and Terry Hoad (Oxford, 1995), pp. 188–205

Brown, A. C. L., 'Welsh traits in Layamon's *Brut*', *MP*, 1 (1903), 95–104

Bryan, Elizabeth, 'Truth and the Round Table in Lawman's *Brut*', *Quondam et Futurus: A Journal of Arthurian Interpretations*, 2 (1992), 27–35

——'Laȝamon's four Helens: female figurations of nation in the *Brut*', *LeedsSE*, n.s. 26 (1995), 63–78

Cannon, Christopher, 'The style and authorship of the Otho revision of Laȝamon's *Brut*', *MÆ*, 62 (1993), 187–209

Davies, H.S., 'Layamon's similes', *RES*, ll (1960), 129–42.

Deskis, Hill T. D., 'The wolf doesn't care: the proverbial and traditional context of Layamon's *Brut* lines 10624–36', *RES*, 181 (1995), 41–8

Donahue, Dennis P., *Lawman's 'Brut', An Early Arthurian Poem: A Study of Middle English Formulaic Composition'* (Lewiston, NY, 1991)

——'The animals tethered to King Arthur's rise and fall: imagery and structure in Lawman's *Brut*', *Mid-Hudson Language Studies*, 6 (1983), 19–27

——'Lawman's formulaic themes and the characterization of King Arthur in the *Brut*', in *Orality and Literacy*, ed. Pilch, pp. 93–112

Donoghue, Daniel, 'Laȝamon's ambivalence', *Speculum*, 65 (1990), 537–63

Everett, Dorothy, 'Laȝamon and the earliest Middle English alliterative verse', in her *Essays on Middle English Literature*, ed. Patricia Kean (Oxford, 1955), pp. 23–45.

Frankis, P. J., 'Laȝamon's English sources', in *J. R. R. Tolkien, Poet and Storyteller: Essays in Memoriam*, ed. Mary Salu and P. T. Farrell (Ithaca, NY, 1979), pp. 64–75

—— 'The social context of vernacular writing in thirteenth-century England: the evidence of the manuscripts', in *Thirteenth-Century England*, I: Proceedings of the Newcastle-upon-Tyne Conference 1985 (Woodbridge, 1986), pp. 175–84

Gillespy, F. L., 'Layamon's *Brut*: a comparative study in narrative art', *University of California Publications in Modern Philosophy*, 3 (1916), 361–510

Glowka, Arthur Wayne, 'Laȝamon's heathens and the medieval grape-vine', in *Orality and Literacy*, ed. Pilch, pp. 113–45

Gray, J. M., 'Tennyson and Layamon', *N&Q*, 213 (1968), 176–8

Guerin, M. Victoria, 'The king's sin: the origins of the David-Arthur parallel', in *The Passing of Arthur*, ed. Baswell and Sharpe, pp. 15–30

Imelmann, Rudolf, *Laȝamon: Versuch über seine Quellen* (Berlin, 1906)

Johnson, Lesley, 'Reading the past in Laȝamon's *Brut*' in *Text and Tradition*, ed. Le Saux, pp. 141–60

—— 'Tracking Laȝamon's *Brut*', *LeedsSE*, n.s. 22 (1991), 139–65

Keith, W. T., 'Layamon's *Brut*: the literary differences between the two texts', *MÆ*, 29 (1960), 161–72

Kirby, Ian, 'Angles and Saxons in Laȝamon's *Brut*', *SN*, (1964), 51–62

Korrel, Peter, *An Arthurian Triangle: A Study of the Origin, Development and Characterisation of Arthur, Guinevere and Modred* (Leiden, 1984), pp. 102–72

Kossick, S., 'The *Brut* and English literary tradition', *Unisa English Studies* 15:1 (1977), 25–32

Le Saux, Françoise, *Laȝamon's 'Brut': The Poem and its Sources*, Arthurian Studies 19 (Cambridge, 1989)

—— 'Laȝamon's Welsh sources', *Engl. Studies*, 67 (1986), 385–93

—— 'Narrative rhythm and narrative content in Laȝamon's *Brut*', *Parergon*, 10 (1992), 45–70

—— 'Paradigms of evil: gender and crime in Laȝamon's *Brut*', in *Text and Tradition*, ed. Le Saux, pp. 193–206

—— 'Relations familiales et autorité royale: de l'*Historia Regum Britanniae* au *Brut* de Layamon', in *Les Relations de parente dans le monde médiéval*, ed. from the Centre Universitaire d'Etudes et de Recherches Mediévales d'Aix (Aix en Provence, 1989)

——'Transition or rejection? French cultural concepts in Layamon's *Brut*', *BBIAS*, 40 (1988), 341–2

——, ed., *The Text and Tradition of Laʒamon's 'Brut'* (Cambridge, 1994)

Lewis, C. S., 'The genesis of a medieval book', in *Studies in Medieval and Renaissance Literature*, collected and ed. W. Hooper (Cambridge, 1966), pp. 18–33

Loomis, Roger Sherman, 'Layamon's *Brut*', in *Arthurian Literature in the Middle Ages: A Collaborative History*, ed. Roger Sherman Loomis, (Oxford, 1959), pp. 104–11

McNelis, James I., 'Laʒamon as *auctor*', in *Text and Tradition*, ed. Le Saux, pp. 253–72

Morris, Rosemary, *The Character of King Arthur in Medieval Literature*, Arthurian Studies 4 (Cambridge, 1982)

——'Uther and Igerne: a study in uncourtly love', *Arthurian Literature*, 4 (1984), 70–92

Noble, James, 'Laʒamon's "ambivalence" reconsidered', in *Text and Tradition*, ed. Le Saux, pp. 171–82

——'Patronage, politics and the figure of Arthur in Geoffrey of Monmouth, Wace and Laʒamon', in *Arthurian Yearbook*, 2 (1992), 159–78

O'Sharkey, Eithne M., 'King Arthur's prophetic dreams and the role of Modred in Layamon's *Brut* and the alliterative *Morte Arthure*', *Romania*, 99 (1978), 347–62

Pearsall, Derek, *Old English and Middle English Poetry* (London, 1977), pp. 80–1, 108–12

Pilch, Herbert, *Laʒamons Brut: eine literarische Studie* (Heidelberg, 1960)

——, ed., *Orality and Literacy in Early Middle English*, ScriptOralia 83 (Tübingen, 1996)

Putter, Ad, 'Finding time for romance: medieval Arthurian literary history', *MÆ*, 63 (1994), 1–15

Rider, Jeff, 'The fictional margin: the Merlin of the *Brut*', *MP*, 87 (1989–90), 1–12

Ringbom, Håkan, *Studies in the Narrative Technique of 'Beowulf' and Lawman's 'Brut'* (Åbo, 1968)

Salter, Elizabeth, *English and International: Studies in the Literature, Art and Patronage of Medieval England*, ed. Derek Pearsall and Nicolette Zeeman (Cambridge, 1988), pp. 48–70

Schirmer, W., 'Layamon's *Brut*', *MHRA* (1957), 15–27

Shichtman, Martin B., 'Gawain in Wace and Laȝamon: a case of metahistorical evolution', in *Medieval Texts and Contemporary Readers*, ed. Laurie A Finke and Martin B. Shichtman (Ithaca, NY, 1987), pp. 103–19

Stanley, E. G., 'The date of Laȝamon's *Brut*', *N&Q*, 213 (1968), 85–8

—— 'Laȝamon's antiquarian sentiments', *MÆ*, 38 (1969), 23–37

Swanton, Michael, *English Literature before Chaucer*, Longman Literature in English Series (London, 1987), pp. 175–86

Swart, J., 'Laȝamon's *Brut*', in *Studies in Language and Literature in Honor of Margaret Schlauch*, ed. M. Brahmer (1966)

Tatlock, J. S. P., *The Legendary History of Britain: Geoffrey of Monmouth's 'Historia Regum Britanniae' and its Early Vernacular Versions* (Berkeley and Los Angeles, 1950), pp. 483–531

Visser, Gerard J., *Laȝamon: An Attempt at Vindication* (Utrecht, 1935)

Weinberg, Carole, '"By a noble church on the bank of the Severn": a regional view of Layamon's *Brut*', *LeedsSE*, n.s. 26 (1995), 49–62

Wickham-Crowley, Kelley M., 'Laȝamon's narrative innovations and Bakhtin's theories', in *Text and Tradition*, ed. Le Saux, pp. 207–25

Willard, R., 'Laȝamon in the seventeenth and eighteenth centuries', *Texas Studies in English*, 27 (1948), 239–78

Wright, Neil, 'Angles and Saxons in Laȝamon's *Brut*: a reassessment', in *Text and Tradition*, ed. Le Saux, pp. 161–70

Wyld, H. C., 'Layamon as an English poet', *RES*, 6 (1930), 1–30

SUMMARY OF WACE'S TEXT

Note Most of Lawman's additions to Wace take the form of supplying speeches, identifying speakers and adding characters' names, so imparting a more dramatic quality to the narrative. His more substantial additions are indicated here within square brackets, as are his line references.

Preliminaries to the Arthurian section

The Romans have departed and left Britain to fend for itself against the attacks of Huns, Picts, Scots and Scandinavians. The British elect Constantine, brother of the king of Brittany, as their king.

6424–686 Constantine arrives in Britain and defeats its enemies. He marries and has three sons, but after only twelve years is murdered by a treacherous Pict [called Cabal]. The Welsh Count Vortigern persuades Constans, Constantine's eldest son, to leave his monastery and become king. The inexperienced Constans leaves the control of the kingdom to Vortigern, who first advises him to invite Pictish mercenaries into Britain, to repel invaders, and then has him murdered by them [under Gille Callaet]. Constans' two brothers, Aurelius and Uther, flee to Brittany, and Vortigern, having silenced the assassins with death, becomes king. [6388–853]

6687–7018 Saxons, led by Hengist and Horsa, arrive in Kent. Vortigern invites them to stay and help him against marauding Picts and Scots. Having built his own stronghold in Thongcaster, Hengist sends for his daughter Ronwen. Vortigern desires her and marries her, and gives her father Kent as dowry. [6854–7184]

7019–186 [Urged by the Britons, after a fruitless appeal to Vortigern], Vortigern's three sons by his first wife, Vortimer,

Paschent and Katiger, rebel against the ever-increasing numbers of Saxons. The British make Vortimer king and he defeats the Saxons in four battles, driving them out of Britain [and enacting religious and legal reforms]. Ronwen poisons him [at a feast] and he dies. [7185-521]

7187-354 King once more, Vortigern sends for the Saxons, who return in huge numbers and, under cover of a truce at Amesbury, murder the British nobles with their knives. Vortigern is spared and flees into Wales, where he tries to build a tower to defend himself. The tower continually collapses and he is told it needs the blood of a boy born without a father to enable it to stand. [7522-757]

7355-652 A search for such a boy ends in discovering Merlin, son of a nun and incubus. He confounds Vortigern's soothsayers by revealing two fighting dragons and a large pool underneath the tower, the cause of its collapse. Merlin prophesies, and warns Vortigern of the arrival of Aurelius and Uther. The British support the brothers, who burn Vortigern to death in his castle by the Wye. [7558-8100]

7653-8178 Once king, Aurelius marches against Hengist and captures and beheads him at the siege of Conisbrough. He is merciful to Hengist's son, Octa, and grants him land near Scotland. Desiring a fitting memorial at Amesbury, he is advised by Merlin how to remove the Giants' Dance from Ireland and to re-erect it: this is Stonehenge. [8101-739]

8179-540 Vortigern's son Paschent allies himself with an invading Irish force and has Aurelius poisoned [by a Saxon]. A comet appears to Uther, and Merlin interprets its rays as imminent victory over the Irish and the birth of two notable children. Uther defeats [and himself kills] Paschent. Aurelius dies and is buried inside Stonehenge. With the [morale-boosting] advice of Gorlois, count of Cornwall, Uther defeats a rebellious force of Saxons and imprisons their leaders, Octa and his cousin Eosa. [8740-9221]

8541-822 At Uther's coronation feast, he is captivated by the beauty of Gorlois's wife, Ygerne. Gorlois at once leaves and puts his wife in the castle of Tintagel. Uther besieges Gorlois at the count's other castle, but is desperate to possess Ygerne. Merlin [who has been fetched from a forest] changes the shape of Uther and his attendants to resemble Gorlois and his men, and thus the king is able to enter Tintagel, seduce Ygerne and beget Arthur. Gorlois is killed in battle, Uther marries Ygerne, and Arthur and Anna are born. [Arthur is blessed in his cradle by fairy-folk.] [9222-619]

8823-9032 After a long reign, Uther sickens, and Octa and Eosa escape and invade Scotland. [Uther's son-in-law proves ineffective against them.] Carried into battle in a litter, Uther still manages to defeat them, but [in a plot] is poisoned by agents of the Saxons. He is buried at Stonehenge and his son Arthur is crowned at Silchester [and Arthur and his barons swear an oath of allegiance]. [9620-981]

9033-406 Arthur and his allies, Cador of Cornwall and Hoel of Brittany, defeat the Saxons Colgrin, Baldulf and Cheldric at Lincoln and Colidon Wood. The Saxons are allowed to leave, but treacherously return and besiege Bath. In the ensuing battle at a nearby hill [beside a river] Arthur is victorious. [9982-10795]

9407-730 Arthur attacks the Scots, allies of the Saxons. He pens them in and starves them at Loch Lomond, but ultimately treats them with mercy. He describes the marvels of Loch Lomond and two other lakes to Hoel. At his Christmas feast in York, he gives the three brothers Angusel, Urien and Loth (the latter his brother-in-law) the domains of Scotland, Moray and Lothian. He takes Ganhumare as his queen. The conquests of Ireland and Iceland follow, and the kings of Orkney, Gotland and 'Weneland' become his vassals. [10796-11336]

9731-10170 There are twelve years of peace, and in these Arthur establishes the Round Table at his court, attracting knights from far and wide. [The Round Table is built by a Cornishman after a Yuletide riot in the hall over precedence.] Then Norway resists Loth succeeding as its new king, and Arthur compels it to accept him. Denmark's king prudently becomes Arthur's vassal. Arthur invades France and defeats

Frollo, vassal of the Roman emperor. Frollo flees to Paris and challenges Arthur to single combat, but loses and is slain. The rest of France is conquered for Arthur by his vassals Hoel and Guitart of Poitiers. He gives Anjou to his seneschal, Kay, and Normandy to Bedoer, his cup-bearer. For nine years Arthur remains in France. He rewards his men with lands. [11337–12073]

10171–11204 Arthur returns to England and at Pentecost holds plenary court at Caerleon. All his vassals gather for the feast, at which the king and queen are crowned, and there are games and music. Twelve messengers from Lucius, the Roman emperor, appear and deliver an angry demand for tribute and submission. [They are nearly lynched by Arthur's court.] Arthur takes counsel and returns word that he will come to demand tribute from Rome himself. Lucius and Arthur gather their allies for war and Arthur, leaving his kingdom in the charge of his queen and his nephew, Modret, embarks at Southampton. [12074–735]

11205–608 The fleet sails for Barfleur. During the night Arthur has a dream of a dragon fighting a bear. On arrival, he hears that a giant has raped Hoel's niece [daughter] Eleine, and taken her to Mont Saint-Michel. Accompanied by Kei and Bedoer, Arthur climbs the mountain and kills the giant. [12736–13049]

11609–12082 Arthur travels through France, making for Burgundy and Lucius' army. He sends his nephew Walwein, Gerin of Chartres and Bos of Oxford on an embassy to Lucius. A quarrel breaks out and the Romans pursue the fleeing messengers, who are aided by a British contingent sent out to reconnoitre the situation. A full-scale battle is only ended when Bos abducts Petreïus, leader of the Roman troops, which are now in disarray. [13050–399]

12083–518 Petreïus and other prisoners are taken to Paris, their escort fighting off a Roman ambush *en route*. Lucius decides to move to Autun by way of Langres, but Arthur travels ahead of him and blocks his way in the Soeïse valley. King and emperor arrange their troops and exhort their men. [13400–687]

12519–13009 Battle begins. Bedoer and Kei perform great feats but are slain. Walwein fights Lucius. The Romans rescue the emperor and are winning the field, when Arthur rallies his troops. The tide is turned by Arthur's reserve detachment under Morvid of Gloucester. In the rout of the Romans, the emperor is killed. Arthur buries Kei at Chinon, and Bedoer at Bayeux. [13688–947]

13010–130 Arthur's plan to advance to Rome is checked by the news [brought by a timid messenger] that Modret has usurped his throne and his queen [as foreseen by Arthur in a prophetic dream]. He returns and makes for Romney, where Modret and his Saxon allies attack Arthur's disembarking soldiers. Walwein and Angusel are killed [after the former has killed the Saxon king's son], but once on firm ground Arthur routs Modret's inexperienced troops. [13948–14160]

13131–298 Modret flees to Winchester, which Arthur besieges. Modret escapes and flees to Cornwall, where he enlists all Arthur's enemies as allies. Arthur gives Scotland to Angusel's nephew Ewain. The queen, distressed at the news of Modret's reverses, flees from York to Caerleon and there takes the veil. King and nephew join battle at Camble in Cornwall. In a bloody struggle Modret dies and Arthur is mortally wounded. The king is carried to Avalon; [two queens convey him there by boat]; it is said he still lives there [with Argante among the 'elves'] and will one day return. The kingdom passes to Cador's son, Costentin of Cornwall, in the year 542. [14161–297]

SAGAS AND OLD ENGLISH LITERATURE
IN EVERYMAN

Egils Saga
translated by Christine Fell
A gripping story of Viking exploits in Iceland, Norway and Britain
£4.99

Edda
SNORRI STURLUSON
The first complete English translation of this important Icelandic text
£5.99

Anglo-Saxon Prose
edited by Michael Swanton
Popular tales of Anglo-Saxon England, written by kings, scribes and saints
£4.99

The Fljotsdale Saga and The Droplaugarsons
translated by Eleanor Howarth *and* Jean Young
A brilliant portrayal of life and times in medieval Iceland
£3.99

Anglo-Saxon Poetry
translated by S. A. J. Bradley
An anthology of prose translations covering most of the surviving poetry of early medieval literature
£6.99

Fergus of Galloway: Knight of King Arthur
GUILLAME LE CLERC
translated by D. D. R. Owen
Essential reading for students of Arthurian romance
£3.99

Three Arthurian Romances from Medieval France
translated and edited by Ross G. Arthur
Caradoc, The Knight with the Sword *and* The Perilous Graveyard – *poems of the Middle Ages for modern readers*
£5.99

All books are available from your local bookshop or direct from:
Littlehampton Book Services Cash Sales, 14 Eldon Way, Lineside Estate,
Littlehampton, West Sussex BN17 7HE *(prices are subject to change)*

To order any of the books, please enclose a cheque (in sterling) made payable to
Littlehampton Book Services, or phone your order through with credit card details (Access,
Visa or Mastercard) on 01903 721596 (24 hour answering service) stating card number
and expiry date. *(Please add £1.25 for package and postage to the total of your order.)*

In the USA, for further information and a complete catalogue call 1-800-526-2778

MEDIEVAL LITERATURE
IN EVERYMAN

The Canterbury Tales
GEOFFREY CHAUCER
The complete medieval text with
translations
£4.99

The Vision of Piers Plowman
WILLIAM LANGLAND
edited by A. V. C. Schmidt
The only complete edition of the
B-Text available
£6.99

Sir Gawain and the Green
Knight, Pearl, Cleanness,
Patience
edited by J. J. Anderson
Four major English medieval
poems in one volume
£5.99

Arthurian Romances
CHRÉTIEN DE TROYES
translated by D. D. R. Owen
Classic tales from the father of
Arthurian romance
£5.99

Everyman and Medieval
Miracle Plays
edited by A. C. Cawley
A fully representative selection
from the major play cycles
£4.99

Anglo-Saxon Poetry
edited by S. A. J. Bradley
An anthology of prose translations
covering most of the surviving
poetry of early medieval literature
£6.99

Six Middle English Romances
edited by Maldwyn Mills
Tales of heroism and piety
£4.99

Ywain and Gawain,
Sir Percyvell of Gales,
The Anturs of Arther
edited by Maldwyn Mills
Three Middle English romances
portraying the adventures of
Gawain
£5.99

The Birth of Romance:
An Anthology
translated by Judith Weiss
The first-ever English translation
of fascinating Anglo-Norman
romances
£4.99

The Piers Plowman Tradition
edited by Helen Barr
Four medieval poems of political
and religious dissent – available
together for the first time
£5.99

All books are available from your local bookshop or direct from:
Littlehampton Book Services Cash Sales, 14 Eldon Way, Lineside Estate,
Littlehampton, West Sussex BN17 7HE (*prices are subject to change*)

To order any of the books, please enclose a cheque (in sterling) made payable to
Littlehampton Book Services, or phone your order through with credit card details (Access,
Visa or Mastercard) on 01903 721596 (24 hour answering service) stating card number
and expiry date. (*Please add £1.25 for package and postage to the total of your order.*)

In the USA, for further information and a complete catalogue call 1-800-526-2778

DRAMA
IN EVERYMAN

The Oresteia
AESCHYLUS
*New translation of one of the
greatest Greek dramatic trilogies
which analyses the plays in
performance*
£5.99

**Everyman and Medieval
Miracle Plays**
edited by A. C. Cawley
*A selection of the most popular
medieval plays*
£4.99

Complete Plays and Poems
CHRISTOPHER MARLOWE
*The complete works of this great
Elizabethan in one volume*
£5.99

Restoration Plays
edited by Robert Lawrence
*Five comedies and two tragedies
representing the best of the
Restoration stage*
£7.99

**Female Playwrights of the
Restoration: Five Comedies**
edited by Paddy Lyons
*Rediscovered literary treasures
in a unique selection*
£5.99

**Plays, Prose Writings
and Poems**
OSCAR WILDE
*The full force of Wilde's wit
in one volume*
£4.99

**A Dolls House/The Lady from
the Sea/The Wild Duck**
HENRIK IBSEN
introduced by Fay Weldon
*A popular selection of Ibsen's
major plays*
£4.99

**The Beggar's Opera and
Other Eighteenth-Century Plays**
JOHN GAY et. al.
Including Goldsmith's She Stoops
To Conquer *and Sheridan's* The
School for Scandal, *this is a volume
which reflects the full scope of the
period's theatre*
£6.99

**Female Playwrights of the
Nineteenth Century**
edited by Adrienne Scullion
*The full range of female nineteenth-
century dramatic development*
£6.99

All books are available from your local bookshop or direct from:
Littlehampton Book Services Cash Sales, 14 Eldon Way, Lineside Estate,
Littlehampton, West Sussex BN17 7HE (*prices are subject to change*)

To order any of the books, please enclose a cheque (in sterling) made payable to
Littlehampton Book Services, or phone your order through with credit card details (Access,
Visa or Mastercard) on 01903 721596 (24 hour answering service) stating card number
and expiry date. (*Please add £1.25 for package and postage to the total of your order.*)

In the USA, for further information and a complete catalogue call 1-800-526-2778

SHAKESPEARE
IN EVERYMAN

*Edited by John Andrews, the Everyman Shakespeare is the
most comprehensive, up-to-date paperback edition of
the plays and poems, featuring:*

face-to-face text and notes

chronology of Shakespeare's life and times

a rich selection of **critical and theatrical responses**
to the play over the centuries

foreword by an actor or director describing
the play in performance

up-to-date commentary on the play

Antony and Cleopatra £3.99

Hamlet £2.99

Julius Caesar £3.99

King Lear £2.99

Macbeth £2.99

Measure for Measure £3.99

The Merchant of Venice £2.99

A Midsummer Night's Dream
£1.99

Othello £3.99

Romeo and Juliet £2.99

The Tempest £2.99

Twelfth Night £3.99

The Winter's Tale £3.99

All books are available from your local bookshop or direct from:
Littlehampton Book Services Cash Sales, 14 Eldon Way, Lineside Estate,
Littlehampton, West Sussex BN17 7HE *(prices are subject to change)*

To order any of the books, please enclose a cheque (in sterling) made payable to
Littlehampton Book Services, or phone your order through with credit card details (Access,
Visa or Mastercard) on 01903 721596 (24 hour answering service) stating card number
and expiry date. *(Please add £1.25 for package and postage to the total of your order.)*

In the USA, for further information and a complete catalogue call 1-800-526-2778

CHARLES DICKENS
IN EVERYMAN

*The Everyman Dickens is the most comprehensive paperback
edition available, with all the original illustrations*

Bleak House
edited by Andrew Sanders
A great mystery unravelled
£5.99

Great Expectations
edited by Robin Gilmour
*From Newgate prison to society
drawing rooms – Pip's hopes and
dreams of becoming a gentleman*
£3.99

Hard Times
edited by Grahame Smith
*Dickens's bleak vision of
mid-Victorian England*
£3.99

Oliver Twist
edited by Steven Connor
*An innocent's journey through
London's underworld*
£4.99

Martin Chuzzlewit
edited by Michael Slater
*Classic examination of greed
and hypocrisy, by turns disturbing
and hilarious*
£4.99

Nicholas Nickleby
edited by David Parker
*An exciting tale of the young
Nicholas making his way in
the world*
£5.99

The Old Curiosity Shop
edited by Paul Schlicke
*A story that has provoked more
extreme responses than anything
else Dickens wrote*
£5.99

A Tale of Two Cities
edited by Norman Page
*The classic English evocation
of the French Revolution*
£3.99

**Holiday Romance and Other
Writings for Children**
edited by Gillian Avery
'Holiday Romance', The Life of
Our Lord', 'A Child's History
of England', *available only in
Everyman*
£5.99

All books are available from your local bookshop or direct from:
Littlehampton Book Services Cash Sales, 14 Eldon Way, Lineside Estate,
Littlehampton, West Sussex BN17 7HE (*prices are subject to change*)

To order any of the books, please enclose a cheque (in sterling) made payable to
Littlehampton Book Services, or phone your order through with credit card details (Access,
Visa or Mastercard) on 01903 721596 (24 hour answering service) stating card number
and expiry date. (*Please add £1.25 for package and postage to the total of your order.*)

In the USA, for further information and a complete catalogue call 1-800-526-2778

FOREIGN LITERATURE IN TRANSLATION IN EVERYMAN

A Hero of Our Time
MIKHAIL LERMONTOV
*The Byronic adventures of
a Russian army officer*
£5.99

L'Assommoir
ÉMILE ZOLA
*One of the most successful novels
of the nineteenth century and one
of the most scandalous*
£6.99

Poor Folk and **The Gambler**
FYODOR DOSTOYEVSKY
*These two short works of doomed
passion are among Dostoyevsky's
quintessential best. Combination
unique to Everyman*
£4.99

Yevgeny Onegin
ALEXANDER PUSHKIN
*Pushkin's novel in verse is Russia's
best-loved literary work. It contains some of the loveliest Russian
poetry ever written*
£5.99

The Three-Cornered Hat
ANTONIO PEDRO DE ALARCÓN
*A rollicking farce and one of
the world's greatest masterpieces
of humour. Available only in
Everyman*
£4.99

Notes from Underground
and **A Confession**
FYODOR DOSTOYEVSKY *and*
LEV TOLSTOY
*Russia's greatest novelists ruthlessly
tackle the subject of their mid-life
crises. Combination unique to
Everyman*
£4.99

Selected Stories
ANTON CHEKHOV
edited and revised by Donald
Rayfield
*Masterpieces of compression and
precision. Selection unique to
Everyman*
£7.99

Selected Writings
VOLTAIRE
*A comprehensive edition of
Voltaire's best writings. Selection
unique to Everyman*
£6.99

Fontamara
IGNAZIO SILONE
*'A beautifully composed tragedy.
Fontamara is as fresh now, and as
moving, as it must have been when
first published.'* London Standard.
Available only in Everyman
£4.99

All books are available from your local bookshop or direct from:
Littlehampton Book Services Cash Sales, 14 Eldon Way, Lineside Estate,
Littlehampton, West Sussex BN17 7HE (*prices are subject to change*)

To order any of the books, please enclose a cheque (in sterling) made payable to
Littlehampton Book Services, or phone your order through with credit card details (Access,
Visa or Mastercard) on 01903 721596 (24 hour answering service) stating card number
and expiry date. (*Please add £1.25 for package and postage to the total of your order.*)

In the USA, for further information and a complete catalogue call 1-800-526-2778